Splattered Ink

Splattered Ink

Postfeminist Gothic Fiction and Gendered Violence

SARAH E. WHITNEY

UNIVERSITY OF ILLINOIS PRESS
Urbana, Chicago, and Springfield

1 2 3 4 5 C P 5 4 3 2 1
∞ This book is printed on acid-free paper.

Library of Congress Cataloging-in-Publication Data
Names: Whitney, Sarah E., 1976– author.
Title: Splattered ink : postfeminist gothic fiction and gendered violence / Sarah E Whitney.
Description: Urbana : University of Illinois Press, 2016. | Includes bibliographical references and index. | Description based on print version record and CIP data provided by publisher; resource not viewed.
Identifiers: LCCN 2016018900 (print) | LCCN 2016005497 (ebook) | ISBN 9780252098895 (E-Book) | ISBN 9780252040467 (hardback : acid-free paper) | ISBN 9780252081927 (paper : acid-free paper)
Subjects: LCSH: American fiction—Women authors—History and criticism. | Gothic fiction (Literary genre), American—History and criticism. | BISAC: LITERARY CRITICISM / Gothic & Romance. | LITERARY CRITICISM / Feminist. | SOCIAL SCIENCE / Feminism & Feminist Theory.
Classification: LCC PS374.W6 (print) | LCC PS374.W6 W47 2016 (ebook) | DDC 813.009/9287—dc23
LC record available at https://lccn.loc.gov/2016018900

To my family—
James and Mary Whitney
Craig Warren
Jack and Reid Warren
In the order in which we first met

Contents

Acknowledgments

My interests in gothic literature and in women's literature have been shaped by many wonderful teachers from grade school to graduate school. Thank you to them all, most especially to Ann Connolly, Susan Dale, Susan Fraiman, Terri Goldrich, Nancy Gray, Elizabeth M. Hull, Deborah Morse, and Kim Wheatley. Thanks also to my Virginia mentors, Sharon Davie and Ginger Moran.

I sincerely appreciate the support, encouragement, and cups of coffee provided by my colleagues in the English Program and the wider School of Humanities and Social Sciences at Penn State Erie, the Behrend College.

Nearly all sections of the manuscript were presented and workshopped over several years at both the College English Association and National Women's Studies Association; I always received constructive suggestions from panelists and audience members. The manuscript reviewers delivered perceptive comments in a helpful manner, for which I am much obliged. I want to thank Astrid Henry in particular for her kind, insightful suggestions about strengthening the manuscript.

I'm indebted to Kristina Peszel for her outstanding technical work preparing the manuscript. Many additional thanks go to Jennifer Clark, Anne Rogers, and Roberta Engleman for their vital expertise. Working with the University of Illinois Press has been a very rewarding experience. Larin McLaughlin provided great support initially, and Dawn Durante has been a perceptive editor with invaluable suggestions and guidance.

A revised version of chapter 2 was previously published in *Tulsa Studies in Women's Literature* 29.2 (Fall 2010). I am grateful to the University of Tulsa for permission to reprint the work.

Thanks beyond words go to my family. My parents, James and Mary Whitney, have always modeled love, support, and a lifelong devotion to books. My husband, Craig Warren, makes me better in all ways. Both my beloved sons were born during the writing of this manuscript, and I can't wait to see how their stories turn out.

Finally, thank you to the writers analyzed in this book, all of whom have created spellbinding tales. I have been privileged to learn from your work.

Splattered Ink

1

Terror and Brightness

What Can Postfeminist Gothic Do?

The winding roads outside Charlottesville, Virginia, curve around a quiet, pastoral landscape. But on January 26, 2010, during a routine check of his fields, the owner of a remote farm in the area stumbled upon a terrible discovery. The skeletal remains uncovered by the homeowner were identified as belonging to college student Morgan Harrington, whose baffling disappearance from a Metallica concert months earlier had garnered national attention. After the necessary forensic tests were completed, Morgan's mother, Gil Harrington, viewed the remnants of her daughter's body. "I can tell you, having seen them, that girl even had some lovely bones," she disclosed to the press in striking language (Spencer, "Black Ribbon"). Later, on the *Today Show*, Harrington added that "I have reviewed images of my daughter from her pre-natal ultrasounds to looking at her empty eye sockets of her cranium. Yes, I have seen . . . lovely bones. Lovely girl" (Silverman, "Morgan Harrington's Parents"). Harrington's comments deliberately evoke Alice Sebold's 2002 best-selling novel *The Lovely Bones*. In that work, Sebold's narrator, Susie, a raped and murdered teenager narrating her story from heaven, uses the titular phrase to describe her skeletal body as a site of "connections—sometimes tenuous, sometimes made at great cost, but often magnificent—that happened after I was gone" (320).

Gil Harrington's descriptions of her daughter's body provide poignant moments of sorrow and recognition. When she borrows Sebold's novel's term to describe Morgan's bones as "lovely," she affirms, profoundly, how much her daughter *mattered*. "I can only respect where she has gone," muses writer Ginger Moran, "gazing at her baby, absorbing her—taking her in, seeing the loveliness still in what remains of a body left out in the cold four months—reabsorbing her, taking her back in, saying there is nothing about her she will turn from, saying her name again and again" ("Mother Gaze"). Morgan Harrington is, of course, a real young woman who suffered unimaginable trauma. She is also part of a larger American women's story of loss and violence. This book is about a subgenre of literature called *postfeminist gothic* that attends to that story.

Postfeminist gothic is a powerful but underacknowledged strain of American women's fiction that tells tales of gendered violence and pain. Menaced and victimized women are, of course, staples of the gothic genre. Yet the stakes for telling these stories are distinctly different in postfeminist culture, which proclaims loudly and consistently that the struggle for women's freedom is finished. *Postfeminism*, which is certainly a contested word, is used throughout this book to describe a powerful cultural sensibility that assumes that gender equity has been achieved, and that feminism is now both obsolete and undesirable.[1] Postfeminist gothic novels, however, violently intrude on the well-constructed fantasy of a safe and equitable world. They feature abject protagonists who are socially invisible, physically broken, or speaking from the grave. Emphasizing women's *dis*empowerment, they go against the grain of a victim-resistant, empowerment-oriented age. In their very narratives, which often foreclose happiness, these works also eschew the therapeutic structures embedded in postfeminist popular culture. While not claiming victimhood as an organizing identity (which feminists are often accused of doing in contemporary culture), postfeminist gothic novels ask us as readers to textually inhabit women's experiences of suffering and to arrive at the uncomfortable conclusion that to be female, even today, means to live with terrible risk. They thus both continue the female gothic literary tradition, which Benjamin Brabon and Stéphanie Genz, following the work of Ellen Moers, have called the "mode par excellence that female writers have employed to give voice to women's deep-seated fears about their own powerlessness," and respond to the particular cultural conditions of postfeminism ("Introduction," *Postfeminist Gothic* 5).

Splattered Ink analyzes how female gothic fiction of the twenty-first century both powerfully critiques postfeminism's candy-colored world and uneasily lives within it, proffering strategies to manage women's fears in dangerous times. The writers studied here address palpable horrors, including sexual assault, incest, domestic violence, and the feminization of poverty, which have been minimized within a postfeminist framework. Furthermore, the novels and memoirs bend, twist, and play with language in distinct ways that challenge postfeminist rhetorics of, among other things, empowerment, progress, objectivity, and the value of "balance." The author Sapphire, for instance, generates verbal explosiveness to illuminate the struggles of a girl hidden from society by racism, poverty, and abuse. Fellow novelist Alice Sebold employs metaphors of burial to explore the self-abnegating costs of postfeminism, while Susanna Moore layers textures of sinister whispers in her tales to aurally represent misogyny's persistence. Other authors use modalities of ambivalence to express the difficulty of living with postfeminism's complexities. Author Jodi Picoult, for instance, tends to defuse thorny questions of gender violence, reaching toward "humanism" by flattening differences and employing multiple perspectives. Mystery writer Patricia Cornwell appears to emotionally wall her readers off from sexual violence, switching late in her career to a mechanized third-person narrative style that bespeaks numbness. These texts' moments of struggle, or even retreat, are powerful reminders of how women negotiate their own fears about violence and victimization in postfeminist times.

The works studied here occupy different niches in the literary marketplace; some are highly acclaimed, while others cleave to conventions of genre fiction. Taken together, they create a broader picture of postfeminist gothic congruities. These texts are united in their bleakness, though, and engaging with postfeminist gothic texts can offer relatively few straightforward aesthetic pleasures. For feminist critics trained to read for moments of female textual agency, and for contemporary readers who value the elastic concept of female "empowerment" so central to postfeminist popular culture, postfeminist gothic novels can seem disconcerting.[2] These works emphasize *dis*-empowerment and brutality, and produce in their readers feelings of anxiety, fear, anger, and perhaps despair. Such affects can be difficult to experience within a culture where optimism sometimes seems mandatory. Sara Ahmed cautions that although those who "cause disturbance" by refusing our culture's "happiness wish" are often labeled as killjoys, such resistance can "also turn disturbance into a cause" (32). Postfeminist gothic novels do precisely this—unearthing the prematurely silent ground of postfeminist culture.

Splattered Ink is one intervention in the increasingly rich academic study of gothic and postfeminism. The term *postfeminist gothic* served as a subject of inquiry in a 2007 issue of *Gothic Studies*. There, Benjamin Brabon and Stéphanie Genz's introduction noted both terms' flexibility, arguing that they are "linked by their transgressive and boundary-defying capabilities, their eschewal of a binary logic and their embrace of pluralism" (1). The notion of an inherently gothic relationship between feminism and postfeminism is also discussed here, primarily in the work of Fiona Tolan (45). Many of the writers in Brabon and Genz's subsequent collection *Postfeminist Gothic* (2007) assess the postfeminist gothic's potential to radically *destabilize* norms of gender and sexuality; Judith Halberstam, for instance, writes of the neo-splatter film's turn to queerness as "the antidote to the 'horror' of heteronormativity or marriage, domesticity, monogamy and family" ("Neo-Splatter" 31).

Other writers interrogating postfeminist gothic, such as Helene Meyers (*Femicidal Fears*, 2001), explore how authors like Edna O'Brien and Muriel Spark perpetuate the female gothic tradition during inhospitable epochs. Like Meyers, whose work is very helpful to my own, I seek to investigate how "women writers adopted and adapted the tropes of an already gendered literary tradition to address the sexual politics of their own time" (19). If postfeminism is haunted (to borrow a gothic concept) by feminism, then the authors studied in *Splattered Ink* haunt back. They challenge its dominant grammars, which include a sanguine focus on empowerment, postracial assumptions and other obliterations of intersectional identity, and a fascination with women's transgressive "badness." Whereas the most familiar icons of postfeminist popular culture are the warrior woman, the "mean girl," and the compulsive shopper and dieter, postfeminist gothic novels give us the basement captive, the incest survivor, and the murdered young woman. It is my hope that these stories are recognized as potent forms of literary activism.

Much of my personal interest in postfeminism has come because of teaching women's literature and studying, alongside my students, the ways that messages about gender continue to matter deeply. I have found that most students are quite interested in novels about female struggle across eras, races, and classes. They frequently voice their approbation of characters who are "strong women," and they express familiarity with concepts of choice and empowerment.[3] Yet students often feel more comfortable skating over moments of gendered conflict in texts. Traumas are seen as valuable only insomuch as they lead to an empowered overcoming; for instance, a character who is sexually assaulted "becomes a stronger person" because of her experience of violence. Students' simultaneous valorization of the heroine's ability to triumph and their reluctance to address the systemic barriers that she confronts illustrate the complexities of a postfeminist culture. Beth DeVolder trenchantly observes that our culture's investment in the overcoming narrative (which has been widely critiqued within disability studies and other fields) "robs us of a legitimate space to grieve, and to get mad, and to bear witness" to violence and discrimination (750). The writers in this project address these issues head on, explicitly dwelling on episodes of gendered violence in order to affirm that they still happen, and that traumas are more intricate, messy, and raw than pop-culture models of "closure" and "moving forward" would have us believe.

Gothic Novels, Gothic Lives

To understand the concerns of postfeminist gothic, it is necessary to more closely examine each of these slippery terms. The *gothic* is notoriously difficult to define; critics regularly disagree on its formal characteristics and historical applications. Yet most feminist critics agree on its subversive potential, which Kate Ellis calls "a resistance to an ideology that imprisons [women] even as it posits a sphere of safety for them" (x). Because it investigates the limits of gendered identities and roles, the gothic has proved to be fruitful ground for feminist studies. Donna Heiland describes gothic fiction as fundamentally "about transgressions of all sorts: across national boundaries, social boundaries, sexual boundaries, the boundaries of one's own identity" (3). From Mary Shelley to Margaret Atwood, there exists a rich tradition of women writers considering the implications of gender and sexual violence in the gothic vein. At heart, then, postfeminist gothic plots belong to a tradition that stretches back centuries. Despite the early dominance of male writers like Horace Walpole, Charles Robert Maturin, and Matthew Lewis, gothic has been widely interpreted as a "woman's genre." Helene Meyers writes that gothic has, "from its inception, been seen as feminine and female: it privileges emotion and the domestic sphere, and middle-class women have obsessively written and read it" (25).

Feminist criticism has long assessed the gothic, particularly because it is penned by women, as a site of patriarchal critique. "Across the theoretical spectrum, feminist criticism views the Gothic novel as a story of gender role inequalities and their concomitant anxieties," summarizes Karen Stein ("Left-Handed Story" 137). The development of a "female gothic" school of analysis can be traced to Ellen Moers's influential reading of Mary Shelley's *Frankenstein* as a birth myth in *Literary Women* (1976). Moers, argue Andrew Smith and Diana Wallace, "engendered a body of critical work which focused on the ways in which the Female Gothic articulated women's dissatisfactions with patriarchal society" and "placed the Gothic at the center of the female tradition" (1). In the female gothic's fever dreams of gloomy castles and mad wives was an embedded critique of the world as it was. The gothic plot, Michelle Massé argues, is "not an escape from the real world but a repetition and exploration of the traumatic denial of identity found there" ("Gothic Repetition" 688).[4] Very often, the terror in female gothic fiction came not from tall dark strangers, but from somewhere closer at hand. Joanna Russ's cheekily titled 1983 essay "Somebody's Trying to Kill Me and I Think It's My Husband: The Modern Gothic" epitomizes the domestic or marital gothic subgenre that was popularized by Victoria Holt, Phyllis A. Whitney, and others beginning in the 1960s. Such works gesture to real life where, as feminist geographers and activists have long pointed out, domestic space is statistically far more threatening to women's safety than are deserted playgrounds and parks after dark.[5] In Joan Lidoff's words, domestic gothic "penetrates the surfaces of personal sentiment and social pretense to expose secret cruelties of family life" (111).

Gothic thus has been and continues to be abundant ground for the working out of fears about sexual violence. Diana Wallace writes that "the Female Gothic is always 'going back': texts are haunted by their predecessors and, in turn, haunt their descendants" (132). Postfeminist gothic fiction builds upon the work of its ancestors, particularly a prior generation of women writing gothic tales in the shadow of civil rights and feminism's second wave.[6] Such authors, including Joyce Carol Oates, Margaret Atwood, and Toni Morrison, adroitly critiqued the endurance of sexual violence against women in Western life while also creating innovative literary strategies to capture trauma's devastating and ongoing impact on victims.

Few authors chronicle the dark corners of America's violent past better than Morrison and Oates. Morrison's novels bear witness to slavery's calamitous legacy, and in particular women of color's relentless experiences of sexual violence. Her reluctance to place her work, which is based on real-life tragedies, within a literary gothic tradition associated with magic and an "apparent lack of connection to reality and intellectual purpose" has been chronicled by Teresa Goddu (*Gothic America* 140). With this reservation acknowledged, Morrison's canon also renovates gothic, pushing out the borders of this historically white tradition. It demands that the distressed maiden archetype central to female gothic be recentered on women like *Beloved*'s (1987) Sethe, who is handled "like I was the cow, no, the goat" as she is robbed of breast milk by white boys on the plantation where she is enslaved (200). Or women like the unnamed, gang-raped mother of *A Mercy*'s (2008) protagonist Florens, who facilitates the sale of her own daughter in colonial America to remove her from a place where "to be female" is "to be an open wound that cannot heal" (163). As Katherine Weese argues, Morrison's novels reframe gothic to "call attention to the fantastic, gothic horror inherent in slavery itself" while subverting "those conventions in a gendered context to advance her feminist treatment" of enslaved women's lives (140).

Whereas Morrison's gothic forces readers to confront the haunting legacy of slavery and racism, Joyce Carol Oates's gothic twists the knife into Americana, dissecting nostalgia-laden epochs and probing the often repressive gender ideologies at their cores. In *We Were the Mulvaneys* (1996), an immensely popular Oprah's Book Club selection, Oates investigates how the social mores of small-town 1960s America compel the titular family to shamed, and ultimately toxic, silence about the daughter's rape on prom night. *Black Water* (1992) retells the Chappaquiddick tragedy from the point of view of the young girl left to drown in an overturned and submerged car by a U.S. politician, while *My Sister, My Love* (2008) fictionalizes the brutal sexualized murder of child pageant queen JonBenét Ramsey. Oates, who has been described by Mary Allen as "an author to read if one dares to know the particular fear there is in being a woman—here and now—even when the surface of life may appear as familiar and safe as a supermarket on a sunny day," returns frequently to narratives of female sexual assault and murder within her prodigious canon of more than forty novels (159).[7]

Postfeminist gothic authors are indebted to their predecessors for their intersectionality and critique of gender inequities; they also take up their forebears' literary innovations in depicting trauma. As Evelyn Jaffe Schreiber notes, Toni Morrison's work has ushered in a paradigm shift in trauma studies; an impressive number of books and dissertations have been galvanized by her work (177). Morrison's writing, argues Schreiber, testifies to the idea that "trauma, whether initiated by physical abuse, dehumanization, discrimination, exclusion, or abandonment, becomes embedded in both psychic and bodily circuits" (2). The concept of "re-memory" explored throughout *Beloved*, where the traumatic past returns in the literal body of the lost daughter, is the most famous; other hauntings in Morrison's work take place in her characters' fragmented minds. The outcast, raped child Pecola Breedlove of *The Bluest Eye* (1970) takes refuge in psychosis, conversing with an imaginary voice who assures her that she now, magically, possesses blue eyes that "get prettier each time I look at them" (201). Oates's work also addresses the psychic trauma of sexual violence, often exploring victim-blaming through the uncomfortable use of refrain. *We Were the Mulvaneys*'s Marianne obsessively repeats the mantra "I was drinking. I was to blame. I don't remember" in the wake of a classmate's violent rape (142). In *Rape: A Love Story* (2003), a lacerating communal voice whispers "she had it coming, she was asking for it" in the wake of a gang rape of a young mother (4). Oates's novels, asserts Tanya Horeck, screen "the thoughts and feelings of victims of violence as they look back over moments of their lives" in a manner similar to the experiences of many survivors of sexual and domestic violence (28). Postfeminist gothic fiction also frequently employs traumatic refrain; in Sapphire's novel *Push*, for instance, torrents of prose repetitions—like the alphabet or the phrase "I want die I want die"—represent protagonist Precious Jones's entrapment within a vortex of incest recollections (53).

Acknowledging the oversimplification, it is perhaps fair to say that while Toni Morrison's and Joyce Carol Oates's gothics hold up mirrors of the violent past and present, Margaret Atwood's gothic oeuvre speculates on a postfeminist future's continued misogyny and threat. Atwood has been long riveted by the social vulnerability of women's bodies; nowhere is this more evident than in *The Handmaid's Tale* (1985), a dystopic novel about a theocracy that has stripped women of jobs, financial credit, and public power, deeming them valuable only as reproductive breeders. Protagonist Offred, a concubine to a military officer, carefully negotiates a world that sees her as "merely a usable body . . . a boat with no cargo, a chalice with no wine in it, an oven—to be crude—minus the bun" (211).

Atwood has frequently linked the disavowal of feminism to personal and social catastrophe. In *Bodily Harm* (1981), a journalist who has made a name for herself proclaiming feminism's death undergoes a series of frightening experiences, including cancer, sexual aggression, and being held hostage. The novel's conclusion suggests a change of heart, in the words of Elaine Tuttle Hansen, where "the stories women told in the 60s and 70s are still true, terrifying, and subversive, as [protagonist] Rennie in the end admits" (5). Atwood has also famously stated that *The Handmaid's Tale* "is an imagined account of what happens when not uncommon pronouncements about women are taken to their logical conclusions" (qtd. in Bloom 2). Within that novel, the fairly conventional Offred's relationship with her feisty feminist protester of a mother reenacts the wave metaphor of generational difference between second and third wave feminists.[8] Indeed, Offred's mother refers to her somewhat derisively as a "backlash" (156). Offred's refusal to heed her mother's warnings about women's progressive loss of social rights has devastating consequences, as she is separated from her family and pressed into sexual labor as one of few alternatives to death.

Postfeminist gothic work is thus beholden to feminist gothic's foregrounding of patriarchal critique and to its literary model of rendering trauma's intense impact. The latter point still resonates today, perhaps counterintuitively. In the twenty-first century, general consciousness of abuse is higher than in the past, and public and private services for survivors of sexual and domestic violence proliferate. Yet our national resistance to the concept of victimization has put a time stamp on survivors' relationship to their trauma.

Psychological terms have morphed into pop phraseology, reframing traumas as things that need to receive "closure." Empowerment within postfeminist iconography, as I discuss later, has become defined primarily by one's ability to rout and quickly forget upsetting experiences. Postfeminist gothic disrupts this dominant affect, interrogating unburied pasts and exploring ongoing hauntings of traumatized lives. It is reflected in the neo-captivity genre, where chronological gaps and fissures rent the texts of kidnapped women, and in the mystery fiction of Patricia Cornwell, whose compulsion to rewrite horrific sexualized murders speaks to misogyny's enduring violent spectacle. The conviction that past is very much present inhabits the worlds of feminist and postfeminist gothic.

As powerful as feminist gothic work has been, however, its inhospitable vision has been interrogated by several critics. Some have questioned the gothic form's political efficacy, deeming it a conservative genre that illuminates inequities but does not show how to transcend them. Michelle Massé, for instance, suggests that the gothic teaches a heroine the masochistic pleasures of self-sacrifice and alienation while dissuading her from pursuing "systemic inquiry about the source of her suffering" (*In the Name of Love* 3). Susanne Becker similarly sees marital gothic as encouraging self-adjustment rather than resistance, which departs from a feminist understanding of "the articulation of private problems and their recognition as collective" (87). Diane Long Hoeveler and Helene Meyers have both proffered concerns about the intractability of gendered gothic scripts. Hoeveler writes:

> The ideology that seems to ground the female gothic novel tradition is the same one that grounds one version of white, bourgeois Western feminism, the belief that women are victimized and oppressed not simply by gender politics but by the social, economic, political, religious, and hierarchical spaces that bourgeois capitalism—and by extension the patriarchal family—has constructed to contain them. (*Gothic Feminism* xiii)

Meyers concurs that "indeed, the script of male vice and female virtue that is oft used to describe cultural feminism is an apt description of the literary Gothic" (18). Hoeveler, in particular, distrusts the gothic's presentation of blameless heroines being cruelly terrorized, warning that it feeds into the suspicion that "women earn their superior social and moral rights in society by positioning themselves as innocent victims of a corrupt tyrant and an oppressive patriarchal society" (*Gothic Feminism* 2).

Postfeminist gothic, which seeks to develop a portrait of violence survivors as resilient, must negotiate around such overdetermined heroine/villain scripts while also avoiding contemporary culture's hostility to the concept of victimization. Authors in the genre therefore devise literary strategies to hinder overly sentimentalized or hagiographic readings of their traumatic tales. Some even demolish their own narratives; Sapphire, for instance, constructs a sequel designed to blunt any oversimplified reading of her novel *Push* as empowering, while Alice Sebold moves from engaging sentimental melancholia in her first novel toward a more pointed and savage critique of postfeminism in her second. Other writers satirize the faux-compassionate "commodified genres of intimacy," to borrow from Lauren Berlant, that make up feminized popular culture (*Female Complaint* x). In Emma Donoghue's neo-captivity novel *Room*, for instance, a formerly kidnapped woman mocks a television reporter who deems her a saint and a beacon of light. This difficulty of talking about gendered victimization while avoiding clichés is crystallized by the words of Elizabeth Smart, the schoolgirl held hostage and repeatedly raped for nine months in 2002. Smart, now a victim's advocate, has said postabduction that "I'm a stronger person than I would have been." Yet she immediately continues, "I wouldn't wish it on anybody, though. I don't think anybody needs to become strong that way" (qtd. in Talbot 38).

Situating Postfeminism

The story of how postfeminism emerged is itself a gothic one featuring villains, frightened maidens, coffins, and charges of excess. Many critics have even resorted to gothic metaphors when considering the relationship between feminism and postfeminism. Sarah Kornfield, for instance, suggests we consider postfeminism as "a *spectral* figure of feminism, a doppelganger portrayed in media entertainment" (448; emphasis added). Meanwhile, bell hooks frames postfeminism as *vampiric* in a critique of Naomi Wolf's popular manifesto *Fire with Fire* (1993). "By rejecting feminism as a political movement that seeks to eradicate sexism, sexist exploitation, and oppression and replacing it with the notion that feminism is simply 'a theory of self-worth,'" says hooks, Wolf drains not only racial and class specificity, but also the political foundation of antisexism, out of its vision. What is left is a movement that "can embrace everyone, since it has no overt political tenets" ("Dissident Heat" 63).

The complex relationship between feminism and postfeminism has been elucidated in many other texts; my brief historicization emphasizes the development of two facets of postfeminist cultural expression that are relevant to the novels studied here. One such element is the cultivation of a sparkling, ebullient affect that skates over discussions of inequity, preferring to focus on narratives of "empowerment" and success. The other is a concomitant disdain for *victimization* that downplays, or even rejects, women's vulnerability to sexual and domestic violence.

In recent years, there has been much linguistic play surrounding feminism's first letter. The "F word" (subject of books, magazine articles, and blog posts) has come to be both derided and proudly reclaimed. Few words stir controversy as much as feminism does, but oddly, this also reifies its materiality. It is hated and it is loved, but very few people deny its historical *existence*. *Postfeminism* is far more of a phantom term; in fact, it shares gothic's mutability. Often, postfeminism's existence is denied outright or ironized through quotation marks. Some writers equate postfeminism with antifeminism; Fred Botting, for example, suggests that the prefix *post* "conceals a dismissive and restorative reaction" and "constitutes a 'backlash' or 'misogynistic turn'" (171). For other critics, like Ann Brooks, postfeminism is a promising meeting ground at the juncture of feminism, postmodernism, and postcolonialism; it signals feminism's "maturity into a confident body of theory and politics, representing pluralism and difference" (1).

Since the 1990s, there has been increased scholarly attention to theorizing postfeminism as it operates in popular culture, with some scholars distinguishing it from the more affirmatively, feminist-identified "third wave."[9] Following the lead of scholars such as Angela McRobbie, Diane Negra, Yvonne Tasker, and Rosalind Gill, I emphasize postfeminism as a popular cultural framework for making sense of gender relations in the contemporary moment. Gill succinctly defines a postfeminist sensibility as being informed by, among other things, "the notion that femininity is a bodily property; the shift from objectification to subjectification; the emphasis upon self-surveillance, monitoring and discipline; a focus upon individualism, choice and empowerment" as well as "an emphasis upon consumerism and the commodification of difference" ("Postfeminist Media Culture" 149). Postfeminist cultural subjects are encouraged to revel in their gender equity and spend the capital that comes with their citizenship freely. Tasker and Negra further assert that "postfeminism is white and middle class by default, anchored in consumption as a strategy" and that it assumes "full economic freedom for women" (2). Kellie Bean adds that postfeminism calls "for women to embrace domesticity, sexual display, the production of children, marriage, fashion and/or sex work as empowering" (5). In other words, postfeminism is invested in refashioning traditionalism as newfangled, and most of all in developing a relentlessly positive worldview. A postfeminist sensibility means always choosing to view oneself as empowered, even in situations when, fairly clearly, one is not.

Postfeminism remains rooted primarily in the cultural sphere. Sarah Projansky reminds us that it is "useful to approach postfeminism as a cultural *discourse*—an attitude, a reaction formation, an always available hegemonic response to feminism—not entirely linked to any historical moment" (88). While postfeminist rhetoric may be injected into political appeals (in the United States, for instance, female voters are often told that they should look "beyond" reproductive issues of birth control and abortion and focus on economic ones, as if one had nothing to do with the other), postfeminism itself has few recognizable landmark institutions or identifiable political-action items. Furthermore, while comparatively fewer young women may self-identify as feminist (a topic widely analyzed in popular media), even fewer utilize the term *postfeminist* as a badge of identity.[10]

Though it may be difficult to pin down the dawn of a postfeminist era, Susan Bolotin's oft-cited 1982 *New York Times Magazine* article "Voices from the Post-Feminist Generation" is an instructive window on its early days.[11] The conclusions drawn by the young women interviewed in Bolotin's essay—that we inhabit a new political age in which feminism as a political and social movement must be disavowed, both because it is "finished" and it is unproductively "angry"—remain influential in the dissection of postfeminist thought. Interviewing women aged eighteen to twenty-five whose worlds had been reshaped by second wave feminism's shockwaves, from Title IX to *Roe v. Wade*, Bolotin discovered many "women who disavowed a connection with feminism while praising its political effects." Among the young women's rationales for feminist disavowal included the perception that it was synonymous with lesbianism, the construction of feminism as "an exclusively radical, separatist, bitter movement," and the women's fears that it would alienate men (30).

Bolotin's article shows effectively how 1980s rhetoric demonized feminist ideas. It is also valuable because it articulates the *ambivalence* felt by young women toward feminism. "I do feel gratitude towards these women in terms of the actual political changes that have taken place," says one woman, who proceeds to express her sorrow "that so few had to fight so hard to get what they got for so many" (29). Bolotin's subjects believe it is easier to not explicitly identify with feminism. However, traces of their ambivalence and even their sorrow about this disidentification remain; this melancholy is also reflected in the feminist "death narrative" that has held court in the media throughout the postfeminist age.

The young women profiled in Bolotin's article came of age in a decade when political and social progress toward women's equality stalled. Sara

Evans comments that "the new surge of feminism just a decade earlier had seemed invincible, growing by leaps and bounds after 1970, ticking off legal and judicial victories that shattered traditional modes of discrimination in education, jobs, sports, and reproductive rights" (85). Pushback in the succeeding decade took many forms, including the slow death of the Equal Rights Amendment, violence toward and harassment of women's health clinics, challenges to Title IX, and the rise of the New Right, buoyed by a popular president "whose social mores were rooted in a vision of small-town America that predated the convulsions of the 1960s" (Martin 146). Working and unmarried women of the eighties were demonized by media-driven social panics ranging from "man shortages" to barren wombs, as Susan Faludi painstakingly chronicled in her oft-cited work *Backlash* (1991). The eighties did see women breaking new barriers of representation in vice presidential politics, the Supreme Court, and elsewhere; some feminist projects, including the institutionalization of women's and ethnic studies in the academy, also gained ground. Nevertheless, says Bradford Martin, feminist work often "added up not to monumental gains in women's status, but rather to defending the hard-won gains of the previous decade in a gritty war of position" (147). In the cultural sphere, Sara Evans adds that the divisive "women v. women" rhetoric in the media served to "make feminists more invisible in the media and even to themselves. The result was that thousands of women were creating new patterns with few models and little support" (88).

The loss of feminist visibility has continued though the present day, although the 1990s saw a resurgent wave of self-defined "third wave" activism.[12] It is safe to say that young women and men coming of age in the period from the late 1980s onward are shaped *both* by the legacy of feminism and the ideology of the backlash. The postfeminist aesthetic contains this same push-pull tension. It openly rejects some elements of feminism, and yet it needs feminism in order to carry out its oppositional arguments. This complicated dynamic plays out in literary and cultural terms through two interrelated modalities. The postfeminist popular sphere leans toward lighthearted narratives of uplift that are best expressed by the visible subgenre of "chick lit." It also repeatedly trots out a darker feminist death narrative, which eulogizes feminism for a "victim-centered" mentality, and celebrates liberation from its overbearing politics. Postfeminist gothic fiction questions the ebullience of these empowerment narratives, even parodying their conventions. Simultaneously, it utilizes either the end-of-life or posthumous subject position to creatively respond to the notion that the need for feminism is "dead." Emphasizing women's disempowerment through accounts of violence and pain, these works ask us to reconsider our culture's sneering rejection of the word *victim* and to reconsider the postfeminist promise of equality and triumph.

It's All Good, Postfeminist Style

"Women," writes Abigail Bray, "have long been the smiling class" (*Misogyny Re-Loaded* 56). Postfeminist popular culture exhorts women to curate a physically and emotionally robust self, optimistically oriented toward choice and skeptical of "negative" or darker emotions. In keeping with the neoliberal and consumerist philosophies from which it draws, postfeminist popular culture eschews, in particular, discussions of vulnerability. Such dark matters are strategically dispersed onto feminism, which surfaces continually in postfeminist discourse as a gothic double.

Postfeminism's cultivation of what Bray mockingly deems a "wide-eyed blank Powerpuff carefree confident girly ideal" is related both to national character and to the infusion of therapeutic discourses into postmodern life (*Misogyny Reloaded* 59). We Americans, as Barbara Ehrenreich observes, "smile a lot and are often baffled when people from other cultures do not return the favor. In the well-worn stereotype, we are upbeat, cheerful, optimistic, and shallow" (1). Positive-thinking movements have emerged regularly throughout modern history, led by groups like Alcoholics Anonymous and charismatic individuals such as Norman Vincent Peale or the 1980s television evangelists. Women in particular have been addressed by these discourses, in feminized outlets like talk shows and magazines that encourage being, to borrow Oprah Winfrey's phrase, one's "best self." Lauren Berlant has described such feel-good culture as an "intimate sphere of femininity," where a "kind of soft supremacy rooted in compassion and coercive identification wants to dissolve all that structure through the work of good intentionality, while busily exoticizing and diminishing the inconvenient and the noncompliant" (*Female Complaint* 6). To feminist critics' chagrin, the postfeminist intimate sphere often reframes conflicts of race, gender, and structural inequities through the personalized language of self-help and self-esteem.[13]

Postfeminism's message of female success through privatized self-transformation resonates in many keys. Therapeutic rhetoric and consumerism have united in the fitness and beauty complex, which, as many critics have noted, positions itself as a new site of empowered choice-making.[14] The cheery postfeminist mind-set is even present in the decidedly less fashionable world of popular economics, where, in spite of a global recession, a new narrative of female uplift and progress is being written.[15] A recent pair of highly cited books—Liza Mundy's *The Richer Sex* (2012) and Hanna Rosin's *The End of Men* (2012)—have spearheaded a cultural narrative of women's projected economic dominance, theorizing that women will soon outearn men, forcing them into the domestic sphere. Both works, while containing illuminating glimpses into how women's educational persistence will reshape economic opportunities for some, envision a painless ride to the top that elides distinctions of race and class. Rosin, for instance, portrays the postrecession economy as "a kind of traveling sisterhood" where "upper-class women leave home" for the workforce, "creating domestic jobs for other women" to fill (5). Additionally, both authors gloss over discussions of antagonistic reactions to such changes in traditional roles. In *The Richer Sex*, Mundy theorizes that men will feel "liberated and enlarged" by becoming homemakers, in part because they will be given social approbation for doing so (224). Rosin recounts, without comment, how a male support-group instructor lectures his charges to acquire paid work in order to avoid being the "bitch" in the relationship (90). Punditry about women's dominance and men's woes is not new, of course, but traditionally it has focused upon the disadvantages of men and boys.[16] Postfeminist manifestos like those of Rosin and Mundy emphasize the chipper conviction that women are uniformly excelling.[17]

As these examples illustrate, many pictures of the postfeminist present do not disaggregate women's privileges, especially with regard to race. Postfeminist thought thus overlaps with "postracial" rhetorics; Ralina Joseph, among other critics, has carefully explicated both ideologies' petulance that race and gender continue to be analyzed as sites of structural oppression *at all* in the supposedly color-blind twenty-first century ("Tyra Banks Is Fat" 239).[18] Sometimes merely eliding differences *between* women and postfeminist and postracial discourses also often valorize concepts of hybridity and diversity at the *expense* of talking about how race affects women's lives. Issues of poverty, violence, and institutional discrimination receive short shrift within postfeminist popular culture, yet women of color who have achieved celebrity are hypervisible to support the argument of a smiling meritocracy.[19]

Postfeminism's sunny affect even has its own theoretical application, "choice feminism," which mandates the embrace of all lifestyle, professional, and political courses of action undertaken by women.[20] Choice feminism bolsters the postfeminist affect of positivity both by foreclosing dissent and ostensibly supporting all women, conveniently ignoring the social contexts and barriers that shape and bind "choices." As I discuss later in more detail, this remaindering of feminist thought has profound consequences within the popular sphere. Postfeminist gothic authors use their narratives to challenge this powerful claim. The strange literary legacy of *The Lovely Bones*, where teen white girls embrace *death* as a narrative space that is not culturally predetermined for them, problematizes the idea that choosing is itself joyous and freeing. In another example, author Susanna Moore's work repeatedly assails both postfeminist overconfidence in women's ability to make uncoerced decisions and choice feminism's assertion that all life decisions must be supported. Finally, Sapphire's tales of a mother and son in trapped circumstances questions the racial and class privileges inherent in the assumptions of choice feminism. Taken together, these varied critiques disrupt the surface of the "smiling class."

One of the most confounding aspects of postfeminism is its ability to repurpose painful and difficult circumstances as positive "challenges." Barbara Ehrenreich has examined this attitude within the culture of breast cancer, which has been rapidly consumerized with pretty and pink products over the past few decades. Ehrenreich, who is herself a breast cancer survivor, is sympathetic to but critical of intragroup pressure to view the disease as a gift or as "a chance for creative self-transformation—a makeover opportunity, in fact" (31). Such "sugarcoating," she maintains, encourages women who struggle with insurance tangles, fear, and debilitating pain to bury such feelings under "a cosmetic layer of cheer" (41).[21]

The sublimation of negative emotions in postfeminist culture is, of course, a complex process; believing that a painful experience has a higher meaning can be a profoundly helpful process for people struggling with illness. Furthermore, it is not my intention to suggest that in their determination to look on the bright side, postfeminist subjects merely exhibit mindless naïveté. I know from pedagogical experience that undergraduate students who have grown up internalizing postfeminism's contradictory messages are often savvy deconstructors of pop culture. Sarah Banet-Weiser has written of postfeminism's deployment of cynicism, irony, and camp in order to let women in on the joke of their own objectification, thus defusing it and rendering it "even ironically empowering" (211). Postfeminism thus mobilizes a range of affects to maintain its buoyancy *strategically*, sometimes accepting what is demeaning in order to be cool, and often displacing darker matters, such as discussions of sexual victimization and violence, onto the specter of feminism.

If gothic produces, as Judith Halberstam has remarked, "the deviant subjectivities opposite which the normal, the healthy, and the pure can be known," then a feminism constructed as wounded serves a gothic function, haunting the robust postfeminist self (*Skin Shows* 2). Since the women's movement, a deeply troubling association of feminism with victimization (itself a toxic word) has crept into the popular lexicon.[22] Feminist theory has itself held lively debates on these issues, as seen, for example, in the work of Wendy Brown, who cautions women that constructing "a certain injury-forming identity" adjudicated by the state risks codifying "within the law the very powerlessness it aims to redress" (21). Yet the pop understanding of feminism as victim-centric was most heavily influenced by a coterie of female critics in the 1990s. Writers like Rene Denfeld, Camille Paglia, Katie Roiphe, Christina Hoff Sommers, and Naomi Wolf argued that feminists promulgated a weak and powerless identity. As Roiphe famously put it, the framework of feminism "transforms perfectly stable women into hysterical, sobbing victims" (*Morning After* 112).[23]

Such arguments have been taken into account and criticized in much contemporary feminist writing, yet they "have been remarkably influential and continue to shape many people's perceptions of feminism," in Rebecca Stringer's words (20).[24] In the revisionists' writings, we can also glimpse postfeminist rhetorical moves that today, twenty-odd years after their initial publications, have become nearly reflexive. Wolf's enthusiasm for what she calls the "genderquake" of legal and social victories won by 1990s women, and her subsequent call for a feminism with "little heavy base ideology beyond the overarching premise 'More for women,'" captures postfeminism's preferences for premature celebration and just lightening up (*Fire with Fire* 138). Roiphe's *The Morning After*, a caricature of college women obsessed with sexual harassment and Take Back the Night marches, features one student who demonstrates "an admirable flair for putting offenders in their place" by pouring milk over sexual harassers' heads and intimidating obscene callers with boasts about her sexual prowess (101). This elegant shrug, this "so what" as response to misogyny, is a technology of postfeminism as well.[25] Similarly, Paglia's exhortation of "warrior heroines" who "spot trouble coming or boldly trounce their male assailants," in contrast to "passive, drippy" counterparts who "constantly get themselves into rape scenarios," resonates in the butt-kicking heroine, a major icon of postfeminist film and television (304).

Social degradation of the word *victim*, and the concomitant yoking of victimization to feminism, continues unabated in twenty-first-century culture. Columnist George Will, writing in reaction to increased federal attention to higher education's sexual assault policy, famously suggested that colleges have made "victimhood a coveted status that confers privilege" ("Colleges Become the Victims"). Reactions online to the opinion piece reaffirmed the vibrancy of the feminist blogosphere in eloquent postings and sarcastic dissections of "#SurvivorPrivilege."[26] Yet the suggestion that rape victims luxuriate in unearned benefits illustrates how embedded cultural contempt for victims—particularly female ones—has become.

The concept of victimization, writes Carine Mardorossian, "assumes an obviousness that obscures its historicity and the theoretical difficulties it presents" ("Toward a New Feminist Theory" 766). An intersectional analysis must remind us that not all women have been historically eligible for victim status in the first place. Women of color are often not considered "legitimate victims" in the context of sexual violence. Linda Meyer Williams has traced the impact of antebellum hysteria about black female hypersexuality on black women's marginalized status today: "If black women are viewed as always desirous of sex, then sex in any form will be viewed as acceptable to black women and the charge of rape denied," she writes (12). Native American women are similarly invisible, as witnessed recently by congressional resistance to including limited domestic-violence protections into the 2013 reauthorization of the Violence Against Women Act.[27] Class and occupational status also further impact our conceptions of who counts; activist Rachel Lloyd reminds us that within the sex industry, women of color "are not believed to be capable of being hurt or raped" and are thus "seen as willing participants in their own abuse" as opposed to victims of violent crime (126). The relationship of women to sexual victimization is thus fragmented, but nearly always negative. Some women are condescended to as victims, and even more troublingly, others' injuries are not recognized at all.

American antipathy to victimhood coexists, strangely enough, with increased knowledge of and services for survivors of sexual and domestic violence. The nomenclature involved today is often more gender neutral; second wave terms like *rape crisis* and *women's shelter* are increasingly replaced with terms like *crime victim service* or *battering intervention*.[28] The gender-neutralizing of much of this discourse is due to antiviolence activists' essential, ongoing work to acknowledge and respond to the sexual and domestic victimizations of many men and LGBTQ survivors. Today we have greater consciousness of men's and boys' ability to be victims of sexual violence (whether of women or of other men) and increased, though not yet adequate, support services. As Molly Dragiewicz notes, the contributions of feminists and their allies has "actually helped to open a discursive space where it is possible to talk about the fact that men are not invulnerable and that women are not incapable of violence" (84).

Still, there is also a troubling undercurrent that decontextualizes gendered violence by contending that it is a "human" problem perpetrated equally by the sexes. In recent years a new approach to domestic violence has arisen, which argues that women commit as many violent offenses (if not more) than men within intimate relationships. Many critics have taken issue with the "gender-symmetry" thesis, particularly its avoidance of the context and severity of violence at issue; both Dragiewicz and sociologist Michael Kimmel provide helpful inquiries into the subject in academic discourse. Gender-symmetry arguments also tend to, in the words of Ta-Nehisi Coates, engage in "annihilation of inconvenient history," erasing the "tradition of men controlling women through violence" ("No, Hope Solo"). *Salon*'s Katie McDonough compares them to "derailing tactics"—defensive eruptions about false rape-abuse accusations and the notion that "women do it too" whenever acts of violence against women briefly take the public spotlight ("Domestic Violence Gender Trap").[29]

While it can be powerful and inclusive to deem sexual violence a "civil rights" or "human rights" issue, Rebecca Solnit reminds us that the "so-called war of the sexes is extraordinarily lopsided when it comes to actual violence" ("Longest War"). Twenty-first-century America has weathered revelation after revelation of widespread abuses of women by members of the military, professional athletes, protestors, coworkers, and suburban teenagers with cell phones and Twitter feeds. We have become desensitized to rampage shooters, who, as did George Sodini in 2009 and Elliot Rodger in 2014, justify mass murder of strangers based on their perceived romantic rejections. The increasingly common phenomenon of girls and women emerging from long-term sexual exploitation in captivity—precisely the stuff of which gothic novels are made—is explored in *Splattered Ink*'s closing chapter. The list could go on and on, testifying to the fact that the female gothic is not so fictional after all.

Rebecca Solnit points out that by obfuscating the role of gender in the experience of sexual and domestic violence, we escape other conversations. "If we talked about crimes like these and why they are so common, we'd have to talk about what kinds of profound change this society, or this nation" needs, she muses, and "we'd be talking about masculinity, or male roles, or maybe patriarchy, and we don't talk much about that" ("Longest War"). Post-feminist discourse about sexual and domestic violence is indeed fragmented. Hypersexualized images of women saturate the media, often connected to discourses about empowerment. Popular culture looks askance at discussing women in terms of vulnerability and victimization (although of course some women aren't eligible to be considered victims in the first place), and suggests instead that they are equal perpetrators of violence. Yet our headlines belie this placidity, providing monstrous tales of rampage shootings, rapes, and femicides. Thanks to the information age, we are awash in knowledge and "awareness" of sexualized violence. It seems, though, that we have increasingly little to say.

Postfeminist Literature, Light and Dark

Postfeminist gothic steps into this cultural silence, testifying to the powerful ongoing realities of rape, assault, and other forms of horror. Attending to such dark topics is difficult not only given the postfeminist mind-set, but also because of literature's changing status as an object of feminist analysis. Embedded in this project is my conviction that the world of contemporary fiction continues to be a vital place for meaningful discussions of gender.[30] On balance, however, twenty-first-century feminist cultural analysis is moving beyond the world of books, increasingly investigating electronic media for bellwethers in the landscape. To date, many of the leading explications of postfeminist culture look to television, film, and other sites for their iconography. Diane Negra's work *What a Girl Wants?*, for instance, examines film, television, and lifestyle brands like those associated with Oprah Winfrey, and Yvonne Tasker and Negra's edited collection *Interrogating Postfeminism* surveys popular culture's mass magazines, punk music, and cinema. Fashion photography and makeover programs are sites of inquiry for Angela McRobbie's *The Aftermath of Feminism*, Joanne Hollows and Rachel Moseley's compendium *Feminism and Popular Culture* interrogates cooking shows and other new paradigms of the domestic arts, and Rosalind Gill and Christina Scharff's edited volume *New Femininities* explores global beauty norms in forums such as pageants and the popular program *Top Model*. The most recognizable icons of postfeminist cultural criticism are characters in a television show, *Sex and the City* (1998–2004), which is, as of this writing, the subject of more than twenty-five scholarly articles and several critical books.

In this vibrant and expansive archive of postfeminist cultural practice, what is the role of *fiction*? In earlier eras, particularly during the 1970s heyday of second wave feminism, stories and novels captured the kinetic energy of the times. Maria Lauret asserts that second wave women's novels "transformed the literary arena and willfully made it a gendered, political space in which women's issues could be discussed and a feminist readership constituted" (1). Writers such as Rita Mae Brown, Marilyn French, Alice Walker, and more, asserts Lauret, showed "the political discourses of Women's Liberation and

Black feminism informed imaginative new reconstructions of the condition of women in American society" (1). Several critics have pointed to the encoding of bildungsromanesque struggles of consciousness-raising in second wave fiction while others appreciate the period's frank attention to formerly taboo topics like sexual assault.[31]

The transformative energy within second wave feminist novels seems harder to locate in their twenty-first-century counterparts. Some works do break through, of course, and the commercially successful young-adult (YA) literature sector is bustling with capable female heroines like *The Hunger Games* series' Katniss Everdeen. While acknowledging the altered expectations of a digital age, where books compete for cultural capital with multimedia, it still seems fair to say that the role of women's novels within postfeminist cultural studies feels somewhat tentative.

There is, of course, one quite visible subgenre of postfeminist fiction: "chick lit," a wry, fizzy cocktail of romance, consumerism, and professional travails. In chick-lit's ur-narrative, a neurotic middle-class white subject stumbles, bumbles, and shops her way through romance with a wealthy and dashing man. The subgenre is both lucrative and visually identifiable; as Elizabeth Merrick observes, "soon after the millennium, it became nearly impossible to enter a bookstore without tripping over a pile of pink books covered with truncated legs, shoes, or handbags" (viii). Chick lit's ascendancy did not occur overnight. Women novelists in the Reagan era continued to explore female gothic themes of misogyny and sexual violence, as the critical work of Helene Meyers, Roberta Rubenstein, and Timothy Melley has shown.[32] Yet the shifting politics of the backlash echoed on bookshelves as well, and, increasingly, manifestos were replaced by frothier genres like the "bonkbuster," an epic of sexual and retail conquest that clearly prefigures chick lit.[33] Much like the word *postfeminism*, *chick lit* has fuzzy origins.[34] James Wolcott's oft-cited *New Yorker* piece on the "kittenish" and "softened and juvenilized" style of women's journalism in feminism's wake neatly prefigures the fictional aesthetic of chick-lit fiction blossoming at the same time (57).

The plethora of Prada shoes, Cartier jewels, and other markers of luxury spilled across the pages of chick lit marks it as an aspirational, rather than a realistic, genre. Yet it also mirrors dominant concerns within postfeminist popular culture, including fabulous consumerism, individual achievement, white insularity, and marriage-focused heteronormativity. Such is the case with Helen Fielding's *Bridget Jones's Diary*, a first-person chronicle of a weight-obsessed urban professional's romantic pratfalls in London, which is widely hailed as an exemplification of the genre. Shelley Cobb muses that

"*Bridget Jones's Diary* holds a privileged place in cultural debates about feminism, women, and gender relations in the current postfeminist climate" ("Adaptable Bridget" 283). Stéphanie Genz similarly refers to Bridget Jones as a "poster child of this self-absorbed postfeminism" (137).

The cultural dominance of chick lit within postfeminist literature has proved to be an interesting conundrum for feminist critics. Some have wisely warned against viewing any feminized genre with patronizing disdain, and have placed the genre within larger traditions of women's writing.[35] Others view the form itself as condescending to women; Elizabeth Merrick, for instance, goes so far as to assert that the "chick-lit deluge has helped to obscure the literary fiction being written by some of our country's most gifted women" and that the genre's "formula numbs our senses" (ix). Pamela Butler and Jigna Desai trenchantly observe that since critique of chick lit operates almost exclusively from a framework of gender, excluding other axes of difference, it thus re-centers "white women as the subjects of feminism who must be saved from the threat of postfeminist apoliticism, and from the popular culture that is imagined as a cause and/or symptom of that apoliticism" (6). It is not my intention to make chick lit a bogeyman. Instead, following Stephanie Harzewski's claim that chick lit "is not the only existing type of postfeminist novel, but it is the *most culturally visible* form of postfeminist fiction," I would like to create equally visible space for a genre that defies the dominant affect of postfeminist literature and paints a very different picture of late capitalist life for women (8; emphasis added). The authors studied in *Splattered Ink* drag women's ongoing experiences of spectacular violence up from the basement, forcing our postfeminist culture to confront the monsters it denies.

I firmly believe that literature remains a meaningful sphere of influence within postfeminist culture. Katherine Payant has written that "it is important for women to name their experience, to evaluate their suffering and joys, their weaknesses and strengths, and to see how these are reflected in other women's lives." Fiction, she continues, "because of its capacity to represent experience, has the ability to help women do this" (221). Postfeminist gothic novels bring to the surface the fears that still grip women while exploring the complex rhetorical strategies undertaken by postfeminism to manage those fears. We begin with the story of teenager Susie Salmon, heroine of Alice Sebold's best-selling novel *The Lovely Bones*, who speaks from an unquiet grave.

2

Uneasy Lie the Bones

Alice Sebold's Postfeminist Gothic

"I was so alive then," narrates the murder victim Susie Salmon in Alice Sebold's best-selling novel *The Lovely Bones* (2002). "I thought it was the *worst thing in the world* to be lying flat on my back with a sweating man on top of me. To be trapped inside the earth and have no one know where I was" (12; emphasis in original). Caught underground with Susie in a psychopath's subterranean lair, readers know that they are in dark territory indeed. Sebold's books—her memoir *Lucky* (1999) and her novels *The Lovely Bones* and *The Almost Moon* (2007)—certainly provide the ingredients for what Eugenia DeLamotte terms the "shopping-list" of gothic literature (*Perils* 5). Reading Sebold, one encounters mysterious and imprisoning domiciles, ruins, uncanny doubles, women in peril, and the acute threat of male violence.

Sebold's literary work uses different modalities to bring the strains of gothic and postfeminist thought into dialogue. Her elegiac best seller *The Lovely Bones* can be profitably read as a gothic tempered by postfeminist ideals. The novel's unique posthumous narrative voice challenges the "victim/agent" debate dominating late feminist discourse, and creates agency for silenced women. But the narrative of *The Lovely Bones* also minimizes anger over gendered violence; it employs digressive subplots that drain narrative momentum, and it funnels readers' outrage and desire for retribution into a single politicized feminist character. By contrast, Sebold's second novel, *The Almost Moon,* reveals postfeminist dreams to be gothic nightmares. Its main narrative evokes a postfeminist fantasy of matricide, but Sebold consistently undercuts the murderous narrator Helen Knightly's claims. By making her heroine a gothic madwoman, Sebold positions Helen as the monstrous extension of the postfeminist woman whose smiling, compliant visage hides a cesspool of hatred.

Alice Sebold has not previously been analyzed within the frame of postfeminist gothic—reviews of her work have stressed her biography (as a college student, she survived a brutal rape and successfully prosecuted her attacker) or ascribed the popular success of her writing to implicitly gendered rhetorics of "therapy." *The Lovely Bones* is understood by many critics as literary comfort food for a post-9/11 public desperate to believe in the happy afterlife of its lost citizens. *The Almost Moon* has been accused of exploiting the American fascination with tragedy to achieve "moral seriousness, soft reviews and brisk sales" (Siegel, "Mom's in the Freezer"). Sebold's fictional universe deserves a closer, historicized investigation; her compelling works show how one woman writer responds to gendered violence in an age that prefers to disengage from questions of gender altogether. Should we continue to deny the materiality and impact of sexism and gendered violence, she suggests, we will make gothic novels of our own lives, and monsters of ourselves.

Elegy for a Buried Girl: *The Lovely Bones*

Sebold's engagement with the macabre, and her abiding interest in the issue of violence against women, began with her wrenching personal experience as a rape survivor. The rape and its aftermath is the subject of *Lucky*, an eloquent memoir that precedes *The Lovely Bones* but which found commercial success after the latter's publication. Early in *Lucky*, a police officer tells Sebold that she is comparatively fortunate; she left the underground tunnel of her rape alive, whereas another girl was dismembered and killed there. The dead girl's specter haunts *Lucky*'s opening preface, in which Sebold recalls lying on the tunnel floor and seeing a pink hair tie. She remembers: "I will always think of her when I think of the pink hair tie. I will think of a girl in the last moments of her life."

Some critics have suggested that *The Lovely Bones*, a fictionalized account of rape and murder, is an attempt to write the experience of the murdered girl with whom Sebold is forever linked. Speaking with Katharine Viner, Sebold observed: "It was never a conscious thing to tell [the other girl's] story. . . . I didn't know the details of her case . . . but obviously I'd be an idiot to deny that inside my unconscious there's something like that going on" (Sebold, "Above and Beyond"). The books do share several commonalities. The first chapter of *The Lovely Bones* (in which Susie is raped and murdered) echoes

Lucky in its use of graphic, straightforward language that foregrounds the experience of bodily pain. Both works also assert that violence against women in suburbia is not anomalous, but alarmingly frequent. In *The Lovely Bones*, a mild-mannered old bachelor to whom the local children sell Girl Scout cookies is revealed as a serial rapist and killer. In *Lucky*, Sebold juxtaposes her own assault at Syracuse University with eruptions of gendered violence in her suburban hometown; these include the arrest of a minister's son for brutally mauling a woman and a childhood friend's revelation that his mother survived a gang rape.

There is, however, a distinct tonal difference between the memoir and the novel. In *Lucky*, Sebold's anger at her rapist is palpable throughout the text. She writes poems about his evisceration and vows to "murder [him] back" through her convincing testimony on the stand (113). This lacerating rage is not present in *The Lovely Bones*; it has been replaced by melancholy. Memoirs and novels belong to different literary genres, of course, and readers need not expect Sebold to replicate one mood in the other. But the choice of elegy over anger in the later (and fictional) book points to the difficulty of writing about women's violence in postfeminist culture.

Sebold's portrait of a brutally violated girl must be set against a postfeminist cultural mood that is deeply hostile to the idea of women's "victimization." As previously discussed, in the early 1990s the assertion that feminism was overly invested in women's vulnerability and victimization took root. In her book *The Morning After* (1993), pundit Katie Roiphe indicted feminism for propounding a new kind of female gothic heroine. "The image that emerges from feminist preoccupation with rape and sexual harassment is that of women as victims, offended by a professor's dirty joke, verbally pressured into sex by peers," Roiphe remarked. Such an image, she continued, "bears a striking resemblance to that fifties ideal my mother and the other women of her generation fought so hard to get away from . . . here she is again, with her pure intentions and her wide eyes. Only this time it is the feminists themselves who are breathing new life into her" (6). Naomi Wolf's book *Fire with Fire* (1993) similarly juxtaposed a "victim feminism" that stressed women's oppression with a forward-thinking, optimistic (and rather politics-free) "power feminism." The accusation that feminism promotes victimist thinking lingers to this day, and it has become a cornerstone of postfeminist ideology. Thus, postfeminist gothic must negotiate between the heroine's experience of terror and the current antivictimist mood; the heroine must suffer, but not become a victim.

This is a tall order, and it is evident from the continuing popularity of women's genres—like television's Lifetime channel—that the *popularity* of the woman-in-peril story remains strong. What has happened, then, is a rhetorical shift in the heroine's presentation; she is now less a victim than a survivor. "The valorization and lionization of survivorship in politics, popular culture, popular psychology, and religion is quite new," writes Alyson Cole, "as is its contemporary coupling with victimhood in expressions such as 'victim/survivor' or 'from victim to survivor" (139). While the term *survivor* has a long history (it is perhaps most often associated with Holocaust memorialization), its current vogue in postfeminism also signals the profound cultural influence of therapeutic discourses. These discourses map a narrative in which a traumatized subject moves from psychological fragmentation to health. The act of naming oneself a survivor symbolically places the subject's trauma in the past and denies the event the ability to "define" her.

The Lovely Bones would seem to present a dilemma for postfeminist analysis because the victimization of the deceased narrator cannot be easily translated into survivorship. Sebold herself has pointed to the difference between her rape and the finality of Susie's fictional trauma. When a radio host suggested during an interview that Sebold and Susie Salmon were both "raped" and "[in many ways] dead," she firmly rejected the idea. "I'm sorry, there's a big difference between me and a dead woman," she responded. "I'm here talking to you, for a start" (Sebold, "Above and Beyond"). In her employment of a posthumous voice, though, Sebold has created a unique form of literary survivorship for the heroine.

The Lovely Bones is one of a small handful of texts practicing *autothanatography*, or first-person accounts of death. Ivan Callus claims that since autothanatographic texts push the boundary between death and life, they should employ a different literary mode from mimetic realism. If the works are "too neat and decorous, if they retain too much of the cadences, shape, idiom and language of the narratives of the living, the memoirs written by the dead in and from their death will disappoint because they fail to convey the absolute challenge to verisimilitude," he asserts. Sebold's "very readable *The Lovely Bones*," Callus continues, "risks a failure of the imagination" by hewing largely to realism (428). Ruediger Heinze, however, cautions us to remember that the cozy realism of Susie's posthumous narration follows, strange as it may seem, from the fact that she did not survive her assault. "Supposing that [Susie] had survived but suffered atrocious physical violence, her narrative would be that of a seriously traumatized teenager, with the consequence of it likely being labeled unreliable," Heinze asserts. "By transporting her to heaven, and thus into a narrative position of alleged otherworldly serenity and peace and of privileged observation, her narrative is, paradoxically, rendered reliable" (288).

The respite of the afterworld does indeed provide Susie's narration with reliable ballast, but most important, her cheerful, self-assured posthumous voice provides emotional relief for readers. As horrifying as it is to be trapped under the earth with Susie in her murderer's subterranean lair, we know that she continues a pain-free "existence" after death. Her family on Earth does not have this sense of catharsis. Indeed, only fragments of Susie's body are ever recovered, leaving her fate suspended in a state of instability that torments her parents. In a troubling passage, Mrs. Salmon dreams of sati (an outlawed funeral practice in which a widow is immolated with her husband's body) because she finds the corporeality of this horrible death strangely comforting. "The girl was being burned alive," Abigail thinks in her dream, "but, first, there had been her body, clean and whole" (173).

The literary survivorship established through Susie's posthumous narration restores some dignity and agency to those silenced by violence. In her memoir *Lucky*, Sebold expressed anger at how the events of her rape were appropriated as student gossip. "Magically I became story, not person, and story implies a kind of ownership by the storyteller," she wrote (97). By placing Susie at this book's center, Sebold puts the person back in the equation; she also creates literary empathy for the most abject class of the murdered. It would, of course, be ludicrous to call Susie's posthumous narration a triumph. As a dead girl, she is largely ineffective in her efforts to influence life on Earth. Nevertheless, the expanded consciousness granted to her by Sebold allows Susie certain privileges. She possesses fluid abilities that allow her to gain access to minds and memories at will and to interpret events that preexist her birth. Through this process, Susie can investigate the inner life of her murderer, Mr. Harvey, as well as the intricate dynamics of her parents' marriage. Sebold's posthumous mythology also places heaven above Earth; from her perch in the afterlife, Susie frequently observes earthly behavior in an affectionate, slightly indulgent way.

Susie is an unusual example of the postfeminist survivor mystique because she suffers the ultimate trauma but evades death's finality through expanded consciousness and narrative control. Diane Long Hoeveler sees a similar fascination with this figure in the traditions of the female gothic. Hoeveler argues that the "core fantasy" of a female gothic novel such as Ann Radcliffe's *Mysteries of Udolpho* (1794) is that "one can tell one's story in a way that the victim triumphs over the victimizer, the weak overcome the strong" (*Gothic Feminism* 101). This creative rescripting is at work in postfeminist culture, too. Hoeveler writes that postfeminism depicts women as "canny, flexible survivors of a patriarchal system that *they actually dominate and manipulate* through a variety of passive-aggressive behavioral strategies that are passed on through cultural systems such as female Gothic novels" ("Postfeminist Filmic" 100–101; emphasis added). Susie Salmon "survives" not only in her narrative, but also in her passive, limited, earthly agency. By accidentally touching a classmate at the moment of her death, she inspires the young girl, Ruth, to become an avenger of violence (more on Ruth later). The text also hints coyly at Susie's possible involvement in her murderer's eventual death. In the conclusion, Mr. Harvey dies by blunt-force trauma caused by a falling icicle. Icicles are discussed earlier in the novel as young Susie's weapon of choice in a how-to-commit-murder game. Sebold renders the language of Harvey's death scene in the passive—"the icicle fell"—which hints at, but does not confirm, Susie's participation (327). In his review of the novel, Daniel Mendelsohn deems the death scene "a laboriously constructed joke" that points to Sebold's overplotting ("Novel of the Year"). But the moment's open-endedness reveals *The Lovely Bones*'s investment in the ideology of the postfeminist survivor. Heretofore, Susie has not been rendered as particularly influential in earthly affairs; it is *unlikely* that she is the agent responsible for Harvey's death. But the possibility remains, and with it the implication that in her place among the clouds, Susie possesses the last laugh.

Susie's posthumous narration is structurally innovative, and it also engages a range of postfeminist moods. Deborah Silverton Rosenfelt has argued that postfeminist novels are "more skeptical than optimistic, more aware of limits than transgressive of traditional boundaries, more elegiac than 'bildungsromanic'" (270). This somber assessment might seem quite distant from the upwardly mobile rhetoric of postfeminist survivorship, but the two are linked. The polite disengagement of many postfeminist works—in other words, the strategic not-seeing of gender inequity—works to *preserve* the "mission accomplished" illusion that is so entrenched in postfeminist thought. *The Lovely Bones* manifests this disengaged aesthetic by dissipating anger over Susie's horrific death. Sebold cannily funnels readers' desire for vengeance into a single politicized feminist character—Ruth Connors, Susie's classmate and friend—and its story line dissolves into circular, digressive plotlines that sap the crime-solving momentum. The novel's inward turning is further complemented by other postfeminist moments of retreatism, including skepticism toward public authority—such as the police—and a revived interest in the home as the feminine center of fulfillment.

Sebold plays with the detective novel's traditional suspense-building apparatus by introducing both a deceased narrator *and* the murderer's identity in the book's first two pages. There is, of course, still room for *The Lovely Bones* to veer into thriller territory; family members' suspicions soon turn toward the villainous neighbor Mr. Harvey, and a police investigation begins. But here too Sebold defies our narrative expectations. After the blistering first chapter depicting Susie's death, the succeeding chapters do not deal with the detectives overmuch; instead, they present short, haiku-like flashbacks of Salmon family life. Each scene contains an object lesson. When Susie narrates a powerful memory about taking a candid photograph of her mother, she comes to the epiphany that Abigail Salmon had a separate adult identity aside from her role as a parent.[1] Other scenes in this section feature Susie playing with snow globes and ships in bottles in order to emphasize the fragility of life. While these fragments provide context into daily life in the Salmon household, they also startlingly dilute the narrative momentum surrounding Susie's murder.

Daniel Mendelsohn has found these brief, gossamer-like scenes to be reminiscent of "the pat, artificial rhythms of television" ("Novel of the Year"). But their digressiveness recalls gothic conventions as well. Lucie Armitt suggests that the cul-de-sac—an uncanny return to the starting place—"can also signal the presiding pattern of melancholia" in contemporary women's gothic (19). *The Lovely Bones* is replete with such inscrutable moments of repetition; for example, the candid photograph of discontented mother Abigail resurfaces again and again, prompting new realizations from each family member who views it. Later in the novel, Abigail and her mother literally walk in circles around the cul-de-sac of their development, ending up where they began. Taken together, these narrative digressions reduce the immediacy and rawness of Susie's assault and murder.

This tonal dampening is further emphasized by Sebold's turn inward toward the space of private memory and away from public authority. In the novel, only civilians (including Susie's father Jack and her grandmother Lynn) correctly intuit that Susie has been killed by Mr. Harvey. The police initially focus on Susie's boyfriend, Ray Singh. As racial outsiders in a 1970s white subdivision, the Singhs encounter behavior that ranges from indifference to prejudice in the wake of Susie's disappearance. Ray's beautiful, aloof mother Ruana dazzles and confuses the police, who "had expected her to fall into the grooves of the patter they relied on with all attractive women," but find instead that "she only grew more erect in posture as they tried harder and harder to ingratiate themselves" (85). For his part Ray both self-dramatizes his outsider status (he refers to himself as "the Moor" and wears smoking jackets to school) and tries hard to fit in (he delivers a lecture on "The Suburban Experience" at a local college). The police's suspicion of Ray is nominally based on the discovery of his love note to Susie, but it is also clearly bound up with racism. "The police descended on his house," Sebold writes, "leaning heavily on him, insinuating things. They were fueled by the guilt they read into Ray's dark skin, by the rage they felt at his manner, and by his beautiful yet too exotic and unavailable mother" (26).

Through the Singhs' struggle, Sebold comments on the privilege of white suburban insularity. Ray's family's outsider status makes them the focus of police suspicion, while the murderous George Harvey, quite literally the "man next door," wears suburban banality like a cloak to deflect attention. Lead detective Len Fenerman dismisses Mr. Harvey as a harmless old man, and his evaluation of Harvey's alibi as "compelling" allows the murderer time to escape (63). The neighbors mourn and hold memorial services, but the crime inspires no foundation of public anger or activism. The novel's reticence toward public authority is not necessarily postfeminist, of course. Historically, women have had good reason to beware the criminal-legal complex, particularly with regard to issues of sexual assault. In *Lucky*, Sebold eloquently articulated her own difficult experiences with the police and law officers tasked with helping her in the aftermath of her rape. But the way in which *The Lovely Bones* turns away from the public sphere does suggest the delicate disengagement of postfeminist fiction that Rosenfelt describes.

Susie's freewheeling and cheerful narration contributes to this aesthetic. Sometimes the character is grandiose; she dreams of "having a body that the boys wanted and the girls envied, but [being] so nice on top of it all that they would feel too guilty to do anything but worship me" (16–17). This self-aggrandizement is typical of adolescent thinking, but the playfulness of Susie's voice becomes jarring when extended to descriptions of the violence done to her. She recalls her dismembered self in a highly understated way: "He carried me back to his house, where, while he went inside to wash up, I waited for him" (16). She even finds a bright side to having her bloody remains placed in a sinkhole where they will never be found: "Ultimately it was the memory of those very moles—and the pictures of their blind, nosy, toothsome selves that I sought out in books—that made me accept more readily being sunk in the earth in a heavy metal safe," she observes. "I was mole-proof, anyway" (293–94).

There are a few fleeting references to Susie's desire for Charles Bronson–style vengeance for her rape and murder, but there are many *more* moments of accommodation to the state of death and passivity (58). Susie's counselor in heaven, Franny, tells her that she will find peace "if you *stop asking* why you were killed instead of someone else, *stop investigating* the vacuum left by your loss, *stop wondering* what everyone left on Earth is feeling" (120; emphasis added). Quicker than we might think, Susie "stops asking" questions about her fate, assuming a position of contented omniscience in the celestial realm. Here, the disengagement of postfeminism overlaps with popular therapeutic discourses of grief. Susie becomes a sage who has "let go" or "moved beyond" her trauma, becoming tempered with wisdom through the years.

The heroine's ready accommodation to posthumous existence calms the audience by reassuring them of meaningful life after death. Indeed, many critics connected *The Lovely Bones*'s commercial success to a post-9/11 public's desire for visions of a peaceful afterlife. Daniel Mendelsohn asked: "For who is Sebold's public, but one that has very recently seen innocents die, horribly, one to whom Sebold's fantasy of recuperation and, indeed, an endless, video-like replay has a vital subconscious appeal?" ("Novel of the Year"). In Britain, Katharine Viner noted, critics tended to "put the book's success down to September 11 and the consolation that, even if nearly 3,000 people were vaporised at their desks, they're alive and well upstairs somewhere" (Sebold, "Above and Beyond"). The novel's invocation of therapeutic language has gendered consequences as well. As previously discussed, feminist critics have warned that therapeutic structures threaten to replace political action with individualized self-work or corrective behavior. Jillian Sandell observes that "built into the structure of therapy and recovery is a belief that society per se *cannot* be changed and it is futile for us to think that it can be. We have control over only our own individual acts of transformation" (23). This attitude can be particularly dangerous for women (more frequent therapeutic subjects than men) by encouraging them to adjust to, rather than to change, inequitable elements of the world. Susie evinces this philosophy in the novel's conclusion, when she reinterprets her death as a beautiful "sacrifice" necessary to bind her family together. She observes:

> These were the lovely bones that had grown around my absence: the connections—sometimes tenuous, sometimes made at great cost, but often magnificent—that happened after I was gone. And I began to see things in a way that let me hold the world without me in it. The events that my death wrought were merely the bones of a body that would become whole at some unpredictable time in the future. The price of what I came to see as this miraculous body had been my life. (320)

Elisabeth Bronfen has written that throughout Western literary history, "the sacrifice of the virtuous, innocent woman serves a social critique and transformation" (181). The striking titular image of the lovely bones foregrounds the theme of feminine self-sacrifice for the sake of the family. Other women are similarly silenced. Susie's mother Abigail survives the book, but is not heard from again in the final chapter. Ruth, the lesbian-identified classmate who swaps bodies with Susie in the novel's magical ending, is "straightened" and returned to a heterosexual coupling with Ray. Deborah Silverton Rosenfelt has remarked that postfeminist novels "tend to reinstate . . . heterosexual passion and heterosexual love, as well as familial relations, perhaps especially motherhood" (270). Indeed, *The Lovely Bones* returns (or resigns) Abigail and Ruth to traditional roles at the novel's end, which is particularly intriguing given these characters' overt connections to second wave feminism.

Ruth, who is inexplicably afforded limited powers of vision when she brushes by Susie's ghost fleeing Earth, operates as a nostalgic representation of the lesbian feminist whose political desires to help women are aligned with her sexual longings. Brian Norman deems her a "cardboard cutout version of 1970s protofeminism" (152). A political outsider from the start, Ruth, who is described by Susie as "the quietest kind of rebel," restores pubic hair and wrinkles to airbrushed female nudes copied from *Playboy* pictorials (77). Sebold notes that Ruth "did not believe in makeup. She thought it demeaned women" (110). A sexual outsider too, Ruth recalls feeling at age eight a "fuzzy feeling of difference, that her crushes on female teachers or her cousin were more real than the other girls' crushes. Hers contained a desire beyond sweetness and attention, it fed a longing, beginning to flower green and yellow into a crocuslike lust, the soft petals opening into her awkward adolescence" (117–18).

In a novel focused on private and often frustrated responses to trauma, such as Jack Salmon's heartbreakingly ineffectual attempt to confront Mr. Harvey, Ruth connects Susie's suffering to a larger political context of female vulnerability and the "many little-girl losts" (209). While still a teenager, she manifests a fascination with the missing Susie that allows her sexual and sociopolitical interests to overlap. Her romantic longings for Susie are triangulated by the latter's boyfriend, Ray Singh; Ruth convinces Ray to engage in sexual play with her, wheedling that "you can pretend I'm Susie and I will too" (201). Simultaneously, the mystery of Susie's presumed death becomes increasingly *vocational* for Ruth. She develops a worldview of female vulnerability; Susie describes watching the New York City–bound Ruth "pound the cement in her defiant boots, sure that women were being murdered wherever she went" (226).

Ruth experiences women's violent memories in "bright flashes—a fall down the stairs, a scream, a shove, the tightening of hands around a neck" (251).

Her notebook is filled with snippets of these scenes: "Domestic. Ave. C. Husband and wife. Roof on Mott Street, a teenage girl, gunshot" (313). These narrative scraps harmonize with the novel's textual rhythm that, as I have already discussed, features short scenes and fragmented imagery.[2] Ruth's visions also complement Susie's own growing understanding of herself as one murdered girl among many; several months after her murder, Susie intuits Mr. Harvey's fellow victims and calls out their names: "Jackie Meyer. Delaware, 1967. Thirteen. . . . Flora Hernandez. Delaware, 1963. Eight. . . . Leah Fox. Delaware, 1969. Twelve" (181).

Wandering the streets and bearing witness in her journal, Ruth aims to "place those pieces back together, to set them firm, to make murdered girls live again" (313). Her voice is the most political in the novel, connecting her source inspiration, Susie, with untold numbers of other victims of male violence. Ruth's avenging arc absorbs much of the anguish readers feel over Susie's fate. As a somewhat heavy-handed representation of lesbian feminism, she is also a specter haunting postfeminist thought. While there is room within postfeminist ideology for a certain kind of lesbian chic, postfeminism is also forged against the "ghost of the scary lesbian/feminist," writes Jane Gerhard; the figure is a "nightmarish vision of autonomous womanhood," with "a man-hating, definitely humorless, and certainly fashion challenged caricature" (37).[3] The "bad political lesbian" has enjoyed a similarly apparitional effect within queer theory, where she is often summoned as the humorless retrograde foil.[4] Such figures insist, as Ruth Connors does, on continuing to read the world through a politics of gender. Ruth's overwrought odes to murdered women, whose titles include "Beside Her Now" and "The Lip of the Grave," signal her belatedness (114).

The character of Ruth Connors is thus loaded with symbolic freight, making the end of her story all the more intriguing. In a finale of magical realism, Ruth swaps bodies with Susie for an evening. While Ruth enjoys the celestial company of the women she avenges on earth, Susie has her first experience of consensual sex, with Ray. This sequence could be read, alternatively, as queer, postfeminist, or as participating in rape culture. Ann Bliss points out that "the text indicates that this possession happens with Ruth's consent and Ray's awareness that he is sexually intimate with Susie, not Ruth" (878). Indeed, Sebold writes, the body swap is "a marvelous possibility that Ruth had dreamed of since our meeting in the parking lot," one that leaves Ruth in its aftermath "more tired and more happy than she had ever been" (310–11). In this moment when she is unhinged from her sexual body and ascends to heaven, Ruth attains her own desires to meet the women and girls who haunt her (it is a moment of comic deflation, compared by Susie to a *Teen Beat* fan event). The sequence also fulfills the teenaged Ruth's earlier promise to Ray that "you can pretend I'm Susie and I will too" (201).

However, despite its playfulness, the body-swapping scene is disconcerting when placed in context of the novel's politics. *The Lovely Bones* soberly and straightforwardly addresses the physical and psychic damage of rape in its opening pages, thus making Susie's invasion of Ruth's body, and her later borrowing of the body to engage in sex, problematic.[5] Additionally, the sequence "straightens" Ruth, if only temporarily. Elizabeth Tallent notes that "the particular body borrowed by Susie in order to experience the loss of virginity has been carefully constructed as lesbian." Such a borrowing, Tallent adds, risks implying that "a lesbian body, by virtue of not 'belonging' to any male, [is] more available for appropriation" ("Trouble with Postmortality"). The body-swapping plot's sexual straightening and problematic politics of consent are indeed troubling. What is perhaps *most* characteristic of the novel's engagement with postfeminist concerns, however, is Ruth's self-abnegation for a perceived greater good. Throughout the novel, Ruth longs to satisfy the dead Susie's perceived needs. "I've written poems for you. . . . Don't you want anything, Susie?" she speaks aloud in the days before the ending swap sequence (295). Much like the narrative arc of Susie, who cheerfully declares the titular lovely bones of her absence a fair exchange for her life, and that of her mother Abigail, who is uneasily returned to the family after trying to slip the bonds of motherhood, Ruth's story simply *ends* in the willing sacrifice of her body.

If Ruth Connors summons the black-clad, chain-smoking, lesbian-identified feminist, Susie's mother Abigail represents another key figure in feminist history: the dissatisfied housewife. Abigail Salmon's trajectory from domestic discontent to reclamation is particularly trenchant given the novel's 1970s setting. "If you were to set [the book] in 2002," Sebold told an interviewer, "the media would have to be part of the novel. And I already knew I didn't want the media to be the focus. I wanted simply to get to the heart of the matter, which was the family and the friends" (Sebold, "Summer Must-Read"). Besides avoiding the ruthless glare of modern media, Sebold's retroactive setting allows her to connect the story of Abigail's untapped intellectual potential to larger issues of second wave feminism.

Many of the novel's arcs harmonize with moments of feminist history. Susie, for instance, experiences a literal "click moment" behind her camera when, during an impromptu photography session, she recognizes Abigail as "in that moment, not my mother but something separate from me" (43). As

Ann Bliss has eloquently noted, the photograph resurfaces throughout the novel, eventually prompting Susie's father to recognize his wife's dissatisfied domestic existence. Abigail Salmon, for her part, could be on loan from the pages of *The Feminine Mystique*. A woman who loved to hold forth to her children on a spectrum of issues from Greek mythology to women's liberation, she had "gotten her master's in English—having fought tooth and nail with Grandma Lynn to go so far in school" (149). Her dreams of teaching are stifled when Abigail becomes unexpectedly pregnant with a third child. Susie ruefully reflects that "if I had paid attention, I would have noticed signs. Now I see the shifting, how the stack of books on my parents' bedside table changed from catalogs for local colleges . . . novels by James, Eliot, and Dickens, to the works of Dr. Spock. . . . When she realized she was pregnant for the third time, she sealed the more mysterious mother off" (151–52).

While Susie interprets her own violent death as a necessary sacrifice, Abigail believes the murder is retribution for her undesired maternity. "She now knew that being a mother was a calling, something plenty of young girls dreamed of being," Susie recounts. "But my mother had never had that dream, and she had been punished in the most horrible and unimaginable way for never having wanted me" (266). Abigail leaves her family and seeks solace on the coast, whereupon Sebold connects her to another icon of trapped domesticity, *The Awakening*'s Edna Pontellier. Abigail, who is repeatedly referred to throughout the novel by the nickname "Ocean Eyes," ruminates about meeting Edna's watery fate. She muses about "the books she had read in college. *The Awakening.* And what had happened to one writer, Virginia Woolf. It all sounded so wonderful back then—filmy and romantic, stones in the pocket, walk into the waves" (222). Yet unlike Woolf and the fictional Edna, this outcast mother is instead "rescued" by the crisis of her husband's heart attack, which brings her back to stay. At the novel's end, Abigail—the same character who "despised the word [Momma]"—quietly rejoins the family and drops out of the final chapter altogether (62). The taming of Abigail mirrors the gendered domestication of Ruth.

Lev Grossman points out that Sebold's "unblinking authorial gaze is her hallmark: where lesser writers would turn away from things too horrible to see or feel or admit, her scrutiny never wavers" ("Fall Arts Preview"). Yet despite the novel's brutal opening scene of violence, much of the narrative does indeed "turn away" in a disengaged, passive, and elegiac fashion. Brian Norman comments that "Susie is not interested in justice within a legal framework, political calls for systemic change in response to cultures of sexual vulnerability and predation, or a critique of suburban fiction of safety and the economic inequality and razing of history that sustain them" (144). The heroine and her mother succumb to the impulses of self-sacrifice and self-abnegation; readers' anger over the catastrophe of Susie's death is channeled into a stock character's vengeance plot. It is as if Sebold had written a gothic novel that desperately wanted to be something else. This curious mixture of lugubriousness and pacification illustrates postfeminist culture's ambivalence about reconciling the enduring fact of sexual violence with a chipper worldview on gender. But where *The Lovely Bones* is delicate, Sebold's second and less critically acclaimed novel *The Almost Moon* is jarring and chaotic, suggestive of a shift in her theoretical trajectory. We begin again with the direct words of a postfeminist heroine, but in this novel, her dreams of a shiny, happy future are revealed to be gothic nightmares.

Postfeminist Monstrousness: *The Almost Moon*

Narrated by a woman on the verge of madness, *The Almost Moon* is a tale of matricide, seduction, emotional abuse, and domestic ruin. Like its predecessor *The Lovely Bones*, the novel begins with a terse acknowledgment of violence to come. "When all is said and done, killing my mother came easily," begins Helen Knightly (3). But the novels quickly part paths. Whereas *The Lovely Bones* portrays a difficult but ultimately loving relationship between mother and child, *The Almost Moon* features a dysfunctional, embittered mother and the daughter who suffocates her. Through the story of the once-beautiful Clair's grotesque decline, Sebold criticizes postfeminism's obsession with youthful beauty and its disdain for aged femininity. She also uses the trope of the doppelgänger to bind Helen to Clair, thus dismantling the postfeminist myth of generational difference. Finally, in the novel's first-person fragmented narration we find Sebold's most frightening indictment of postfeminism. In Helen, Sebold has created a heroine whose madness is far from meaningless (as some critics implied). Rather, her insanity serves as a gendered critique of a postfeminist world gone mad. Helen, in other words, loses her grip on reality *because* she tries to enact the postfeminist fantasy of gender.

The relationship between *The Almost Moon* and *The Lovely Bones* is complex; although they share an overriding concern with women and violence, the former has a sharpness of tone that is, as I have discussed, oddly missing from Susie Salmon's story. While both novels trade in horrors, *The Lovely Bones* possesses an endearing narrator and several textured, interesting supporting characters. Readers find no Susie in *The Almost Moon*; both narrator Helen and her mother Clair are acidic figures. Indeed, save for a redemptive final scene, sympathy and compassion are as absent in this novel as they are present in *The Lovely Bones*. Perhaps Sebold deliberately scoured away any trace of sentimentality in order to avoid the same criticisms that confronted her first novel. Yet the shift in tone between the books is actually more organic than it might at first appear. *The Almost Moon* amplifies Sebold's anxiety, previously expressed in both *Lucky* and *The Lovely Bones*, about excessive feminine self-censorship. By creating a new novelistic structure that relies on alienation rather than the compassion seen in her other works, Sebold uses the gothic lens to scrutinize postfeminist beliefs.

The Almost Moon is set in a suburban community where, as Helen puts it, "daggers awaited behind every smiling face" (154). Locked in their homes of quiet desperation, feeling alienated from other women, Helen and her mother Clair recall other such figures in Sebold's universe, most notably *The Lovely Bones*'s Ruana Singh and Abigail Salmon, and the teenaged author herself in *Lucky*. Several gothic motifs from the earlier two books, including visits to decaying ruins, also recur in the world of *The Almost Moon*. The most intriguing thread of connection, though, is Sebold's ongoing insistence that feminine performativity in our culture shapes both violence and our response to it. As both *The Lovely Bones* and *Lucky* make clear, compliance and social politeness can be lethal for women. Susie, trained to be a nice young girl, pays dearly when Mr. Harvey invites her to visit his "little hiding place" in the cornfield. Harvey's "natural authority," she observes, "rooted me to the spot" and prevented her from following her instincts that something was amiss (*Lovely Bones* 7). In *Lucky*, not only must Sebold bargain with her rapist for her life with "pleases" and "thank yous," but she must also conform to public expectations for "acceptable" victimhood if she is to defeat him in the courts. Reflecting on her judicial performance, Sebold writes: "I was authentic. I had been a virgin. . . . I was also a good girl, and I knew how to dress and what to say to accentuate that. . . . While still in court I thanked the jury. I drew on my resources: performing, placating, making my family smile. As I left that courtroom I felt I had put on the best show of my life" (144). Only when she is alone does her "authentic" self surface: "I called Madison a 'motherfucker' in the privacy of my dorm room while I pounded my pillow and bed with my fists. I swore the kind of bloodthirsty revenge no one thought possible coming from a nineteen-year-old coed" (144).

Years later, in *The Almost Moon*, Sebold unleashes Helen as a monstrous rebuke to the self-censoring mask that postfeminist culture presses on women. Caretaker, wife, mother, and putative "good girl," Helen allows her internalized resentments to bubble over with disastrous consequences. However, such a cultural critique is possible only when there is distance established between the character in question and the author and audience. Because Helen is neither plainly autobiographical nor indubitably linked in readers' minds to the author (as is Susie Salmon, perhaps unfairly, due to the profusion of media discourse about Sebold's rape), she allows Sebold the textual freedom to move in a new direction. And because she is alienating, unreliable, and half-mad, Helen encourages readers to disidentify with her claims and to view the novel's psychological landscape with suspicion.

From the time she was a young girl, Helen Knightly manifested vicious antipathy toward her mother Clair. A former lingerie model trapped in an unhappy suburban life, Clair's self-worth is rooted in her sense of femininity, which she defines as enduring sexual appeal to men. As Helen recalls it, her mother's narcissism led her to shroud the mirrors of the house and adorn the living room with still photographs of herself in her prime. Clair's obsession with physical beauty poisons her relationship with her daughter; she is driven to starve Helen with "meals" of celery sticks and marshmallow fluff, and to harangue her about her appearance. Clair manifests great antipathy toward the daughter whose birth signaled the end of her youth and freedom; even on the last day of her life, she calls Helen a "bitch" while having her soiled diaper changed (5). As Clair's beauty fades with age, she cloisters herself from the world. Helen compares her to a "dog trained not to go beyond the boundary of his own yard" (98). In one brutal passage, Clair allows a young child who has been hit by a car to bleed to death in front of her because she is too panicked to summon help. Ultimately, the neighborhood siren barricades herself inside her house, mourning her lost sex-symbol youth. She ends her days in mental and physical decay.

Clair's narrative of hyperfemininity and its decline has particular resonance for postfeminist culture. It is commonly accepted that postfeminism valorizes overt displays of femininity, often construed as either a reaction against or an "evolution" from the supposedly frumpy feminist age. Kirsty Fairclough points out that postfeminist discourses urge women to "engage in the constant maintenance of the self in order to remain beautiful, employable, marriageable and ultimately happy." She continues that "the voracity of the empowerment or 'you're worth it' rhetoric has propelled this to the point where women are often considered as 'letting themselves go' if they have not continuously participated in rigorous beauty regimes" (sec. 8). The obsession with staying youthful also surfaces in the discourse of "Girl Power," a primarily white, middle-class commercial movement that celebrates positive thinking and the purchasing power of preteen and teenaged girls. As a philosophy, Girl Power casts its influence far beyond its purported demographic. Sadie

Wearing observes that postfeminism has a tendency to stretch the category of "girl" into "age ranges that would previously have been understood as unambiguously adult" (284). Popular fictional icons like Bridget Jones, Ally McBeal, and others well into their thirties testify to the enduring power of youthful femininity.

But the dark double of postfeminism's glamorization of youthful beauty is its horror of age. Rebecca Traister characterizes this double whammy as "the desire to sexualize and spoil [young women] while young, and to degrade and punish them as they get older" (qtd. in Fairclough sec. 16). In Helen's disdainful telling, the aged Clair is grotesque. Her coquettishness is creepy rather than seductive, and she is an infantilized burden to her husband and daughter. "I had warmed baby food and fed it to her with long pink spoons pilfered from Baskin-Robbins. I had carted her to doctors' appointments, first with blankets and then towels to hide the world from her," Helen complains (273). Clair's senescent body is also a source of contempt for the lean, well-exercised Helen. During an "autopsy" scene in the beginning of *The Almost Moon*, Helen strips and coolly examines her murdered mother postmortem. Clair gives off a "fecal-mothball combo" scent (Helen frequently mentions her mother's incontinence) (43). She dwells on her mother's breasts and the "hole that had given birth to me," noting that the primary markers of Clair's femininity are now jiggly, hairless, limp, and pathetic in their old age (44). In constructing the story of these two women, Sebold plays with postfeminism's monster—the "hag" in the mirror—and the monstrosity of that fear itself as it is expressed through Helen's narration.

Helen's terror of mature femininity is expressed through the particular juxtapositions Sebold uses to emphasize generational difference. Building a generational identity through the rejection of "older" values is hardly unique to postfeminism, of course; in fact, mother/daughter tension is a prominent trope in self-identified third wave feminist writing and the subject of a great deal of analysis.[6] In such writings, Astrid Henry observes, second wave feminism is personified as variously "puritanical, dated, dowdy, asexual" and more, making her a figure who "stands in the way of the daughters' freedom" (11). The mother/daughter trope of feminist waves is frustrating for a number of reasons: overgeneralization, historical inaccuracy, racial and ethnic insularity, and more. Yet it is also a point of differentiation from postfeminist discourse; whereas many third wave texts portray conflicts in feminism as moments of familial dispute, and thus filled with exasperation and with the continued expectation of dialogue, postfeminist discourse is often dismissive toward its antecedents.

Helen's disidentification from her mother in *The Almost Moon* does not play out along expected lines. Clair is no hairy-legged second waver; instead, she is meticulously made-up and, in her youth, curvaceous. Helen, by contrast, pursues a less markedly feminine look by cropping her hair and obsessing about her lean, muscular look achieved with yoga and weights. These efforts, she crows, "keep my muscles teeming just below my skin" (89). Margitte Kristjansson has written that "the slender body codes the tantalizing ideal of the well-managed self in which all is kept in order despite the contradictions of consumer culture," and Helen engages in similar delusions of self-righteousness throughout the novel (131). "Thank you, Stella, at World Gym!" she cheers as she hoists her old out-of-shape mother's body around the house (11). Clair's metaphorical uselessness and belatedness is literalized as *dead weight* when she is unable to resist suffocation by her fit daughter. Incredibly, Helen reflects that "if I were less flexible, less in shape, I would not have been able to commit" the crime "of which I now stood guilty" (183).

Yet despite Helen's rigid constructions of daughterly difference, Sebold reveals her to be, in fact, a gothic doppelgänger for Clair Knightly. Helen displays an athletic rather than a curvaceous physique, but the corporeal self-discipline she exhibits recalls Clair and her strict dietary limitations. Both women also modeled their bodies for primarily male consumption (Clair in a lingerie showroom, Helen as a nude model in art classes). In fact, Helen shows off smug pride in the proof of her desirability as an artistic muse; she is fond of reminding her mother that "a painting of *me* existed in the Philadelphia Museum of Art" (145; emphasis added). Furthermore, mother and daughter each marry emotionally unavailable artists; both also seduce their male neighbors. The text, then, continually undoes Helen's avowals of mother-daughter difference. As Helene Meyers suggests, "Doubling—an obvious staple of the gothic—puts into question the autonomy and integrity of the subject" (17). Sebold uses the doppelgänger motif to call into question Helen's maternal contempt as well as the postfeminist blindness preventing her from understanding her own reenactment of Clair's life.

The Almost Moon also critiques Helen's myopia about male heroism; in this modern gothic, men are relegated to the sidelines. Benjamin Brabon and Stéphanie Genz write that critics "have drawn on the female gothic to describe a familiar set of narratives that revolve around an innocent and blameless heroine threatened by a powerful male figure and confined to a labyrinthine interior space" ("Introduction," *Postfeminist Gothic* 5). For gothic heroines of old, like Catherine Morland of *Northanger Abbey* or Emily St. Aubert from *The Mysteries of Udolpho*, the terror of the world stems in part from the difficulty of distinguishing between male savior and male foe. However, since postfeminist rhetoric is interested in appeasement, it plays down male villainy to sidestep the "man-hating" stereotype that has become indubitably fixed to feminism. The novel's men—Mr. Knightly and Helen's ex-husband Jake—are spectral presences of absent cruelty. Ultimately, though, Helen's hagiographic impressions of her father and husband are textually unraveled every bit as much as her fantasy of difference from the mother.

"He carried the burden of her . . . this body had folded into his over and over again like so much batter until the two of them became one," remarks Helen of the father she idolized (8). The family surname, Knightly, deliberately references Jane Austen's *Emma* to reinforce Helen's misperceptions—unlike the hero and champion of Emma Woodhouse, Sebold's Mr. Knightly is a paragon of wisdom and balance only in his daughter's mind. Helen's vision of him as a protector is thrown into question by his pronounced absences from home (later revealed to be mental hospitalizations). It is young Helen who absorbs the duties of caretaking for the indigent Clair; it is teenaged Helen who is left alone, in a terrifying scene of threatened sexual assault, to fend off a mob of men seeking to punish Clair in the wake of the hit-and-run accident.

Both men who are dear to Helen build artistic fantasy lives that help them evade domestic responsibility. Mr. Knightly retreats into the condemned building of his childhood home, where he builds large, surreal plywood cutouts of people as therapeutic release. Helen's husband Jake, too, leaves his family life for the outdoors, where he builds elaborate ice sculptures. "I thought he would come back to me," Helen muses. "But then he began building things out of earth and ice, sticks and bones, and left all human flesh behind" (221). Although the neglect exhibited by both men is evident to readers, Helen—like a good postfeminist heroine—extends to them the forgiveness she cannot grant her mother Clair. Even when Mr. Knightly cruelly shoots himself in front of Clair, Helen asserts that she will never blame him for "his absence, his weakness, or his lies" (203).

Readers of *The Almost Moon* thus find themselves locked in a gothic textual prison as they tenderly feel out the trapdoors and rotten foundations of the world narrated by Helen. Sebold compounds this confusion by invoking the madwoman narrative, common to the female gothic tradition, to explore the cultural consequences of postfeminist compliance with the status quo. Helen's mental instability is made evident quite early in the novel. "When I was a teenager," she reminisces, "I thought every kid spent sweaty summer afternoons in their bedrooms, daydreaming of cutting their mother up into little pieces and mailing them to parts unknown." Helen's fantasy of Clair's dismemberment continues: "As I agreed to take out the trash, I cut off her head. As I weeded the yard, I plucked out her eyes, her tongue" (58). Such psychotic eruptions continue into Helen's adulthood, where she dreams of being carved up into "Scarsdale diet patties" of beef and later of giving out bags of her own "effluvia, shit and urine, saline and blood" in a bizarre martyrology (205, 251). While Helen does not dismember Clair postmortem, she considers it. Instead, she settles for slicing and dicing her mother's braid, the symbol of her prized femininity.

Helen, the mad heroine, was coolly received by critics of *The Almost Moon*. Asserting that the book "demonstrates none of the psychological acuity or emotional chiaroscuro of [*The Lovely Bones*]," Michiko Kakutani assailed Helen Knightly as a "talkative monster, whom the reader never comes to understand" ("Instability Passes"). Lee Siegel dismissed Helen's disjointed narrative style as "really like one very long MySpace page" ("Mom's in the Freezer"), while Sharon Dilworth added that Sebold has "left out the crucial components of empathy and cogency. . . . Insanity can only be meaningful as a literary device if it reflects our own sense of well-being" ("There's Nothing Lovely"). Yet the trope of insanity has long been valued in women's literature as an imaginative alternative to prescriptive gender roles. Karen Stein reminds us that in gothic literature, a literary madwoman such as Bertha Rochester of *Jane Eyre* or Esther Greenwood of *The Bell Jar* provides a "critique of the society which has prevented her from developing her full human potential" ("Monsters and Madwomen" 126).

Helen Knightly's fractured narration reveals the simmering anger and resentment bred of a lifetime of compliance, acceptance, and filial servitude. After her father's abdication of responsibility, it is Helen who administers enemas, feeds Clair baby food, and performs the many other tasks assigned to caretakers. Sebold highlights the difficult and unrewarding nature of Helen's day-to-day duties in a world where elder care is still inequitably distributed by gender. But it is in the *language* Helen uses in self-description that we can find a critique of postfeminist accommodation. Helen imagines her own epitaph as reading "SHE LIVED SOMEBODY ELSE'S LIFE" (90). She frequently uses metaphors of imprisonment and servitude to describe her lot. Most strikingly, she self-identifies as a soulless "robot that had gone off the rails . . . after serving its master faithfully for years" (271). Some of these moments seem to be calculated bids for reader sympathy. One need not fully accept them to recognize that Helen's life has been spent in silent obedience of others' wishes, particularly her father's. Indeed, her ex-husband and others are particularly horrified by the circumstances of Clair's murder because of Helen's reputation as a saintly, obedient child. In the end, we can read Helen's madness as a cautionary tale of the postfeminist position of self-censorship. Those who smile brightly and keep silent, Sebold warns us, may hide a reservoir of hate beneath.

In *The Lovely Bones*'s finale, skeletal connections are made between everyone except the self-sacrificing heroine. The denouement of *The Almost Moon*, by contrast, finds Helen developing her own spine and making needed connections to the outside world. "I knew what held me," she muses, coming to a decision to eschew suicide and take responsibility for her mother's death (289). Helen's final revelation takes place in the home of her mother's elderly neighbor, Mrs. Leverton. In her creation of this environment, Sebold signals the hybrid possibilities of postfeminist gothic. "Home" has distinctly different resonances for the two genres: it is often marked as the solution for all women's problems in postfeminism, but it is too often a chamber of horrors for the female gothic. Mrs. Leverton's home represents neither of these polarities, but represents a messy, lived-in form of domestic space. Being in this environment for a time helps Helen "wake up" from postfeminism as she gains perspective on her life and comes to terms with the enormity of her crime.

Throughout *The Almost Moon* the Knightly house is portrayed as a family prison. "'There are secret rooms inside us,'" Helen tells her therapist, adding that "in my house we never left them . . . in my house my mother and father preferred them to everywhere else" (279). Clair Knightly, the "totemic presence," monstrously consumes space, while Mr. Knightly regularly flees to his childhood home to escape the pressures of responsibility (4). Helen frequently comments on her sense of childhood imprisonment: Stonemill Farms, the name of their housing development, "had always sounded like the name of a medieval jail to me," she avers (142). Yet as a grown woman, Helen rattles around as the sole inhabitant of a too-large house that was paid for by her father. The description of Helen living in her overbuilt suburb needs to be read within the context of the postfeminist domesticity fetish that has gripped the popular media for the past two decades. Diane Negra has chronicled how "popular cultural narratives centralize/idealize a woman's apparently fully knowledgeable choice to retreat from public sphere interactions in favor of domesticity" ("Quality Postfeminism?" sec. 3).[7] Home, writes Elspeth Probyn, becomes in postfeminist ideology a woman's "natural choice" and "a reaffirmation of what has supposedly always been there" (152). Though it invokes the rhetoric of "choice feminism," the retreatism narrative gracefully backs away from the "trouble" of career professionalism and seeks refuge in the old ideas of separate spheres. But if postfeminism locates the solution for everything in "going home," the gothic tradition has always looked askance at domestic beatification. For writers as diverse as Mary Shelley, Angela Carter, and Toni Morrison, home is not a refuge but rather the place where violence strikes in the night.

Helen flees to Mrs. Leverton's in order to end her life; because Mrs. Leverton has herself recently died, Helen knows that the house will be empty and not yet occupied by mourners. Although the body of Mrs. Leverton may be gone, her presence within the home exerts a powerful and clarifying influence upon Helen. Upon her entrance, Helen comments that she was "in the house, finally, of the Other" (288). For Helen, this exoticized "Other" (a charged concept in feminist and postcolonial rhetorics) represents a new kind of home for women. Sebold portrays the Leverton home as no well-tended paradise; it is a jumble of crayons, shawls, teakettles, ladies' magazines, and other pieces of everyday domestic detritus. "Tchotchkes is the woman's middle name," Helen recalls Clair saying dismissively of the neighbor—but to Helen, the house is warm and alive because of the activities of its owner (284). Mrs. Leverton, a devoted mother and grandmother, fought off dementia each day by listing the names of presidents, capitals, and family members. "Every day, Mrs. Leverton wrote again the things that kept her tethered to the outside world," Helen muses. "No matter how frail, she had not relinquished her hold" (289). In a final and perhaps unintended gift, Mrs. Leverton bequeaths the lessons of living gracefully to Helen, and the latter finally confronts her own demons. She grieves for Clair's loss, and decides to follow Mrs. Leverton's example and connect to the larger world by accepting punishment and planning a post-prison life of service. The conclusion of *The Lovely Bones* is defined by Susie's *absence*, but the end of *The Almost Moon* finds Helen becoming finally *present* and accountable for her own life. This is made possible by the new paradigm for home that Sebold creates—one that evades the polarities of the gothic castle or the postfeminist McMansion.

Misha Kavka writes that feminism has "set itself the task of accosting social structures" to "define the relation between . . . the institutional and the intimate" (39). Long an imaginative repository for gendered fears, gothic literature too asks us to interrogate the places women cannot go and the punishments for their gendered transgressions. Female gothics written in a postfeminist age must confront their culture's deaf ear toward gender inequity and violence. It is all the more important, then, to listen to what they have to tell us. Alice Sebold's *The Lovely Bones* articulates the melancholia that lies beneath postfeminist culture. Susie Salmon is buried too soon, and though Sebold provides imaginative new possibilities for Susie through her posthumous narration, the story is quick to throw dirt over any lingering expressions of trauma or rage. By contrast, *The Almost Moon* reveals postfeminist heroine Helen's life to be a hall of mirrors and shows how the postfeminist gothic can be used to interrogate a world in which feminism has been unfairly demonized. Sebold's fictional compliance with *and* critique of postfeminism indicates how much of a vexed, ambiguous genre the postfeminist gothic remains. Her compelling work urges feminist critics to examine the monsters we think we have buried and to be watchful mourners at the cemetery.

"Maybe for You There's a Tomorrow": Dead-Girl Fiction and the Susie Salmon Effect

Alice Sebold's work continues to resonate in popular culture in ways that she could not have expected. Much as Susie Salmon maintains a vibrant literary presence after her corporeal death, *The Lovely Bones* is experiencing a robust, though strange, afterlife in the wake of its 2002 publication. Peter Jackson directed a very different film adaptation of the novel in 2009. Susie has also acquired a rash of YA literary descendants. These works about dead teenaged girls, which include Gabrielle Zevin's *Elsewhere* (2005), Gayle Forman's *If I Stay* (2009), Lauren Oliver's *Before I Fall* (2010), and Jess Rothenberg's *The Catastrophic History of You and Me* (2012), are, unlike Sebold's novel, written and marketed for an adolescent audience.[8]

The dead-girl genre, as explored both in Jackson's film and the subsequent novels, envisions the posthumous space as a wellspring for creative rewritings of adolescent female lives. Here, the afterlife is *not* a place for reflection and memory (as it is for Sebold's Susie) but rather a place of vigorous industry, self-development, and new promises of reincarnated happiness. The troubling appeal of posthumous-girl stories for an adolescent audience, I argue, responds to the overdetermination of the white middle-class teen girl figure in postfeminist popular culture. Writing of famous nineteenth-century girls' deathbed scenes, from Little Eva to Beth March, Elisabeth Bronfen observes that dying "functions as these women's one effective communicative act, in a cultural or kinship situation otherwise disinclined towards feminine authorship" (141). Two centuries later, girls confront a postfeminist popular culture that talks endlessly *about* them, but still offers them very little cultural authority. Dead-girl narratives, then, allow readers to gracefully "bow out" of predetermined stories framing them as in crisis, fully empowered, and/or "mean." By replacing the feminine ur-plot of marriage and childbearing with a cemetery plot, they also reveal anxieties about the expectations for adult female sexuality in postfeminist times.

The dead-girl genre has also altered the cultural status of Alice Sebold's *The Lovely Bones*. Sebold, of course, did not write a YA novel; her text features a young protagonist, but it is written for adults. However, *The Lovely Bones* is increasingly interpreted as a "youthful" book because of several factors. These include the particular vision of Peter Jackson's film, a radically revised marketing campaign to attract teenaged girls to the movie, and other novels' selective adaptation of Sebold's ur-narrative for a younger reading audience. All of these rewritings of *The Lovely Bones* borrow its cheerfulness and humanism while eschewing its sexual violence and discussion of gender politics. Layered over the original source, they muffle the novel's disruptive potential and illuminate the tendency in postfeminist popular culture to "lighten up" narratives of gendered trauma.

Susie Salmon launched a thousand screenwriting ships even before the publication of Sebold's manuscript. In 2000, before the novel's release, an unfinished film treatment was sold to a British film company. Financial problems led to the script being passed between acclaimed directors, including Luc Besson, Lynne Ramsay, and Steven Spielberg, before *Lord of the Rings* saga director Peter Jackson took the helm. Shot on location both in Pennsylvania (where the novel is set) and New Zealand, *The Lovely Bones* boasted a budget of "$70 million in production and an additional $85 million in worldwide marketing and distribution" (Fritz and Eller, "Paramount Nixes Plan"). The film received a passel of poor reviews and it narrowly avoided commercial disaster, saved only by an innovative marketing campaign. My intent here is not to offer a full cinematic critique, but rather to focus on two meaningful elements. The first is Jackson's artistic decision to de-emphasize conflicts of gender and sexuality, and the second is Paramount's strategic readjustment of the film's target demographic from adults to adolescent girls. Both choices have significantly altered how *The Lovely Bones* is perceived in popular culture, morphing it from a novel critical (albeit in a problematic way) of how violence silences women into a teen vehicle envisioning the afterlife as a land of delights.

The film version of *The Lovely Bones* modifies Sebold's narrative by minimizing adult relationships and dampening sexuality in particular. Foregrounding the father-daughter relationship, the movie accords negligible space to adult women. Abigail is seen infrequently, and Ruana Singh, the chronicler of alienation and racial difference, is omitted altogether. The other major departures from Sebold's text all involve subduing sexual elements. Most startlingly, Susie's rape is absent from the film version, which fundamentally alters the narrative. On-screen, the physical violence begins and ends with Mr. Harvey grabbing her. Consensual sexuality is also tamped down in the PG-13 film. Encounters between Susie's sister Lindsey and her boyfriend Samuel, the mother Abigail and adulterous detective Len Fenerman, and Ruth and Ray are missing. So too is any mention of Ruth's lesbianism. The film uses a kiss as a synecdoche of sexuality; upon her return in Ruth's body, Susie merely smooches Ray, while in the book they "made love in the shower and in the bedroom and under the lights and fake glow-in-the-dark stars" (308). As Laura-Marie von Czarnowsky observes, the adaptation "needs a prettier heaven, a safer environment, an ultimately more black and white take on the story" for its audience (sec. 17).

Yet while the film version condenses and subdues many important narrative elements, it foregrounds visual pleasures. Jackson depicts the celestial realm as both impressionistic and frantic; lovely light-bathed landscapes come and go rapidly, reminiscent of time-lapse photography. Susie encounters shifting lands of looming cliffs and flowing waters, where flowers blossom in the sky and under the ice as rainbows float and ambient synthesizer music croons. In an interview with Scott Bowles, Jackson describes this filmic heaven as "ruled by Susie's unconscious desires" and "a powerful, beautiful and mysterious place . . . a young 14-year-old girl's idea of 'heaven'" (Jackson, "Peter Jackson"). Jackson's heaven is also always associated with intense physical activity. Susie falls through a wheat field into water, drops to the bottom of an ocean, runs frantically to a tree whose leaves blow off before her, and dances with her fellow victims in a field. This kinetic vision of the afterlife creatively responds to a source text that contains few actions and extensive interior monologue. It departs significantly, though, from Alice Sebold's contemplative heaven, where Susie takes pleasure in watching, listening, and quietly waiting for souls drifting "like snowflakes" away from Earth (155).

Critics of the film pounced on Jackson's amplified visuals. A. O. Scott wrote in the *New York Times* that the film reminded him of "a mid-'70s art-rock album cover brought to life," adding that "while its trippy vistas are sometimes ravishing, they are also distracting" ("Gazing Down"). Others were blunter. Todd McCarthy complained in *Variety* that "Jackson undermines solid work from a good cast with show-offy celestial evocations that severely disrupt the emotional connections with the characters" ("Review: 'The Lovely Bones'"). The *Chicago Sun-Times*'s Roger Ebert, the most vitriolic of all reviewers, zeroed in on the perceived moral effect of making heaven preferable to earth.

"If you're a 14-year-old girl who has been brutally raped and murdered by a serial killer, you have a lot to look forward to," he jeered. "Sure, you miss your friends, but your fellow fatalities come dancing to greet you in a meadow of wildflowers, and how cool is that?" ("The Lovely Bones").

Strange as it might seem, Paramount Pictures's marketing team adopted the "how cool is that" tone in the fall of 2010 during a marketing shakeup. Widely anticipated for months, the film of *The Lovely Bones* had been viewed by Paramount Pictures as a candidate for awards season. Opening in limited release in early December—the season for heavyweight dramas seeking Oscar acclaim—it underperformed. Instead of accepting the film as a fiscal disappointment, Paramount radically altered the marketing, positioning the film as a father-daughter story and resetting their target demographic to teenaged girls. Pamela McClintock reported in *Variety* that Paramount "began surveying people in shopping malls about TV spots for the film" ("'Lovely Bones' Does About-Face"). While adults were noncommittal, teenagers responded enthusiastically. Homing in on the demographics' expressed interest in "the film's spiritual themes, and the father-daughter relationship," McClintock writes that Paramount "cut ads playing these up and began airing spots on female-skewing channels, including Lifetime and Lifetime Movie Network." Journalist Irin Carmon noted that the new trailer juxtaposed the words "A father's search" with Susie's portrayer, actress Saoirse Ronan, intoning, "My murderer couldn't understand . . . how much a father could love his child." Another preview highlighted the teenaged romance between Ray and Susie while music that "seems taken out of a CW drama" soared in the background ("*The Lovely Bones* Wins"). These revamped trailers were also attached to the lucrative teen-market film *Twilight: New Moon*, which raked in $72 million on its opening weekend.

Paramount's about-face saved a film in trouble. *The Lovely Bones* "stunned box office observers in coming in No. 3 for the four-day weekend, grossing an estimated $20.5 million from 2,563 theaters for a total [cumulative gross] of $21 million," writes McClintock ("'Lovely Bones' Does About-Face"). She quotes a studio rival's admiration: "'I think they did an amazing job of changing gears from trying to sell a pre-sold literary title, to selling a film that appeals to younger females. Kudos to them for recognizing their weakness and turning it into a strength.'" The spending power of adolescent girls ultimately gave the film a needed second act, and yet the perception that they were a last-ditch audience after the literary crowd turned away speaks to their "weakness" or lower cultural status.

In light of the repurposing of the film as a teen vehicle, *The Lovely Bones* is somehow becoming a cultural artifact *for girls*. The source material, while no doubt read *by* many girls, represented the posthumous young female voice in all its complexity to a mainstream adult audience. Furthermore, the impulses that the film amplifies have been recirculated by YA fiction. To be sure, the YA world has lately been gripped by a girls-confront-doom aesthetic, as seen in dystopian series such as *The Hunger Games* and *Divergent* and in death-driven vampire chronicles like *Twilight*. Yet the *specific* influence of *The Lovely Bones* on these novels is striking. All feature an attractive, white, middle-class heroine with loving parents, a school crush, and an otherworldly attuned younger sibling. All must negotiate the border between life and death. Some of the novels even invoke Sebold's visual cues. The original cover art for the paperback release of Gabrielle Zevin's *Elsewhere* features a ship in a snow globe. The snow globe is, of course, a key image in *The Lovely Bones*; it is also the first scene in the film. Featured in the prologue during a conversation where Susie's father reassures her that the penguin trapped inside "has a nice life" in his "perfect world," the snow globe foreshadows Susie's far less perfect experience in her own hermetic heaven.

It is vital to note that these dead-girl novels are not gothics; although they deal with wrenching loss, they do not chronicle acts of malevolence or discuss dark desires. In fact, they are tonally light and often humorous. Whereas Sebold's Susie suffers graphic sexual assault and murder, these heroines are usually killed instantly in vehicular accidents (or in one memorable case, by an actual broken heart). Like the film version of *The Lovely Bones*, these stories present worlds scrubbed clean of rape, teenaged sexuality, racial difference, and more, and consequently they reflect dominant postfeminist aesthetics.

While the dead-girl genre explores the fictional perils and pleasures of adolescent femininity in the afterlife, teenaged girls on Earth have been subjects of an ever-increasing amount of popular attention. Kimberley Roberts asserts that "in the nineties teenage girls acquired a self-conscious political identity separate from women for the first time" (*Girls in Black and White* 4). In dramatic fashion, the popular press has hailed the figure of the white middle-class teenaged girl as, alternatively, being in crisis, fully empowered, and engaged in verbal and emotional destruction. Sinikka Aapola, Marnina Gonick, and Anita Harris suggest that in twenty-first-century popular culture, "two discourses about girlhood have taken hold as key explanatory devices for understanding young women's lives. These are the stories of 'girl power' on the one hand, and 'crisis' on the other" (194).

Psychologist Mary Pipher's groundbreaking *Reviving Ophelia* (1994) crystallized the narrative of "Girl Crisis," which warned of a profound loss of self-esteem and identity upon puberty in girls, and subsequent destructive behaviors, including disordered eating, cutting, and substance abuse. As Emilie Zaslow chronicles, Pipher's book inspired more than forty titles on adolescent female crises in the 1990s. During this period, Zaslow continues, "adults interested in girls' lives were suddenly barraged with academic and institutional reports that warned against a growing crisis in girls' lives. These reports cautioned that as girls approach adolescence, the experience of living in a patriarchal culture catches up with them" (14). Intriguingly, Kathleen Sweeney connects this phenomenon to the literary world as well, noting that more than twenty best sellers of the twentieth-century fin de siècle featured scrappy teenaged heroines in trauma. Five, including Toni Morrison's *The Bluest Eye*, were featured on the highly influential Oprah's Book Club. "These rite-of-passage novels and memoirs tapped into millennial adult female interest in the Girl Icon in literature as a stand-in for their own forms of recovery and power," avers Sweeney, and they mark "a parallel to the overwhelming interest in non-fiction titles dealing with girls in need of rescue" (199). The Girl Crisis narrative has proved helpful in raising public awareness about many problems confronting teenaged girls, including eating disorders and self-mutilation. Yet it has also been the target of considerable criticism. Some feminists view it as a protectivist "doom and gloom" story imposed upon girls; Jennifer Baumgardner and Amy Richards, for instance, complain that "a veritable cottage industry has been forced out of the fertile soil of girls' failing self-esteem" (179). Other more conservative critics assail that Girl Crisis draws focus from boys, who are the real subjects suffering an educational and moral crisis.[9]

In true gothic style, the Girl Crisis narrative also spawned its own doppelgänger in the 1990s via the Girl Power movement. The idea of Girl Power had its roots in an independent "riot grrrl" punk-music scene on the West Coast, but it was quickly co-opted into a marketing phenomenon best exemplified by the Spice Girls. Girl Power asserts that young women have limitless potential and barrages teen consumers with messages to exert their power through "being positive" and purchasing sparkly consumer goods. "If 1970's feminism was built on the ideals of authenticity and solidarity, Girl Power is built on dreams of celebrity and self-advancement," Susan Hopkins wryly observes (11). Most feminist theorists speak of Girl Power as a commodified dilution of feminism. Rachel Fudge writes that "for some people, it's a way to bypass the complexities of feminism. . . . The problem with girl power is that all too often it relies on style over substance, baby tees over action" (18). The caution evinced by the two critics here is not universally shared; Caryn Murphy, for example, argues that "Girl Power, derived from grassroots feminism, is an articulation of the strength and authority of young women" (99). It is true that the discourse of Girl Power can be appropriated for many different and potentially progressive ends. However, as circulated by media icons and in consumer culture, Girl Power relentlessly focuses on the power of the individual, giving little regard to social context, and exudes a somewhat groundless optimistic outlook. What Hopkins calls its "eternal adolescence of fun, fantasy and narcissism" lays out a predetermined pathway for adolescent girlhood that is just as narrowly prescribed as its counterpart Girl Crisis (122).

If girls are neither empowered nor in crisis, perhaps they are just "mean." A third metanarrative focusing on female relational aggression combines the pain and drama of Girl Crisis with Girl Power's strident spirit. A myriad of books in the mid-1990s such as *Queen Bees and Wannabes* (2002) (the basis for the 2004 hit film *Mean Girls*) and *Odd Girl Out* (2002) unveiled the "hidden" world of girls' relationships, dominated as they were by gossiping, backstabbing, cliquishness, and other forms of attack directed at undermining personal bonds. Meda Chesney-Lind and Katherine Irwin argue that there has been a profound shift in the media from a "poisoned girlhood theme" to a "*poisoned girls* theme" (143; emphasis added). One tangible result of popular interest in girls' supposedly toxic behavior has been skyrocketing public interest in bullying in schools and in cyberspace. Chesney-Lind and Irwin take umbrage with the collapsing of physical and nonphysical violence into the umbrella term *bullying*, and argue that "what this area of research is really doing is systematically measuring a set of attributes that have always been associated with girls and women (i.e., their devious and venomous natures) and then intellectually equating these 'aggressions' to boys' violence" (109). In the next chapter, I more fully take up the implications of the postfeminist tendency to falsely flatten out distinctions between male- and female-authored violence. Suffice it to say for now that, just as Girl Crisis and Girl Power before it, "Mean Girls" has become a highly recognizable box in which to place adolescent femininity.

However they are framed, white middle-class adolescent girls have emerged as overdetermined subjects of concern in twenty-first-century popular culture. The resulting dead-girl young-adult fiction of the 2000s and 2010s responds by creating new narrative paths for female protagonists. As relatively powerless, lifeless beings, the protagonists of these novels do not fit easily into the hearty "empowerment" rhetorics of Girl Power, and only one (*Before I Fall*'s Samantha Kingston) dubiously qualifies as a "Mean Girl." The squeaky-clean heroines and the brisk, light tone of the writing also signal that these are *not* narratives of Girl Crisis. In fact, the posthumous narration allows these narrators to step out of any grand cultural narrative about girlhood altogether. Like Harriet Beecher Stowe's Little Eva, Louisa May Alcott's Beth, and other dying heroines before them, they slip out before womanhood, frozen in time; the difference is that protagonists Liz, Mia, Samantha, and Brie don't leave the narrative, but continue to speak from a celestial perspective.

Lauren Oliver's novel *Before I Fall* emphasizes death's instructive qualities. High school senior Samantha Kingston, the passenger in a fatal car crash, relives her final hours seven times over. Each time, she readjusts her desires and gains wisdom and insight. On the last day, she is able to change not the outcome but the circumstances of her death, rewriting it as a sacrifice that rescued an outcast classmate, Juliet. Unlike the other books within this genre, *Before I Fall* anchors its heroine in *purgatory*. There is no heaven here; Sam repeatedly experiences the moment of her death, which is "full of heat and sound and pain bigger than anything, a funnel of burning heat splitting me in two," and the subsequent terror and disorientation that follows the resetting of her day to the morning (80). The book establishes quickly that Sam's death itself cannot be avoided; the extent to which she can alter its meaning, however, depends on her moral growth.

Prior to her accident, Samantha had ruled the school within her high-status clique. "I have first pick of everything. So what. That's the way it is. Nobody ever said life was fair," she snaps at the reader (18). Sam bullies lower-status girls, cheats off her classmates, and plans to lose her virginity to her loutish boyfriend simply to keep up with the sexual experience of her peers. Over the course of the week, Samantha becomes a more thoughtful daughter and sister, dumps the boyfriend, and, most important, acknowledges her abuse of power to Juliet. Sam critically reassesses her own life, musing about adolescent female self-silencing in a way that recalls Mary Pipher's work on Girl Crisis:

> I think of all the times I sat in squirming silence, terrified I would say or do the wrong thing, terrified the dorky, lanky, horseback-riding loser inside me would rise up and swallow the new me, like a snake feasting on something. How I cleared the shelves of my trophies and dumped my beanbag chair and learned how to dress and never ate the hot lunch, and, above all, learned to stay away from the people who would drag me down, and carry me back to that place. (*Before I Fall* 408–9)

Oliver uses direct address repeatedly in the novel to connect Sam's experiences to the readers. Ruminating that readers perhaps feel that her behavior merited punishment, Sam asks: "Let me ask you: is what I did really so bad? So bad I deserved to die? So bad I deserved to die like *that*? . . . Is it really so much worse than what *you* do? Think about it" (80–81). By employing an intimate, confessional tone, Oliver asks adolescent female readers to similarly interrogate and reform their own lives.

Gayle Forman's *If I Stay* similarly plays with the life-and-death border and also emphasizes the importance of good choices. High school senior Mia has a loving family composed of two laid-back, "alternative" parents who nurture her musical talents, and a sweet younger brother. The family is close-knit until a violent car accident kills her parents on impact and her brother soon after. The comatose Mia lingers in between worlds, observing others navigate life without her; soon it becomes apparent that Mia can will herself back to life. A nurse tells her grandparents, "You might think that the doctors or nurses or all this is running the show. Nun-uh. *She*'s running the show" (82). Mia herself avers: "If I stay. If I live. It's up to me. . . . It's not up to the doctors. . . . It's up to me . . . I decide. I know this now. And this terrifies me more than anything else that has happened today" (88).

The story's sole dramatic conflict—Mia's drama of being suspended between worlds—is on one level a metaphor for adolescence, which is poised uncomfortably between childhood and the adult realm. Life is framed here as the "adult" choice, as compared to the comforting sleep of death. "Sleep would be so welcome. A warm blanket of black to erase everything else. Sleep without dreams. . . . Is that what death would feel like? The nicest, warmest, heaviest never-ending nap? If that's what it's like, I wouldn't mind. If that's what dying is like, I wouldn't mind at all," Mia muses (179). By choosing to return to her body at the novel's conclusion, Mia faces pain both physical ("a blinding flash, a pain that rips through me for one searing instant, a silent scream from my broken body") and emotional (233). By assuming responsibility and making the "good" choice to return to corporeal femininity, Mia will be reunited with her boyfriend Adam and form a new family, without adults.

If I Stay and *Before I Fall* are borderlands novels that stress the importance of moral growth and decision making for their heroines. Gabrielle Zevin's *Elsewhere* and Jess Rothenberg's *The Catastrophic History of You and Me* extend posthumous narration fully into the celestial realm. Whereas Alice Sebold's afterlife is a sort of eerily empty memory walk for Susie (the film, of course, enhances heaven's colors and landscape to a garish degree), in these novels heaven is a corporate arm of Earth, complete with gift shops and pizza places. While Susie Salmon lingered and remembered in solitude, heroines Liz and Brie are offered vastly different, and active, choices when they arrive. *Elsewhere*'s Liz learns that heaven is a bustling place where souls age backward until, at seven days old, they float down the river to be reborn. *Catastrophic History*'s Brie discovers that she is, in fact, the recycled soul of someone else. These two novels offer creative visions of an interconnected afterlife in order to provide recompense for the heroine and the reader. Death, it turns out, is truly *not* the end.

"On behalf of the crew of the SS Nile, welcome to Elsewhere," booms the public-address system on a giant boat of dead souls delivering *Elsewhere*'s Liz to an unknown fate. "The local time is 3:48 p.m. All passagers [pun intended] must now disembark. This is the last and only stop" (40). The victim of a bicycle accident, Liz experiences the afterlife as a hyperreal version of Earth. Here Frank Lloyd Wright makes architecture "better than any of the buildings he built on Earth," painful careers get second acts (Marilyn Monroe is now a licensed psychiatrist), and physical injury is impossible thanks to Healing Centers (48). Most curious of all is the reverse aging, which complicates traditional spiritual understandings of heaven as the place where loved ones reunite. In the realm of Elsewhere, one long-dead soul might have gotten so progressively younger as to be a child again when their romantic partner arrives. Liz quickly understands that in heaven, just as it was on Earth, her life will be short. "So nothing matters here, does it? I mean, nothing counts. Everything is just erased. We're all getting younger and stupider, and that's it," she complains (54).

Liz encounters postfeminist forms of address even in the celestial realm. "I think you'll find that dying is just another part of living, Elizabeth. In time, you may even come to see your death as a birth. Just think of it as *Elizabeth Hall: The Sequel*," offers an adjustment counselor (79). In a passage reminiscent of *The Lovely Bones*, Liz's dogs advise her to "stop being lonely. . . . Oh, and be happy! It's easier to be happy than to be sad" (107). She adjusts to the relentlessly positive, industrious work ethic, forgiving her hit-and-run killer, abandoning her memories, and finding a career as a celestial vet. Finally, she comes to reassess her life, valuing quality over quantity. "A life isn't measured in hours and minutes. It's the quality, not the length. All things considered, I've been luckier than most," she muses (266). Maintaining that "there is no difference in quality between a life lived forward and a life lived backward," Liz exits the story as a laughing baby, born anew into waiting arms (274).

Elsewhere contends that young women can find productive happiness in death. *The Catastrophic History of You and Me* makes a similar claim, although its vision of heaven differs. When fifteen-year-old Brie Eagan experiences a breakup, she suffers the medically unusual death by broken heart, which is clearly an adolescent revenge fantasy. Waking up in a celestial pizza shop, she is soon zipping back and forth to Earth, seeking to first punish, and later forgive, the boy who broke her heart. As in the other novels, *Catastrophic History* emphasizes the unpredictability of fate and the importance of listening to teenagers. Brie's father, a cardiologist, says on television that "as parents, we should all be talking to our children about how they feel . . . and we should be listening" (301). At her own funeral, Brie confides that "no matter how much you think you know a person—no matter how pretty they are, or how together they act, or how popular they seem, you can never know what their lives are really like. *Not unless you ask them. And not unless you're listening*" (328; emphasis in original).

Because they are dead, Brie and her fellow protagonists can no longer be listened to on Earth. Leila Sales believes the novel instead grants a different kind of agency. Brie's "actions may no longer have the ability to change the world of the living, but they change *her*," Sales writes. "Brie passes through the five stages of grief—denial, anger, bargaining, sadness, and acceptance—before she can move on to her final resting place. Even in death, she is still able to grow. It's a wonderfully appealing premise" ("Problem with Dead Narrators"). Indeed, Rothenberg utilizes Elisabeth Kübler-Ross's five stages of grief as subheadings in the novel, further emphasizing the arc of forgiveness and growth. In the denouement of *Catastrophic History*, Brie finally recalls a prior existence as "Lily," sweetheart of her celestial guide Patrick, three decades ago. Having been the unwitting architect of her accidental death, Patrick bargained his soul for Lily's reincarnation (as Brie). The revelation satisfies the romantic requirement of the genre, providing Brie with a fulfilling past identity that compensates for the loss of her earthly life and family.

The dead-girl narrative, worked out in different ways in these four books, offers readers a new pathway out of the thicket of teen-girl master narratives. The protagonist provides warm assurance of the continuation of life, as well as the promise of new adventures and relationships in heaven. I have suggested that these novels connect to a postfeminist gothic sensibility by peculiarly figuring the space of *death* (or near-death) as the most productive speaking stance for teen-girl narrators. In their treatment of sexuality and of whiteness, they also reflect postfeminist anxieties.

"I can't imagine you without that thing between your legs," says Mia's friend upon learning that she might give up her beloved cello (128). That quasi-sexual reference reveals the real romance in *If I Stay*, which is between Mia and her music. Music's erotic power is emphasized in Mia's own faltering relationship with her boyfriend, which develops into intimacy only when he asks Mia to play him like an instrument. "I reached for the bow and brushed it across his hips, where I imagined the bridge of the cello would be," Mia narrates, sparking a "surge of love, lust, and an unfamiliar feeling of power" (61). For his part, Adam "plucked at my chest and my belly, but I could feel him in places his hands were nowhere near . . . and when I felt like I could not take it one more minute, the swirl of sensations hit a dizzying crescendo, sending every nerve ending in my body on high alert" (61–62). *If I Stay* circumspectly replaces images of sexuality with cadences of music, and sexual reticence is similarly embraced by the other novels. *Elsewhere*'s virginal Liz finds love, but soon falls into a second childhood. Her last moments with her boyfriend are decidedly unerotic, as baby Liz is swaddled off down the river while her toddler boyfriend wails "Gonegonegonegonegone" (272). *Catastrophic History* mitigates Brie's sexuality by revealing that the boy who took her virginity turned out to be gay. In death, Brie is able to rewind time, and she recasts herself as Jacob's buddy, subordinating her own romantic needs and telling him that "I'll always be your friend" and "Just be yourself" (354–56). Sam's romance in *Before I Fall* is perhaps the most circumscribed of all. Moving from her oafish, sexually aggressive boyfriend to her childhood best friend, Sam must be content with thrilling looks and touches over the span of four repeated days. Elisabeth Bronfen has written that for a dying young heroine in literature, part of the "convention of a good Christian death" is being "transported to heaven before she has become too contaminated by the world," especially in terms of sexual purity (91). Indeed, all the texts in this young-adult subgenre struggle to keep adult sexuality at bay; this marks a significant departure from Sebold's novel, where Susie first experiences violent rape and, later, inhabiting Ruth's body, actively seeks a sexual encounter with Ray Singh.

The space of near-death and post-death compels the postfeminist gothic because it promises release from the female body, marked as vulnerable because of its gender. The heroines of dead-girl narratives spend time contemplating their disconnection from their physical selves. "I'm staring at myself, at the 'live' Mia now, lying in her hospital bed. I feel a burst of fury. If I could slap my own lifeless face, I would," narrates Mia (161). Brie describes her burial, feeling "haunted by the smell of rotting flowers . . . scraping shovels, and rain falling on headstones, and the slamming of cold, hard cemetery gates, locking me in for good" (291). Yet they do not *inhabit* their bodies, and thus they are freed from what Kathleen Sweeney calls our "overloaded pop culture image banks" with their images of intensely sexualized "Lipstick Lolitas" (49). The unconventional romantic narratives branching out of these novels suggest the genre's desire to think its way out of sexual expectations for women in postfeminist culture.

Sociologist Lorraine Kenny describes white middle classness as a "life intentionally taken for granted" (2). Similarly, when Liz reflects on her earthly life in *Elsewhere*, she comes to the realization that "her life had been entirely without obstacle" (76–77). Whereas *The Lovely Bones* critiques the insularity of suburban America through the travails of Ray Singh and his mother Ruana, the YA variants present worlds scrubbed of racial difference. In *Catastrophic History*, Brie's celestial experience is dominated by a handful of white, middle-class, pizza-shop kids. African American women appear only as caretaking nurses in *If I Stay*, lavishing attention on the comatose Mia. *Elsewhere* creates a black best friend for Liz in the afterlife. Thandi's life story is composed of stereotypical circumstances; she was felled by a drive-by shooting in Washington, D.C. (9). "Aw, it's nothing special. Happens pretty regularly where I come from," Thandi demurs (16). The voice of the socioeconomically deprived, she encourages Liz to be as happy as she is in a land of material opportunity and freedom from violence. Most peculiarly, Zevin includes a speculative passage telling us what would happen "if we were to read the book of Thandi." Among the things we would learn is that she had an unfaithful boyfriend named Slim and a dead *and* deadbeat father. "But because this is not Thandi's story, we join her on a rather unremarkable day. For her, at least," the passage concludes (189).

In the United States, preferred media narratives about dead and lost girls have also *not* featured stories like Thandi's. Instead, JonBenét Ramsey, Natalee Holloway, Madeleine McCann, Elizabeth Smart, and other Caucasian blue-eyed blondes have represented what Rebecca Wanzo calls "the universal sign of the endangered child" (*Suffering* 185). Wanzo points out that according to Department of Justice figures, more than three-quarters of the children murdered between 1980 and 2000 were male, and the victims were also disproportionately of color, thus presenting a very different face from the dominant media coverage ("Era of Lost [White] Girls" 114). Yet something about vulnerable white girls provokes what journalist Eugene Robinson deems "the full damsel treatment" in American society (qtd. in Wanzo, *Suffering* 208). The protagonists of postfeminist dead-girl novels do not suffer torture or deliberate violence, and they cannot be precisely equated with famous real-life victims. But in death they do control their narratives, and their whitewashed heavens, like their earthly existences, reflect the general tendency within postfeminist popular culture to exclude "other stories" like Thandi's.

What hath Susie Salmon wrought? More than a decade after the publication of Sebold's novel, popular fiction and film are rife with images of cheerful dead white girls waving good-bye and dispensing their wisdom from heaven. Angela McRobbie has argued that popular culture markets sickness (as best exemplified in the listlessness of today's skeletal fashion models) as an expectation for girls. By becoming accustomed to pathology, she writes, young women "become used to the idea that self-harming, or being depressed or grieving that they have 'left it too late' to have children" are "all part and parcel of women's lives, and that there is no solution beyond those on offer, no radical alternatives" (112). Sickness, of course, is not the same as death; in fact, illness is markedly absent in these novels where girls move swiftly from the bloom of health to a deadly accident. But we can interpret the dead-girl genre within McRobbie's framework of adjusting to pathology. If sickness, strife, and pain are to be inevitably drawn to the corporeal female body, then death's breezy, bodiless buoyancy is indeed cause for girls' cheerfulness. In an attenuated way, this conclusion echoes many other writers of the postfeminist gothic who envision the post- and near-death space to draw attention to violence against women. Alice Sebold's Susie, of course, desperately wants to be part of the story on Earth. But in leaving the story altogether, her younger contemporaries suggest that the "elsewhere" following this life might offer teenaged girls a frightening and unorthodox place of freedom and self-development—a grave of their own.

3

A Woman Might as Well Be Brave

Susanna Moore's Ambient Fright

Alice Sebold and the young-adult novelists who followed in the wake of *The Lovely Bones*'s success employ imagery of graves to ask readers to question what postfeminism buries. Novelist Susanna Moore, who has penned five novels about endemic sexual violence, is similarly focused on what lies beneath.[1] Moore's literary mode dismantles; her lacerating words lay bare the insidious climate of postfeminist popular culture, and her heroines are verbally, and even literally, dismembered. The corpus of her work represents what Judith Halberstam has called "shadow feminisms," ways of interrogating gender that "take the form not of becoming, being, and doing but of shady, murky modes of undoing, unbecoming, and violating" (*Queer Art* 4).

In particular, Moore critiques the postfeminist ethos of "empowerment." She problematizes the Teflon nature of contemporary popular culture's "warrior woman" icon through her accounts of gendered asymmetries of power. The question of female vulnerability, Moore has noted in an interview, "is the only thing that interests me." Women, she continues, "are completely disadvantaged—despite what men will say. It is not a fair fight. . . . My only method of survival is in taking it . . . on, facing it, thinking about it" ("Write the Good Fight"). Most controversially, Moore assails the overreach of postfeminist narratives that fetishize "choice," and she suggests that in reality, the world is far from a free marketplace. As a whole, her work connects the realities of women's physical, social, and sexual disempowerment—all of which are written on the bodies of her broken heroines—to the false promises of postfeminism.

The Hawaiian Trilogy: An Education in Loss

In the popular press, Susanna Moore is sometimes unfairly deemed a shock jock. This reputation derives from the sexual explicitness and homicidal ending of the novel *In the Cut*. Bret Easton Ellis, Moore's friend and the author of the notoriously violent *American Psycho* (1991), told her that the novel disturbed even *him* deeply.[2] *In the Cut*, which was later unsuccessfully adapted as a Meg Ryan film vehicle in 2003, may be Moore's most famous production. Her work, though, is varied, spanning genres from the historical novel to contemporary horror to the coming-of-age tale. Raised in Hawaii, Moore turned to writing after a series of bohemian careers that included modeling and script reading for actors like Jack Nicholson and Warren Beatty. Her Hawaiian trilogy—*My Old Sweetheart* (1982), *The Whiteness of Bones* (1989), and *Sleeping Beauties* (1993)—features three heroines passing from largely idyllic childhoods into the stormy seas of adulthood, where they are alternately berated, beaten, and raped by the men in their lives. This unwelcome entrance into adult femininity is witnessed by a gothic figure, Claire Clark, whose excess epitomizes the storm, noise, and emptiness of postfeminism.

Tracing the physical, spiritual, and moral journey of an "apprentice" moving through the world, the Hawaiian trilogy invokes the bildungsroman, a literary tradition that is, in Susan Fraiman's words, "bound up with a process of canon formation" (136). Ellen McWilliams asserts that the model is "recognized throughout the world as a synonym for exploring aspects of human progress and development" (12). Yet as Fraiman and other feminist scholars have noted, applying the bildungsroman's apprentice-to-adult trajectory to female literary subjects has always proved difficult. Gender expectations rendered the heroines of eighteenth- and nineteenth-century novels less mobile than male counterparts; women, particularly women of color, were also highly circumscribed in the public sphere. Feminist scholars have thus theorized a female bildungsroman with different contours. Marianne Hirsch has claimed it as a "discontinuous, circular path which, rather than moving forward, culminates in a return to origins," using "structures of repetition rather than structures of progression" (26). Susan Roskowski adds that such a trajectory follows "a pattern in literature by and about women: movement is inward, toward greater self-knowledge that leads in turn to a revelation of the disparity between that self-knowledge and the nature of the world" (49).

Decades of feminist activism have, of course, reshaped expectations for female subjects, yet the bildungsroman tradition still informs contemporary reading practices. In 1972, amid a flourishing of feminist literary production,

Ellen Morgan wrote that the female bildungsroman was "the most salient form for literature influenced by neo-feminism." The "novel of apprenticeship," she continued, was "admirably suited to express the emergence of women from cultural conditioning into struggle with institutional forces, their progress toward the goal of full personhood, and the effort to restructure their lives and society according to their own vision of meaning and right living" (qtd. in McWilliams 19–20). Deborah Silverton Rosenfelt agrees that coming-of-age novels from the 1960s and 1970s "take their textual life from an encoding of the dynamic of women's oppression and women's resistance" (269). In its own way, the more contemporary chick-lit genre also echoes the female bildungsroman. Novels like *Bridget Jones's Diary* (1996) or *The Secret Dreamworld of a Shopaholic* (2000) feature women who progress from corporate novice to professional (often through comic ineptitude) while simultaneously undergoing self-transformation in grooming and appearance.

Susanna Moore reorients the contemporary female bildungsroman away from the concepts of agency and self-work, creating somber moods and ambivalent endings. Her dark tales begin, somewhat incongruously, in an island paradise. "Hawaii was a ravishing little world. It was an isolated place, redolent with romance," Moore comments in her memoir *Light Years* (4). The land of her childhood is fragrant, fertile, and free, particularly for the girls who explore its shores in wonder. "There were no fences, no locked gates, no marked boundaries of property lines," she remembers in another memoir (*I Myself Have Seen It* 150). Hawaii is not a social paradise; Moore admits that it was "an hierarchical, snobbish, and quietly racist society" (123). The islands do, however, remain places of physical freedom and maternal nurturing for her young heroines, and they spend their youth surrounded by the powerful, feminine image of the sea. "No memory presents itself of my first acquaintance with the sea. It was always there, and I was always in it," Moore writes (*Light Years* 1). Bodies of water hold hypnotic significance for the narratives of female bildungsromans; often they are vehicles of escape for heroines, like Rachel of Virginia Woolf's *The Voyage Out* (1915), George Eliot's *The Mill on the Floss* (1860), and Kate Chopin's *The Awakening* (1899), who are at odds with their societies. In Moore's Hawaiian novels, the protagonists voyage out to the mainland for an education in misogyny and violence. When they return home, they are wiser but spiritually drowned.

In the first and least gothic novel of Moore's Hawaiian trilogy, *My Old Sweetheart*, the young heroine, Lily, watches as her mother, Anna, is mentally tormented by her husband's coldness. Anna is a formidable beauty brought to the Hawaiian islands by her physician husband, Sheridan, whom Anne

Tyler describes as exhibiting "an almost sadistic detachment toward his family" (14). Anna does not fit into the local community, and Sheridan "grew to be embarrassed, and, eventually, contemptuous of her efforts to keep him interested. His delicacy, his discernment, were repelled by her" (33–34). A deeply observant young bystander, Lily observes the impact of her father's cruelty on her mother. Anna confides in her daughter inappropriately, and hounds her for information about her father's infidelities. Teaching Lily about the mechanics of assisted suicide, Anna also holds Lily responsible for preventing her overdose. Despite such histrionics, Anna's daughter remains fiercely devoted to her. "Anna had so drawn Lily into her maternity, into her femaleness and her magic, that Lily could not be faulted for wanting to fix everything," Moore writes (33). After her suicide, Anna haunts the novel as a ghost, metaphorically reincarnated as Lily's own daughter, "the other Anna" (193). The melancholic *My Old Sweetheart* recounts a young woman's bearing witness to male emotional savagery; this narrative is further intensified in Moore's linked novels *The Whiteness of Bones* and *Sleeping Beauties.*

Sleeping Beauties, which is the final of the three Hawaiian novels, but considered here for reasons of thematic congruity, embellishes Moore's themes of brittle gender relations and violence. The heroine Clio is described repeatedly as an island girl, an archetype characterized as "resilient, courageous, kind, generous" (175). Like many heroines of fairy tales and female bildungsromans, Clio is motherless. At the cusp of young adulthood she seeks out her Aunt Emma, a self-appointed guardian of native ways. Descended from both native Hawaiian and white bloodlines, Emma "talked to Clio of the things she had come to fear would be lost," like "the long songs without rhyme or meter called *meles*; the hulas and oral genealogies; the very history of her passing race" (8).

Emma is the mouthpiece for Moore's dark view of female social limitation. She warns Clio of the great "discovery, hardest for a woman, of the chasm between expectation and reality," adding that "one is thrown into the ocean almost at birth and a girl is deceived into thinking that because she can hold her head above water, she will stay afloat" (56). Clio, for her part, describes the "tremendous" revelation learned in adolescence that "being a girl was going to be held against me." (70). Yet she persists in a quest for romantic love. Falling for Tommy, a young film star visiting the islands, Clio sets off for the self-mythologizing realm of Hollywood. Everything she encounters there is garishly artificial. Lying at the pool one day, Clio is struck by "the bright orange cheese on the plastic grass, and the pale green of a piece of lettuce lying across [friend] Mimi's big toe, the nail painted fire-engine red"

(88). Clio's new husband Tommy is fully a creature of this landscape. He has obliterated his own history, repackaging his sister into his personal assistant, and he has even created his house in his own image, selecting "the carpet to match his eyes." (85). Clio begins to recognize, too late, her husband's emptiness.

Abused and belittled by Tommy, Clio is also viciously beaten on-set when she refuses her husband's request to participate in bestiality. Kept prisoner inside the hotel to prevent the prying questions of the press, Clio escapes. She is threatened with recapture at the airport by male security guards curious about a pair of handcuffs in her suitcase (placed there by Tommy as an ominous warning). Clio convinces them that the handcuffs "which I didn't want and had never wanted" are erotic gifts. The guards "nodded in understanding and even sympathy with my husband" and let her go (174). What did the soldiers think when they saw her bloody clothing and purpled face, Clio wonders, in a moment that gestures to misogyny beyond the boundaries of her personal experiences. "All these men threatening women," Clio muses later, upon hearing of her cousin's marital difficulties (213). She wonders, Moore writes, "what it was that women did to men that was worse than beating them?" (222).

Clio decides to move home, retreating to Hawaii after her realization that defending herself against Tommy's battering would be impossible. "I wouldn't be able to beat him senseless," Clio thinks. "I am not strong enough. That is why it doesn't work that way. It never has, and it never will" (222). Clio's ruminations on the lopsided physical matchup between husband and wife are echoed by her cousin Mamie, the major protagonist of *The Whiteness of Bones*. There, Mamie takes umbrage with feminism for its "refusal to admit the superior, undeniably superior, strength of men—not economic or political strength, that was another thing altogether—but the simple fact that at any moment" a man could "reach over and snap her narrow wrist in two" (216).

Moore's literary musings on gendered physical inequities within the context of violence responds to a particular postfeminist moment that has conflated women's political empowerment with robust athleticism. In policy terms, this has often meant proffering self-defense or "assertiveness" classes for women as *the* premier antirape strategy, as opposed to an array of approaches including analysis of rape scripts and rape culture. The "woman warrior," arguably the most visible female icon in postfeminist television and film, epitomizes what Stacy Gillis calls a "competitive postfeminism" that "endorses a 'survival of the fittest' model and which encourages women to kick ass" (8). The tradition of lithe, fantastical heroines equipped to fight threatening men has brought characters like Xena, Buffy, (La Femme) Nikita, Beatrix Kiddo/The Bride, Lara Croft, and more to household-name status. A thorough exploration of this figure's ideological contradictions is beyond my scope here, and much engaging and insightful scholarship on the oeuvre exists already.[3] At their best, warrior-woman films and television programs root the characters' physical aggressions in a larger discussion of social inequities. *Buffy the Vampire Slayer*, for instance, routinely builds its plots around the heroine verbally and physically demolishing misogyny uttered by men in all sectors of society, from frat boys behaving badly to fervent preachers. But like all interesting ideas, the postfeminist warrior woman has been copied into oblivion, and the just-warrior aspect of the character is often jettisoned. "Girls kick ass. Isn't that what the t-shirt says?" sneers the jaded heroine of a television program (*Dark Angel*, 2000–2002) that capitalized on Buffy's success. Melanie Newman bemoans the fact that so many of these characters "resemble cartoons" full of girl-power sloganeering. "The kick-boxing girl has become a 21st century literary cliché," she proclaims ("Feminist or Misogynist?").

The woman-warrior archetype in fiction is aptly represented by Lisbeth Salander, the antisocial, punked-out computer hacker known more commonly as the "girl with the dragon tattoo." Salander, widely embraced as an iconoclastic heroine, is the crime-fighting vigilante at the heart of the late Swedish author Stieg Larsson's globally best-selling *Millennium* trilogy. The first and most popular book in the sequence—originally titled *Men Who Hate Women*—involves two narratives of sexual violence. Salander helps solve the case of a woman who vanished, it is revealed, after killing the father who repeatedly raped her. She further avenges her own brutal rape at the hands of her corrupt legal guardian. Reenacting the particular nature of the assault, Salander anally penetrates her attacker and tattoos words of shame into his body as a permanent reminder of his crimes.

In one of the book's most famous passages, Lisbeth Salander dismisses the idea of seeking help from a women's crisis center after being raped. "Crisis centers existed, in her eyes, for *victims*, and she had never regarded herself as a victim," writes Larsson. Salander instead chooses to "do what she had always done—take matters in her own hands and solve her problems on her own" (189). The character's disdain for collective social justice, and her pursuit instead of private revenge, recalls the antivictimist debates that have framed popular (mis)understandings about Western feminist thought since the late twentieth century. Claire Henry provocatively argues that Larsson uses Salander's story to present "the idea of revenge as the *responsibility* of the rape victim, a notion that resonates with the threads of anti-victimism and individualism in post-feminist and neo-liberal cultures" (178). Similarly, Melanie Newman's scathing review of *The Girl with the Dragon Tattoo* (which Henry references) draws from Larsson's work the underlying belief that "if only females would stop acting as 'victims' and discover their own capacity for violence, the aggression visited on them by men would disappear" ("Feminist or Misogynist?").

This chilling assertion serves as yet another addition to a laundry list of things women should do to prevent their own violations. Susanna Moore cynically examines the idea that a capacity for violence is a woman's best form of protection in *Sleeping Beauties*'s final confrontation between Clio and her abusive husband Tommy. Tommy tries to justify his beating of Clio on the generic grounds that "women do things just as bad to men," adding, "Sometimes worse things. It fucking evens out" (222). Clio pushes the limit of his contention, querying: "If I beat you up and leave you bleeding in the Sunrise Suite at the Kahala Hilton, we'll be even? We could stay together?" Tommy's answer, accompanied by derisive laughter, is that "I don't think it works quite that way" (222).

In a postfeminist culture that looks to televisual and cinematic icons as models of female agency, Susanna Moore's heroines seem like outliers indeed. Unlike Xena, they cannot and do not fight back. In the wake of a sexual assault by her employer, *The Whiteness of Bones*'s Mamie reports that "she was ashamed of her naïveté, and she was ashamed of her physical helplessness . . . she had not even tried to defend herself . . . she did not understand that her silence had come from a falsely guilty sense of her own complicity" (219). Furthermore, Moore refuses to provide the requisite happy ending for her battered protagonists. At the end of *Sleeping Beauties*, Clio finds peace only by avoiding her husband and returning home to the islands' richly restorative, matriarchal space, where "the salt and the *limu* and the sun healed her" (109). But the price of Clio's recovery is retreat from the larger world; she now knows better than to be, in her wise Aunt Emma's words, "deceived into thinking that because she can hold her head above water, she will stay afloat" (56).

Spiritual drowning similarly affects Clio's cousin Mamie Clark, the heroine of Moore's Hawaiian novel *The Whiteness of Bones*. "This is my fault," thinks Mamie, as a drug fiend rapes her with a plastic tiki. She continues her apologia: "This is my penance for the time I rode my bike too slowly past the boys in the workers' camp, and walked too slowly past the construction workers on Fifty-fifth Street, and because I wasn't smart enough to understand about the hotel room" where her employer assaulted her, and because "I am a woman and I deserve no better" (255–56). Mamie has, prior to this scene, endured childhood molestation by a beloved servant, sexual harassment from numerous sources, and sexual assault. Ultimately, she internalizes the rules of a victim-blaming culture, viewing her own body as a battleground for others to claim. Moore contrasts Mamie's worldview with that of her sister Claire Clark's, a woman as sharp and cutting as her name. Repeatedly described as the modern woman, Claire is sexually indiscriminate and emotionally abusive, verbally wielding the concept of "choice" like a bludgeon. Through the productive tension between Mamie's and Claire's characters (Claire also appears in all three Hawaiian novels), Moore explores postfeminist responses to male violence.

The Hawaii of Mamie's and Claire's childhood is a fecund, generous paradise. "Piles of rotting mangoes, black with drunken fruit flies, lay under the big trees," Mamie observes. "The branches drooped low, heavy with fruit. The spoiled mangoes smelled like sweet jam" (5). Racially and economically privileged, but also possessing a child's lack of self-consciousness, Mamie easily navigates the various milieus of her upper-class parents, the native family housekeeper, and the day-labor camps filled with local boys. Her time in this physical Eden, though, is exceedingly short. Eleven pages into the novel, a beloved caretaker named Hiroshi molests her while they sit under a banyan tree. "She felt as though her body, by some mistake or accident, had passed out of her keeping," Moore writes of Mamie's reaction. "I did not have it very long, she thought" (11). Mamie internalizes the abuse; Moore relays that "the almost unbearable weight of grief and regret brought on by her assumption of responsibility would nearly crush her" (22).

Mamie and her sister exchange one idyllic island for an altogether different one when they move to Manhattan after college. The "fall" into urbanization has spiritual overtones as well as gendered ones; Mamie leaves the fertile realm of fierce matriarchs and island girls for a bleaker realm. The heady smell of flowers, she is disappointed to learn, is replaced by "the more prosaic smells of this new city—urine, diesel fuel, warm pizza, dry-cleaning fluid" (84). Mamie contemplates her newly altered expectations when she stands behind the rail at Gracie Square and wonders "if she would see a corpse float by, or the bloated body of a dog" (83). The girls' New York residence with their maternal aunt Alice (self-christened "Alysse") is bildungsromanic. "Mamie, an apt student," Moore writes, "was beginning her course of New York lessons" (68). Mamie first learns that the women around her, including Alysse, have leased their sexual services in exchange for financial security. Alysse opines that men are "jobs. Work. And if you're any good at what you do . . . you're promoted" (119). One of her compatriots, called Bones Washburn, so nicknamed for her sexual expertise, is described thusly:

> She had paid with every stupefying dinner party; every aggrieved and vicious stepchild; every arduous performance of fellatio (tens of thousands of them); every holiday spent killing scared, hot, plains animals; every perjury; every bad beating. She did not complain because she understood that those were the terms of her arrangement. The women who were jealous of her, and said viperish things about her, did not have any idea of the discipline required by Bones' line of work. (80)

The marriage plot has long held great significance in women's literature, for in eras of limited economic opportunity and legal rights, women depended upon their husbands for their very livelihood. Stereotypes about gold diggers and sugar daddies may have not disappeared entirely, but certainly the decades since the mass migration of women into the labor force have changed the terms of marriage. It is striking that in Moore's New York landscape of liberation and wealth, the same old story prevails. Violence and mistreatment are conditions to which upper–West Side matrons must adjust in order to gain financial security.

The New York lessons, however, do not simply highlight the endurance of prefeminist narratives about marriage as economic exchange. Moore develops an aesthetic of reverberation, expressed in anecdotes and side stories that amplify the main narrative's concerns. Mamie is repeatedly verbally assaulted by strangers or near-strangers telling her unsettling anecdotes about adult femininity. These frightening confidences, murmured by women with flat affects, create an electric sense of unease. By way of creating Mamie at a society lunch, Alysse mentions that her friend "Appollonia was just telling us about her rape" (93). Another acquaintance introduces herself to Mamie by telling her about a method of vaginal stretching. Alysse discusses a friend's incontinence, the by-product of years of raging bulimia, casually over drinks. A woman describes, in a banal tone of voice, how a female friend self-immolated because her husband wouldn't pay attention to her. Another blithely recounts how her husband likes to photograph animals with erections and to re-create famous car accidents. The collective force of these utterances is depicted as a kind of bodily assault perpetrated against Mamie. If she leaves New York, Mamie imagines that "she would be cleansed of the semen running down her hips, and cleansed of the city. . . . [She] did not know how to scrape herself clean except by casting herself away" (232).

The Whiteness of Bones's use of vicious background noise summons the gothic in its excess and its intrusiveness. Moore utilizes it to critique the confessional culture that has become a recognizable element of postfeminism's pop sphere. Confessional content, as practiced on talk shows and in web therapies, magazines, and other mass-market platforms, can, as Christine Marshall and Kiran Pienaar point out, showcase the suffering individual with an aim to "initiate change and validate the agency of the victim in overcoming their suffering" (526). Second wave feminist practices of consciousness-raising were similarly rooted in this kind of transformative change. Much contemporary confessional culture, though, is stripped of social context, emphasizing instead the notion of self-improvement as synonymous with empowerment. When the New York ladies in *The Whiteness of Bones* confess tales of rape, eating disorders, and fear of vaginal tearing and domestic violence, they are not seeking alliances with other women who have experienced similar suffering. They are merely talking to talk, and through their banalized whispers, Moore comments on the numbing effects of life in misogynist culture.

Reflecting on past experiences including "the Chinese driver who politely asked if she was good for sucking; the boys . . . who turned a shortcut through the camp into a ritualistic hazing; [employer and sexual offender] Mr. Felix, who believed in a good diet and moderation in all things, even ejaculation; the men who whispered to her in the street," Mamie concludes that "it is necessary for a woman" to "be very, very careful. Always ready to run" (260–61). Her viewpoint contrasts with that of her sister Claire, through whom Moore examines postfeminist discourses of risk and choice. Claire represents female modernity in ways that Mamie simultaneously admires and fears; she is often described in scientific metaphors like "a Darwinian adaptation" and a "wonderful mutant . . . some genetic She-of-the-Future" (91, 105). The adult Claire returns in the novel by casually announcing to Mamie, while removing her soiled underwear, that she has just undergone an abortion financed by her sister's money. In short order Claire takes a job servicing Japanese businessmen at a cross-dressing bar, wrecks the sisters' rented apartment, and engages in drugs and S&M. When Alder, Mamie's lover, meets Claire for the first time, she is swollen, twitching, and covered in cuts and bruises. After a few halfhearted stabs at conversation, she farts loudly: "'I'm sorry, but I just got fucked in the ass,' Claire said. She gave them a satisfied, insolent smile and went to her room" (239). Claire claims her behavior as rooted in choice and empowerment; she also is insistent on displaying her bruises and buttock welts (from S&M encounters) to her recalcitrant sister.

When Mamie recoils, Claire lectures that she should not mind, since Claire herself does not mind showing off private scars. "Mamie hesitated," Moore writes. "She was confused as to why she should mind, especially since Claire had spent years trying to convert her to the belief that, as Claire put it, 'if it doesn't hurt anyone, it's okay'" (206).

Moore's attitude toward Claire's sexual freedom is not censorious; she is critical, however, of postfeminism's fetishizing of choice, and of its overreliance, at least in the popular sphere, of using sexuality as the hallmark of women's freedom. "You still don't get it, do you? It's my choice. Mine," Claire says to Mamie when her sister questions the wisdom of staying in a violent relationship (243). As a concept, *choice* is both totemic and problematic in postfeminist culture. It has supplanted earlier terms, such as *rights* and *justice*, in both the abortion rights movement and within feminist discourse more generally. Reproductive rights historian Rickie Solinger explains that "choice" became the dominant concept of the abortion rights movement because it was "a term that evoked women shoppers selecting among options in the marketplace" and as such was perceived as "an easier sell . . . a package less threatening or disturbing than unadulterated rights" (5). Its influence has spread more generally into popular understandings of feminism. Elspeth Probyn coined the term *choiceouisie* to define a postfeminist sensibility that sees the world as a buffet of equal, nonideological options, and Linda Hirshman popularized the term *choice feminism*, defining as a mind-set where all of a woman's professional and personal decisions "counted as 'feminist' as long as she *chose* it" ("Homeward Bound" sec. I; emphasis in original). Such politics are even memorably satirized in the iconic postfeminist television series *Sex and the City*. When the conservative character Charlotte is needled by her friends for quitting her job to stay home at her husband's request, she cries "I choose my choice! I choose my choice!" (in the episode titled "Time and Punishment"). For Charlotte, as for *The Whiteness of Bones*'s Claire, any behavior is legitimized if it is freely chosen.[4]

Choice feminism's ascendance has strong ramifications for feminist theory. Many scholars have critiqued choice feminism's inattention to the way that "the challenges of racism, sexism, classism, and cultural hegemony profoundly interfere" with pursuing "autonomy, freedom, and independence" at the choice buffet (Pastor, McCormick, and Fine 76). In particular, cultural analysis of what Michele Wallace called the black "superwoman"—the woman who must make all choices and decisions to survive, as opposed to selecting lifestyle options—has highlighted the privileged nature of this discourse.[5] Others have interrogated the power dynamics inherent in choice feminism's supposedly flexible framework, focusing on its minimizing of dissent as well as the social pressures conscripting what appear to be "freely chosen" options (Gill 154).[6] Choice is a problematized concept, and when Mamie "minds" Claire's self-destructive actions, despite understanding them as voluntary, she counters the claim that choice is itself inherently validating.

By considering, and criticizing, some of Claire's choices, Mamie treads on dangerous ground. Confronting her sister after Claire returns home bruised and beaten, she snaps: "Your choice? Is masochism a choice? Selfishness? Get out! Get out of here!" (244). Masochism has emerged as a lightning rod in feminist debates, including the series of internal feminist theory in the 1980s over pornography, prostitution, and other aspects of sexuality that are often known as the "sex wars."[7] Rita Felski wryly observes that "a survey of the writing on female masochism turns up wildly diverging propositions: masochism is a natural urge in women; epitomizes women's oppression under patriarchy; is an empowering form of sexual experimentation; does not exist" (127). Mamie and Claire enact the polarity that Felski describes within their narratives. For Mamie, masochism becomes a fatalistic framework to make sense of her continued misfortune. Michelle Massé has argued that gothic heroines are trained to reinterpret suffering as "really the love and recognition for which they long or at least its prelude" (*In the Name of Love* 3–4). While Mamie takes no pleasure in the assaults perpetrated on her, she comes to recognize the ubiquity of gendered violation, and even expect it. "In the end, the world wins," she tells her boyfriend in a bleak assessment of the female body. "You start out thinking that your vagina is all right, harmless even, and then something happens when you're about thirteen, actually happens, and it all changes. It's as if it's turned inside out and suddenly it seems ugly and shameful and not at all harmless" (200). In the wake of her sexual assault, Mamie again says to her lover: "'It is what started everything, you know, all my trouble, a vagina. That's how it began. . . . The bad thing is, I don't know what I can do about it.' Physiognomy as fate, she thought. Vagina as fate. Vagina as fight. Vagina as fête" (266). This linguistic play prefigures Moore's later work *In the Cut,* where female genitalia are indeed fate, fight, fête, and ultimately fatal.

In contrast to Mamie, Claire Clark embraces masochism as, in Felski's description, an "artful choice" that is the "quintessence of sexual boldness and erotic fluidity" (136). In the novel's finale, the weight of Claire's cumulative "choices" lands fully on Mamie. Claire's dealer beats, rapes, and sodomizes Mamie while the strung-out Claire watches with no reaction. The bruises that Claire once proudly displayed are now textually rewritten onto Mamie's broken, punished body. The scene marks the break between the two women. Mamie rescues both herself and Claire (who later claims no memory of the incident) but leaves her sister on the street to finally fend for herself. Mamie's bildungsroman is complete, as she has received a moral education in the gothic nature of gender relations in the novel and has come to believe that sexual violence is inevitable.

As a reader, it is difficult to view Mamie's final return to Hawaii with anything except great relief. Moore's signature lush imagery returns, and Mamie is bathed in silver rains. The cost of her safety, though, is infantilization, as Mamie returns to sleeping in her childhood room, nursed to health by her mother. "The body that used to be her body was thankful to rest," Moore narrates, implying that the adult female version of Mamie cannot find peace and safety in such a vicious world (259). Mamie and her fellow heroines certainly attain an education in human cruelty and in sexual violence during their forays at home and abroad. Their collective educations show, however, that there has been shamefully *little* human progress and development when it comes to ending misogyny. Despite their fertile settings, the novels are ultimately saddened and resigned, viewing violence as a rhythm as regular as waves upon the shore.

Disarticulation and *In the Cut*

Susanna Moore's most famous heroine to date does not stay afloat. Frannie, the creative-writing professor narrating *In the Cut*, exits the novel in pieces that are about to be sunk beneath the Hudson River. The novel's plot revolves around Frannie's witness of a sexual act between two strangers in a bar. When the female stranger is murdered, Frannie is subsequently drawn into the police investigation. Erotically drawn to the lead detective, Malloy, she nonetheless worries that he is actually the killer. Ultimately, Frannie runs from Malloy and seeks assistance from his partner Rodriguez, which proves to be a fatal mistake. Describing the shift from her Hawaiian trilogy to the harsh world of *In the Cut*, Moore reminisced that "I was considered to be a 'women's writer,' which meant that I wrote poignantly about children and flowers and mothers. And that irritated me. . . . I remember very consciously thinking, 'Oh really? You think that's all I can do? You think that's all that interests me, all I can write about?'" (Moore, "Kind of Craziness" 2). *In the Cut*'s invocation of dark, menacing urbanity seems to contrast with the Hawaiian novels' pastoral abundance. Yet *In the Cut* also builds on Moore's interest in gothic feminism, amplifying her themes both in consequence (Frannie is murdered) and in texture. "I wanted to show in *In the Cut* the subtle and constant violence that is displayed everywhere in our culture—in language; in attitudes, of course; in popular films and music," Moore has commented ("Kind of Craziness" 2). She thus creates a sinister milieu where whispered threats and recurring images of "disarticulated" women lurk around every corner. Language *lacerates* in this narrative; characters' control over linguistic power is directly connected to their survival. John Hodgkins writes that Moore "pares her prose and disarticulates her sentences" to create in Frannie a sense of "raw, wounded narration" (51–52). Frannie is robbed first of her language and then of her bodily integrity through murder and dismemberment.

In the novel's opening pages, Frannie studies poetry placards on the New York City train cars. Like the subway itself, language is an itinerant vehicle. Parsing her student Cornelius's use of the word *vex,* Frannie imagines it is "a word his West Indian grandmother might use. Vex. Like cutlass. Probably brought to the Caribbean by Walter Ralegh [*sic*], who was now [on a poetry placard] in the subway" (35). Language also travels through slang, which is Frannie's research interest. *In the Cut* is punctuated by her lists of collected terms, which often ominously focus on female genitalia. "Virginia, n., vagina (as in 'he penetrated her virginia with a hammer')," reads a typical entry (54). Meghan Freeman observes that Frannie's collected lexicon highlights "the vulnerability of the body in language, the endless ways in which it can be used, co-opted, appropriated, violated, damaged, and destroyed" (127). That abstract body is gendered female; by the end of *In the Cut,* Frannie will have suffered the *enactment* of many of the baleful scenarios she collects. Early in the novel, for instance, she expresses delight at a malapropism she has collected, wondering "what could be more alluring than *breastesses*?" (27; emphasis added). The word recurs horrifically in the course of Frannie's murder, as her killer slashes off her nipple. "My breastesses," she cries out, referencing both her corporeal pain and her murderer's deliberate obliteration of the site of her femininity (176).

Michael Gordon writes that "language has come to be defined as a resource, full access to which has been historically denied to women" (16). *In the Cut* connects linguistic power to survival through the idea of "disarticulation." First introduced by Detective Malloy to describe female murder victims' dismemberment, the word reverberates throughout the novel, suggesting a quick step from loss of linguistic control to physical obliteration. Because she is an academic and a renowned authority on slang, we might suppose that Frannie would seem to exert some *mastery* over language. In fact, when we first meet Frannie she is being accused by a student of failing to recognize her racial and her educational privileges. Her African American student Cornelius complains about her request for him to "trash-talk" for her anthropological benefit. "People like you think the brothers are guinea pigs. The way we talk and shit," he protests (5). Yet Frannie's privileges are progressively dismantled throughout the novel, and she is increasingly silenced, to use a well-worn feminist literary term.

As she did in the earlier *The Whiteness of Bones*, Moore creates an ambient texture of threats and whispers to underscore Frannie's sexual and physical vulnerability. She layers the utterances and actions of all the novel's male characters on a backdrop of unease that threatens Frannie in both public space and behind her own locked doors. In so doing, Moore comments on the pervasiveness of sexual intrusion experienced by women. Anna McCarthy has written that the broadcasting of television in open, public, nondomestic space—locations such as the doctor's office, the corner bar, the shopping mall food court—has made "the relationship between authoritative public voices and private, localizable meanings seem more like a movable threshold than a binary determination" (228). While language has never been rooted to electric cords as has television, Moore too uses the idea of ambience to create a landscape where words travel and diffuse across public and private realms. Both within her apartment and on the street, Frannie is threatened.

Frannie's personal interactions with men are marked with linguistic and corporeal danger. Her confounding relationship with Detective Malloy is the most obvious example. Malloy has a tattoo similar to the one that Frannie spied on the ostensible murderer in the bar; nevertheless, she is drawn to him. Meghan Freeman states that their relationship is "carried on almost entirely using rhetorical tactics that are meant to restrict or withhold access to sensitive information about themselves that the other seeks" (129). Each continually fails to understand the other, and Moore uses these slow, circular exchanges to replicate Frannie's frustration at Malloy's dangerous opacity. "I been in the fucking tunnel all day," Malloy begins to tell Frannie after coming home. She does not glean that he is using the epithet as an intensifier, but thinks instead of a tunnel devoted to sex. "A fucking tunnel?" she wonders in response. "Sometimes I hear language in a way that causes me to appear to be more literal than I am" (37). In another example, Frannie has been informed that Malloy was "going to another murder." It becomes a significant phrase, repeated and puzzled over by both characters. "Another funeral, maybe," says Malloy in response. "Not another murder." And later—"Listen, when did he [the student] say I was going to another murder?" (39). "I believe what I said . . . is I was going to another funeral . . . not quite the same thing" he muses again (40). One interpretation of the phrase in question simply describes a social ritual after a death, while the other is far more sinister.

Frannie is imperiled not only by her unfathomable lover; the other men in her life, including her student Cornelius and her old friend John, also menacingly resurface at key points. Cornelius is inappropriately attentive, popping up at subway stops to "escort" his teacher and following her home against her will. Even his words are laced with uneasy sexual suggestiveness. Frannie remarks to herself that Cornelius "says he has something to show me" (146). Their relationship plays off of combustible racist fears of African American men menacing white women, but Moore also emphasizes the significance of Cornelius's gender-based physical privilege. As Cornelius follows her into the ostensible sanctity of her own building, Frannie realizes that "any fragile authority I might once have had, based on my position as a thirty-four-year-old teacher and his position as a nineteen-year-old man, was no longer in force. Didn't mean shit in the hot and airless front hall" (106). Frannie deliberately uses the slang tag word *shit,* previously associated with Cornelius's speech patterns, to emphasize his dominance over her in this isolated space. Even more bellicose than Cornelius is Frannie's old friend John Graham. John admits to walking by Frannie's apartment, stalking her, and harassing her ex-boyfriends and colleagues after she rejects him romantically. Exhausted by his surveillance and manipulation, Frannie asks him if it wouldn't "be easier if you just hit me once in the face, and got it over with?" (139).

Like Alice Sebold, Moore uses digression in these narrative arcs, but whereas *The Lovely Bones* blunted the momentum of a murder mystery, *In the Cut*'s red herrings amplify Moore's point that sexual menace lurks everywhere. The side stories of Cornelius and John supplement the most intense exploration of misogyny through the character of Detective Rodriguez, Malloy's partner and the man who will murder Frannie. Recently reassigned to desk duty after trying to kill his wife over a petty argument, Rodriguez is startlingly open about his brutality. Upon first meeting Frannie in a bar, he minimizes his domestic-homicide case as "some spic [who] did his wife." The woman in question, he adds, "must not of known when to shut up" (51). Dismissing Frannie as "one of those feminist broads," he proceeds to tell her that all he requires of women is "two tits, a hole and a heartbeat" (51). Even Rodriguez's final act of murder itself is laced with misogynistic observations. A killer who cuts with words as well as with blows, Rodriguez even cracks jokes about how vaginal odor will impede his plans to dump Frannie's remains.

New York offers no safe spaces for Frannie, as earlier evidenced in her encounter with Cornelius in the hall. Sue Thornham has effectively argued that the film version of *In the Cut* (2003) constructs a gritty Big Apple in deliberate juxtaposition to the "bright safe city" of postfeminist imaginings seen on television's *Sex and the City* (34).[8] Moore's New York is indeed dank and menacing. Thornham notes that the film's buildings "are daubed with sexualized graffiti, its streets suffused with the threat of male violence. Women walk arm in arm, in pairs; when we glimpse them alone they are running, in flight from something we do not see" (37). Specters of male violence haunt the novel's backdrop as well. A man on the subway points and leers at Frannie, saying that there is "not enough meat on your bones yet" (62). Glimpses of famous murder cases are woven into the narrative; Detective Malloy, for instance, recounts the 1986 "Preppy Murder" case, in which a well-connected young man received relatively little jail time for the strangulation of a woman who, he falsely claimed, desired "rough sex." Frannie's student Cornelius pens a piece of creative writing about John Wayne Gacy, serial rapist and killer of young men. Malloy leaves an FBI primer on "lust murderers" on his desk; within its pages, Frannie reads a murderer's confession that mirrors her own future killing. "I wanted to cut her body so she would not look like a person and destroy her so she would not exist," reads the anonymous murderer's entry. "I began to cut on her body. I remember cutting her breasts off. After this, all I remember is that I kept cutting on her body. I did not rape the girl. I only wanted to destroy her" (137). By the book's end, Frannie, the language professor who bears the word, becomes a statistic and a story authored by Detective Rodriguez's knife.

In keeping with postfeminist wisdom, which places responsibility for sexual-violence prevention in victims' hands, Frannie constantly takes safety precautions. Moore writes several sentences about locks, as if to linguistically capture the (false) security they provide the novel's women. "I closed the door behind [Cornelius], and locked it, and because the bolt makes a loud sound when it is turned, I knew that he would hear it sliding into its rusted grooves, and I was glad," says Frannie (14). A few hours later, she describes having "closed the heavy street door behind me, pushing it with my shoulder to make sure that it was locked" (14). Frannie's friend Pauline, another murder victim of Rodriguez, "has seven elaborate locks on her door. It takes her several minutes to open them" (28). These locks fail to protect Pauline from a gruesome beheading. Moore herself dismisses the idea of "preventative" behavior, adding in an interview that "they're going to get you either way. It doesn't matter what you do, they're going to get you [even if] you don't go out of your house, you hunker down, you're very careful, you've got a pit bull, you have 15 locks on your door" (Moore, "Dead End" 15).

Danger comes for Frannie, as it did for Angela Sands, a gothic figure haunting the novel's edges. Sands, the dead woman whose fate prefigures Frannie's own, is a doppelgänger whose loss of language and life is expressed through the trope of disarticulation. In her first and only living incarnation, Sands forms part of a voyeuristic tableau that Frannie stumbles upon in a bar's back room. She is mesmerized by the woman's sexual subservience and finds herself borrowing Sands's mannerisms in an encounter with Malloy, "moving my head in the same slow dipping way that the girl with the red hair had moved her head, wondering if he [Malloy] had taught her" (85). Angela Sands's *disarticulated* body (to borrow Malloy's term) also serves as a grim reminder of how the novel links women's corporeal autonomy with access to language. "What a good word, I thought. Disarticulated," Frannie muses (19). The term resonates for her, notes Meghan Freeman, for "what is to be feared more by those whose power resides in words than the deprivation of speech?" (131). Soon enough, Frannie too is literally and metaphorically dismembered. Detective Rodriguez precedes his murder with sadistic play, tearing Frannie's clothes and assaulting her breasts. Diane Naugler has written that in the popular imagination "it is not the vagina but the breasts that have come to operate as the central symbol of femaleness. . . . In the arithmetic of gender, breast is to female as penis is to male" (100–101). Rodriguez tears apart the physical symbol of her femininity; even through intense pain, Frannie wonders at the ramifications of a loss of a breast, "lighter without the rose nipple to give it weight, to give it meaning" (177).

Moore's earlier description of male/female conflict as "not a fair fight" recurs in the book's death struggle. Frannie is placed into linguistically and physically subordinate positions. She narrates how her murderer "grabbed me by the hair and threw his legs around me. Riding me. My hair his reins." She bites him "just like a girl," and pleads. "I asked him not to hurt me," Frannie recalls. "It seems to be what women say. And men. It did not stop him" (179). As she is being slashed, Frannie thinks disjointedly: "Cutting me . . . I have a new word for the dictionary. . . . In the cut. From vagina. A place to hide. To hedge your bet. But someplace safe, someplace safe from harm" (179). Frannie *is* cut (by Rodriguez) because she is *in possession of* a cut/cunt; in other words, because she is female.[9] The novel's famous last line switches pronouns, moving from "I know the poem" to "she knows the poem," thus confirming Frannie's disarticulation. "Just as her body is dismembered by Rodriguez' razor," writes John Hodgkins, "so is Frannie's already destabilized and fragmented subjectivity permanently riven, as the narrating 'I' is joined in the concluding sentence by the more remote, impersonal 'She'" (55–56).

Readers have witnessed Moore's earlier attempts, in the Hawaiian trilogy, to counter the postfeminist discourse of empowerment by frankly discussing female *dis*empowerment. In this, her most self-consciously literary novel, Moore plays with the concept of *enacting* the prefix *dis*. *In the Cut* depicts a contemporary world that dismisses and dismembers women, from the disarticulated female corpses scattered regularly in the Hudson River, to Pauline's decapitation, to the "two tits, a hole and a heartbeat" that characterizes Rodriguez's perfect woman. Moore has in the past contended that Frannie is misconstrued by reviewers as either naive (for her romantic involvement with a potentially dangerous man) or masochistic. Her behavior, she contends, is motivated by "her refusal to be afraid" (Moore, "Kind of Craziness" 3). Lest this come uncomfortably close to butt-kicking babe territory, Moore returns us to her dark worldview. "What is so bleak about *In the Cut* is that even when a woman makes that determination, they'll still get you," she remarks. "'They' being the patriarchy, the establishment, those who hold power. So a woman might as well be brave" (3).

"I Hate the Victim More": The Big Girls

The background texture of *In the Cut* is staccato, focusing on clean, sharp movements like the click of a lock, the tap of a stiletto walking quickly at night, and the whistle of a knife. By contrast, Moore's subsequent novel, *The Big Girls*, set in a dank and festering women's prison, features ambient noise of a more dripping, leaking sort. Inmate whispers and the snatches of guard conversation caught by the prison therapist Louise all deride the soft feminine body, associating it with haplessness and vulnerability. In true gothic style, *The Big Girls* features three doppelgänger female protagonists. Helen, a woman in prison for filicide, symbolically overlaps with both her therapist Louise and Angie, a famous actress with biological and marital ties to the other two women. Moore's fracturing of the main subject blurs and destabilizes the narrative while also suggesting the commonality of female abjection across class lines. Drawing from famous legal cases, including the narratives of Andrea Yates and Sylvia Likens, *The Big Girls* critiques postfeminism's misplaced investment in the discourse of female "badness," both in terms of women's actual violence and as a cultural fetish that is sometimes conflated with empowerment and equality. The "bad girl" archetype also blinds us, she reminds us in an echo from her earlier Hawaiian novels, to the realities of women's victimization. Moore forces us to look critically at how postfeminist grammars of empowerment and glorified female transgression (badness) work to deride women's bodies.

Badness, the word I have chosen to represent the target of Moore's critique, is certainly clunky and imprecise. It is not synonymous with *evil* or *atrociousness,* but rather it connotes a sexy, or at least harmless, kind of rebelliousness. As already discussed, postfeminist popular culture tends to fetishize female "badness" as part of its project to neutralize discussions of inequity. The sword-wielding woman-warrior genre in film and television is one example of this tendency. The wide-ranging embrace of female relational aggression, which is rooted in psychological observations about adolescent girls' competitive behavior but has become a sort of catchall to describe the duplicitous, catty, and verbally violent American woman, is another. In a postfeminist landscape in which gender equality and gender neutrality are presupposed accomplishments, American ideas about women's capacity for *criminality* have also greatly expanded. In *The Big Girls*, Moore explores the increasingly popular contention that women's violence occurs at equivalent rates and outcomes as does men's.

When *The Big Girls*'s prison therapist Louise delves into the history of women in prison, she learns that inmates were allowed to have children accompany them, and no woman was incarcerated for filicide until 1930. "Any mother who killed her child was, by the very nature of her crime, out of her mind and needed treatment, not punishment. The public was more forgiving of these women than they are now," Louise notes (54). That "forgiving" nature is a vestige of protectivism, and criminologists Katherine Stuart Van Wormer and Clemens Bartollas have noted that women "who presented an image of helplessness when prosecuted for misdemeanors and felonies, including homicide," might be given relatively light sentences, keeping racial and class privileges in mind (16). The removal of women from the pedestal of preferential treatment began in seriousness during the 1970s, due in part to feminist protest against protectionist legislation. In postfeminist culture, the trend now seems to be going the other way.

Criminologists Barbara Bloom, Meda Chesney-Lind, and Joycelyn Pollock-Byrne have popularized the terms *vengeful equity* and *equality with a vengeance* to describe the process in which punitive sentences are handed out to women as a purported form of gender equity with men.[10] This process, in the eyes of many criminologists and sociologists, flattens out gender distinctions in method and manner of crime and reifies a narrative of "bad girls" that has had disturbing consequences.

Violent crime remains a highly gendered enterprise. According to the FBI "Crime in the United States" report for 2009, of 8,654 arrests for murder/nonnegligent manslaughter, 931 were female offenders (10.75 percent of the total). The gender gap is even more pronounced in sexually based offenses: 187 of 15,093 arrests for forcible rape were female (1.2 percent of the total) ("Crime in the United States"). Nevertheless, the presumption of women's criminality in popular culture seems to loom ever larger. For some, the effort to represent women's violence as equivalent to men insinuates, as Lynn Harris puts it, "that this is the dark price we pay for female empowerment. As in, *hey, feminism, thanks a lot*" ("Is Female-on-Male Violence on the Rise?"; emphasis in original). Sociologist Jennifer Schwartz has contrasted two reactions to the historical increase in women's arrests: a behavioral hypothesis that "evolving gender roles could 'masculinize' female behavior, increasing female motivations for physical aggression or attack," and a social-constructionist theory that heightened crime awareness and proactive school interventions have expanded the definition of crime "to include more minor acts of aggression and violence, the sorts of crimes in which women are more likely to be involved" (790–91). Her research, which includes analyses of several nations with gender-egalitarian policies and cultures, belies the behavioral interpretation that women's equality "causes" violence. Nevertheless, the narrative of "bad girls" continues unabated in both news reports and within the postfeminist cultural landscape. Jennifer Pozner writes of "salacious narratives on crime dramas" that attempt "to create a false equivalence, discussing the few women who have been violent and using those women's stories as proof that A) there's 'just as much' female-to-male domestic violence as male-to-female, and B) domestic violence isn't a problem that women have to deal with as victims anymore" (qtd. in Harris, "Is Female-on-Male Violence on the Rise?"). The allure of female badness, as Lynn Harris mentions, is its disruption of the cultural scripts of victimization. "Both partners are equally to blame, both partners are equally abusive; women are strong enough to punch, women are not—or no longer—the only victims," she notes ("Is Female-on-Male Violence on the Rise?").

Such narratives also whet the cultural appetite for punishment. Ike Bradshaw, prison guard in *The Big Girls*, notes that attitudes toward female prisoners have drastically changed in recent times. "Look," he says. "They just weren't that crazy about sending you girls to the gas chamber . . . but it's changing. They're really starting to like it" (89). The public is not alone in this sadistic pleasure; throughout Moore's novel, the guards are shown offering disparagement and outright cruelty to the prisoners. The women kept behind the bars of New York's Sloatsburg Prison, though, are far from being empowered antiheroines who have taken advantage of the law. Their stories are bound up in questions of race, gender, and limited access to power. Stacey D'Erasmo remarks that "the women-in-prison genre, even at its most blatantly exploitative, can't escape the political. The collective female experience, what we're allowed and what we're forbidden, is distilled into the image of rows of women behind bars doing time for crimes that often seem to be entangled in questions about gender and power," including "the much-beaten woman who finally kills the abusive husband or boyfriend, the prostitute, [and] the drug mule for male gangsters" ("Jailhouse Flock").

Many cases featured in *The Big Girls* reflect the sexual exploitation that D'Erasmo captures. The main character Helen suffered repeated rapes as a child. Her fellow inmates are similarly traumatized: Shayna was forced into prostitution at the age of eight, Darla is raped in jail, and the elderly Mary suffered an ear sliced off by her own son. Most of the inmates are further disadvantaged by their race and class. When she first arrives at the prison, the therapist Louise notices that there are no guardhouses along the river and cracks a cynical joke: "Do they think black women can't swim?" (3). The prisoners are, as in real life, disproportionately women of color and women living in poverty.

Helen herself is an abused wife who killed her children during a psychotic break. Her story draws on other narratives of murderous mothers, most particularly that of Andrea Yates. Yates, who methodically drowned her five young children in 2001 while suffering from psychosis and depression, became notorious around the world. Like Yates, Helen experiences depression and religion-inspired hallucinations. Both women also lived in rigidly traditional marriages where they were assigned the bulk of the child rearing. Many columnists and some women's organizations, such as NOW, used Yates's case as a platform to draw attention to postpartum depression and the unacknowledged burdens of maternity. Anna Quindlen, for instance, indicted the "insidious cult of motherhood" in which women are "meant to be all things to small people, surrounded by bromides and soppy verse and smiling strangers who talk about how lucky we are" (62). Of course, there were many in the public sphere who felt that Yates served as a poster girl for feminist claims of victimization and who chided, as the *Spectator*'s Mark Steyn did, "the new generation of sob sisters" who deemed "infanticide an understandable byproduct of contemporary lifestyle" (19).

Moore has commented in an interview that in *The Big Girls*, "one of the things that I set out to write about was motherhood, that's really what interested me; what it is to be a mother, what does it mean to be a mother? And almost everyone in the book, all the women, are mothers" (Moore, "Birnbaum v. Susanna Moore"). By using a doubling motif that links Helen to two other women, the successful professional therapist Louise and the celebrity actress Angie, Moore suggests the commonality of maternal desperation amid staggering cultural expectations. In one example of doubling, both Helen and Louise suffer postpartum psychotic breaks. Louise's involved thoughts of harming her son. She thinks: "If I really had thrown Ransom [her son] out the window, I might be dead now" (54). Increasingly, the two women blur together, referring to each other as "sisters." Louise confesses that she's "been dreaming about my patient Helen. She told me that she dreams about me, too" (63). The doppelgänger effect is further complicated when Moore introduces the perspective of Angie, who has ties to both women. Angie, a famous actress, dates Louise's ex-husband and may or may not be Helen's long-lost biological sister. Susanna Moore has said that Angie was created to explore "the obsession with celebrity that we now suffer" that leads to "the dissolution of the line between ourselves and others" ("Birnbaum v. Susanna Moore"). The novel's gothic hall of mirrors, which blurs three women who are distinctly different in class and educational status, makes Helen's abjection free-floating rather than bound to prison walls. She could be, literally, any woman.

Helen and her fellow prisoners are labeled "big girls" by one of the corrections officers. As felons, they have committed big crimes; yet the phrase also has other connotations. "Big girl" can serve as a derisive euphemism for an overweight woman. It can also condescendingly refer to someone behaving like a little girl. Both of these alternate meanings are at play in the novel, where Helen and her fellow inmates are patronized by a staff revolted by their softness, weakness, and ripe feminine physicality. "They [the guards] hate being here. They hate working with women," Louise reflects early in the novel. "They would rather have a hundred male prisoners than one woman prisoner. It's the women's voices that get on their nerves, they say" (39). The female voice is a persistent source of vexation throughout the novel. One therapist uses tapes of singer Yoko Ono to torture male offenders. Louise herself comments that it is "common knowledge" that female inmates "cannot be compelled to silence, unlike men" (20). Male guards are quick to denigrate the prisoners. When a guard cracks a joke about a prisoner's escape attempt, Louise "realized that he assumes I share his feelings of contempt" (84). Although she considers herself a sympathetic, socially progressive woman, Louise too comes to be revolted by her charges. An elderly inmate piques her disgust because "her support stockings had slipped to her ankles, and I saw that her swollen legs were mottled brown and gray. Her eyes were bloodshot. Her breath was disgusting—it smelled of Pepto-Bismol and garlic" (154). Louise also admits hating another former patient "because she was fat" (192).

An embedded anecdote in the center of *The Big Girls* epitomizes social contempt for the weakness and vulnerability that is so often gendered feminine. One of Louise's colleagues, Dr. de la Vega, tells her of his female patient, a woman who violently tortured a young girl named Judy. Judy's story is Moore's fictionalization of the 1965 Sylvia Likens case, in which a fourteen-year-old, left with a neighbor woman by her itinerant parents, died of unspeakable brutality. Bound in the woman's basement, Likens was subject to branding, scalding baths, object penetration, beatings, feces consumption, and more; she finally died of shock and a brain hemorrhage. The case has been the topic of endless true-crime treatments throughout the years.[11] Notably, Likens's torture and murder was examined by Kate Millett in her semifictional 1979 work *The Basement: Meditations on a Human Sacrifice.* In an interview with the *New York Times*, Millett called the case "the story of the suppression of women. Gertrude [Baniszewski, the lead perpetrator] seems to have wanted to administer some terrible truthful justice to this girl: that *this was what it was to be a woman*" (Broeske, "Midwest Nightmare"; emphasis added).

Millett's analysis of the case resonates strongly with the themes of Susanna Moore's own dark aesthetic. However, the most significant aspect about the Likens narrative in *The Big Girls* is how Louise's colleague makes sense of it. What "disturbs Dr. de la Vega," Louise narrates, "is that the dead girl *did nothing to save herself.* He cannot bear it, and his distress causes him to entertain his own fantasies of torture, which alarm him. He is so angry with her for not going to the police, for not running away, for not fighting back, that he cannot sleep at night" (119; emphasis added). She understands the depth of his distress when "he said, gazing at me as if he had never seen me before, 'She could have called me. Why didn't she just pick up the phone and call me?'" (119). Judy, of course, did not know Dr. de la Vega. Yet startlingly, he transfers his anger about her torment back onto her. "As much as I can't stand the sight of [my patient]," he tells Louise, "*I hate the victim more*" (118; emphasis added). In an age of supposed gender equality, women and girls are presumed to have an arsenal of tools—both physical and verbal—to fight off the physical and sexual violence that they experience disproportionately. By not fighting back, Judy/Sylvia Likens reveals the soft underbelly of feminine vulnerability that postfeminism presents itself has having transcended.

Helen and her fellow big girls cannot escape their festering prison home. Louise, though, can, and in the second half of the novel she begins full-scale retreat, disidentifying with the prisoners and embracing a conservative heterosexual relationship with guard Ike Bradshaw. Bradshaw, for whom prisoners exist as "women whose opinions and feelings don't count for anything," soon has hold of Louise (79). He maintains the upper hand in their sexual relationship, opining that "she's nice to fuck. A little eager, but that can be fixed" (121). Louise's relationship with Bradshaw offers her "liberation" from serious work and from social activism:

> I realize for the first time in almost a year I'm not thinking about the women. Now I find myself distracted by the niceties that engage the attention of a middle-class lady who's getting laid—my Brazilian wax, for example. . . . So this, I say to myself in amazed triumph, is what I needed! All those years [in academia] when what I really wanted was a pedicure. That chilly Palo Alto summer spent on a theory of moral rationalism when what I wanted was new underwear. New sheets. (99)

Louise's postfeminist holiday and subsequent detachment from her patients means that she overlooks Helen's increasing instability. As the doppelgängers disengage, Helen becomes psychotic and commits suicide. The novel ends on a note of separation, with Louise envisioning her former patients' daily lives while she, "here, in this world," tends to her son and lover (224). Sherryl Connelly reads the ending as partially redemptive, arguing that Louise "cannot save [Helen] or any of the women condemned to the grim depravity of Sloatsburg. But from their lives it seems she may learn her way around her own" (15). While this may be true, it is difficult to read the melancholy ending as anything but a loss for the big girls of Sloatsburg Prison, now left in an even more isolated purgatory.

Susanna Moore's work is often unfairly portrayed as masochistic and nihilistic because it plumbs depths of sexist hatred and contempt. "In studying fictional violence," writes Michael Kowalewski, "one must explore the power of words to sicken and befoul as well as freshen and redeem" (11). Moore addresses endemic misogyny both through her narratives, which are punctuated with blood-soaked acts, and also through miasmatic landscapes that teem with risk and threat. The man in the subway leering at Frannie to put meat on her bones; Dr. de la Vega railing about his hatred for a murdered girl who "failed" to protect herself; the professor who waylays Mamie to ask if he can look at her breasts—all testify that the toxicity of contemporary culture lies in words as well as in acts. "The hatred and the violence is so deeply ingrained, and so much a part of our culture, that I would rather go down brave," Moore has said (Moore, "Dead End" 15). Many years before Moore wrote about "Judy," Kate Millett wrote of the real-life Sylvia Likens that "you have been with me ever since, an incubus, a nightmare, my own nightmare, the nightmare of adolescence, of growing up a female child, of becoming a woman in a world set against us, a world we have lost and where we are everywhere reminded of our defeat" (11). Decades later, Moore's defeated protagonists fracture the brittle mantle of physical, linguistic, and social empowerment maintained in postfeminist popular culture.

4

Break Through to Me

Sapphire's Ghost in the Postfeminist Machine

Just as Susanna Moore's "Judy" (and the real-life Sylvia Likens) was trapped in a claustrophobic space of horror, so too is Claireece "Precious" Jones, narrator of Sapphire's 1996 novel *Push.* Confined to a cramped apartment in Reagan-era New York City, Precious tells readers by way of introduction that "I was left back when I was twelve because I had a baby for my fahver." She continues: "This gonna be my second baby. My daughter got Down Sinder. She's retarded" (3). Raped by her father, abused by her mother, HIV positive, rejected by the school system, obese, and living in poverty, Precious continues the postfeminist gothic tradition of abject heroines.

As critics have noted, *Push* is a social call to arms on many levels, targeting unresponsive educational institutions, the failure of the social safety net, and more. It is also an intervention in the framing of postfeminist blackness, particularly as it relates to display of public suffering and abuse. *Push* is an incest narrative, and as such it is enmeshed in gendered debates about temporality, memory, and veracity. Public skepticism and scorn about incest revelations, though, is also complicated by postfeminism's voracious appetite for narratives of black female suffering and by pop culture's legitimizing of black women as neospiritual leaders who will assist other (white) women negotiating trauma. Sapphire undertakes specific literary strategies to challenge postfeminist resistance to incest trauma, to deconstruct its preoccupation with the black female body as a site of suffering, and finally to foreclose a reading of her novel as an uplifting tale of exceptionalism.

Tackling the controversy about "recovered memories" that has dominated the recent cultural discussion of incest in literature, and which is often invoked to signify women's mendacity, Sapphire shows how memory can shift in meaning with the benefit of educational resources. *Push*'s literary form is experimental; told at first by a preliterate narrator, it moves from near-incoherence to clarity. The novel's plot mirrors the narration's slow evolution. With the benefit of education, Precious's inchoate sense of injustice helps her to redefine herself as an incest survivor and to access resources to help herself and her son. *Push* also speaks directly to postfeminism's tendency to make black women into gothic dark doubles. Assailing the discourse of the teenaged welfare "breeder," Sapphire makes of her heroine a capable, empowered mother *and* student. Throughout the text, she also foregrounds sexually explicit, genitally focused language of the vagina and the anus. One effect of this strategy is to compel readers' attention to incest's intimate pain. Another is to raise and disrupt painful stereotypes about black female hypersexuality as well as to call postfeminism to account for its frequent regard of black women as disposable. Finally, Sapphire's reworking of her source material in the 2011 sequel *The Kid*, which chronicles the unhappy life of Precious's son Abdul, signals her refusal to accept a neoliberal or postfeminist reading of *Push* as an up-by-the-bootstraps tale of hard work and meritorious victory. In writing *The Kid*, Sapphire speaks to the need for radical changes in the American social safety net and precludes readers from considering Precious's struggles as consigned to the past.

Vampire Sucking the System's Blood: On Gothic and Postfeminist Blackness

In an oft-cited passage from *Push*, young Precious Jones recalls watching a television show in which it is revealed, thanks to a photo taken at a party, that most of the guests were vampires. "The other peoples did not exist. They vampires," she muses. "They eats, drinks, wear clothes, talks, fucks, and stuff, but when you git right down to it they don't exist" (31). Precious maps this moment onto her own social invisibility, adding: "Don't nobody want me. Don't nobody need me. I know who I am. I know who they say I am—vampire sucking the system's blood. Ugly black grease to be wipe away, punish, kilt, changed, finded a job for" (31). Precious is thus positioned within and without; she not only identifies *with* one of the key gothic tropes of outsider difference, but also emphasizes the way parasitic discourses are often racially applied to *ostracize* welfare mothers like her.

For writers of color, the gothic has occupied a similarly doubled status. America's racist past provides endless grist for a gothic mill of terror and fear. Richard Wright famously wrote in the conclusion to his 1940 essay

"How 'Bigger' Was Born" that the tragic past and continuing oppression of black Americans cast a shadow so profound that "if Poe were alive, he would not have to invent horror; horror would invent him." Yet as a form developed primarily by white authors, and as one associated with fanciful and often supernatural trappings, gothic often provided a poor fit for literary projects about slavery's material horrors. The slave-narrative tradition in particular utilized realism to convey the quotidian horrors of enslaved life, employing what Avery Gordon deems "a plain unembellished style of writing that conveyed only the believable facts" and "nothing that smacked of 'the imagination'" (145). Furthermore, the gothic's dark racial Others are often its ciphers and villains. From Bertha Mason haunting the attic to the devilish Zofloya, from Heathcliff's mysterious appearance on the moors to *Nosferatu*'s ratlike Orloff, classic gothic literature and film often draw on ethnic and racial difference to produce their monsters and ghosts. Eugenia DeLamotte has suggested that "behind the fears of dark, racialized others on which the Gothic construction of whiteness hinges is the unspeakable Other of that construction: the fear that there is no such thing as whiteness, or even race" ("White Terror" 17).[1] Ideologies of gender have, historically, further exacerbated the gothic's racial divisions because women of color have traditionally been excluded from consideration as the distressed damsel.

Writers of color compelled by the gothic, therefore, must negotiate against historical inhospitalities in both its form and content. Nonetheless, the gothic's affective power to shock and terrorize was, and remains, politically useful for narratives about racism. Teresa Goddu observes that the "iconography of imprisonment, the fear of retribution, and the weight of sin" in nineteenth-century gothic fiction "provided a useful vocabulary and register of images by which to represent the scene of America's greatest guilt: slavery" (*Gothic America* 133).[2] In their political critique of white patriarchy, antislavery authors also shared some similarities with white women's female gothic. Kari Winter has persuasively argued that "more than any other literary genres of the period, the female Gothic and slave narrative genres focused on the terrifying injustices at the foundation of the Western social order" (2). Both traditions "powerfully dramatize the need for solidarity among women," although the dynamics of race and class often disrupt the realization of this ideal (110).

Above all, writers of color have *renovated* gothic traditions, emphasizing, in Maisha Wester's words, "the sense of horror in the very issues of ownership and (dis)possession at play in the process of writing the gothic" (28). They resituate key gothic topoi. The female gothic, for instance, often utilizes gloomy, haunted mansions to signal the frightening nature of supposedly safe domestic space for women. Yet urban gothics, like Sapphire's *Push*, illustrate the terror of home by limning a cramped, claustrophobic apartment where the incestuously abused heroine's bedroom is the site of evil. Evie Shockley has also foregounded the need for intersectional readings of gothic tropes, analyzing how "live burial," a staple white gothic punishment for transgressive nuns, cannot be read simply as "repressed sexuality" (444). Such an arc in Ann Petry's *The Street* (1946), which features the African American heroine Lutie experiencing sexual threat in the very apartment she rented in order to fulfill a domestic ideal, highlights "the ghastly gap between the efficacy of Lutie's determined performance of the gender, race, sexuality, and class identities that she desires and the results that such behavior *promises* to bring in terms of the rhetoric of domestic ideology" (Shockley 447–48; emphasis in original). Precious Jones expresses similar frustrations, voicing the desperate hope early in *Push* that if others realize she "is a beautiful chile like white chile in magazines . . . a blue-eye skinny chile," her abuse would be stopped (64).

By tapping the gothic icons of vampires and other things that are "spooky an' shit," Sapphire appropriates a literary language that conveys fear and terror; she also updates, in the dark-skinned and large-framed Precious Jones, the archetypal gothic heroine. Like the other texts in this book, *Push*'s use of the gothic must be filtered through a postfeminist lens that resists acknowledging and discussing gender-based victimization. Women of color, and black women in particular, are addressed paradoxically by this antivictimist discourse; while their claims to injury are often minimized, they are simultaneously overrepresented in popular culture as "wise women" and authorities on suffering. To more fully contextualize the literary strategies embedded within Sapphire's *Push*, it is useful to unpack some of these disjunctions in more detail.

Kimberly Springer has commented that most cultural investigations of postfeminism seem to have "dwindled to a whimper" past the point of acknowledging the absence of women of color ("Divas" 249). It is true that the most visible icons of postfeminist popular culture, whether girls at risk or fun-loving women having sex in the city, are overwhelmingly white (this pattern holds true for postfeminist literature, including the books in this study as well). Postfeminism offers haunting specters of silence when it comes to dealing with survival issues. As Springer points out, "the discourse of having it all" that dominates postfeminist popular media has "always been a bit lost on black women and anathema to black feminism, which aimed, in the 1970s, to *dismantle* the idea that black women could be superwomen" (252;

emphasis added). Yet black women are also instrumental figures in certain postfeminist *grammars*, following Rebecca Clark Mane's definition of the term as a set of "strategies for sublimating and containing challenges to racial inequality" (73).[3] Extraordinarily high-achieving celebrities such as Oprah Winfrey, for instance, are often used as evidence of the bountiful opportunities available in a postracial, postgendered society.

Postfeminism fashions itself as postracial, frequently trumpeting the achievement of a color-blind society. Another postfeminist grammar of talking "around" race is the veneration of the mixed-race heroine, a figure extremely visible in television and literature since the late 1990s.[4] As many critics have pointed out, the unproblematized celebration of the mixed-race heroine's "hybridity" does not de-center whiteness, and can risk blithely masking, as Isabelle Thuy Pelaud notes, "the immense difficulty, stress, pain, and contradictions that arise to various degrees when the people involved are located on the margin at the intersection of cultures" (50).[5] When postfeminism does speak *to*, and not around, blackness, it often falls back on familiar stereotypes. As previously discussed, a key element of the postfeminist aesthetic is creating distance from anger, an emotion that is stereotypically associated with feminism. The continued existence of the brash, castigating "Sapphire" stereotype illustrates how black women, regardless of their individual relationships to feminism, are collectively misrecognized as always already angry. As articulated by Michele Wallace in *Black Macho and the Myth of the Superwoman* (1979), the Sapphire archetype is "too domineering, too strong, too aggressive, too outspoken, too castrating, too masculine" (91). Many black feminist critics have catalogued the continuing iteration of this figure in popular forms of media.[6] *Push*'s author Sapphire, the former Ramona Lofton, thus chose a culturally loaded pen name. In an interview, she not only jokes about being inspired by New Age symbolism, but also adds that "at one time in African American culture, the name . . . had a very negative connotation. Sapphire was, like, the evil, razor-toting type of belligerent black woman, which was somehow attractive to me" (Sapphire, "Sapphire's Big Push" 29).

Lofton is not the only one to find Sapphire's energy appealing. It is an oddity of postfeminist culture that while black female subjects are frequently demeaned and have little political power, white female audiences often covet their strength and endurance, perceiving them as what Susan Douglas calls "a jailbreak from demure femininity" (128). Douglas cautions that what white women covet about the "sassy black woman" trope is its perceived assertiveness, and not the lived reality of black female experience. For those who "walk away from the TV or out of the movie theater as a white woman in a white world," she adds, "such images have few consequences" (132).[7]

Public fascination with black women's physical and verbal displays of strength is rooted in American history. Slave women performed physical, sexual, and emotional labor, taking care of white families while enduring their own unimaginable losses. Lauren Berlant has chronicled our nation's tradition of spectacular black female suffering on page and screen, from the slave narrative of Harriet Jacobs to the contemporary congressional testimony of Anita Hill, which galvanized a national public discussion of sexual harassment in the workplace (*Queen of America Goes to Washington City*). Black women have been at the forefront of the incest-survivor movement, both in the production of acclaimed literary narrative and in public disclosures of abuse by luminaries like Oprah Winfrey and the late Maya Angelou. Today, Melba Wilson adds, a predominantly accepted cultural view is that "black women are strong and can handle anything that life throws at them—whether rape at the hands of white slaveowners; the trauma of being separated from their children in slavery; racism; violence against us within our communities, or sexual abuse" (10).

The problematic "naturalization" of black female suffering contributes to the popularity of the female-led neospiritual movement that has permeated popular television and literature since the 2000s. Karlyn Crowley has argued that, whether expressed in goddess feminism, in appropriation of Native American imagery, or in secular Oprah worship, "many white women believe that a more powerful spiritual gender identity is found in the superior spirituality and indigenous traditions of women of color" (163–64). At the pinnacle of this intimate sphere of femininity is the multimedia entity Oprah Winfrey. Drawing on intense personal charisma, neosacred texts like her book club, and other church-inspired elements, Winfrey blends spirituality and self-help psychology into a powerful brew. And while she may stand atop popular culture's pinnacle of black female neospiritual power, she is not there alone. Others, including literary titans Alice Walker and the late Maya Angelou, as well as motivational speaker Iyanla Vanzant, also wield influence.[8]

To put it bluntly, many white readers and viewers seem comfortable talking about personal trauma as long as those conversations are facilitated by supportive, sympathetic black women. The idea that "random but interested dark women are watching over us, ready to pop in just when we are in deep, deep trouble and in need of advice or sanctuary" is deeply attractive to mainstream popular culture, Sheri Parks contends (xv). This dynamic is important when considering the divisive reception of incest claims since the women's movement. When she entered the 1990s book marketplace with

Push, Sapphire's race and gender constructed her, in public terms, as part of a sagacious authority on suffering. It also placed her within a mainstream public struggling to grapple with the legacy of incestuous violence. It is to that contested terrain that we now turn.

Rolling the Eyes: Incest and Postfeminist Culture

Incest strikes at the safety of familial and domestic space; educational campaigns about it cannot focus, as they too often do in discourses of sexual violence, on the "othered" stranger in the bushes. The female gothic has long argued, of course, that home is among the least safe locations for women and girls; Ruth Perry has even averred that incest or its threat is a *foundational* motif of the eighteenth-century gothic novel (272). But beginning in earnest in the 1970s, the topic of incest spilled from the pages of gothic novels into the public domain, bringing with it skeletons of all kinds. Second wave feminist activism, in conjunction with a post-Vietnam public's greater awareness of trauma, led to heightened public consciousness of the crime and its aftermath (Harkins xiv). Janice Doane and Devon Hodges have carefully documented how feminists like Florence Rush, who identified child sexual abuse as a major feminist issue, were at the forefront of public education and the development of crisis services, and helped to frame incest as a crime of abuse rather than one of mental illness. Inspired by women's movement activism, public discussion of incest moved into the mainstream; *Ms.* magazine published its first article on incest in 1977, and a plethora of books followed, including the survivor's compendium *Kiss Daddy Goodnight* (1978). By 1984, even the thoroughly middlebrow subculture of made-for-TV movies had caught on, airing the incest drama *Something about Amelia* and fielding thousands of help-line calls in its aftermath (Whittier 121). In a twenty-first-century moment where we have become somewhat oversaturated with, and cynical about, phrases like *breaking silence* or *speaking out*, it is vital to recognize the contributions that feminist activists and their allies made that have helped family-abuse survivors to do just that.

As the antivictimization rhetoric of the backlash era began to spread, however, public support for survivor stories began to erode. Nancy Whittier has analyzed the dampening effect of self-help's ascent in incest recovery, arguing that it tended to unmoor discussions of sexual abuse from familial and patriarchal power structures.[9] Additionally, the notorious day-care abuse cases of the 1980s, and in particular the McMartin preschool trial's unfounded rhetoric of satanic panic, unsettled the public. No flashpoint about incest was more controversial than that of recovered memory, the idea that accounts of childhood sexual abuse may not initially be subject to conscious recall but can resurface in the course of therapy. Feminist therapists Ellen Bass and Laura Davis's book *The Courage to Heal* (1988), an incest-survivor recovery classic, served as a lightning rod in the debate because of its oft-quoted line (revised in subsequent editions): "If you think you were abused and your life shows the symptoms, then you were" (22).[10] The idea that "long-forgotten childhood events may be unearthed and later recollected with considerable accuracy" was explosive (Haaken 14). Many media outlets ran stories about families riven by accusations of buried childhood abuse; some accusers eventually recanted.

The controversy over recovered memory represents a small portion of overall abuse claims, but its impact was profound. By the 1990s, a countermovement was under way, pioneered by the False Memory Syndrome Foundation (FMSF) and other organizations propounding the theory that abuse memories were largely planted by therapists. Sociologist Richard Ofshe and journalist Ethan Watters describe the process thusly: "Convincing a client that she has a memory of abuse can be a simple two-step process. First, the therapist assures her that a symptom is a reliable indicator of abuse. Then he or she proceeds to change the client's definition of memory so that the indicator can be defined as a memory" (83). Public skepticism, in Rosaria Champagne's estimation, denied abuse survivors "the legitimacy to bear witness to their own lives and histories" (9). It also raised larger concerns about women's suggestibility as hapless dupes of manipulative therapists. In some ways, the trope of recovered memory has come to represent its own discursive shorthand for the complex subject of child sexual abuse. During a screed against incest narratives (including *Push*), critic Katie Roiphe criticizes the use of recovered memory in literature as a late-breaking "bargain-basement epiphany" where "the entire story is reduced to a riddle" and incest's discovery "is like a flash of lightning illuminating the entire book" ("Making the Incest Scene" 68).[11] The use of recovered memory as deus ex machina is quite common in television procedurals, where genre convention requires a whiplash of a twist in the episode's final five minutes. This method leads to a dramatic flourish, but misrepresents the complication, pain, and confusion of real-life victims.

In the early twenty-first century, discourses about incest are mixed, to say the least. Governmental watchdog groups and social services for survivors have exponentially proliferated. Nevertheless, a kind of cultural disdain for child sexual-abuse victims continues to predominate, expressed in several different ways. Roiphe's comments remind us of the trivializing of incest narratives in the popular media. Public skepticism, mixed with contempt for claims of victimization, also impacts survivor recovery. Abigail Bray, for instance, has warned of a dismissive discourse of "tolerant openness" that ascribes child sexual abuse to moral panic and views "children's sexual liberation and agency as a form of individual self-empowerment" ("Governing the Gaze" 175).

Sapphire's novel *Push* thus enters a marketplace in which incest is simultaneously hypervisible and treated with derision. Within the world of literature, incest narratives have a history spanning from at least the twelfth century, and a particular connection, as I have already mentioned, to the gothic tradition.[12] Critically acclaimed fiction about incest was at its zenith in the 1990s—perhaps in counterreaction to public skepticism about abuse claims. Other such works include Carolivia Herron's *Thereafter Johnnie* (1991), Jane Smiley's *A Thousand Acres* (1991), Liza Potvin's *White Lies (For My Mother)* (1992), Dorothy Allison's *Bastard out of Carolina* (1993), E. Annie Proulx's *The Shipping News* (1993), and Paula Vogel's play *How I Learned to Drive* (1997). Evidently, these stories of pain and loss still resound with audiences. For black women writers, the stakes of writing incest narratives are heightened both by a presumption of pathology by some white audiences and the burdens of respectability politics on the other. As previously discussed, Sapphire also faces the prewritten script of the "wise woman," spiritually leading readers in traumatic terrain.

Janice Doane and Devon Hodges write that black writers "have sometimes felt that incest in the black family cannot be discussed without confirming myths of black deviance" (32). Myths about the prevalence of black father-daughter incest have become woven into social and medical discourse. Lynn Sacco, for instance, has documented differing early American twentieth-century medical practices involving the treatment of girls' gonorrhea; while physicians went to ludicrous lengths to disavow the sexual origin of gonorrhea in white girls, they *assumed* that black girls with the medical symptoms were incest victims (108). The assumption of black hypersexuality continues to shape legal and psychological interventions into incest today. Carolyn Thornton and James Carter, who have analyzed how Child Protective Services intervenes (or fails to do so) in incestuous black families, contend that "when incest is reported in black communities," it is often "minimized or disregarded by agencies assigned to investigate and treat the problem" (50). In her groundbreaking work *Crossing the Boundary: Black Women Survive Incest*, Melba Wilson forthrightly addresses the "damaging myth" that "it is normal practice in black communities for little black girls to be sexually manhandled by their fathers, grandfather, uncles, and friends of the family" (7).

The fear of reinscribing racist assumptions has heightened the stakes for the discussion of incest in black women's writing. In fact, the *Push*-connected satirical novel *Erasure* (2001), directly addresses the risk of offering up pathologized black families for white entertainment. In Percival Everett's novel, a black academic, frustrated by the sensational financial and critical success of a female-authored urban novel, pseudonymously writes an over-the-top satire about an urban rapist. To his horror, his parody is fêted in the press by reviews that deem it "a true, raw, gritty work," "more like the evening news," and "the truest novel I've ever read" (254, 260–61).[13] Everett told the *Observer* that he has "nothing against ghetto novels" but is troubled by the public's perception that, within African American literature, they are "the only representations out there" ("Colour Bind"). His warning about the danger of creating tragedy porn for a voracious reading public is well taken, although I agree with Latoya Peterson that his critique "misfired at *Push*," underestimating the novel's complexity and introspection ("Of Push").

The act of writing incest narrative is, then, a complex negotiation of both fear of silence and fear of overexposure. In her introduction, Melba Wilson addresses the tension involved in "airing publicly some of the uncool stuff that goes on in our communities" and "exposing the dirty linen that we all know and keep quiet about" (1). The domestic metaphors Wilson uses reference the politics of respectability, a discourse that, in Evelyn Higginbotham's words, emphasized "temperance, cleanliness of person and property, thrift, polite manners, and sexual purity" in order to "refute the logic behind [black women's] social subordination" (193).[14] Even in contemporary times, argues Candice Jenkins, many texts express a "longing to protect or save black women, and black communities more generally, from narratives of sexual and familial pathology, through the embrace of conventional bourgeois propriety in the arenas of sexuality and domesticity" (14). Toni Morrison addresses the impetus to remain mute about issues of sexual abuse in what is arguably the most famous novel in incest literature—1970's *The Bluest Eye*—with a narrator who beckons her audience with a secret "quiet as it's kept" (1).

Push, with its gothic excess, raw sexual imagery, and scatological emphasis, is the very opposite of quiet. Sapphire has found new and innovative ways to navigate the quagmires of postfeminist incest fiction deftly. While skeptics contend that women dwelling on the past have whimsically undertaken accusations of abuse through handily recovered memories, Sapphire uses the very structure of *Push* to illustrate that for some survivors, memories are never *buried*, but rather only partially *interpretable*. Until she has engaged with education, Precious is unable to fully articulate and understand her experiences of abuse and to access resources that would help to change her life. The literary form of *Push*, then, mirrors the unfolding of the incest narrative. As Precious's narration moves from preliteracy to written expression, she also moves from having little understanding of injustice to reconceiving herself as a crime victim. The relationship between education and the incest revelation continues to be cyclical, as Precious's newfound knowledge further galvanizes her education, making her into the primary educator for her son Abdul. Gillian Harkins notes that Sapphire consistently connects "the scenes of reproductive and intellectual labor, a model and imitation through which Precious comes to articulate her agency" (219).[15] By linking maternal power to productive citizenship, the novel speaks back both to racist caricatures of young black women as indigent "breeders" and to postfeminist assumptions about incest victims' wallowing in the past.

Dorothy and Anthony Hurley observe that *Push* "is first and foremost an incest story. Incest is foregrounded and generates all the developments in the plot" (90). Precious Jones's opening statement, "I was left back when I was twelve because I had a baby for my fahver," offers absolutely no doubt about the centrality of incest both within her memory and within the narrative (1). The opening line serves as a moment of intentional difficulty—the reader stumbles over "fahver" and has to translate to the nearest known English word—father. Subsequently, the reader experiences another shock at the *content* of the sentence. Additionally, the construction of "*for* my father"—that is, by him and beholden to him—shows Precious's lack of agency.

While Precious shows she is aware of and subject to her father's sexual control, it is not until a key moment later in the book that she fully understands the concepts of rape and incest. These moments of illumination are not the sort of "a-ha" moments that Katie Roiphe scorns, but rather naturally born of the feminist, Afrocentric education she receives in an alternative school at the age of sixteen. Socially promoted but illiterate, Precious arrives in Ms. Rain's classroom, where writing and reading are prized. Ms. Rain insists that even preliterate students write in journals, corresponding with them in return. As critics have noted, Ms. Rain's pedagogical practices introduce Precious to historical knowledge of racism and sexism; she uses this knowledge to name her own experiences of abuse and to develop communal relationships. "Farrakhan's insistence on black pride, Tubman's efforts to free slaves, and Walker's affirmation of personal change and growth all stand in mimetic relation to Precious' own processes of empowerment and liberation," notes Ann Folwell Stanford (131).[16]

As she gains the tools to express herself through writing, Precious's literary capacities expand. She shows off technical skills such as intensification ("Capital letter is how you start off sentence or say something with deep shit meaning like Fuck with capital F") as well as disambiguation ("to too two. Three different 2 words" (82, 98). Her spelling improves through practice: "Rite wRite write" (99). Most strikingly, though, Precious moves into expressive language and poetic abstraction. Of course, even her preliterate utterances are gifted with rhythmic cadence. Wendy Rountree and Brittney Cooper have illuminated the different musical aesthetics at play in the novel, and Sapphire has told Rountree that *Push* can be considered a "blues/hip-hop/jazz novel," noting "the transcendence in the blues" as well as hip-hop's "open defiance" and social justice focus as pertinent to Precious's transformation (133).[17]

Letters rule the story of *Push*. Not all of them are as hopeful as *ABC* or *GED*; *HIV*, for example, threatens Precious's health by the novel's close. But the ABCs, which Precious recites at regular intervals in the book to calm herself, hold special power. Her alphabet is crafted to reflect her own personal experiences (*E*, for example, stands for "evil like mama") as well as black cultural iconography, such as *A* for Africa and *Q* for musician and actress Queen Latifah (65–66). As she repeats her ABCs, Precious begins to put her life into alphabetical order. By this I mean both that she is able to reconceptualize herself as an abuse survivor, and in so doing she becomes not fixated on the past (as a skeptical postfeminist reading might assume), but instead focused on integrating her traumatic past with her present and future. In one of the novel's most moving passages, Precious speaks to her unborn child. "Listen baby, Muver love you. Muver not dumb. Listen baby: ABCDEFGHIJKLMNOPQRSTUVWXYZ. Thas the alphabet. Twenty-six letters in all. Them letters make up words. Them words everything" (66). The passage poetically expands from the fundamental building blocks to an embrace of "everything" that language offers. It is a lullaby intended for a baby who is crucial for Precious's educational development and for her self-reclamation. "Ultimately, Sapphire shows that the route to fair representation for young African American mothers is not simply through gaining a voice, but through accessing literacy," Toni Fellela comments. "Women must be able to read and write in order to gain control over their destinies" (39).

In *Push*, "incest is the optic that sheds light on the wider social, cultural, and political problems that black communities face, including abject poverty and the failures of the social system," argue Dorothy and Anthony Hurley (114). The biggest turning point in the novel is Precious's revelation, in the course of analyzing her relationship to her newborn son, that "I was rape" (68). This moment allows her to radically revise her self-conception from abject girl to incest survivor. It is literally inconceivable without Abdul's presence, for it is in puzzling out the circumstances of his birth that Precious comes to fully understand the crime perpetrated against her. By using maternity as a site of transformation with respect to Precious's self-understanding and development, and by refusing to distance Precious's mothering from her education, Sapphire invests her subject with dignity while combating the racist stereotype of young black women as indigent breeders.

Within the supportive, female-led community of Each One Teach One, Precious gives birth to Abdul, and this galvanizes her revelation that she is an incest survivor. Looking at him, she muses: "He's a good baby. But he's not mine. I mean, he is mine. I push him out my pussy, but I didn't meet a boy 'n' fall in love, sex up 'n' have a baby. I think I was rape" (68). Precious cradles in her arms the *product* of sex (Abdul), but because she never participated in the *process* of consensual sex, she experiences cognitive dissonance. A careful student of Ms. Rain, Precious proceeds to connect her experience as an incest survivor with the historical sexual exploitation of black women. "I think what my fahver do is what Farrakhan said the white man did to the black woman," Precious muses. "Miz Rain say we is a nation of raped children . . ." (68–69). The unusual grammar of her statement "I was rape" also bears further scrutiny. By refusing temporal closure ("I think I was *raped*"), it implies that sexual violence is ongoing and widespread. Precious comes to understand the ubiquity of sexual assault. Brought to an incest survivor's group, she is amazed to see women of all races and identities present. "All kinda women here. Princess girls, some fat girls, old women, young women. One thing we got in common, no *the* thing, is we was rape," she narrates, again repeating the unusual construction (130). Furthermore, the stories of Precious's classmates, brought together in the collection of memoirs that ends the novel, reaffirm that sexual violence is depressingly commonplace. "I am sick with the walking dicks of Harlem," classmate Rhonda (another survivor of incest) writes. "Everywhere is a hand rubbing, a dick going psst psst come here come here." Her friend Jermaine's story is equally bleak; raped by her girlfriend's father at the age of fourteen, she escapes her father's molestation attempts only to be gang-raped by six men. The placement of the group journal after the conclusion of the narrative, argues Susana Morris, "purposefully underscores the women's shared experience of destructive family life" and jars readers "out of the Madonna and child symbolism to (re)consider the stark reality" of the girls' experiences (123).

Precious's revelation that "I was rape" allows her to reconceive of herself as a survivor; part of the work entailed by this realization includes a painful reevaluation of her bleak childhood. When a nurse expresses sympathy for the twelve-year-old mother Precious and asks her, "Was you ever, I mean did you ever get to be a chile?" she responds, "Thas a stupid question, did I ever get to be a chile? I *am* a chile" (13). L. H. Stallings writes that "Sapphire uses the exchange to demonstrate that perhaps the very notion of childhood is racialized and not as universal as some assume" (116). For Precious, there has *never* been any demarcation between the developmental phases of childhood, adolescence, and young adulthood. "I'm twelve now, I been knowing about that since I was five or six, maybe I always known about pussy and dick. I can't remember not knowing. No, I can't remember a time I did not know," she muses (12). *Push* reveals a fundamental schism inside a young woman who was denied the basic experiences of childhood, but who remains in a youthful phase of educational developmental.

The novel ends with the words *tick/tock*—a comment that each moment is worth savoring for the protagonist, whose prognosis as impoverished AIDS sufferer in the 1990s would have been uncertain at best. But the ticktock of the biological clock is most commonly understood today as referencing women's *reproductive* time. Diane Negra has eloquently argued that anxiety about women's time, and in particular their reproductive cycle, is a significant element of the postfeminist aesthetic. Analyzing among other things the contemporary prevalence of biological-clock metaphors, the rhetoric of Botox, and "deadline" films about unintended pregnancy, Negra describes a "distinct feminization of the time crisis" in postfeminist culture (*What a Girl Wants?* 48). This crisis may be expressed through discourses of fertility (a biological clock), aging (turning back the clock), or increasingly lavish celebrations of "demographic-defining rituals including sweet-16 parties, bridal showers, weddings and baby showers which are positioned as markers of female identity legitimation" (50). Whatever its form, Negra illustrates that the "time crisis" of postfeminism is geared toward preserving and extending the chronological period from adolescence through the midthirties—in other words, the years of women's lives most socially geared toward romance, marriage, and childbearing.

To be sure, the subjects addressed by these forms of media are mostly white and upwardly mobile, *not* the Precious Joneses of the world. Indeed, the feminized time crisis that Negra has identified serves to highlight just how differently postfeminist culture addresses young white and black women. Whereas white women are subjected to pressures to reproduce (including the popular-media surveillance technique called "bump watch"), black women face judgment about their fertility, particularly if they are poor. From the days of President Reagan's "welfare queen in a welfare Cadillac," the specter of the poor black mother has been used to symbolize teeming waste, fraud, and a host of other social disorders. Emilie Zaslow contends that "two models of motherhood exist in postfeminist media: 'good' mothers are valued power brokers who negotiate social systems by summoning their personal resiliency and 'bad' mothers are women in the inner city who are (unworthy) dependents surviving off of the welfare system" (107).

White maternity continues to be celebrated on-screen and in public life, even when unintended. Pamela Thoma has drawn attention to the 2000s cohort of unplanned-pregnancy films featuring "young, white, American-born women who demonstrate their privilege as consumers and their modern feminine subjectivity through choosing to reproduce" ("Buying Up Baby" 409). These upbeat films, as well as the real-life public embrace of potential vice presidential daughter Bristol Palin, who was an unmarried pregnant teenager during her mother's 2008 campaign, offer a sharp contrast to pathologized images of nonwhite young women. "In the popular media and political imagination, teen mothers are black," contends Tricia Rose, "and black teen single (usually unmarried) mothers are the cause of their own poverty: they are living, breathing examples of black women's wanton sexuality and generally irresponsible behavior" (173).

The notorious stereotype of the welfare queen frames black women as both large (through repeated pregnancies) and living large (off the largesse of government assistance). To the outside world, Precious is an always-hungry, never-empty womb. "If the desires of middle-class white women have been constructed via anorexia and bulimia, so the desires of lower-class black women have been constructed in terms of motherhood and matriarchy," Doris Witt remarks. "Young white women purportedly want nothing more than to be thin; young black women, nothing more than to have babies" (192). In *Push*, a variety of voices, from Precious's official file to Ms. Rain, all imply that motherhood will fundamentally impede Precious's professional aspirations. By juggling her babies and the ABCs, Precious challenges all these bromides about the black teenaged mother.

"I'm gonna start going to Family Literacy class on Tuesdays. Important to read to baby after it's born," Precious writes as Abdul's birth impends (64). Via education, Precious reinforces her own capability and by extension her ability to provide a stronger intellectual foundation for her son. "Soon as he git born I'ma start doing the ABCs. This my baby . . . I am comp'tant," she avers (64). Other characters, however, express doubts about Precious's capacity to combine motherhood and education. Ms. Rain urges her to prioritize school above all else, telling her that "I think your first responsibility has to be to yourself" and that "if you keep Abdul you might have nothing. You are learning to read and write, that is everything" (70). Precious feels the weight of these choices too and she rhythmically juxtaposes them in her writing. "Now instead of life for me I got Abdul," she muses. "But I love Abdul. I want go school love abdul schoolabdulschoolabdul" (69). At another point, she asks herself, "What I gonna be, queen of babies?" "No, I gonna be queen of those ABCs—readin' 'n' writin,'" she decides (75). A few pages later, she again deems herself "queen of the ABCs" (81).

The "queen of babies" comment directly summons the poisonous stereotype of the welfare queen. *Push* was written in the shadow of President Clinton's 1996 Personal Responsibility and Work Opportunity Reconciliation Act, which fundamentally changed welfare by, among other things, limiting federal benefits and quickly moving recipients to low-wage jobs. Sapphire has spoken of how this political moment shaped her work, asserting to interviewer Owen Keehnen that "every time Newt Gingrich opens his mouth it's about a welfare mother. I wanted to shed additional light. I wanted to show something behind the statistic. So yeah, I'm on a mission" (Sapphire, "Artist with a Mission"). The intrusions of the state are personified in the novel by "the file," which is first kept at Precious's school and subsequently by her caseworker Ms. Weiss (whose name, as Monica Michlin points out, deliberately references the "white power-system") (178). The newly literate Precious is now able to read what the state has in store for her. Ms. Weiss's report minimizes her client's stated desires to pursue a GED and college; she writes that "in keeping with the new initiative on welfare reform I feel Precious would benefit from any of the various workfare programs in existence. Despite her obvious intellectual limitations she is quite capable of working as a home attendant" (119). As Michlin asserts, "behind the well-written, technocratic language, lies a social death sentence" (178).

Precious thus faces a two-pronged attack on her ability to mother and go to school. Ms. Weiss's criticism of Precious's balancing act is bolstered by the weight of state power. Precious uses her education to critique the state's plan for her to become a home attendant (a historically raced form of employment, as she points out). Putting her mathematics acumen on display, she calculates not the workfare wage but the real wage, which includes child care and transportation, that is involved in being "on call" for nursing-home residents. She comes out with a net profit of $1.12. "Who will take care of Abdul? . . . And what about school?" she asks. "How would I keep up with my reading and writing if I can't go to school?" (121).

In contrast to Ms. Weiss, Ms. Rain is a deeply sympathetic character in the novel; her advice that Precious should put her education first is genuine and well-intended. But when she says that "being a good mother might mean letting your baby be raised by someone who is better able than you to meet the child's needs," she underestimates how Precious's maternity *informs* her educational goals, and vice versa. "I is best able to meet my child's need," Precious writes to Ms. Rain (72). Punctuating her retort not by "Precious Jones" but rather "Ms Precious," in imitation of "Ms Rain," the moment illustrates Precious as maternal pedagogue, meeting her teacher and mentor on equal terms.

The consistent linkage of educational and maternal success in *Push* defies stereotypes of the pathological single black mother. *Push* depicts, through its titular verb, the *effort* involved in both educational and childbirth labor. Sapphire further ties the two by linking Ms. Rain's teachings about history with Abdul's birth and Precious's subsequent reconceptualization of herself as an incest survivor. Ms. Weiss urges Precious to take (unwanted) first steps into the world of workfare at the same time that Abdul is described as a "toddler" taking his first steps as well (73). And the main narrative of *Push* concludes with Precious acceding to his request to "read him a story before bedtime" (139–40). Subsequently, the literary labor of Precious and Each One Teach One—a collection of first-person stories—closes the novel.

Sapphire's construction of Precious's powerful maternity is, interestingly, partial. Abdul is Precious's *second* child; his older sister, the disabled Little Mongo (her birth name, if different, is never known) hides in the shadows. Described as a "flat-faced" and "ugly" bundle at birth, Little Mongo is thoroughly unwanted (17–18). In *The Kid,* Precious's grandmother Toosie, who took care of Little Mongo, opines that "she was retarded. She shoulda died. . . . I tell you I miss my record player more than I miss yo' mama 'n dat damn Mongo" (175). Katrine Dalsgard provocatively claims that "the lasting implications for Precious of her parents' abuse are given physical form" in the novel in both Little Mongo's Down syndrome and Precious's HIV-positive diagnosis (185). Precious expresses some identification with her neglected daughter, noting that the name "is short for Mongoloid Down Sinder, which is what she is; sometimes what I feel I is. . . . So ugly, worth nothin'" (34). Yet the little girl is largely invisible in the text. Lee Daniels's 2009 cinematic adaptation,

Precious, features Little Mongo more, allowing audiences to glimpse her in Toosie's care. In the final shot, Precious carries *both* her children away from Mary and into the cityscape. The movie's departure from the book in this regard may be an attempt to answer the lingering question of why Precious draws strength only from her son and not her neglected daughter.

I would argue that while Little Mongo does not compel her mother's attention or sympathy in any sustained way within the frame of the novel, she is a textual ghost in both *Push* and *The Kid*. She repeatedly appears or is invoked in conjunction with the number twelve (the age at which Precious gave birth to her). Thus she becomes a sort of gothic trope, haunting the text as her mother grows to understand the incestuous horror that has been perpetrated upon her. "When I have a baby at twelve," Precious begins in her journal, unable to go on. Later, she adds "I just want to say when I was twelve, TWELVE, somebody hadda help me it not be like it is now. . . . Why no one put Carl in jail after I have a baby by him when I am twelve?" (125). Little Mongo is later inadvertently summoned in *The Kid* when her teenaged brother Abdul is told for the first time of her existence. Abdul becomes entirely disoriented when hearing that his mother birthed a child at twelve. "I'm thirteen, twelve, thirteen, twelve, thirteen, twelve?" he asks, comparing his current age to that of his mother (110). Abdul's repetition of Little Mongo's number—twelve—gothically reaffirms the horror of sexual violence that haunts the family.

"Cultural myths offer comfort that the parent-child relation is one of pure and uncomplicated love," says Jen Shelton. "Any time a victim of incest speaks out and tells the story of what has happened to her, the willful ignorance that allows incest to happen is shattered, however briefly. Thus, it is through narrative rather than laws that the system of incest is most directly disrupted" (18). Sapphire uses the powerful feminist concept of "coming to voice" in narrating Precious's story. In a skeptical postfeminist moment, where the trustworthiness of women's memory is assailed and child abuse dismissed as past trauma, Sapphire illuminates how education influences Precious's understanding of the past.

"Wide as the Mississippi": Sexual Shame and Anxiety in *Push*

Postfeminist culture exhibits delicate sensibilities when it comes to the discussion of past traumas, and *Push* violates those sensibilities not only in its narrative but also in its explicit language. Sexual and excretory epithets dominate the opening pages. Precious's first five pages of narration include the expression "mutherfucker" six times, and repeated references to "fuck" and "shit" in a variety of grammatical forms. Precious's early interactions with people are almost exclusively expressed through turns of phrase that focus upon the genitals. Her principal, for instance, is "a cunt bucket" who looks at her like "I wanna suck a dog's dick or some shit" (7). This kind of language dominates her thinking because, since childhood, her parents' genitals have battered the boundaries of her bodily autonomy and life experience. Much as she used experimental literary form to demonstrate the shape of Precious's journey toward understanding and stopping her abuse, Sapphire here uses the language of private parts to refute the idea of incest as "private business." Foregrounding and repeating images centering on the vagina and anus, she creates two distinct narrative motifs within the novel's cacophony of sexual explicitness. On one hand, the text's preoccupation with vaginal smell and size signifies Precious's survivor's shame and guilt; on the other, the anus literalizes Precious's standing, both within her family and by society at large, as disposable filth. Utilizing these two sites of the body, Sapphire confronts and disrupts painful stereotypes about black women's hypersexuality while refusing to let the reading public look away from the intimacy of incest's violation.

The sexual abuse that both of Precious's parents inflict on her crowds her cognitive space to the point where she cannot learn, thus setting into motion her academic and social poverty. Thinking back to her childhood, Precious remembers:

> I see me, first grade, pink dress dirty sperm stuffs on it. No one comb my hair. Second grade, third grade, fourth grade seem like one dark night. Carl is the night and I disappear in it. And the daytimes don't make no sense . . . talking, bouncing balls, filling in between dotted lines. Shape? Color? Who care whether purple shit a square or a circle, whether it purple or blue? . . . I disappears from the day, I jus' put it all down—book, doll, jump rope, my head, myself. (18)

Precious's description of her dress dirty with semen stains also illustrates the extent to which she functions as a *waste* receptacle for her parents. Throughout the novel, vaginal imagery is associated with filth and is used to reference both Precious and Mary pejoratively. Mary's sexual abuse of Precious takes the forms of vaginal molestation and oral sex. Sapphire's depiction of this maternal assault breaks narrative taboos; Janice Liddell asserts that never before "in African American literary history has a Black mother been accorded such conscious agency over the brutal downfall of her own flesh and blood, especially her only daughter" (143).[18] Precious's disgust for her mother is most frequently articulated by referencing her unbearable feminine stench. "I know she got pussy odor . . . I'm ashamed, this is my Mama," Precious reflects (84–85). During a memory of abuse, she recalls that "Mama jaw open like evil wolf. *The smell deeper than toilet.* Her fingers pick apart my pussy. Night. Poisoned rat" (133; emphasis added). In this recollection, Mary's mouth, the instrument of both verbal and sexual abuse, gives off the smell of "toilet," most commonly associated with the genitals. Thus jumbled, Mary becomes a symbol of the *vagina dentata*, mouth/vagina/anus/fingers grabbing for Precious's bruised skin. For her part, Precious distinguishes herself from the abusive Mary by citing her proper feminine hygiene, indicating that "I wash serious between my legs . . . I don't smell like my muver. I *don't*" (36).

Sapphire associates Mary with grotesque vaginal odor to demonstrate the character's offensiveness on many levels. However, Precious's own disgust and anxiety about her vagina illustrates both her abuse survivor's guilt and the stereotypes of hypersexuality that confront her. One of the most controversial moments in *Push* is Precious's bewildered description of a rape in which she experiences an orgasm. "I feel the hot sauce hot cha cha feeling when he be fucking me," she narrates. "I get so confuse. I HATE him. But my pussy be popping. He say that 'Big Mama, your pussy is popping!' I HATE myself when I feel good" (58). Elizabeth Donaldson points out that *Push*'s project is "to speak plainly about the shame surrounding incest and about a female sexuality that cannot be passive and refuses to be silent" (55). Charting Carl's continuing control over Precious in the passage just quoted, Donaldson also contends that "her orgasms are scripted by him, despite her attempts to take ownership. . . . Her father therefore determines how she thinks of her orgasms and her sexuality" (57).

Precious is upbraided in a particular way when she resists her father's rapes. "You wide as the Mississippi, don't tell me a little bit of dick hurt you heifer," he snaps (24). Carl demeans his daughter by comparing her to a cow and her vagina to a river. The invocation of the Mississippi River in particular is also significant. Sapphire's work, which focuses on Northern and urban African American life, is sometimes placed in an oppositional literary tradition from writers such as Alice Walker and Maya Angelou, whose work derives from more Southern and rural traditions.[19] Yet the word *Mississippi* appears significantly in both of Sapphire's novels, summoning not pastoral bliss but something darker. In *Push*, the Southern nurse who feels sorry for the postpartum Precious but fails to assist her is referred to by the phrase "Mississippi self" (17). Mississippi is also at the literal center of *The Kid*. In an embedded tale, Toosie (Precious's grandmother) narrates the violent history of the Jones women, including lynchings, starvation, and her own rape and impregnation at age ten.[20] Mississippi symbolically represents a site of poverty and sexual violence.

Carl's insults about the supposedly outsized nature of his daughter's genitals are part of a larger discourse about girls' and women's predisposition for sexual penetration. Assessing gendered historical discourses about AIDS, Paula Treichler and Catherine Warren have pointed out that some early articles "argued with great clarity and few qualifications that a crucial physiological dichotomy between the rectum and the vagina protected women from HIV; unlike the 'vulnerable rectum,' the 'rugged vagina' was built by nature to take abuse, and was therefore too tough for the virus to penetrate" (92). The discourse of the "rugged vagina" seems to surface often, as seen in 2012 electoral debates about whether forced vaginal ultrasounds (for women seeking abortions) "really" hurt. As Frank Smigiel points out, "This enigma of women's sex simply demonstrates how *her body can take it*—not only penetration and reproduction, but also commodification, exchangeability, and spectacularization" (258; emphasis added).

Carl is not the only one to attempt to stigmatize Precious in this manner. In an interview with social worker Ms. Weiss, Mary narrates how Carl penetrated Precious with his finger before removing her diaper and attempting intercourse with his infant daughter. "You know what trip me out is it almost can go in Precious! I think she some kinda freak baby then," says Mary (135–36). When describing her as a "freak baby," a "heifer," or "wide as the Mississippi," her parents' implication is clear: the preternaturally sexualized Precious possessed an accommodating anatomy, thus invalidating the question of her consent. Melba Wilson has written that "another myth in [black] communities views sexual abuse and incest as the 'schooling' of young black girls about matters which are sexual" (13). Because black girls are additionally saddled with the image of promiscuity, Wilson adds sarcastically, "why make a fuss about their daddies breaking them in early, I mean, it's better to keep it all in the family, right?" (14). In *Push*, Carl exemplifies this view; as he sexually molests his toddler daughter, he tells his common-law wife that "this is good for her" (135).

Sapphire's discussion of hypersexualization stereotypes loaded onto black girls is not limited to vaginal imagery alone; it also involves "the other end." Janell Hobson writes that the construction of black female bodies as grotesque is rooted in the "problematic fetishism of their rear ends" (*Venus in the Dark* 88). Surveying iconic figures including Nanny of the Maroons,

Saartjie Baartman (the so-called Hottentot Venus), Josephine Baker, Venus and Serena Williams, Lil' Kim, and Foxy Brown, Hobson argues that the rear end has "historic and cultural tropes of rawness, lasciviousness, and 'nastiness'" (102). Not only can the butt commodify black women, it can also metaphorically swallow them up. "This single body part comes to represent [women of color] and, by extension, racialized sexuality," Magdalena Barrera observes of the buttocks (408). As linguist Eric Hyman observes in his exhaustive explication, the word *ass* is expansive: "a piece of ass" can mean a woman's genitals or an entire woman (207).[21]

Both older Jones women utilize anal imagery when referring to Precious in order to shame her. Mary calls her daughter a "Jezebel ass," ignoring her husband's rapes of her daughter and suggesting instead that Precious seduced him (19). In *The Kid*, grandmother Toosie similarly deems Precious "Fast Ass" and explicitly blames her for her rapes, saying scornfully: "She act like her fast tail ain' de cause of a lot of what happened. Carl did it by himself? Twice? I don' think so" (176). The association of Precious with the rectum recurs again when Mary tells her daughter to get an HIV test because Carl has died from AIDS. Mary avers that she herself will test negative because she and Carl did not engage in sex "like faggots, in the ass and all" (86). Whether Mary knows or suspects that Carl forced Precious into anal sex (which she incorrectly assumes to be the only transmission vector) or whether she simply sees her daughter as "Jezebel ass," Mary connects Precious to anality. It is important to point out that *Push* contains no discussion of how Carl contracted AIDS. Yet simply because he is an HIV-positive black man, he summons up the stereotype of the *down low*, a slang term referencing a publicly heterosexual male who engages in same-sex activity. Nels Highberg, commenting on the overrepresentation of this figure in popular culture, sees it as an insidious image by which "the generically pathological African American family has transformed into something out of a horror film, with down-low men as the killer and HIV as the weapon" (6). Down low or not, Carl is a textual phantom within the narrative of *Push*; Precious observes that he "come in the night, take food, what money they is, fuck us bofe" (85).

Sapphire's linguistic play on the ass highlights the way it is often used to control and denigrate the sexuality of black women. The *excretory* functions of the rectum have racialized significance as well. In the escapist dreams that sustain her during sexual traumas and flashbacks, Precious often fantasizes about being white, slender, blonde, and blue-eyed. These are physical attributes that are socially valued, according to her televisual knowledge. Precious sees these images everywhere, even in unexpected places; she admires, for instance, blonde white children pictured "on toilet paper wrappers" (65). Sapphire's use of the controlling Caucasian image in popular culture draws on Morrison's work in *The Bluest Eye,* where the protagonist ingests gallons of white milk and envisions a blue-eyed self who, like Precious, is free from neglect and sexual violence. In *Push,* the white children on the toilet paper rolls connote health, prosperity, and hygiene even as they advertise a product associated with waste; similarly, white people with disposable income will outsource their waste to home health-care workers. Precious realizes that "all she [social worker Ms. Weiss] see for me is wiping ol white people's ass" and changing "white woman's diapers" (121).

During one of the most memorable and controversial scenes in *Push,* Precious seems to accept her association with the fecal. In the aftermath of one of Carl's rapes, she narrates that "I go bafroom. I smear shit on my face. Feel good. Don't know why but it do" (111). But as Elizabeth Donaldson points out, the incident is a moment of resistance. "By smearing feces on her face," Donaldson writes, "Precious symbolically makes her most private business public. The hidden becomes manifest; the unspeakable is spoken" (56). Once again, Sapphire forces attention to the physical and psychic violence of incest through the most graphic of images.

In the novel's conclusion, vaginal imagery is reclaimed on Precious's terms, through the contexts of childbearing and motherhood. In an interview about *Push,* Sapphire asserts that "there is something very aggressive and assertive about being a female. We're taught to be very laid-back and passive, but if we're to survive, if we're to move forward, we have to have that pushing energy" (Sapphire, "Sapphire's Big Push" 29). The parallel narratives of childbirth and self-birth via education have pushed Precious to new places in life, and they help her to reclaim her body for herself. During an incest survivors' meeting at the end of the novel, Precious agonizes about speaking in public. "To talk I have to tell how I feel in my body," she laments. "My body my head I can't say it right" (129). When she finally raises her hand to speak, Precious aligns body and head in a specific way: "I raise my hand. My hand is going up *through* the smell of Mama, my hand is pushing Daddy's dick *out* my face" (130; emphasis added). In this moment, she both pushes out *and* through, shutting off her father's control and "birthing" an autonomous self. In the wake of breaking her family's incestuous silence, Precious begins to reconceive her own body. She thinks of "how *alive* I am, every part of me that is cells, proteens, nutrons, hairs, pussy, eyeballs, nervus system, brain" (137). In this self-conception, the vagina is neither monstrous nor absent. It is present and a part of her, along with her other organs. Precious here has gained what L. H. Stallings calls "erotic literacy," a "life skill of reading and comprehending the various scripts around sexuality, and taking the most relevant or useful ideas and mediating them through an individual's gender and sexual identities and desires" (115).

Opening Up Endings: *The Kid*

The last glimpse of Precious Jones in *Push*'s main narrative is a hopeful one; Abdul, the golden child, smiles and coos in the warmth of late-setting sun, safely curled up in his mother's lap as she contemplates his future. Abdul is the source of his mother's intellectual drive and the pride of her heart. A decade and a half after the publication of *Push*, Sapphire returned to the story of Abdul Jones's life, revealing it to be a downward spiral from his mother's deathbed to a series of predatory, abusive homes, and finally to a mental institution. Just as the word *push* rang through the novel of the same name in order to symbolize Precious's ongoing reproductive and educational labor, *The Kid* too has a signature phrase: *opening up*. The phrase does not describe amenability to new communities and ideas, as it might have for the intellectually curious Precious Jones. Instead, *opening up* references the violent sexual penetration of bodies. The distinction between the two books' key phrases is significant. In penning this lonely, alienated sequel, Sapphire "opens up" the wound of Precious's story once more, this time adding an unhappy ending that involves her difficult death and the loss of her son. Through the story of Abdul's sexual victimization and perpetration, Sapphire addresses the continuing feminization of sexual violence. Most crucially, *The Kid*'s dark narrative prevents readers from understanding *Push* simply as a postfeminist/neoliberal success story of black female exceptionalism.

Sapphire signals her novels' continuity both by plot and by structural repetition. Precious and Abdul experience many similar events growing up, including sexual violence at the hands of guardians, legal confusion over their multiple given names, racial self-denigration, and refuge in the performing arts. Most reviews also yoke the two novels and explicitly compare the two protagonists' circumstances—a process that disadvantages the sequel. Writing in the *Washington Post*, DeNeen Brown asserts that "unlike *Push*, which, despite its grim tale of pathologies, offered slivers of hope, *The Kid* provides little if any relief for its characters or its readers. It's packed with the cyclical pain of generations of sexual abuse suffered by characters who in turn inflict pain on others . . . there are no redeeming characters, no saviors, no person who is good enough to save Abdul—not even Abdul himself" ("Book Review:

'The Kid'"). Michiko Kakutani of the *New York Times* adds that "while the reader felt enormous sympathy for Precious—who was repeatedly raped by her father, molested by her mother and who gave birth to her first child at age 12—it's hard here not to feel revulsion" for Abdul's depictions of sexually assaulting others or disrespecting his grandmother ("He's a Vessel"). Fellow *Times* critic Danielle Evans contemplates the possibility that "the mission of 'The Kid' is to punish those readers of 'Push' who found even the faintest glimmer of hope in Precious' journey, as if Sapphire were daring anyone to make this novel into a Hollywood story" ("In Sapphire's New Novel"). Indeed, the explicit painfulness of *The Kid* is meant to indict readers who viewed *Push* as an up-by-the-bootstraps triumph of individual will. By killing off Precious in the novel's first pages and subsequently ending the tightly knit community of Each One Teach One, Sapphire challenges the audience to move beyond simply viewing *Push* as inspirational narrative.

"I never wanna leave you," Precious tells her beloved son early in *The Kid* (7). It is evident that had his mother lived, Abdul Jones would have enjoyed a loving childhood. Early in the novel, he recalls a birthday where his mother was "holding me in her arms kissing me and dancing with me" and the "house is smelling like lasagna, wine, and people. . . . Everyone is laughing" (3). Precious emerges as a disciplined, calm, caring parent who not only promises to take Abdul to Disneyland but also makes him drink milk and lectures him about doing homework. Like Ms. Rain, Precious transmits the importance of cultural history and knowledge; she introduces Abdul to Aretha Franklin and Langston Hughes, speaks to him frankly of racial injustice, and stimulates her son's sense of spiritual wonder. Finally, she emphasizes sexual autonomy and self-respect, telling Abdul to "just remember your private parts are yours an' no one is supposed to touch 'em 'less you say so, hear? Hear?" (10–11). Precious's lingering influence is seen in Abdul's pronounced early intellectual curiosity, his love for the arts, and even his physical appearance. "I'm like my mom, soft, dark, and beautiful," he remarks (143).

But AIDS claims Precious, and the moment of her funeral (the only textual space where the major characters of *Push* reunite) closes the door on Precious's story of triumph against the odds. Although Precious was enrolled at City College, worked as a counselor, and, in the words of Ms. Rain, showed "what a good game you can still play when the deck is stacked against you," she still faced many obstacles (19). "I'm not supposed to mention Medicaid didn't want to pay for her [AIDS] drugs," her old classmate Jermaine says, "or that the 'fare was threatening her again to leave school or lose her benefits, that there's a padlock on her door and that she died broke and depressed, deeply depressed" (20). On that note, the once-unified characters of Each One Teach One exit the novel. Ms. Rain goes off on a trip to London, while Precious's closest friend Rita, herself dealing with complications from AIDS, surrenders Abdul to the state. There are vague unkept promises to visit Abdul, but the supportive community that transfigured Precious's life in *Push* is scattered.

Many horrors follow. A glitch in the social-service paperwork sends Abdul to foster care, where he is beaten to a pulp and raped by an older child. He spends his adolescence in a Catholic boy's home, and while the daytime brings intellectual stimulation, the nights are filled with sexual abuse by the administrators. Expelled for raping a fellow student, Abdul is reunited with his great-grandmother Toosie, but he rejects her attempts to parent him and strikes out on his own, funding his dance education by trading sexual favors. This is no typical *Künstlerroman*: Abdul ends the novel in an institution, unsure of his very reality. While the narrative of *Push* moves toward literal and temporal order (as epitomized by the repetition of the ABCs), in *The Kid*, time and meaning collapse inward. Abdul frequently sleepwalks, loses and regains his memories, and becomes profoundly disoriented. His fractured state of mind is rendered in jagged, sex-obsessed, stream-of-consciousness form, as the following passage illustrates:

> Why can't I move? Do I have a name? Arf! Arf! Meow@ Am I a cat, a nigger, a boy, a man? What's the difference between a cat and a nigger? And a man? Why is everything so bleary? Where is yellow? Pineapple? Green? Trees? Ice cream? The pink bulb of My Lai's clit, her deep pussy, why isn't she here? If someone is yours, why don't you own them? If you're free, an American, why can't you leave when you want? I must be someplace else. Where the fuck is here? (318)

Erica Galioto remarks that the various "violent assault[s] on [Abdul's] identity from the outside" result in a "lack of psychological and emotional stability," making it difficult for readers to "locate a core with whom to attach and identify" (140). Her observation bears fruit in the novel's reviews; *Kirkus Reviews*, for instance, deems Abdul a "narrator who has difficulty distinguishing his dream life from the shifting realities of his existence" ("Kirkus Review: *The Kid*"). Michiko Kakutani characterizes him as "an angry, abused and abusive character, who recounts his violent acts and fantasies in graphic and repetitious detail, delivers lots of caustic rants about women and homosexuals, and who often seems less like a coherent individual than a cobbled-together pastiche of a focus group of tormented teenagers" ("He's a Vessel").

"There's just no glimmer of humanity left in Abdul's soul," agrees Tina Jordan of *Entertainment Weekly* ("Book Review: *The Kid*").

The repetition and lack of self-illumination in *The Kid* can indeed make it an exhausting novel to read. Of her decision to make Abdul a perpetrator, Sapphire has said: "This is what happens to a vast majority of people who have been abused. There is a cycle of abuse that is very much above water, and then there's another area of the cycle that is very much hidden. That's part of what I wanted to bring out in the text" (Sapphire, "Sapphire Releases Graphic Sequel"). It is also significant, though heretofore unremarked upon, that Abdul uncritically accepts the *feminization* of sexual violence. He is rightly outraged when he is victimized by older males, but thinks nothing of preying on smaller, weaker children in acts that are described in typically gendered terms of domination and submission. Schooled haphazardly by a series of abusive men and absent female mentors, Abdul is unable to empathize with his mother's experience of incest, which he discovers through her journal, or with his girlfriend My Lai's accounts of sexual abuse at the hands of her adoptive father. Through her problematic protagonist, Sapphire critiques the persistent gendering of, and disdain for, victimization in postfeminist culture.

From adolescence, Abdul has been culturally conditioned to see white women as icons of desire and symbolic displacements; in his fantasy it is they, and not he, who must sexually serve more powerful men. Abdul dreams of a girl with a "banging body" in a "white minidress" who will "rub me up rub me down" (69). When he is about to have sex with Amy, a beautiful fellow dancer, he defies the ambivalence of his wilting erection by reminding himself: "She's all white and blond. I feel a surge of what, power? I don't know: Joy? Power? This is the ultimate, ain't it?" (251). Abdul's blurred vision of sexual power expressed by domination is also echoed in his fantasy about raping and burying a body that is "not me, it's a girl, little storybook girl golden" (123).

Language about "opening up" recurs repeatedly in the novel; while sometimes it describes the turnout and technical mastery associated with Abdul's passion, dance, more frequently it describes the violent penetration of *people*. Great-grandmother Toosie, for instance, describes her rape at the age of ten as "Nigger Boy bustin' me open" (182). Until adulthood, Abdul's only sexual experiences have included being sodomized by his teachers and raping fellow schoolboys. His romantic yearnings focus on forceful penetration. "I want someone to open me up like I did the kids and [his abuse victim] Jaime," he muses. "Ram me up with love . . ." (122). When Abdul becomes involved with My Lai (the chosen name of Noel Orlinsky, an incestuously abused rich girl), his fantasies take this form as well. "I call up the picture of her in my mind laying on my bed, her thighs open as a baby's," Abdul thinks (343). He dreams of "charging across the floor, a tiger taking her like an animal from behind, sinking my teeth into [My Lai's] neck, busting her open" (362).

The recipient of the "opening up" is implicitly feminized, regardless of his or her actual gender. Abdul's first victim, a younger child named Jaime, moves "like a little kitten skittering down the hall with his backpack bouncing over his butt" (66). Abdul further clarifies the power differential, adding, "He's like a little child. I'm like the big father" (66). He refers to raping Jaime as "riding my horse," emphasizing his positional dominance, and he complains about his victim's cries (84): "I really do wish he would shut up, his crying getting mixed in with my good feeling of . . . of being *a king*" Abdul snaps (54; emphasis added). In his dreams, Abdul also dreams of revenging himself on the pedophile Catholic brothers, who appear in this context as *women*. "Pull up the skirt, bitch! You heard me, bitch, pussy! Pull that goddamned skirt up and let me see them cupcakes," he rants (72).

Throughout the novel, Abdul remains characterized by persistent myopia about his sexual culpability. He is outraged to encounter a child pornographer and beats him until near-death. Yet he does not recognize his own criminality as a rapist. "They were having fun too. They loved it!" Abdul tells his therapist about his victims (359). The therapist, Dr. See, repeatedly tries to make Abdul see parallels between his own experience of sexual abuse and that of his girlfriend, My Lai. Abdul opines that My Lai's experience was not as traumatic as his because "I'm a man, I'm not supposed to have to put up with that shit!" (368). My Lai, being female, is inherently susceptible to being "opened." His comment seems to echo Susanna Moore's character Mamie—here too, it seems, vagina is fate.

Just as Precious's death unmoored Abdul's life, her reappearance—as a textual ghost—exhibits the potential to draw him back. Toward the novel's end, Precious returns through her journal; when Abdul discovers this piece of the past, it radically reshapes his world. "My sun my lilte sun my lif *his dady mine*," he reads (238; emphasis added). This incest revelation unravels Abdul's carefully sanitized family fable, where his "father got killed in the war" (203). In an act of rejection, he dumps his mother's journals onto the subway tracks, another alienating moment that, as Erica Galioto points out, is a "complete annihilation of the 'You' Precious envisioned as her own audience" (141). But the enduring impact of Precious's words is manifested later, when Abdul listens to his girlfriend My Lai stage a public reading of her own journal. My Lai's account of her father's rapes, and her mother's complicit silence, parallels Precious's incestuous abuse by Mary and Carl. Hearing his girlfriend's words, Abdul remembers "tearing another woman's notebook to bits in Central Park and throwing the bits in the howling subway tunnel" (294). Abdul's ability to connect the words of these two women hints at his capacity for empathy with victims of sexual violence. This is dependent, of course, upon his ability to admit responsibility for sexually abusing other boys. Sapphire acknowledges this urgency in an interview, saying that "if he is willing to go back with the truth about who he is, we get the feeling that he can begin to get a life" (Sapphire, "Sapphire Releases Graphic Sequel").

The Kid flips the script of gender victimization by focusing on the trials of Precious Jones's son. But whereas mainstream postfeminist discourse likes to insist on the "equality" of violence suffered by women and men (an issue also taken up by Susanna Moore and Jodi Picoult), Sapphire demonstrates that victimization remains linked to *feminization*, irrespective of the sufferer's actual gender. The ongoing horrors perpetrated on and by Abdul also testify to incest's long traumatic reach. As inspirational a figure as Precious Jones is, her death and her son's subsequent unraveling in *The Kid* remind us that personal resilience, without widespread social change, is simply not enough.

Writing the stories of Abdul and Precious is a dangerous enterprise. Their incendiary legacy of incestuous violence and trauma cuts across the grain of a forward-focused postfeminist age. Additionally, Sapphire must navigate around postfeminist culture's tendency to assign black women the responsibility for healing psychic wounds, as well as its preferred reading of *Push* as confirming the triumph of individual persistence. She looks askance at simply raising "awareness" (to borrow an empty word circulated frequently throughout postfeminist culture) of Precious's and Abdul's plights. Heather Hillsburg argues that "while compassion can function as a stepping stone toward moral action, disrupting the negative stereotypes that plague black women," it can also be insufficient, merely "support[ing] someone's claims to being a moral actor on the premise that she has identified oppression and is now displaying the correct social response" (125). Instead, Sapphire strategically uses negative affects to challenge readers' responses to the Joneses. By killing readers' relationship with Precious and creating narrative intimacy with a troubled and often cruel victimizer, Sapphire pushes for readers to think through the cycle of abuse in a way that is more profound than the issuance of greeting-card sympathy.

I close with a small but illuminating moment toward the end of *Push* when Precious discusses therapy with the Each One Teach One class. "I'm going to start going to meetings wif Rita for insect survivor," she mentions. Her classmate Bunny informs her that the correct word is incest. "Thas what I mean," Precious muses, to which Bunny replies, "Well, it ain't what you been saying." This play on *insect/incest* is one more manifestation in *Push* of how letters and words matter. It is also an affirmation that education is now allowing Precious to put into dialogue what she has "meant" all along. Yet Precious's subsequent reaction when she learns the difference between the two words is equally notable. "One's where your parents molest you, the other is like a roach or bugs," Bunny tells her. "I crack up laffing," notes Precious, adding that "you can't get all hung up on details when you trying to survive" (123–24). Finding unlikely humor in the situation is characteristic of Precious. The moment also serves as a microcosm of what *Push* can do, as explained by Lauren Berlant's concept of diva citizenship. "Flashing up and startling the public," writes Berlant, the subaltern subject "puts the dominant story into suspended animation . . . and she challenges her audience to identify with the enormity of the suffering she has narrated and the courage she has had to produce, calling on people to change the social and institutional practices of citizenship to which they currently consent" (*Queen of America* 223). These incandescent glimpses, Sapphire suggests, may be all many readers can access of Precious Jones in this world of deep racial and gender inequality. But the challenge remains, issued by Precious herself at the beginning of her story: "I'm gonna break through or somebody gonna break through to me" (5).

5

Waking the Dead

Patricia Cornwell's Forensic Imagination

The posthumous voice of Susie Salmon, the dying utterances of Frannie, and the ghostly glimpses of the socially marginalized Precious Jones remind us that the postfeminist gothic is a toxic landscape. The heroines of this tradition often live on the borders of life and death; some, though, make death their salaried occupation. Within postfeminist popular culture, the figure of the female death professional—a Charon figure who stoically witnesses and bears pain and who provides maternal care and solace for victims of sexually violent crime—is quickly becoming just as archetypal as the woman warrior or the singleton in the city. Dr. Kay Scarpetta, who is featured in twenty-three novels (and counting) written by Patricia Cornwell, epitomizes this figure.

Cornwell is often credited with ushering in the forensic turn in mystery fiction, which has made millions of readers into what Jean Murley deems "violent crime pseudoexperts . . . able to speak intelligently about blood-spatter patterns and 'organized' versus 'disorganized' serial killers" (3). The public appetite for the female death professional, this indelible cultural icon that Cornwell has created, illustrates how postfeminist gothic aesthetics can be understood in complex ways. For instance, Dr. Kay Scarpetta's composure in the face of frightening scenes of femicide can be read as a *critique* of the postfeminist promise of a secure, equal world, or as *sanctioning* increasingly sadistic tableaux. Although her corpus of work is immense, Cornwell is drawn to reworking the familiar gendered narrative of Jack the Ripper, but with a postfeminist twist. Her plots pit prototypical "singleton" victims (white, beautiful, professional) against psychotic males who mutilate their faces and skin. Cornwell's autopsy narratives are dark doubles of the aspirational makeover narrative that promises women transformative change both inside and out in postfeminist culture. Rebuking the postfeminist conception of the body as disciplined, youthful, and increasingly plastic, Cornwell moves, via Scarpetta's Stryker saw, toward ever more disarray. Her critique suggests that the regimes of bodily discipline that are so central within postfeminism's conception of contemporary femininity are in fact lethal.

The bleakness and despair inherent in Cornwell's slashing, murderous world is not fully managed by the ministrations of the female death professional, Scarpetta. I read the profound aesthetic changes and narrative shifts of Cornwell's post-2003 novels as representations of Scarpetta's submergence in postfeminism's violent landscapes. The series's twelfth book, *Blow Fly*, marks Cornwell's move from first- to third-person narration; this change wrenches the audience from intimate identification with Scarpetta to a more clinical remove. The plots similarly alter course from thrillers to meditations, often rendered in opaque and leaden prose, about sinister encroachments of technology. Scarpetta herself moves from the subject ruling the morgue to the object dissected on the Internet. Such changes can make the reading of Patricia Cornwell's later work difficult going. Yet her benumbed aesthetic, and her turn toward an unembodied digital world rather than one of blood and guts, is worth exploring because it captures the consequences of turning away from gendered violence.

Autopsy Chic: The Female Coroner in the Popular Imagination

Chic, intelligent, wisecracking women heading up sleek and professionally equipped medical facilities are ubiquitous in twenty-first-century popular culture. On the small screen, this type of character is found in the various *Law and Order* franchises (1990–); the *CSI* franchise (2002–); *Crossing Jordan* (2001–7); *Cold Case* (2003–10); *NCIS* (2003–); *Bones* (2005–), *Rizzoli and Isles* (2010–), *Body of Proof* (2011–13), and more. Female forensic pathologists have an equally storied representation in mass-market fiction, appearing in the best-selling works of Tess Gerritsen, Kathy Reichs, and, most of all, Patricia Cornwell. The mother of the genre, Cornwell has received the rare "grand slam" of mystery accolades, winning the Edgar, Creasey, Anthony, and Macavity awards. In the decades since, she has built a literary empire with multimillion-dollar sales and translations into thirty-six languages. According to Nigel Farndale, she is "the biggest-selling crime writer in the world (and the second biggest-selling female writer in any genre, after J. K. Rowling)" (Cornwell, "Killer Queen"). No interview with Cornwell occurs without a recounting of her gothic personal history. It includes childhood poverty; a close relationship with evangelists Billy and Ruth Graham; a disastrous marriage to her college professor; a notorious same-sex affair; being stalked online; high-powered Republican friendships (including one with George H. W. Bush); battles with anorexia and depression; and extreme wealth. She has achieved a level of personal celebrity unknown to most authors, bolstered by her television appearances about forensic issues. Harriet Lane writes: "As well as being one of the richest crime novelists in the world, with a fortune of $100 million, Cornwell is probably the most *conspicuous*: posing for her portrait beside her beloved Bell helicopter, sinking millions into a crusade to prove that Walter Sickert was Jack the Ripper, and having an affair with a female FBI agent whose husband ended up going berserk with a gun at the Prince of Peace United Methodist Church outside Washington" ("Tough on Crime"; emphasis added).

Cornwell's creation, Dr. Kay Scarpetta, is nearly as memorable; she is indubitably the most successful and well-known of the female medical examiners that dominate much of popular detective fiction today.[1] A petite, blonde, blue-eyed Italian who moved from working-class stock to riches, Scarpetta's life trajectory mirrors elements in Cornwell's own life. This fact is not lost on critics: Nigel Farndale writes that "to sit opposite Patricia Cornwell is to sit opposite a character she created 20 years ago, Dr. Kay Scarpetta" (Cornwell, "Killer Queen"). A feature in *Vanity Fair* notes that Cornwell has a "gold Scarpetta ring" and "black Scarpetta jacket" that "the author had designed specifically to celebrate her fictional heroine" (qtd. in Susan Ford 33). Intriguingly, Cornwell publicly disavows the resemblance; she told interviewer Farndale that "I don't even remember why I decided to make her blue-eyed and blonde-haired. I don't think it came from me. When I envision Scarpetta, she doesn't look like me. She is not a projection of me" (Cornwell, "Killer Queen"). Nevertheless, the critical perception of overlap between creator and subject persists; as Linda Mizejewski observes, "Cornwell consistently offers her own image as the correlative of her heroine, in book-jacket photographs, web site photo galleries, and popular journalism" (7).

Cornwell's ur-narrative of the female death professional blends feminist narrative with the faith that scientific crime-solving can manage women's very real fears of violent injury. Stefan Timmermans has argued that because medical examiners, unlike the coroners who preceded them, are required to have medical training, they represent "an expansion of scientific power and a curtailing of political power" (5). Scarpetta herself snipes that "some coroners were consummate politicians who did not know an entrance from an exit wound, or care" (*Point of Origin* 254). Medical examiners employ forensics, and in so doing offer, in Mizejewski's words, the promise of a "stable field of reference by which identity and evidence can be measured, recognized, and named" (6).

Female medical-professional novels are further marked by feminist interventions. Kay Scarpetta and Temperance Brennan (a similar character in a series authored by Kathy Reichs) are in their fifties with grown children/wards.[2] They were educated in the crucible of the second wave, and Cornwell's Scarpetta frequently reflects on the sexist treatment she endured. "In an era when women were teachers, secretaries, and housewives, I was going to be a physician," Scarpetta observes in *Body of Evidence* (168). In *Postmortem*, she laments being outside the loop in medical school, where as one of four women, she was subject to verbal harassment and noninclusive treatment by her peers. "It was not chance when old tests made the rounds but were never available to me," she comments. "I was a small insect faced with a formidable male network web in which I might be ensnared but never a part" (92). She later reminisces of her residency days that "one day the head nurse grabbed my arm in the hospital. . . . I'd never forget her hate when she snarled that her son hadn't gotten in because I had taken his slot" (*Unnatural Exposure* 193).

Cornwell's world is populated with sexist dinosaurs. Her police partner, Pete Marino, consistently makes chauvinistic and homophobic jokes, and a lab assistant confides that "it still blows my mind a little to see chicks chasing after killers. Back when you got started, they probably did nothing but check parking meters" (*Black Notice* 93). Peter Messent comments that Scarpetta continually clashes with "men and women who do not expect a woman to be in a position of authority, and Cornwell's novel plays on the gap between such expectations and Scarpetta's challenge to them" (126–27). Scarpetta's infiltration of the "unfeminine" realm of the autopsy lab is, Heidi Strengell asserts, "particularly suspect and dangerous, since she is a woman with a scalpel, which is a phallic symbol" (85). The linkage between Scarpetta's career choice and her inner "steeliness" is made explicit in an exchange when Marino tells her, "I've seen you cut open bodies with a smile" (*Cruel and Unusual* 212). Similarly, Maura Isles (a medical examiner in the popular Rizzoli and Isles series authored by former physician Tess Gerritsen) is derisively referred to in the press as the "Queen of the Dead." In *The Sinner*, Gerritsen zeroes in on the gendered anxieties inspired by a figure like Isles: "Most of all, it's her calmness that disturbs them, her coolly regal gaze as she surveys the horrors that they themselves can barely stomach. Unlike them, she does not avert her gaze. Instead she bends close and stares, touches. She sniffs. And later, under bright lights, she cuts" (7).

No entry in any of these female death-professional series is for the squeamish. "For the most part, I don't spare my patients indignities. I can't," Scarpetta admits (*Predator* 108). At the moment that bodies arrive at the protagonists' morgues, they have been subject to both violence and the decomposition that accompanies death. Postmortem insult is further provided by the medical examiners themselves, who twist, crack, and saw their way through the human form in search of answers. Scarpetta peels off faces and boils bones; Maura Isles breaks a young nun's hips in *The Sinner* in order to give the corpse, in full rigor, a pelvic exam after suspected pregnancy. Bent over a prone body, Stryker saw in hand, Scarpetta at times seems to mirror the serial killer she stalks (a fact not lost on critics). She often bemoans the violence she must wreak, ruing while cooking bones that "what was left of a woman I believed had been murdered began to process in the pot, in what seemed one more indignity and callous slight to who she was" (*Point of Origin* 112).

The female medical examiner may intrude upon a traditionally male space, but the books in such series manage anxiety about potential masculinization by reasserting feminine motifs of domesticity and maternal care. For Scarpetta, refuge from the "dirty work" is found in the domestic arts. Bobbie Robinson notes that "Scarpetta feeds and nurtures constantly. . . . [She is] an Italian mama" (100). Indeed, long passages depicting Scarpetta's Italian meals are featured in nearly every novel, and Cornwell even released a cookbook entitled *Food to Die For: Secrets from Scarpetta's Kitchen* (2003). Scarpetta observes that "preparing food was restorative and soothing . . . it was either cook or clean" (*Scarpetta Factor* 307). This sense of nurturance is easily carried over to her professional life where, as Robinson writes, she "closely identifies with the corpses/victims, who are most often women; she never violates their dignity as human beings and handles the harsh clinical requirements of her job with as much tenderness as the tasks will allow" (99). The medical examiner's dignified handling of the victim taps into a historical health-care narrative where, as Heather Nunn and Anita Biressi remark, "women have been allotted a unique relationship with the dead and dying body." As those who "cleaned, laid out, and presided over the lost relative or community member and have been integral to the death rituals of preparing the 'clean and proper' body for last rites," women occupy a central role in dying. In contemporary culture some have even become, as the celebrity cases of Princess Diana and Mother Teresa illustrate, "stylized as the angelic ministry" (200–201).

To reconcile the opposing gendered scripts of masculinized science and feminized care, female medical-examiner books position their heroines as stoically absorbing and bearing others' pain, often using religious imagery. In *Point of Origin*, Scarpetta upbraids a defense attorney, saying, "I'd like you to spend just one day with the victims. Just one goddamn day, *putting your hands in their blood and touching their wounds*" (314; emphasis added). She also remarks of victims that "I had touched their bodies and translated their pain into diagrams and autopsy protocols and dental charts" (63). At other junctures, Scarpetta speaks of being "haunted" by her dead clients. "You don't put your hands inside their ruined bodies and touch and measure their wounds," she tells Benton Wesley. "You don't hear them speak after they're dead" (*Point of Origin* 12). Christiana Gregoriou writes that "Cornwell remodels the genre by rejecting the concept of the detective who remains unaffected by her work. . . . [Scarpetta] remembers the faces of the victims' parents and is influenced by her work to the extent that she is prone to bad dreams" (145).

The female death professional emerges as a figure that absorbs tremendous suffering but must maintain a professional, unruffled calm. Scarpetta ruefully observes that "I had seen people weep, wail, rant, rage and . . . throughout I was always the physician, always appropriately dispassionate yet kind, for that was what I was trained to be" (*Cause of Death* 125). Tess Gerritsen writes that a forensic specialist is "a woman who could read a lifetime's worth of miseries etched in the bones of the dead. She could look at the skulls on her shelf and see, in each, a personal history of pain. . . . Long after the flesh melts away, the bones still tell their stories" (*Sinner* 196). Scarpetta complains in *The Last Precinct* that "I am supposed to handle any sight, any image, any smell, any sound without flinching. I am not allowed to react to horror the way normal people do. It is my job to reconstruct pain without feeling it vicariously, to conjure up terror and not allow it to follow me home" (135). The violence these doctors encounter is further compounded by its ubiquity; a common complaint in these novels is that the morgue is *never emptied* of murdered women. In Gerritsen's *Vanish* (2006), for example, a still-breathing woman in a body bag is ignored due to the exceeded capacity of the morgue.

In pragmatic terms, the Scarpettas of the world translate their empathic abilities into legal testimony that carries emotional heft. "When the medical examiner isn't in the courtroom, then, in a sense, neither is the body, and jurors don't envision the victim or what she went through during the process of dying violently. Clinical words on protocols simply don't evoke the terror or the suffering," Scarpetta rages (*Last Precinct* 48). Even her own therapist encourages her to amplify and theatricalize victims' suffering for the benefit of the court. "What if you could conjure it up like the footage of a film and watch [victim Diane Bray] being attacked, watch her hemorrhage, watch her being bitten and beaten? Watch her die? How powerful if a jury could see a film like that," she muses (61). Emily Nussbaum has theorized that female professionals' fictional interventions on women's behalf, as epitomized by figures like detective Olivia Benson on *Law and Order: Special Victims Unit*, speak to the fantasy of a supportive and "incorruptible legal system, in which the police are eternally in the rape victim's corner" ("Trauma Queen"). Scarpetta's work is more limited, given that victims are already dead when they come to her table. Nevertheless, she too participates in the victim-avenging narrative.

At the same time, Scarpetta's identification with victims goes beyond the professional; because she is emotionally bound to them, she herself is made vulnerable. Throughout the early novels, she dreams vividly of the dead. In *Postmortem*, she experiences a vision of a rape and murder:

> I saw him with her, inside that bedroom. I could almost see his face, but it had no features. . . . She would try to reason with him at first, after the paralyzing fear of waking up at the feel of cold flat steel to her throat, or at the chilling sound of his voice. She would say things, try to talk him out of it for God knows how long as he cut the cords from the lamps and began to bind her. She was a Harvard graduate, a surgeon. She would attempt to use her mind against a force that is mindless. Then the images went wild, like a film at high speed, flapping off the reel as her attempts disintegrated into unmitigated terror. The unspeakable. I would not look. I could not bear to see any more. I had to control my thoughts. (45)

The identification Scarpetta feels with victims is bound by gender; her male counterparts lack empathy and often deride the female dead. Some are merely insensitive or macabre; Scarpetta remembers shuddering at her predecessor's office, which contained "macho mementos," including "a silicone breast implant from a woman who had been raped and murdered" (*Cause of Death* 149). Other male professionals in the series are more sinister. Recounting a police workshop at which she was the only woman, Scarpetta tells her therapist that "the [photos of] sexual mutilation was arousing to some of them. . . . Do you have any idea what that's like? To see a dead body, to see photographs, videos, of someone brutalized, of someone suffering and terrified and realize that the people around you are secretly enjoying it? That they find it sexy?" (*Last Precinct* 64). In the post-2003 novels, which switch to omniscient narration, we learn that Scarpetta's anxiety is not mere paranoia. For instance, a forensic intern recounts the following fantasy: "He imagines her dead. He imagines her in a pool of blood, shot dead on the floor. He imagines her naked on the steel table. One of life's fables is that dead bodies can't be sexy. . . . To say a man has never had a thought about a beautiful woman who happens to be dead is a joke" (*Predator* 68–69). Textual anxiety that male crime professionals receive voyeuristic pleasure from viewing scenes of violent crime runs throughout many of these series; Gerritsen's Jane Rizzoli, for example, suspects a forensic psychologist of being too eager to view autopsy photos. She wonders, "Did he enjoy the view of atrocities visited on a young woman's body?" (*Mephisto Club* 83).

Cornwell uses male disdain for, and disidentification with, female corpses to reassert the gendered vulnerability of women and, by extension, Scarpetta. Female readers also experience this double bond; they are both the broken body and the professionalized, objective counterpart doing the cutting. As I have mentioned, one of Scarpetta's narrative functions is to neutralize very real fears of violence for women. Like her televisual counterpart Olivia Benson, "the worse the stories get, the stronger she becomes" (Nussbaum, "Trauma Queen"). Laura Browder has theorized that women read true-crime stories for "an existential encounter with the truth," seeing "bravery in their own refusal to avert their gaze" from both "the terror suffered by crime victims" and "their own traumatic memories" (932). This echoes Susanna Moore's position that the only method of surviving a world of profound gender inequality is "in taking it . . . on, facing it, thinking about it" ("Write the Good Fight").

Of course, embedded in any discussion of stoic allies like Scarpetta or Olivia Benson are questions of sadism and exploitation. Alison Winch has defined a "girlfriend gaze" as a faux-friendly discourse about female bodies delivered in commiseration based upon the "shared pain" of having "a female body in a culture that obfuscates its relentless (classed and raced) misogyny" (31). It might seem difficult to apply this kind of discourse to the Scarpetta archetype; after all, the female corpse before her is nonconversant and certainly far past worry about thigh gap, dieting, or gray hair. Nonetheless, Winch's concept of how patriarchal gazes fly under the radar when deployed by women utilizing a soft, nonthreatening register of intimacy applies to the female medical examiner, whose penetrating operations on the corpse are perceived as kinder because of their shared gender. Readers might ask whose interests Scarpetta really serves. Sally Munt, for instance, opines that Cornwell's books "are saturated with the scientific discourse which legitimates the systemic state-sanctified dismemberment of the female body with the kind of empirical details which borders on the fetishistic" (202). In response to such charges of exploitation, Cornwell insists that she is merely a truth teller, reflecting the dangers of contemporary life. She told Janice Turner that "I try to write about crime not to celebrate it and make it sexy, but to condemn it. But I'm going to show it to you. Because it's not pretty. It's ugly and nasty and painful and frightening" (Cornwell, "Patricia Cornwell's Extraordinary Life").

The female medical examiner manifests postfeminist gothic sensibility not only through her stoic caretaking of broken women, but also by her belatedness. Much like Sebold's Susie Salmon or Moore's protagonist Frannie, the Scarpetta archetype is speaking to us from the end of the hourglass. The rise of the medical examiner–as-detective represents a distinct development in mystery fiction; other figures like the private eye have of course investigated murder, but only as one part of a spectrum of crimes. As Susan Allen Ford observes, by going to work postmortem, Scarpetta is "at once part of the investigative process but marginal to its traditional definition" (28). She despairs in *Black Notice* that her victims are "passing through indifferent hands and cold air and water. Everything so cold, cold, cold. . . . It's all so cold in the end" (68). Despite her righteous indignation and authentic compassion for victims, Scarpetta can provide only fragments of comfort, such as a name for an unidentified woman or information about the manner of death. Rooted in her melancholy is the realization that the bodies laid before her table speak similar stories of gendered abuse.

Make Me (Six Feet) Under: Autopsy and Aspiration in Postfeminist Narrative

The phrase *going under the knife* has permeated our popular culture. Most people instantly associate it with plastic surgery, an elective process with the end goal of disciplining (tightening, smoothing, filling, injecting) the human body in some way. Plastic surgery is a key expression of the makeover narrative, which Cressida Heyes calls "a major fetish in western cultures in recent years" (20). Women are the primary addressees of makeover programming, a central element of the postfeminist sensibility. "In the hypervisible landscape of popular culture" today, argues Alison Winch, "the body is recognized as the object of a woman's labour: it is her asset, her product, her brand and her gateway to freedom and empowerment in a neoliberal market economy" (21). The care and upkeep of said body is naturally of extreme importance to its subjects, and the makeover promises physical, psychic, and spiritual benefits for a body that is, in Debra Gimlin's words, "a symbol with an unlimited capacity for alteration and modification" (78).

Feminist critics have developed powerful, elegant analyses of the cultural tyranny of the body that has enveloped women for centuries.[3] Yet the postfeminist makeover movement continues to speak to women, despite the power of these critiques, often by co-opting feminist ideas to present the idea of physical transformation as choice and empowerment. Whereas prefeminist television programs such as *Queen for a Day* (1956–64) would show subjects who undertook body regimes to please their husbands (or to land one), in the twenty-first century, one is much more likely to find an appeal for *self*-improvement couched in feminist rhetoric. Susan Douglas points out that breast-implant manufacturer Allergan, for instance, sells its products with the tag phrases "power, freedom, individuality, and self-confidence" (233). Through cultural influencers like Oprah Winfrey, the makeover has become, in Deborah Caslav Covino's words, "an explicit and perceptive goal, as the achievement of greater psychic health through body and attitude adjustments consistent with a total self-concept that emphasizes individual choice and responsibility" (83).

Often, the self-work industrial complex hooks consumers by portraying the makeover as an alignment process that gives physical form to what was already there, providing, in Cressida Heyes's words, "a body that better represents the moral virtues one has developed" (28). Today, the language and practice of makeovers have fully infiltrated women's popular culture.[4] Susan Douglas points out that in the current climate, *refusing* to seek cosmetic surgery is viewed today as "an admission that you don't care enough about yourself and don't have enough self-esteem to tackle the requisite deferred maintenance" (233). While fewer women engage in cosmetic surgery than, say, dieting or gym memberships, thanks to the relative normalization and greater affordability of certain procedures, we are all "inevitably in a relationship to surgery regardless of whether we actually become surgical" (Blum 44). Virginia Blum speaks of a gaze that "sweeps the world with its inquiry: Did she do it? Or he?" (33). Even Patricia Cornwell is herself framed by this gaze. Janice Turner's profile of the author portrays her as "lean, sinewy and toned" with a face "tightened and evened by surgery, Botox, and collagen until, without make-up at 51, she looks like a slightly freeze-dried Meg Ryan" (Cornwell, "Patricia Cornwell's Extraordinary Life").

In an era where *going under the knife* has become an instantly recognizable phrase, Patricia Cornwell offers us a different meaning. Her autopsy narratives are bent on *disassembling* the posthumous female body. Instead of achieving rejuvenation and redemption, Scarpetta's patients are turned violently inside out, the scalpel traveling through clothing, flesh, and finally to bone. In fact, bones are the autopsy narrative's calling card, featured heavily in Kathy Reichs's series on forensic anthropology and indelibly in *Point of Origin*'s portrayal of Kay Scarpetta boiling flesh off bones in a pot purchased from a restaurant. It would be difficult to conceive of an image darker, or more directly opposed, to the resonant popular images of postfeminism. If plastic surgery represents the domestication of the knife, then Cornwell's autopsy narratives hone its sharp edges.

During an autopsy in *The Body Farm*, Scarpetta "incised the scalp behind the ears, folding it down to expose the skull, and the face suddenly collapsed into a sad, slack mask" (93). Similarly, in *Cause of Death* she watches as a colleague "reflected back the scalp. He pulled it forward over the eyes to expose the skull, and [the victim's] face collapsed, sad and slack, as if he knew what was happening and was grieving" (55). This procedure describes the same technology as the face-lift, but in a radically different context. Everything about Cornwell's autopsy narrative seems to invert the aspirational makeover narrative and to tell a very different story about the female body. The autopsy profoundly changes the status of the corpse, whose body is no longer a space of disciplined control, but rather one of seepage and decay. Female victims have landed on Scarpetta's table because their good looks have prompted male killers to bite, break facial structures, and even remove their visages entirely. The hard work of body maintenance is literally ripped asunder by animalistic violence in narratives that deliberately evoke Jack the Ripper's legacy. Cornwell's autopsy narrative undoes—and at times seems to provide ironic commentary on—the myth of mobile self-transformation lodged in postfeminist popular culture.

A corpse rots, leaks, swells, and bloats; it is the polar opposite of the constructed ideal Western feminine body, which as Susan Bordo writes, is "absolutely tight, contained, 'bolted down,' firm: in other words, a body that is protected against . . . areas that are soft, loose, or 'wiggly'" (190). All bodily discipline regimes come to their end in death. The fictional medical examiner Maura Isles grimly notes of a victim that "her belly had been enviably flat, the reward no doubt of many hours laboring at sit-ups and stomach crunches. How easily all that effort was reduced by a scalpel to incised muscle and gaping skin" (*Mephisto Club* 184).

In *Volatile Bodies*, Elizabeth Grosz theorizes that within Western thought, "the female body has been constructed not only as a lack or absence but with more complexity, as a leaking, uncontrollable, seeping liquid; as formless flow; as viscosity, entrapping, secreting," and exhibiting a "disorder that threatens all order" (203). Prone, helpless, mute, and leaking, the corpse on the gurney before Scarpetta is feminized in its submissive state, regardless of its sex. Furthermore, it is subject to the intrusive gaze of the medical examiner and others who are less sympathetic. Regarding the victim before her, Scarpetta thinks sorrowfully:

> The dead are defenseless, and the violation of this woman, like the others, had only begun. I knew it would not end until Lori Petersen was turned inside out, every inch of her photographed, and all of it on display for experts, the police, attorneys, judges and members of a jury to see. There would be thoughts, remarks about her physical attributes or lack of them. There would be sophomoric jokes and cynical asides as the victim, not the killer, went on trial, every aspect of her person and the way she lived, scrutinized, judged and, in some instances, degraded. (*Postmortem* 9)

Scarpetta's detective work also challenges the postfeminist view of the body as a site of plasticity and alteration. The stories written *onto* the lived body over time prove essential in her forensic investigations. "Anatomical detail—whether it be a hysterectomy, a root canal, or scars from plastic surgery," she observes in *All That Remains*, can "assist in the identification of the body." She further affirms that "teeth have their own stories. Your dental habits often reveal more about you than jewelry or designer clothes" (*Last Precinct* 46). When confronted with alternate theories of the crime or perspectives that differ from her own, Scarpetta returns to one basic principle. "The body doesn't lie" (*Scarpetta Factor* 137).

Through the autopsy narrative, Cornwell constructs the feminized corpse as truth-telling. The stories that the bodies reveal are all too familiar. The victim/killer dyad is almost always gendered in popular crime fiction; as Kathleen Gregory Klein asserts, "the Woman is the body in the library on whom the criminal writes his narrative of murder" (173). Cornwell's oeuvre not only cleaves to the female-victim paradigm, it also adapts one of the most notorious Western crime narratives of all—the story of Jack the Ripper.[5] Cornwell updates her perpetrator/victim dyad with a postfeminist twist of the knife. The beautiful and upwardly mobile white victims in her novels are nearly all "singletons"—a paradigmatic symbol of postfeminist representation and the kind of figure most likely to be beguiled by the makeover narrative's bodily discipline imperatives. Cornwell's rippers viciously maul these women and, with them, the postfeminist belief in beauty's sacredness.

Thought to be responsible for the murders of at least five impoverished women in 1860s London's East End, the criminal known today as Jack the Ripper was never caught. His cultural legacy is fraught. "As the prototype of dozens of filmic and fictional treatments and as the inspiration for numerous real-life 'heroes' of crime, the Ripper has materially contributed to women's sense of vulnerability in modern urban culture," writes Judith Walkowitz (543–44). Yet while his name is synonymous with barbarism and violence, he can also "be made to seem as domestic and ordinary as Jack Sprat, as playful as Jack in the Box" (Caputi 17). Claimed as part of a "vanished Victorian London, a romanticized East End of cobbled streets and gaslights," Jack the Ripper is commemorated in walking tours and memorabilia (Cameron 184). Though he is subject to various interpretations, the killer is unquestionably recollected with far more detail than his victims. As Elyssa Warkentin observes, "Within the field of 'Ripperology,' it is standard practice—indeed, it is nearly a generic requirement—to focus principally on describing and identifying the Ripper, secondarily on explaining his motives and methods, and only reluctantly on his victims" (36).

Patricia Cornwell's killers are overwhelmingly males who, like Jack the Ripper, manifest some kind of alterity, or even monstrosity.[6] The killer in *Postmortem* has a metabolic disorder known as MSUD (maple syrup urine disease) and must shower or wash hands repeatedly throughout the day. Another is a paranoid schizophrenic. The first recurring villain, Temple Gault, is "an exquisitely pretty blond young man" (*Cruel and Unusual* 349). Most striking of all is Jean-Baptiste Chandonne ("Le Loup-Garou" or werewolf), whose hypertrichosis leaves him covered with baby-fine hair seven to nine inches in length. He is repeatedly described in canine terms and possesses "a dirty odor, like a dog that needs to be bathed" (*Black Notice* 329–30). Chandonne, the self-aggrandizing figure most closely patterned after Jack the Ripper, utters psychotic fantasies and intones that "given the opportunity, he would rip women apart as he did in the past, but his electricity is not charged by hate or lust. He would destroy beautiful females to answer his higher calling, to complete a pure circuit that is necessary and godly" (*Blow Fly* 48). Cornwell deploys such figures in the service of the crime narrative that preoccupies her: the physical destruction of a particular kind of woman by a particularly cruel kind of means.

Historically speaking, the women mutilated and killed by Jack the Ripper have been variously conflated, disparaged, and ultimately rendered disposable. Much of their dismissal from public consciousness is class based; Elyssa Warkentin uncomfortably narrates a tourist experience in which the guide "reminded us several times that although the Ripper's victims were prostitutes, we were not to imagine that they were physically attractive . . . in fact, they were ugly, alcoholic, and probably disease-ridden hags—hilarious in their wretchedness and easy sexuality" (36). The women laid out before Dr. Scarpetta, though, are of a different ilk: beautiful and professionally successful. The very first victim, Dr. Lori Petersen of *Postmortem*, is a Harvard graduate and classically trained violinist (the rapist-murderer breaks her fingers out of spite). A bit later, Scarpetta finds the key to solving her case in *Point of Origin* when she realizes her female victims are connected by model-quality good looks. One victim is referred to as "a masterpiece of human flesh, a work of art" (174). In *Black Notice*, an elite police chief and "haughty beauty" is beaten so severely that she is unidentifiable (39). Nearly all female victims are living alone.[7]

The women murdered by violent criminals in Cornwell's work are manifestations of what Stéphanie Genz calls the *postfeminist singleton*, a "young, unattached, and mostly city-dwelling woman who is caught between the enjoyment of her independent urban life and her desperate yearning to find 'Mr. Right' with whom to settle down" (135). The singleton, best personified by Bridget Jones and the women of *Sex and the City*, is overrepresented in the postfeminist popular landscape and is similarly overabundant in Cornwell's work. The character is a type who was raised on second wave feminist gains and fed on the concepts of empowerment and a "just do it" philosophy. She is also usually white (people of color are rarely encountered within Cornwell's corpus, although the cringe-worthy resolution of *Postmortem* depends on Scarpetta's realization that the sole African American victim doesn't "sound black" to a killer who selects victims by phone) (372). Beautiful, professional single women who "transgress the narrow boundaries of home and hearth and dare to enter public space" are uniquely at risk in these fearmongering narratives (Walkowitz 544).

Jane Caputi has asserted that Ripper narratives have made murdered women's postmortem display and humiliation into "fixed iconography . . . to communicate female defeat, degradation, and destruction" (8). Similarly, Cornwell's victims are nearly always nude, propped up, and left for discovery. They are further insulted by a series of bodily mutilations that target the skin. Serial killer Temple Gault bites his victims and removes the skin to prevent dental identification. *Point of Origin*'s Newton Joyce keeps a freezer full of sliced-off faces, displaying some on mannequins. *Book of the Dead*'s Sandman removes women's eyes, fills them with sand, and sews the socket shut. Chandonne uses an iron hammer to "shatter women's heads and bodies to battered flesh and splintered bone, especially their faces" (*Blow Fly* 154). Of course, skin damage is a major motif in horror narrative, where deformed killers on-screen like Freddy Krueger, Leatherface, Buffalo Bill, and Michael Myers envy the nubile bodies and beautiful visages of their victims. "Skin houses the body and it is figured in Gothic as the ultimate boundary, the material that divides the inside from the outside. . . . It offers itself up as text, as body, as monster," writes Judith Halberstam (*Skin Shows* 7). In Cornwell's schema of violence, the Ripper figure expresses rage at and takes aim at femininity—in this case, the particular locus of the face. The sadism of these sequences is unfortunately not new, but it takes on fresh significance in the context of the postfeminist makeover narrative against which it is contrasted. Cornwell's compulsion to repeat this familiar tale speaks not only to its enduring cultural power, but to the contradictory ideology of postfeminist culture itself. The tightened, controlled, youth-displaying body is both an ideal and a death sentence in this world. Plastic surgery and autopsy, it seems, really are only an edge of the knife apart.

"You and All Your Machines": The Flight to Un-Embodiment

Moments of literary dismemberment are common to the work of Alice Sebold, Susanna Moore, Sapphire, and Patricia Cornwell. *The Lovely Bones* depicts loss through its short, choppy scenes that mimic Susie's corporeal fracture and her family's subsequent splintering. Moore's *In the Cut*, meanwhile, tries to make language viscerally represent the acts of dismembering, disarticulating, and otherwise splintering women's sense of safety and authority. In *Push*, Sapphire expresses Precious's preliteracy and traumatic fragmentation through truncated, repeated phrases that later become knit together with educational insight. Cornwell's later work, however, is up to something different. Like the young-adult novels that followed the success of Sebold's novel, Cornwell explores women's flight from corporeality. Unlike the teen heroines of that subgenre, who are bereft of bodies but busily occupied in a hopping afterlife, Cornwell's characters—most especially Scarpetta—become *virtual*, closely identified with their electronics and portrayed as objects of Internet display. Scarpetta's trials at the hands of anonymous hackers, viruses, and gossips illuminate the destruction wrought by a sarcastic, bitchy form of postfeminist discourse online. Cornwell's increasing interest in the vitality of online technologies reflects contemporary culture; in an age where the Supreme Court debates to what extent corporations are people, it is safe to say that lines between the human and the nonhuman are becoming blurred. Given, though, that Cornwell's series is predicated on the materiality of guts and splatter, the series' newfound enthusiasm for discussions of chat rooms, BlackBerries, and other tools of technology is peculiar. The later novels' flight from women's bodies toward a floating network demonstrates an aesthetic of exhaustion that, while problematic, could become a tool of the postfeminist gothic.

Cornwell's abrupt switch from first to third person beginning with the novel *Blow Fly* (2003) has resulted, Beth Head contends, in "altering the dynamic of these texts to a staggering degree" (36). Cornwell reflected that "I somehow felt I'd reached the end of what I could do with the series, so I began to think that I should try the omniscient point of view. I knew that if I didn't get outside of Scarpetta's skull, I was just going to be so cramped" (Lane, "Tough on Crime"). In fact, her later novels drift so far outside of Scarpetta's skull that her always-successful protagonist becomes *iconic*, gaining a unique level of public celebrity that includes a CNN program, FBI consultant status, pop-culture visibility, and near-universal adoration. Angela McRobbie has written that contemporary technologies, such as makeover programs, cast a "spotlight of visibility" on their subjects and lead to a "kind of spectactularisation of feminine subjectivity, which becomes the [desired] norm" in postfeminist culture (125). Scarpetta's body becomes just such an object of pageantry; it is *she* who is now endlessly dissected by a floating "public" emboldened by social technologies. The doctor is loved, but she is also impersonated on the Internet, mocked by gossip blogs, and repeatedly subjected to identity theft. Clearly, Cornwell is critiquing the invasive nature of social technologies. But by moving the emotional center of the novels away from Scarpetta's professional exploits to her own exploitation (online and in person), she eschews textual engagement with bodies altogether.

One staple of mystery fiction holds that the detective figure is always at risk from the criminals that he or she chases. In Cornwell's early novels, Scarpetta too is targeted by the killers she unmasks. In *Postmortem*, for example, Scarpetta feeds the press humiliating medical information about the murderer in an attempt to flush him out, and he attacks her. By contrast, later antagonists are drawn to Scarpetta because of her personal *magnetism*. Serial killer Temple Gault's fixation with Scarpetta leads him to, in Rose Lucas's observation, appear everywhere "with an uncanny ability to know just where Scarpetta is, what she is doing, what she cares about" (214). Gault leaves clues for her at the Italian "Scarletta" restaurant, steals her credit card, and creates a false identity as her fictitious son "Kirk Scarpetta." Scarpetta's therapist even suggests that, metaphorically, she is "his mother, and he brings you what he kills" (*From Potter's Field* 263). Similarly, hypertrichosis-afflicted "wolfman" killer Jean-Baptiste Chandonne dreams only of Scarpetta from his prison. He writes psychotically rapturous letters urging their reunion: "Do you remember that night? You eagerly opened your door and then attacked me because you could not face your longing for me" (*Blow Fly* 153). Chandonne's equally crazed brother, Jay Talley, is no less under the doctor's spell. No other woman satisfies him, and he complains that for "three nights now he has brought [his girlfriend] out here in his boat, hoping that somehow her body will become Kay Scarpetta's, and finally becomes furious because it can't" (*Blow Fly* 8).

Scarpetta's charisma attracts *all* men, to the consternation of other women. Talley's companion "can't control herself when she is forced to think of Kay Scarpetta, who is fine-looking and smart" and she "could cut Scarpetta's throat" (*Blow Fly* 40). In the same novel, another girlfriend opines that "I'm so fucking tired of the Doc this and the Doc that. . . . She's the only woman in your life, if you're honest about it" (326). In *Book of the Dead*, villainess Shandy Snook, *who has never even met Scarpetta*, repeatedly belittles her. "Hickory-dick-or-y-Doc, she's got you by the cock," she tells her boyfriend Marino (93). Cornwell even rescripts past narratives to emphasize Scarpetta's desirability. In the first Scarpetta novel, *Postmortem*, the happily married Benton Wesley shows no romantic interest in Scarpetta, and for her part she admits she'd only "gradually warmed up to" him (98). In 2008's *Scarpetta*, we learn that Benton in fact lusted after Scarpetta to such an extent that he had an erection around her when in the morgue and needed to carry his briefcase with him at all times as a shield (64). Similarly, Pete Marino's enduring crush on Scarpetta becomes an insane attraction that leads him to sexually assault her in *Book of the Dead* (2007).

The price of Scarpetta's personal and sexual aura of magnetism is also found in the virulent belly of the Internet. Although Scarpetta has always had significant professional success, she becomes a national celebrity through her platform on CNN. Subsequently, complete strangers assail her—in *Scarpetta*, one cries: "You're beautiful. Now that I see you in person, I can tell it isn't from some makeup artist or perfect camera angle. . . . I wish you would hug me. I need you to hug me!" (125–26). Beamed through the television, with posters of herself plastered throughout New York City, Scarpetta has achieved a level of celebrity that for some would represent the apex of postfeminist success. Yet Scarpetta is quickly subject to intrusions of social media where she is attacked on the basis of gender. Eluned Summers-Bremner comments that in

Cornwell's novels one senses the "everyday trauma of alienations engendered by the machinic, information-seeking and generating structures of urban-oriented, post-industrial life" (141). Karla Mantilla's term "gendertrolling," a form of misogyny characterized by vicious, coordinated attacks filled with pejorative slurs, describes Scarpetta's online experience ("Gendertrolling" 563).

To briefly contextualize technology within Cornwell's oeuvre, the novels have always featured muscular industrial technologies (detective Pete Marino, for instance, buys ever bigger motorcycles as he ages, as if to ward off the threats of emasculation that preoccupy him) but focused above all on electronics, which are often associated with Scarpetta's computer-expert niece Lucy. The 1990s books capture the awkwardness of "Web 1.0," where networks are slow and halting and dial-up modems plague Scarpetta's investigations. Marino describes his computer as "standard issue, black, boxy, sticky keys, the whole nine yards" (*Postmortem* 18). In later works, the computer becomes a key part of the plot's forensics, but increasingly, it also takes on a sinister cast. Scarpetta is repeatedly impersonated online, beginning in *Unnatural Exposure* when a colleague poses as "deadoc" to dispense medical advice. "Deadoc's saying he's you," Lucy tells her aunt. "In cyberspace, on the World Wide Web, you're both the same person with two different screen names" (109). This baffles Scarpetta, who is "lost again in the dark space of the UNIX environment with its strange symbols and commands like *cat, :q!* and *vi.*" (110). Scarpetta's noted technophobia points to the generational digital divide with her niece, and also emphasizes the distinction between her materially rooted work and the ephemeral worlds of cyberspace. As Linda Mizejewski observes, "Scarpetta is attached to technologies of the body (fingerprints, autopsies, biochemistry), but her lesbian cohort [Lucy] is attached to computer technologies that can imagine, connect, and create scenarios unfettered by traditional assumptions about what is 'real.'" (15). In *Cruel and Unusual*, Lucy solves a potential "hacking" over the phone by directing commands to Kay, who complains about the impenetrability of it all. "I'm not a UNIX programmer. You might as well be speaking Swahili," she snaps (64). She later announces that "computers were the modern Babel, I had decided. The higher technology reached, the greater the confusion of tongues" (*Body Farm* 41).

As old-fashioned as Scarpetta's paranoia about computers might seem, she has legitimate reason to be wary of the black box with the sticky keys. The online attacks that began in *Unnatural Exposure* occur repeatedly, always targeting female authority. In *Black Notice*, she is impersonated by an online medical reference called "Chief Kay" who says things like "I don't have much of a bedside manner" and "women don't do enough anymore to make their men feel important and in charge" (131–32). Queerness is also a locus of professional vulnerability when the duplicitous killer Carrie Grethen faux-romances lesbian Lucy in order to manipulate her computer expertise. The fallout destroys Lucy's self-confidence and career prospects; as Scarpetta notes, Carrie's betrayal "sucked up every drop of Lucy's life" (*Point of Origin* 125).

In the eponymous novel *Scarpetta*, Cornwell again deploys social media to imperil her heroine. While living in New York, Scarpetta becomes the favorite subject of a malicious gossip blog called "Gotham Gotcha." She is spotted by readers who submit tips to the website about her various comings and goings. "Gotham Gotcha" exemplifies an aspect of postfeminist sensibility associated with gossip blogging; this subculture, writes Kirsty Fairclough, uses "derisive and vicious discourse" to "debate aspects of a celebrity's behavior, lifestyle and appearance" (sec. 3). Cyberspace's fluidity may conceal the actual gender of the anonymous author (indeed, Fairclough points out that many celebrity gossip bloggers are male), but the act of policing others' appearance with witheringly sharp dismissal is stereotypically associated with women. Fairclough notes that celebrity icons in this world who do not cleave to traditional ideas of femininity are verbally castigated by terms such as *trannies* and *manly* (sec. 10). Scarpetta too finds that the Internet turns on her quickly. In *Scarpetta*, a female webmaster named "Shrew" seeks to humiliate Scarpetta, for reasons unknown, by leaking intensely personal information about her, including her sexual assault by Marino. Shrew also simply makes up lies about Scarpetta, including the falsehood that she was sexually abused in childhood by nuns. The webmaster sneers that "Scarpetta may live in a world of stainless steel but she's certainly no woman made of steel. She's weak, a disgrace. Guess what, she can be raped. That's right. Just like any other woman" (174). Rapeability emerges as a trump card that can subdue even the highest-flying professional.[8]

Gotham Gotcha also tries out another popular postfeminist refrain: asserting the victim's complicity in her own attack. The blog opines that readers "can blame the victim [Scarpetta] this time. She brought it upon herself. Pushed away, mistreated, and belittled her investigative partner in crime until one drunken night in Charleston when he couldn't take it anymore." Shrew adds that "you have to feel a little sorry for poor Pete Marino . . ." (174). The novel's plot mirrors Shrew's commentary. Scarpetta and a postrehab Marino are gothically doubled by the characters in the main mystery narrative, which involves the violent death of a female dwarf with a pathetically ardent boyfriend. The victim, Terri Bridges, was an obsessive-compulsive, uptight woman who drove everyone crazy with her neatness and her controlling nature. "Makes you wonder if [boyfriend] Oscar finally couldn't take it anymore," Marino observes (363). Chillingly, the investigators restage the crime scene, with Scarpetta sitting at the mirror in front of which Terri met her death and Marino behind her in a simulated strangling. Terri and Oscar—the controlling woman and her besotted man—are obvious stand-ins for the relationship of Scarpetta and Marino, and Scarpetta should, it is implied, be grateful to have escaped Terri's fate.

From "deadoc" to "Gotham Gotcha," every electronic intrusion into Scarpetta's identity robs her of her sangfroid. "Modern technology no longer seemed like her best friend. It bit her often. This time it may have bitten her badly," she concludes in *The Scarpetta Factor* (309). In chronicling Scarpetta's trials by social media, Cornwell references the way the Internet itself has proved gothic for women, sending frightening expressions of anger and contempt via faceless foes. Abuses of power on the electronic frontier are often depressingly familiar in gendered terms, whether conveyed by rape threats, cyberstalking, spamming of pornographic images, or revenge porn (the unauthorized distribution of explicit photos taken for private purposes). The borderless, anonymous, and largely unregulated nature of what Catherine Buni and Soraya Chemaly call the "unsafety net" gives it an eerie feel where intrusions can come from any corner.[9] In subjecting Scarpetta to the humiliations and fears that plague untold women online, Cornwell finds another way to revise the aspirational narrative of postfeminism. Scarpetta's luminous celebrity is no protection against an onslaught of words; her online foes do not just seek to "bite," but instead to wound, to carve, to bring her metaphorically, if not literally, closer to the bodies on her table.

However, Cornwell's social commentary on cybermisogyny is blunted by an increasingly leaden and opaque sense of plot development and writing style that moves further and further from the series' original concerns about gender and crime. The prose style becomes *itself* somewhat "electronic," moving to long, highly technical passages broken only by an occasional melancholic conversation. In *The Scarpetta Factor*, for instance, Scarpetta loses the BlackBerry that Lucy has given her and meditates about the consequences of its theft for an astonishing *five pages*; she is only stopped by e-mails from Lucy, who sends her constantly updated "clues" to the BlackBerry's location via a GPS tracker she has installed. Reading this segment, one directly experiences Scarpetta's electronic headache.

There is an actual victim in *The Scarpetta Factor*; her name is Toni Darien, and she was an avid jogger. Darien was killed by fellow members of a secret society of data-capturing enthusiasts; she would download her daily vital signs every fifteen seconds to a Bluetooth-enabled "combination actigraphy data logger with a highly sensitive accelerometer or bimorph element in a two-layer piezoelectric sensor that basically measures gross motor activity" (488–89). It is difficult to remember, reading these later novels, that Cornwell works in a genre about *bodies* and what happens to them on gurneys. Readers are a long way from the morgue, where boiled bones and sliced faces revealed intimate secrets. Gone too are Scarpetta's anguished screeds about compassion and justice for victims. The data-centric plots of *The Scarpetta Factor* (in which Kay and her crew get to virtually replay the last hours of Darien's life at fifteen-second intervals) and *Port Mortuary* (in which Scarpetta watches via virtual headphones the last minutes of a man's life) offer ghoulish visions of what forensic science can achieve for us. It will be possible to know and experience someone's end—to gorge on information about precisely how it happened. But these novels fetishize the *how* of death at the expense of *why*—something that Cornwell took on, albeit problematically, throughout her earlier career. As I have discussed, victims in the earlier books were killed "in service of" a narrative about male control/sexuality, and often those narratives were overwrought or problematic in their mystification of serial killing. But after Cornwell's shift out of Scarpetta's consciousness, victims tend to lack any sort of narrative complexity at all; they are interchangeable, unmourned, and strictly plot devices. Like the dead-girl subgenre of young-adult fiction, and like prison psychiatrist Louise in Susanna Moore's *The Big Girls*, Scarpetta has taken flight. She has left the crevices of the body on the gurney and sought refuge in blinking screens and data walls.

The later novels' flight toward bodilessness also linguistically mechanizes Scarpetta and her colleagues. A troubled Scarpetta describes her unease to be "as if I am having software problems. All sorts of files are being opened and closed unprovoked, and system messages are flashing" (*Last Precinct* 28). Speaking of being pursued by a serial killer, she muses that "I think the shock of it all causes a disk error and you can't remember with the same degree of intense attention to detail" (146). There are myriad other examples of Cornwell's computerized narrative. Scarpetta describes "beginning to feel unhinged, as if she'd lost her GPS" (*Scarpetta* 393). Sex with her boyfriend Benton is described as "rearming the mechanism" (*Scarpetta Factor* 304). For his part, Marino longs to become a computer, wistfully thinking: "Computers didn't get drunk or forget, had no regrets, didn't care. They connected everything, created logical trees on the data wall. Marino was afraid of his own data wall" (*Scarpetta Factor* 280). Perhaps this language of hopeless mechanization points to depletion in Cornwell's imaginary. After years of being elbows deep in the splatter, readers are now taken to a sterile world. The trade-off, though, is a near-total disengagement with the politics of violence. All that remains is, as one of Lucy's lovers puts it, "you and all your machines" (*Scarpetta Factor* 257).

Conclusion

In an interview about books that have shaped authors' lives, Cornwell claims kinship, both genealogical and metaphorical, with another famous writer, Harriet Beecher Stowe. "I wish I could sit down with her now and talk about the crime that permeates our society, the slavery that may have changed its shape and form but not its fangs," she writes (Coady and Johannessen 57). She is convinced that they have a "shared belief that all unfairness, harshness, and inevitable violence are born of the same original sin: the abuse of power, the ultimate result of which is enslavement, impoverishment, suffering, and death" (58).

Cornwell's articulation of their "shared belief" collapses historical specificity. Stowe's concerns were intimately tied up with abolition and evangelicalism, while Cornwell's (though she does not identify them as such) are galvanized by violence against women. The two relatives would also seem to diverge in terms of their aesthetic style. There is none of Scarpetta's coolness in the tear-stained world of *Uncle Tom's Cabin*. Both, though, have been the subject of literary condescension. Jane Tompkins's influential book *Sensational Designs* (1985) defends Stowe and fellow sentimental novelists against critical scorn deeming them responsible for evils ranging from "anti-intellectual consumerism" to "the propagation of the debased images of modern mass culture" to, finally, the "encouragement of self-indulgence and narcissism in literature's most avid readers—women" (124). As an author working in female-heavy genre fiction, Cornwell too is consigned to a narrow realm of expectations. Her work is largely considered only in terms of its plotting; her "pipe dream," as she tells interviewer James Kidd, "is that someone will notice that one of my sentences is really good" (Cornwell, "I Created a Monster"). The most illuminating comparison between these two literary women, though, may be in their fictional intent. Tompkins's work analyzes how Stowe used feminized emotional appeal to craft political messages; she asserts that her fiction "represents a monumental effort to reorganize culture from the woman's point of view" and "offers a critique of American society far more devastating than any delivered by better-known critics" (124). Stowe wanted to inspire abolitionist conversion in the hearts of her readers, and is memorialized by President Lincoln's (attributed) comment that she was "the little woman who wrote the book that started this great war."

Cornwell's "crusade" against gendered violence, and in particular the cultural fascination with the brutal deaths of young single (white) women, is blunted by the increasing opacity and distance of her language. "If you chomp down too hard on my work," Cornwell mused in an interview, "you're going to break your teeth" (Lane, "Tough on Crime"). Her flinty affect strives to *manage* the horror of sexualized violence, much as does the stoic Scarpetta figure herself. Although Scarpetta's disengagement may be unsatisfying, Cornwell shows it to be understandable, through her repeated scenes of splatter. As long as being female is a risk factor for savage death in her world, then Scarpetta and her fellow medical examiners will have no shortage of patients within the cool, hushed space of the morgue.

6

Hedging Her Bets

Jodi Picoult's Textured Ambivalence

The soft-focused domestic scenes that cover more than twenty novels by Jodi Picoult seem to offer a place of refuge from the spatter and gore of Patricia Cornwell's Kay Scarpetta. Picoult is a staple of the *New York Times* best-seller list and a contributor to Oprah Winfrey's magazine; she is known for well-researched novels about middle-class families awash in legal and moral ethical dilemmas. Her mannered, measured narration would appear worlds removed from the experimental preliterate narrative of Sapphire's *Push* or the ethos of fragmentation that drives the work of Alice Sebold and Susanna Moore. And yet, within Jodi Picoult's corpus, writes Ginia Bellafante, "terrible things happen to children of middle-class parentage: they become terminally ill, or are maimed, gunned down, killed in accidents, molested, abducted, bullied, traumatized, stirred to violence" ("Jodi Picoult and the Anxious Parent"). Whereas the other authors in *Splattered Ink* explore the ramifications of gendered violence perpetrated upon the female protagonist, Picoult's gothic probes another locus of vulnerability—the protagonist's *child*. In one of her novels, Picoult alludes to Mary Shelley's quintessential female gothic text by naming a minor character "Frankenstein." Centuries after Shelley's iconic depiction of anxious maternity, another voice of domestic horror haunts the night.

Much as Patricia Cornwell's female death professional *manages* scenes of barbarity in the mystery genre, Picoult packages her work to raise and defuse fears of gendered violence. Wrapping her main narratives about women and children suffering from sexual assault and trauma within layers of secondary plots, metaphors, and multiple perspectives, Picoult demonstrates a postfeminist investment in the ideals of balance, indeterminacy, and neutrality. Such rhetorical moves create distance from "angry" feminism. Many of Picoult's narratives collapse specifically gendered narratives into stories of everyone's colorless human pain. Postfeminism too routinely dismantles women's issues into a sort of "humanism" that presupposes the death of gendered concerns.

To briefly situate Jodi Picoult in the literary marketplace is to turn toward the loaded and ill-defined term *middlebrow*. Nicola Humble proposes that a middlebrow novel "straddles the divide between the trashy romance or thriller on the one hand, and the philosophically or formally challenging novel on the other: offering narrative excitement without guilt, and intellectual stimulation without undue effort" (11). Long tied to middle-class aspirational values, middlebrow literature, like novel reading in general, has been frequently associated with *women*. "Roughly speaking, what one might call the *average* novel—the ordinary, good-bad, Galsworthy-and-water stuff which is the norm of the English novel—seems to exist only for women," George Orwell famously remarked long ago (244). The many novels of Jodi Picoult are packaged for an upper-middle-class, primarily female audience. Each paperback edition bears her name in a large colored band and contains a gauzy, faceless shot of domestic life front and center. Meg Wolitzer has commented that this type of presentation visually codes a novel as feminine. Featuring images of "a little girl in a field of wildflowers" or "an empty swing on the porch of an old yellow house," such works might "as well have a hex sign slapped on them, along with the words: 'Stay away, men!'" ("Second Shelf"). A favorite of book clubs, Picoult has also found an outlet as a commentator and reviewer for *O Magazine*, part of Oprah Winfrey's empire of middle-class female taste production.

Picoult has used her cultural power to advocate for greater gender and ethnic diversity in the literary marketplace. Most memorably, in a 2010 tweet, she commented that the "NYT raved about [National Book Award–winning Jonathan] Franzen's new book. Is anyone shocked? Would love to see the NYT rave about authors who aren't white male literary darlings."[1] Her remark was widely dismissed in the blogosphere; it even prompted Pulitzer Prize winner Jeffrey Eugenides to state, "I didn't really know why Jodi Picoult is complaining. She's a huge best-seller and everyone reads her books, and she doesn't seem starved for attention, in my mind—so I was surprised that she would be the one belly-aching . . . it [exposure in the *New York Times*] usually has nothing to do with their gender, but just the marketplace" ("I Don't Know Why"). In response, Picoult told an interviewer that "I didn't feel like I was saying something that everyone didn't already know, that women are reviewed less frequently and differently than men and there are fewer female reviewers." She also suggests there is a double standard for literary critique.

"I've heard the word 'formulaic' come up when people criticize my books," she says. "Why? Because I have a trial in many of my books. I don't know that John Grisham is called formulaic very often, so it is kind of interesting" ("Sisterhood's Keeper" MM12). This remark reflects her literary style; after raising the valid comparison to legal-thriller writer Grisham, she trails off without ultimately challenging the inequity she has noted. Nevertheless, Picoult's critiques have shed light on enduring condescension toward the feminine and the popular (two terms that can take on a rather gothic twinning at times) in literary circles.

Picoult's work is also notable for its layered research. To be sure, she recycles certain plot structures in many novels. Her protagonists are nearly always white New Englanders with red hair, and almost every volume is replete with a love triangle involving the protagonist's best friend. However, Picoult's novels are also known for their wide-ranging and detailed explorations of American ethnic enclaves and subcultures. *Second Glance* (2003), for instance, investigates details of the Vermont state government's early twentieth-century sterilization of the Abenaki native people, and *Plain Truth* (2000) delves deep into the customs of the Amish community. Picoult's official website notes praise from *Image* magazine about her "impressive research into wolf biology, hierarchy and pack mentality" in the course of writing *Lone Wolf* (2012). In an interview with Bob Abernethy and Bob Faw, she is commended for doing "extensive research for each book—visiting the Rhode Island Crime Lab for an upcoming novel, spending time on death row for *Change of Heart*, or staying on an Amish farm for *Plain Truth*" in service of "painstaking attention to detail" (Picoult, "Jodi Picoult"). Picoult's research gives her work a level of difficulty that distinguishes it from "beach reads" and other maligned subgenres of women's fiction. It also highlights the breadth of her imagination. However, as I discuss in more detail, Picoult's tendency to have multiple competing narratives within the same novel suggests that the primary plots, which chronicle sexual assault and trauma, are somehow insufficient in themselves and must constantly be viewed through other lenses.

Balancing the Scales: Domestic Disturbance and Warrior Mothers

Catherine Rottenberg has argued that the idea of the middle road, of "balancing private and public aspects of the self," is becoming "the telos of the progressive narrative with respect to emancipated womanhood" (155). The idea that feminism is epitomized by having it all has been recently popularized by the "corporate feminist" manifestos of Sheryl Sandberg, Anne-Marie Slaughter, and others. Sandberg, one of the most elite women in business and technology, authored the working woman's volume *Lean In* (2013) in which she argues that we need "more portrayals of women as competent professionals and happy mothers" (24). Slaughter, whose high-powered career has encompassed the State Department and Ivy League deanships, wrote one of the Internet's most widely read essays, a 2012 opinion piece called "Why Women Still Can't Have It All." Within its pages, Slaughter marshals considerable anecdotal evidence in service of her claim that "a balanced life still is more elusive for women than it is for men." Rottenberg cautions that the repackaging of feminist success as the achievement of balanced well-being signals a fundamental "reorienting of the liberal feminist discursive field away from notions of freedom, equal rights, and social justice," and fails to take into account the material realities of most women's lives (147). In their efforts to "integrate fully into the American system" and better juggle it all, these manifestos also diverge from justice-centered women-of-color feminisms, which, Brittney Cooper writes, recognize "fundamental flaws in the system" and seek "its complete and total transformation" ("Feminism's Ugly Internal Clash").

Of course, the fetishizing of "work/life balance" in postfeminist popular culture is not limited to the sphere of the boardroom. The emerging subgenre of "priv-lit," epitomized by best sellers like Elizabeth Gilbert's *Eat, Pray, Love* (2006), emphasizes white female self-discovery and balance, achieved through spiritualized consumption.[2] Similar concerns have long been exhorted by the Oprah multimedia franchise, which urges viewers to "live your best life" through the curated selection of fitness, health, and mindfulness products.

Jodi Picoult's novels fetishize balance in two distinct ways. Picoult locates value in the *concept* of balance, and expresses it through her multiple perspectives and resistance to truth claims. In an interview with *Religion and Ethics Newsweekly*, she states that if "you can make them [readers] understand why someone with a differing opinion has that opinion and at least come to respect that opinion, I think you make the world a better place. I think I'm still teaching. It's just a really big classroom" (Picoult, "Jodi Picoult"). The challenge for readers, as I discuss in more detail later, is to *judge* among these differing opinions and to struggle against simple relativism, particularly within Picoult's stories of gendered violence. In addition, within her narratives, Picoult also invokes the concept of "balance" in a more traditional postfeminist way, finding meaning and progress in the restoration of domestic equilibrium for career-oriented mothers. As mentioned, Picoult's work often roots itself in maternal anxiety. "Criminals sit next to us on the bus," she writes in *Vanishing Acts*. "They pack our groceries and cash our paychecks for us and teach our children. They look no different from you or me. And that's why they get away with it" (33). Invoking suburban evil in a manner similar to Alice Sebold in *The Lovely Bones*, Picoult avers that "the same man who robs a general store at knifepoint might, at a traffic light, turn and smile. The guy who raped a thirteen-year-old girl might be singing hymns beside you at church. The father who kidnapped his daughter might be living right next door" (*Vanishing Acts* 194). To guard against the wolves at the door, Picoult advocates a form of "warrior" motherhood in keeping with postfeminist logic.

Chris Jenks has argued that in Western postmodern culture, children have become not only profound sources of love but also "partners in the most fundamental, unchosen, unnegotiated form of relationship" because trust "that was previously anticipated from marriage, partnership, friendship, class solidarity and so on is now invested more generally in the child" (111). In Jodi Picoult's work, bonds between children and parents easily eclipse the romantic ties between adults. In *Perfect Match*, Nina Frost confesses that "sometimes when you pick up your child you can feel the map of your own bones beneath your hands, or smell the scent of your skin in the nape of his neck. This is the most extraordinary thing about motherhood—finding a piece of yourself separate and apart that all the same you could not live without" (151). Delia Hopkins rhapsodizes in *Vanishing Acts* that "after giving birth you realize that the biggest part of you is now somehow external, subject to all sorts of dangers and disappearance, so you spend the rest of your life trying to figure out how to keep her close enough for comfort. . . . Until you have a baby, you don't even realize how much you were missing one" (7).

Within postfeminist American culture, as I have already discussed in the context of Sapphire's work, there is intense attention to promoting white women's fecundity through methods as diverse as antiabortion rhetoric, narratives about the ticking biological clock, and celebrity "bump watching." Women of color are not perceived as having a similar "legitimate claim to motherhood," an issue eloquently taken up by Mary Thompson, whose analysis of *Push* contrasts white women's recuperation of the word *breeder* as a hip mothering term with its original reference to slave women's reproductive value (sec. 30).[3] Within postfeminist iconography, singletons, like Bridget Jones or the cast of the television program *Girls* (2012–), are overrepresented. Yet postfeminism's orientation toward domestic fulfillment and a "return to femininity" necessarily addresses mothers as well. Susan Douglas and Meredith Michaels famously coined the term *new momism* to describe the philosophy, spawned against a Reagan-era backdrop of declining federal support for family programs, that "no woman is truly complete or fulfilled unless she has kids, that women remain the best primary caretakers of children, and that to be a remotely decent mother, a woman has to devote her entire physical, psychological, emotional, and intellectual being, 24/7, to her children" (4).

Decades after the 1980s, the shadow of new momism is still very much present. Judith Warner writes that "this widespread, choking cocktail of guilt and anxiety and resentment and regret is poisoning motherhood for American women today" (4). Internet culture has provided a kind of flogging space for women who fail to live up to these internalized expectations. For instance, acclaimed writer Ayelet Waldman's assertion in a *New York Times* piece in 2005 that "I love my husband more than I love my children" met with such online vitriol that Waldman, who described herself as "crushed" by the reaction, subsequently titled her book *Bad Mother* (Luscombe, "Ayelet Waldman: Bad Mother."). Writing of the cyberaggression directed toward mothers of "misbehaving" female celebrities such as Lindsay Lohan and Britney Spears, Shelley Cobb argues that "the association of motherhood with self-sacrifice" has "become particularly virulent in postfeminist new momism" ("Mother of the Year" sec. 12).

Jodi Picoult's novels are also suffused with the ideology of intense mothering, but they are galvanized by plots that jeopardize children's safety, particularly by threats of gendered violence. Mothers, of course, experience a special culturally induced impetus toward domestic safeguarding. As Cobb writes, "Protecting their children, especially their daughters (whether that be from pedophiles or terrorists), has become the current signifying feature of middle-class motherhood. . . . Any suggestion that a mother might not be properly protecting her daughter or, worse, putting her daughter in harm's way, borders on the criminal" ("Mother of the Year" sec. 20). The emergence of "warrior mother" iconography in popular culture within the past twenty-five years serves as another instance, like the warrior woman of television and Girl Power, of postfeminism's embrace of empowerment ideology. Cultural fascination with warrior mothers is observable even in the shifting nomenclature bestowed upon the maternal voting demographic. Many Americans remember the "soccer mom"—defined by William Safire as a middle- to upper-class suburbanite who "often drives a sports-utility vehicle or a minivan, [and] carries snacks and orange juice for the kids"—as a discursive icon in the 1996 presidential election (Safire, "Soccer Moms"). "If you are a soccer mom," reflected pundit Kellyanne Fitzpatrick, "*the world according to you is seen through the needs of your children*" (qtd. in MacFarquhar, "What's a Soccer Mom Anyway"; emphasis added).[4]

Succeeding political cycles have featured other iterations (waitress moms, mortgage moms) but most recently, the "security mom" has had the public ear. She symbolizes a voter who ostensibly prioritizes protection from terrorism over more traditional "women's" concerns like education or health care. Many self-defined security moms adopt a bellicose tone; columnist Michelle Malkin, for instance, opined that "a candidate who underestimates the security mom and her vote this fall may do so at his own peril. Hell hath no fury like a momma protecting her babies" (qtd. in Rodino, "War Mothering" 382).[5] The image of the militant mother protecting her children intensified in 2008. Charismatic and controversial Republican vice presidential candidate Sarah Palin famously introduced herself to the crowds at the 2008 Republican Party Convention as a "hockey mom" who could be distinguished from a pit bull only by her "lipstick." Palin went on to coin another famous term, *mama grizzly*, at an antiabortion political action committee event. Michelle Rodino-Colocino writes that "more formidable than a pit bull, tougher than a hockey mom in lipstick, the mama grizzly represents a tough mother subject position that retains femininity during battle" ("Man Up" 81).

Armed with an array of electronic devices to tag and monitor their children, contemporary security/hockey/grizzly moms are expected to ward off all potential evil in their children's path. Jodi Picoult's novels *Perfect Match* (2002) and *Vanishing Acts* (2005) speak to these issues in complex ways, affirming the warrior mother icon while also upholding Rottenberg's postfeminist grammar of "balance." In *Perfect Match*, Nina Frost, a sex-crimes prosecutor, shoots, in open court, the priest she believes sexually assaulted her son. This drastic act is undertaken to right the heroine's balance; the novel recounts how her child's abuse spurs Nina to recognize her domestic deficiencies and reinvest in home. In *Vanishing Acts*, a warrior mother gets startling news; she *herself* was kidnapped in childhood by her own father. The novel's interrogation of the gender politics of child custody tapers off, avoiding judgment and settling for another balancing of scales, in which the heroine simply exchanges maternal love for paternal love.

In the opening of *Perfect Match*, Nina Frost forces Tylenol down her mildly sick son's throat as she hurries to her job. "You'll just hope that your own son has the good sense to get sick when you're not scheduled in court. . . . How can everyone else's kid be a priority over your own?" her husband lectures accusingly (31). This scene of domestic strife in which Nina ignores her son's strange silence and his bed-wetting, abruptly dumping him at day care, signals a now-familiar theme of the incompetent working mother. Because Nina does not properly attend to the tenets of postfeminist new momism, she exposes her child to abuse. Nathaniel is molested by a priest who, by virtue of his moral authority, is easily able to compel Nathaniel's silence. But it was Nina, we learn, who pushed the unwilling child into the priest's clutches for a special story hour. "Go," she insists, remembering: "Nathaniel buried his face underneath my sweater . . . I had to peel his arms from around me, push him in the right direction. Twice he looked back, and twice I had to nod, encouraging him to get a move on" (216).

Perfect Match emphasizes Nina's work/life imbalance. She is a lawyer specializing in child abuse cases, but she has minimal maternal resources. Despite clear signs that something is wrong with her son, Nina breezes through her morning thinking of her upcoming cases. "Unlike most parents, who lie awake at night worrying about the horrors that could befall a child, I have the chance to do something about them. I'm a white knight, one of fifty lawyers responsible for cleaning up the state of Maine," she boasts (10). But Nina's legal expertise proves far from helpful in her son's case—in fact, it is seen as a *deficit*. She questions the medical expert too aggressively, asking if her son's exam shows "evidence consistent with penetration" and if he can "tell if it was penile penetration? Digital? Or some foreign object?" (42). Nina believes that by collecting information about the sexual assault she has the best chance of finding and punishing a perpetrator (the mute Nathaniel will not, initially, identify him). Yet her response is deemed inappropriately maternal by the examining doctor. "Parents ask whether their children still feel the pain from the assault," the doctor thinks, "if they will remember, in the long term, what happened to them. But these questions, well, they make [me] feel as if [I am] being cross-examined." Upon being dismissed by the medical staff, Nina crumples into a "small keening ball on the floor," and the doctor approvingly notes that "it's the first time that day he has seen her act like a mother" (44). Nina's husband Caleb similarly upbraids her, indicating that Nathaniel "needs a mother more than he needs a mother who is a prosecutor" (119).

Nina blames herself for her lack of balance; her maternal inattentiveness caused her to fail to see "what was under my nose" (71). She adds that "my work, it will have to wait. This all happened to Nathaniel when I wasn't present to bear witness; I cannot risk letting him out of my sight again" (47–48). In the wake of the trauma, Nina hears from several sources that "things happen for a reason." This nearly ubiquitous phrase in contemporary American culture can be profoundly comforting, yet also deterministic, suggesting that some important lesson will always occur to balance the scales in the wake of something terrible. Nathaniel's child psychiatrist, for instance, tells Nina to refocus her energies domestically, observing that "there's a big part of me that also thinks things happen for a reason, Nina. Maybe [Nathaniel's] not the only one who's starting over" (85).

Subsequently, Nina decides to kill her son's abuser. In her mind, this is a heroic maternal act, in line with the ethos of the "mama grizzly." She is willing to endure jail and separation from Nathaniel in order to prevent his testimony and subsequent retraumatization. Picoult's narrative recalls the real-life case of Ellie Nesler, who made national headlines in 1993 for fatally shooting, in court, her six-year-old son's molester. Nesler, like the fictional Nina, rooted her actions in maternity, telling the press, "I'm not a hero, I'm a mother." Sympathetic viewers at least initially agreed; one told a reporter that "this is about a mother protecting her cubs . . . you mess with my young, honey, and you're dead meat" (Frank 209). Nesler's lawyer repeatedly referred to his client as a "she-bear" (an antecedent of the "mama grizzly"), invoking a wild animal protecting her young. In an interview from jail, Nesler herself told Oprah on-screen that "my son was afraid, and now he's not afraid. . . . He's a normal little boy, and he can play. So I am sorry that I killed someone and that I'm not with my children, but on the other hand, I wish the judicial system would have taken care of it. I wish I didn't have to." This sentiment is closely echoed by the fictional Nina, who screams at her husband: "You want me to wait for the courts to get around to charging this bastard? While he rapes ten, twenty other children? And then wait some more . . . and then wait again? . . . I'm already going to prison for killing a man. I don't have a life anymore. But Nathaniel *can*" (242).

Ellie Nesler's profiler Russell Frank reminds us that people want a "simple heroine." Nesler, who turned out to have taken methamphetamine on the day of the shooting and was later jailed for drug dealing, quickly became "a complicated character" (205). The same can be said of Nina, whose self-conception as the mother-hero is severely undercut. Her act is not driven by the ethics of intense mothering that preoccupy "true" heroines in Picoult's oeuvre; rather, it is cannily *staged* using Nina's extensive knowledge of how "temporary insanity" is adjudicated. "I make my eyes flicker from left to right, lighting on nothing," says Nina after being jailed for the priest's murder. "I chew my fingernail till the cuticle bleeds. *I make myself crazy, because this is what I want them to see*" (137; emphasis added). Even now, in the midst of the trauma that most demands her maternal resources, Nina thinks like a lawyer instead.

Furthermore, Nina shoots the wrong man, reinforcing her incompetence as a warrior mother. She misunderstands Nathaniel's confession; hearing "Father Glen" instead of "Father Gwynne," she reveals how little she knows her child. It is left to her husband, Caleb Frost, to pick up the pieces. Caleb executes the vigilante justice that his wife cannot when he quietly poisons Gwynne using antifreeze, the tools of his own trade. Caleb's actions exemplify a postfeminist narrative Sarah Projansky has described in which male characters "return to their traditional roles as 'manly' saviors in order to fix what women/feminists unwittingly have made inoperable" (85).

Perfect Match utilizes postfeminist warrior mother iconography to critique the imbalanced career woman; in her later novel *Vanishing Acts*, Picoult invokes the symbolic territory of the abducted and (perhaps) abused female child to explore the gendered politics of child custody. The abduction of a child remains, thankfully, a relatively rare demographic event. But it is a narrative that, Mary Elizabeth Williams writes, "taps into our absolute most primal dread—the wolf at the door, coming not for you but for a vulnerable child. Your child" ("Why Etan Patz Still Haunts Us"). *Vanishing Acts* exploits this fear in its account of a woman, Delia, discovering that she herself was stolen, dragged across the country decades ago by her father. Oddly, the story does *not* focus on Delia and her self-discovery; rather, it becomes a polemic about father's rights. The abandoned mother's perspective is suborned to the story of Delia's heroic father, who battled a 1970s domestic court system biased in favor of women. The seemingly criminal Andrew undergoes a heroic trajectory of suffering in prison, giving up bit by bit of his painful story fighting for his daughter's safety. Meanwhile, the ostensibly victimized mother, Elise, is progressively revealed as inattentive, alcoholic, and finally unfit.

Child abductions have occurred in America from very early days, as slave narratives and white colonial captivity narratives illustrate. Rebecca Wanzo observes that, during slavery, "black children were the object of sympathy in a very early moment in rhetoric about child abduction. . . . The theme of mothers being torn away from their children and the impact on mother and child was one of the central narratives indicting the slave trade" (*Suffering* 190). Our cultural fascination with child abduction in the modern period has centered on spectacular *individual* disappearances, for instance that of baby Charlie Lindbergh in 1932. The 1979 national news-making case of Etan Patz, a six-year-old who disappeared on his way to school, saw the "endangered or despoiled child [become] such a ubiquitous figure in the media," claim Susan Douglas and Meredith Michaels. The combination of moral panic over the influx of mothers into the workplace, the decimation of federal funding for family programs under President Reagan, and "a news media increasingly infested by the voyeuristic sensibilities of tabloid journalism" fueled the national obsession with abducted children (89).

Because they generate a culture of fear and paranoia in parents' hearts, child abductions have become a powerful representational trope in contemporary literature as well. Lionel Warner observes the prevalence of missing or taken children in British and Canadian works like Graham Swift's *Waterland* (1983), Margaret Atwood's *The Handmaid's Tale* (1985), and Ian McEwan's *The Child in Time* (1987). The motif of child theft, Warner suggests, operates as "part of a web of concerns about the future and the freedom of the individual, in which the theft can be seen as an emblem of those fears" (54–55). On American literary shores, child abduction has been featured in genre fiction such as Dennis Lehane's hard-boiled thriller *Gone, Baby, Gone* (1998). It more commonly occurs, however, in Picoult's realm—middlebrow or "women's" fiction. The paradigmatic example is Jacquelyn Mitchard's *The Deep End of the Ocean* (1996), which was Oprah Winfrey's inaugural Book Club selection, and which became a feature film three years later. Mitchard's novel of a kidnapped son who coincidentally reencounters his birth family nine years later is similar to *Vanishing Acts* in terms of providing a generally happy ending. The reality for many kidnapped children, of course, includes abuse and even murder.[6]

Not all literary examples of this genre emphasize the bereft mother's perspective, but most do. Susan Douglas and Meredith Michaels have suggested that mothers have been uniquely addressed by the media panic around kidnapped children from its inception in the 1980s. The subtext then, they write, was that "working mothers' most unforgivable sin was exposing their children too soon to the 'outside' world, a place of overly commercialized relationships and self-interested predators." Perhaps, they continue, the panics suggested "it wasn't worth it: Equality for women had been too expensive for kids" (107). In *Vanishing Acts*, the mother is not a frantic career woman and the kidnapper is not a stranger but a father. Yet the parental rules defined in the "new momism" still apply. Delia Hopkins is kidnapped by the person who can best provide the kind of intensive, all-consuming, and materially rich mothering that is appropriate—in this instance, her *father*.

Like most of Picoult's protagonists, Delia—herself a young, single mother to a daughter—expresses a lioness's new momism. As a child, we learn that she had shared with her friends "only a single wild wish. *One day*, I'd written, *I will be a mother*" (15). Delia's concept of maternal devotion cleaves to what

Sara Ruddick calls *preservative love,* which is "an *activity* of caring or treasuring creatures [children] whose well-being is at risk" (240; emphasis added). Delia, who has chosen a career as a search-and-rescue expert, ruminates that a mother is "someone who could not be dragged from me, kicking and screaming, no matter how powerful the force of separation was. Someone who would give up her life if it meant I couldn't be a part of it" (76). In one saccharine scene, Delia's daughter Sophie, gazing rapturously at the stars, points out that "WOW, upside down, is MOM" (255). Delia will have to reevaluate her idealized conception of mother love when the circumstances of her own kidnapping are revealed.

As he recounts it, Delia's father Andrew was disadvantaged as a parent by his gender. Despite having more status, money, and resources than his estranged wife, he faced courts who "automatically gave custody to a mother even when the father had a spotless background" (178). Picoult's depiction of the 1970s judicial system as beholden to feminist concerns is curious. Within Western jurisprudence, there is a long and unequal history of parental rights; Carol Smart points out that "until the middle of the nineteenth century it was only possible to speak of *fathers'* rights in respect of legitimate children" because the state of marriage "gave fathers complete legal power over their children" (4; emphasis added). In the Western tradition, the famous 1839 Caroline Norton case in England began to give more weight to maternal claims to the child's best interest. Yet since the women's movement, the public dominant image of the courts is, as Smart puts it, "one in which women are unjustifiably favored, in which fathers are excluded to their detriment and the detriment of the children, and where the interests of the children have been misconceived" (22). Legal scholar Martha Fineman adds that a postfeminist "fetish with gender neutrality" has attacked "the performance of nurturing or caretaking tasks as the basis for preferencing parents," roles historically fulfilled by women (34).

Wealthy, white, and possessed of a stable job as a pharmacist, *Vanishing Acts*'s Andrew would seem to be the parent with the legal advantage. Yet he reiterates that in the 1970s, "no one believed a father could do as good a job raising a kid as a mother . . . even an alcoholic one" (373). Picoult establishes Andrew's paternal bona fides in his backstory; we learn that he is an upstanding community member who runs a senior center. His devotion to Delia overrides any semblance of a personal or romantic life; although many women "would have thrown themselves at a man like Andrew Hopkins, he only dated sporadically, and he never remarried," Delia says proudly. "He used to say that life was all about a boy finding a perfect girl; he was lucky enough to have been handed his in a labor and delivery room" (10). Having provided the perfect childhood for Delia, the jailed Andrew now keeps his silence about the kidnapping. Readers enter into his prison world for an extended time and witness him being subject to attempted rape, near-constant beatings, and other forms of abuse. His heroism even precludes him from revealing pieces of information that would help his defense, such as a childhood incident where Delia was bitten by a scorpion while in her mother's care (256).

This narrative of Christlike suffering displaces the story of the lost mother, torn from her child for more than twenty years. As mentioned, Elise Hopkins is given little textual space in *Vanishing Acts*; we know only that she is Latina and a recovered alcoholic, and that she firmly believes in tarot and mysticism. Delia had imagined "Marion Cunningham and Carol Brady and Ma Walton" as her ideal maternal figures (76). Instead of these bastions of white middle-class suburban television, she gets a mother figure separated both by the passage of years and by socioeconomic stratification. In a troubling passage stressing Elise's ethnic "primitivism," Delia, who has been given a cloth bag by her mother, muses: "I can smell the rotten flesh of mangoes . . . I can taste the bitter blood of a hundred babies being born . . . I smell urine and roasted corn and the smiling raw mouth of a watermelon. It is my mother's world, I realize, in the palm of my hand" (343). When Elise does not meet Delia's expectations, the daughter begins to doubt her mother's fitness.

Acknowledging that alcoholism is a serious problem, the debasement of Elise in *Vanishing Acts* still seems unwarranted. In the most striking example of the text's condemnation of the mother, *Andrew* (the kidnapper) forgives *Elise* for her poor parenting. "I just wish you'd loved yourself a little more," her felonious husband tells her. "I forgive you," Andrew whispers, calling it a "gift" (371–72). In a final twist, is it is revealed that Elise's boyfriend—a man that she chose over Andrew Hopkins—may have sexually abused Delia. "His hands went underneath her skirt . . . he had his hands on her. He touched my daughter. And every time Elise got drunk, or fell asleep, he was going to be there doing the same thing," Andrew says on the stand, to everyone's astonishment (384). Although under cross-examination Delia admits no memory of this abuse, she subsequently believes she might remember. The trigger for her recollection is hearing Spanish (words spoken by Victor Vasquez, her mother's boyfriend). Once again, the world outside of snowy New Hampshire intrudes to symbolize abuse and disorder.

Significantly, Andrew backs off his abuse claim in private; he tells his daughter later that "I honestly didn't know whether it [his allegation] was true. . . . The more time that passed, the more I wondered if I'd jumped to the wrong conclusion . . . because that way I could justify running away with you" (417). Nevertheless, his declaration in court that Delia was abused leads to his legal acquittal; furthermore, it serves as a final breaking point between Delia and her mother. *Elise*, rather than Victor, becomes the target of the daughter's rage because she has failed to live up to the lioness standard of momism. "I wanted you to be my mother. I wanted one so badly," Delia tells her. When Elise responds that "I am your mother," Delia excludes her from that role. "I think of what would happen if someone, anyone, touched Sophie," she rages. "I'd kill him. An icicle through the heart, a car filled with carbon monoxide. He would not take another breath if he touched my daughter" (414–15). Taking her leave, Delia tells her parent that "I wish I could tell you that I know you did the best you could, but I can't" (415).

Vanishing Acts does not definitively determine whether Delia was sexually abused—because it is not interested in the answer. In rather flippant fashion, Delia decides that "there isn't one truth, there are dozens" (418). She does not seek therapy or even appear to dwell on the issue. A friend asks, "What if the whole kidnapping experience isn't the story of Delia? What if disappearing wasn't the most cataclysmic event of your life?" What if, she suggests, "coming back" is? (267). Picoult shows the heroine "coming back" as her good father's daughter, reentering New England life with a toss of her red hair. Delia enacts the process of maternal *disidentification*, described by Astrid Henry as a key dynamic whereby young women establish their own self-concept by rejecting or distancing themselves from their female progenitors. In returning to the snowy-white origins of New England, she restores the identity of "Delia Hopkins," daughter of Andrew Hopkins and no one else.

The sexual-abuse claim in *Vanishing Acts* works very differently than it does in a novel like Sapphire's *Push*. Here, it is the sort of deus ex machina plot twist that Katie Roiphe identified in her survey of incest fiction as being used to distinguish good mothers (Delia) from bad (Elise, the hapless bystander), and to strengthen Delia's sense of identity as her father's daughter. In the novel's conclusion, Delia asks her father why he abducted her if he did not know she was being abused. "Because," he says simply, "you asked" (418). Delia is thus made the *agent* of her own abduction; this is reaffirmed by her lawyer, who asks in court, "What if, to Delia, the kidnapping wasn't something frightening? What if she considered it a relief, a way out from the sexual abuse?" (406). Andrew is thus absolved not only in motive but in responsibility for the crime of child abduction because his young daughter desired it. The frightening narrative of child abduction is neutralized by Picoult's reframing of Delia not as victim, but as empowered agent who has exchanged one parent for another and achieved the ever-elusive "balance."

The "what-if" questions that are posed by Delia's lawyer in court exemplify Picoult's ethics of speculation. *Perfect Match* is similarly overlaid with ruminations on the morality and legality of Nina's act of murder. "What good is the legal process if people can decide their motives are bigger than the law? If you remove one brick from the foundation, how long before the whole system tumbles down?" the heroine muses (287). During closing arguments, Nina similarly addresses the jury. "What if your best friend was being held at gunpoint, and you had a revolver in your own hand? What would you do?" she asks. "What if you came home and found your wife being raped? Where is the line?" (328).

These novels demonstrate the centrality of indeterminacy to Jodi Picoult's aesthetic. Critical praise for Picoult typically underscores her work's open-endedness. The *St. Louis Post-Dispatch* is featured on a back-cover blurb noting that "Jodi Picoult's books explore all the shades of gray in a world too often judged in black and white." She has affirmed in an interview that "I'm not going to tell a person how to think, don't believe in that. What I want to do, when I write these books, is just to say don't be so sure of yourself. Let me pull the carpet out from underneath you, and let's see if you can still find the footing" (Picoult, "Jodi Picoult"). Indeed, Picoult writes in the author question-and-answer segment attached to the paperback edition of *Perfect Match* that her book's "overarching message" is that "we shouldn't rush to judgment. . . . I can't tell you I would do what Nina did in her situation . . . but I can't tell you I wouldn't, either" (n.p.).

Picoult's interest in creating indeterminate stories poses a conundrum for readers. Her desire for readers to carefully consider all sides and come to their own particular solutions to moral dilemmas is well-intentioned and inclusive. By writing open-ended narratives, she promotes ongoing conversation *with* her readers through various media platforms, including her author website and Twitter. On the other hand, it recalls choice feminism, which, as Michaele Ferguson argues, "evinces a fear of politics" and simply "aims to avoid having to make judgments, to avoid taking controversial stands that might offend and exclude, and to de-radicalize feminist claims" (248).

Picoult's 2006 novel *The Tenth Circle* revisits her interest in exploring ethical indeterminacy through narratives of sexually violent trauma. The plot, in baldest form, revolves around a teenaged girl's rape and her family's subsequent ungluing. In *The Tenth Circle*, Picoult explores the contours of an emerging postfeminist discourse about coerced sex, or *gray rape* as it is colloquially named. Multiple and competing narratives of what actually happened to the teenaged victim Trixie are presented, but no resolution occurs; in this case, the author's openness seems far more problematic. In fact, in a digressive move that recalls Alice Sebold's *The Lovely Bones*, the narrative shifts from Trixie's circumstances to those of her father, Daniel, who struggles to contain his avenging desires. In the novel's opening, Picoult writes that "Trixie Stone had been a ghost for fourteen days, seven hours, and thirty-six minutes now, not that she was officially counting" (20). With her story blunted by her father's revenge narrative, Trixie does indeed become a kind of inaccessible phantom to readers.

The Tenth Circle begins with an anecdote testifying, as most Jodi Picoult novels do, to the intense bond between parent and child. In this case the parent is Daniel, a stay-at-home father who is the pinnacle of domesticity. Daniel "never forgot to put out the recycling bin; he set the coffee to brew the night before because [wife Laura] was a bear when she didn't have any in the morning; he never once complained about the fact that it had taken a good decade longer than he'd liked to make a name for himself in the comics industry because he was the stay-at-home parent" (37).

When Trixie confesses to her father that her ex-boyfriend Jason raped her at a party, Daniel reacts violently. In a "tornado of pure fury, Daniel had grabbed the first thing he could lay hold of—a soap dish—and hurled it into the bathroom mirror. Trixie had started shrieking, shaking so hard it took him five minutes to calm her down" (60). In the emergency room, "he balled his hand into a fist and struck it against the cinder-block wall. He pummeled the cement again and again . . . until he knew Trixie wasn't the only one hurting" (67). Picoult constructs Daniel's explosions of violence to parallel the Dante-inspired comic he is drawing, "The Tenth Circle," in which a protagonist literally battles his "beast within" in order to slay demons and rescue his maiden daughter. The novel quickly becomes a vengeance narrative featuring masculine retribution. Daniel acts as a sympathetic male avenger; Lisa Cuklanz has described this archetype as a man who brings an "enlightened and sensitive approach to rape" to the screen, but takes so much textual space that he re-centers masculinity, "marginalizing rape victims and other women in the process" (63).[7]

Rape serves as a plot device for the protagonist to uncork "legitimate" vengeance, but this is not its only novelistic function. "I have always said that I write books about questions that don't have easy answers," Picoult says in the reader's guide to *The Tenth Circle*. "I don't think I have any right to tell a reader what's the 'right way' to think. To this end it's really important to me to put all the different points of view of a situation into a book" (n.p.). To her credit, Picoult goes beyond using sexual assault as simply the "issue of the day" for the multiple-perspective discussion format that she favors. She grapples with Trixie's conflicting feelings about what happened to her, and she pays particular attention to the experience of nonconsenting women who may not have verbalized "no." Her exploration of nuance is not without its problems, though; she depicts teenaged female sexuality as an inevitable, combustible force (much the same way that male violence is apparently naturalized), and she privileges the father Daniel's interpretations of Trixie's sexual assault.

The Tenth Circle does not directly narrate the party sequence between Trixie and her ex-boyfriend Jason. However, the incident is initially depicted as a sexual assault. "Daddy, he raped me," Trixie tells her father (55). Furthermore, Picoult depicts the emergency-room pelvic exam as a direct rewriting of the rape. Trixie is "completely, violently aware of who she was and what had been done to her. There was cold steel, and a rasp of flesh. A push from the outside, as her body struggled to keep the speculum out . . . she was being held down at the thighs and then there was pain and force and *you are breaking me in two*" (71; emphasis in original). The rhetorical slippage to direct address within the final sentence is particularly striking, broadcasting pain directly in this novel that, unlike the vast majority of Picoult's work, has no first-person narrator. A medical professional lends weight to the credence of Trixie's claim as well, telling the police detective that "I've been an ER OB/GYN for fifteen years, Detective, and I have yet to see the woman who'd be willing to suffer through a sexual assault exam just for the hell of it" (141).

Yet as with most social-issue novels written by Jodi Picoult, information is being withheld from the initial narrative. As time passes, Trixie is shown to have provided untruthful statements about the loss of her virginity and about self-inflicted wounds (cutting) that she claimed were marks from Jason's weapon. Additionally, Jason's perspective is introduced; he wonders "what the hell Trixie was trying to pull. They had been going at it, full force—*consensual* . . . if that was how she communicated no, then it was a foreign language Jason had never learned" (93). To her credit, Picoult also calls Jason's own credibility into question, suggesting that the "go out and take it" mind-set he learns in athletics blurs into aggressive sexual behavior (200). However, Picoult also flirts with victim-blaming by emphasizing the combustibility of teenaged female sexuality, mostly through the portrayal of Trixie's best friend Zephyr, a crudely drawn caricature of sex-positive feminism. Zephyr chains pink paper clips to keep track of her sexual conquests and tosses off lines like "a guy can't hurt you if you don't let him" (29). She is fond of sexually explicit party games like "Rainbow" (a supposed group oral-sex game that is widely considered today to have been a moral panic of the early 2000s).[8] Picoult describes the case detective looking at Zephyr in her "stretch button-down shirt and stacked heels, her eye makeup, her scarlet nail polish" and thinking "*This is exactly the problem*" (132). Picoult's end-of-book author interview for *The Tenth Circle* spotlights her take on wanton teen promiscuity: "Instead of relationships, kids have random hookups, or friends with benefits—sexual experiences that the next day they pretend never happened. Oral sex isn't considered sex. At parties, you'll see games like Stoneface and Rainbow. . . . When I've gone to speak to high schools to speak to students and I mention this research, the looks I get from the student audience are priceless—their jaws drop, because (a) I know about it and (b) I'm brave enough to tell them I know" (n.p.).

Faced with a portrayal of aggressive teenaged female sexuality that apparently can confuse or overwhelm male peers, readers must look to Trixie's own articulation of her experience. Yet her memories layer and blur, often conflicting in their interpretations. Initially she tells the lawyer that "it all goes blank . . . I can't remember anything, really, until he was on top of me" (193). The subsequent revelation that Trixie was drugged with ketamine increases the legal sanctions against Jason—but in another twist, it is shown that Trixie bought the drugs *herself* in order to get high. "She couldn't say for a fact that Jason had slipped it into her drink . . . it was possible that Jason had had nothing to do with it at all," Trixie admits (373). Finally, Trixie reflects of the night in question that "it was all mixed up now . . . she couldn't entangle what she'd wanted from what she didn't" (258). Although earlier she had claimed no memory of the assault, now she tells Daniel that Jason "said, 'Don't tell me you don't want this.' And I . . . I didn't" (371).

To Trixie, what is most confusing is the gap between her bodily experience of nonconsent and her failure to verbalize nonconsent. She muses:

> *No* and *know* sounded the same. You were supposed to be able to say the magic word, and that was enough to make your wishes—or lack of them—crystal clear. But no one ever said *yes* to make the sex consensual. You took hints from body language, from the way two people came together. Why, then, didn't a shake of the head or a hand pushing hard against a chest speak just as loudly? Why did you have to actually say the word *no* for it to be rape? (373)

Trixie does not use gendered pronouns in her meditation, but the gendered rules of sexual contact she describes are easy to ascertain. Boys initiate and girls serve as the sexual gatekeepers. A lack of pushback, as opposed to an enthusiastic affirmation, is taken as a sign to continue, because it is not culturally expected or desired for girls to say yes to sexual experience. Trixie understands that her resistant body language might not meet the legal standard of saying no, but she points out that the body has its own intimate codes that Jason, given their previous closeness, ought to have understood and respected.

Trixie's experience engages the question of *gray rape*, a controversial term first identified in a 2007 *Cosmopolitan* article by Laura Sessions Stepp as "sex that falls somewhere between consent and denial and is even more confusing than date rape because often both parties are unsure of who wanted what" ("New Kind of Date Rape"). Stepp lays the blame for gray rape at the feet of "today's hookup culture," which depends on "lots of partying and flirting, plenty of alcohol, and ironically, the idea that women can be just as bold and adventurous about sex as men are." Feminist pushback against the concept of gray rape as Stepp describes it has been pronounced. Tracy Clark-Flory, for instance, writes that Stepp "manipulates women's stories of being raped while incapable of giving consent to fit her own agenda—in other words, to slyly make an argument against casual sex and women's sexual aggression" ("'Gray Rape' Myth"). Others view the concept of gray rape *itself* as diluting the impact of sexual assault in the public consciousness. Jessica Valenti forcefully argues that "the reason we have qualifiers—legitimate, forcible, date, gray—is because at the end of the day it's not enough to say 'rape.' We don't believe it on its own and we want to know what 'kind' of assault it was in order to make a value judgment about what really happened—and to believe that it couldn't happen to us" ("Ending Rape Illiteracy").

Conversely, Linda Martín Alcoff suggests that exploring gradation and ambiguity in sexual violence is fruitful because feminist theory does not have enough languages to discuss such traumas. Alcoff writes that "in order to begin to bring forward the experiences of sexual violence as victims experience them, we will need to allow for variable, even uncertain and ambiguous, formulations, and judgments that may not rise to the level of courtroom adjudication of guilt. If we want to listen to survivors, we will need to prepare ourselves to hear about the gray areas" ("Dear Congressman Akin"). A straightforward "rape is rape" paradigm, such as was verbally expressed by President Obama in response to 2012 senatorial candidate Todd Akin's suggestion that only certain rapes should be considered "legitimate," may dissuade people who are unsure of how to characterize their experiences or who need time and memory to process them.[9]

Shades of gray are precisely the colors that interest Jodi Picoult. *The Tenth Circle* explores nuance in the way Alcoff is suggesting—most particularly in its contention that a bodily language can "speak" a truth that is not necessarily legally admissible. Here again, though, Picoult detours her own argument by abruptly switching to Daniel's narrative, as he returns to his native Alaska to find Trixie, who has run away. Daniel, who was raised by the Yup'ik in Alaska, invokes the beliefs of his upbringing to articulate Trixie's experience. "In [Alaska], people believed that a thought might turn into an action at any moment; a word held in your mind had just as much power to wound or to heal as the one that was spoken aloud," Daniel muses. "In this part of the world, it didn't matter what Trixie had or had not said: What Jason Underhill had done to Trixie *did* count as rape" (377). In her author's afterword, Picoult emphasizes that "just because a word isn't said out loud doesn't mean its intention isn't received. . . . To a Yup'ik Eskimo, then, silence is an act. Words are a weapon. Imagine, then, a case of date rape. Legally it always comes down to whether or not the girl said no. *But to someone who'd grown up among the Yup'ik Eskimos—like Daniel Stone—it wouldn't have mattered if Trixie said it . . . or merely thought it*" (n.p.; emphasis added). Seguing to Inuit perspectives in the novel's conclusion destabilizes the white and Western construction of justice, and Daniel's belief in his daughter is admirable. What is problematic is the novel's determination to return narrative control and the framing of the sexual assault to the father's perspective.

The Tenth Circle reflects Jodi Picoult's investment in indeterminacy. An act of sexual violence against a girl is nested in layers of multiple perspective and interpretation. Readers wade carefully through the bulky narrative, surrounded by passages of specialized knowledge on the Yup'ik cultural practices. By blanketing the main narrative in digressive material and by framing events through multiple viewpoints, Picoult risks blunting her story's traumatic impact. She also chances settling for a kind of moral relativism, a point further developed in one of her most famous novels to date, 2007's *Nineteen Minutes*. In this narrative of a teenaged school shooter and his childhood friend, Picoult raises and smooths over distinctions in gendered violence for her readers.

"You're Strangers Now": The Spectacle of Boy/Girl Violence in *Nineteen Minutes*

In *Nineteen Minutes*, midwife Lacy Houghton, mother to a teenaged killer, has an unsettling message for new parents. "This child you've been waiting for is not who you imagine him to be," she thinks. "You're strangers now; you'll be strangers years from now" (246). *Nineteen Minutes* is one of many dramatizations of school shootings. In the wake of multiple real-life tragedies in the 1990s and 2000s, most notably at Colorado's Columbine High School (1999), such literature has proliferated. Lionel Shriver's acclaimed novel *We*

Need to Talk about Kevin (2003), a mother's account of her murderous son, won the Orange Prize and was adapted as a 2011 feature film. Shriver's protagonist Eva, as Jen Webb reflects, receives "deepest satisfaction . . . in equal parts from her professional engagements and from her sexual relationship with [husband] Franklin, rather than motherhood and domesticity" (134). Through Eva's unreliable narration, readers must decide whether Kevin is a monstrous "bad seed" in a loving family or the product of poor parenting by a distracted mother. *Nineteen Minutes*'s Lacy Houghton, by contrast, epitomizes care-intensive maternity, which makes her son's evil actions all the more devastating. "How could you change a boy's bedding every week and feed him breakfast and drive him to the orthodontist and not know him at all?" Lacy wonders brokenly (59).

Picoult devotes some attention to Lacy's narrative and its attendant fears of raising a monster, but she is far more interested in exploring the teenaged characters' experiences of violence. She rescripts the Columbine narrative to include a second, *female* shooter whose involvement is revealed in the novel's conclusion. In so doing, she borrows a traditionally masculine story of explosive, violent aggression in order to draw attention to the less spectacular, more internally focused narrative of Girl Crisis. Picoult suggests that female pain can also be so unbearable that it would express itself in homicidal anger. She also adapts the popular narrative of bullying (the contention that the Columbine gunmen were bullied has been largely debunked in recent years) in order to explore the gendered norms of victimization.

Picoult's genuine interest in exploring issues of homophobia and sexism exists side by side with her authorial worldview, which stresses nonjudgment, interconnectedness, and cultural relativism. Every choice and every perspective that she presents becomes equally important, and thus equally indistinct. As Lacy Houghton, the gunman's mother, observes, "Isn't it amazing how, when you strip away everything, people are so much alike?" (32). This all-embracing ethos expresses itself in the narratives of Picoult's novels and also in her embellished prose, which is heavy on metaphor and the use of the second person. Her impulse to stress human belonging over the consequences of gender violence is problematic because, as we have seen, women consistently get left behind in her narratives. In *Nineteen Minutes,* Josie's story comes to its violent, hasty conclusion and is tossed aside. It seems that her story can only be told *in terms of someone else*—in this case, Peter—and so in Picoult's rush to be everywhere at once, these interesting and recurring arcs of female self-abnegation and depression fall through the cracks.

It should first be established that Picoult's novel *is* a deliberate rewriting of Columbine. Her trademark scrupulous research is on display in the novel, and the characters' actions largely mirror what is known about the actual crime. Like the real-life killers, Peter Houghton targets the cafeteria and library of the high school. In another parallel, Peter's plot is nearly discovered when a gun-shop employee calls his house to confirm an ammunition order and his father intercepts the call. Picoult also musters other facts in the public record, including the suicide by gunshot of a victim's parent. The biggest distinction in her fictionalization is, of course, that she writes about a *single* killer, as opposed to Columbine's deadly duo. However, even this fact is rescripted late in the novel, when Josie Cormier emerges as a second shooter. The finale is in some ways a surprise, but in others it is not, for the downtrodden boy Peter and the popular girl Josie have been twinned from the very first pages.

Nineteen Minutes opens with a vengeful handwritten note. "By the time you read this, I hope to be dead," the narrator begins. "I guess I should tell you, 'Don't blame yourself: this isn't your fault,' but that would be a lie. We both know that I didn't get here by myself." Similar missives recur throughout the novel—seven in all—and their narrator and audience are ambiguous. At certain points they seem to reference the world of Peter, the shooter. Yet at other times their phrasing and content appears to come from his childhood friend, the popular Josie. Josie, too, is suicidal, and the antagonism displayed in the first note seems to better fit her fraught relationship to her mother (Peter, by contrast, gets along well with his parents). Janet Maslin's review of the novel recognizes this narrative opacity. "Who wrote the journal entry about schadenfreude?" she asks. "Maybe Peter, maybe not; it doesn't sound like him . . . there are a lot of women in 'Nineteen Minutes,' and both the book's masculine and feminine voices favor womanly turns of phrase" ("After the Shooting Is Over"). Maslin's comment reveals the degree to which Picoult has deliberately established a hybrid voice—Josie/Peter—to equate the experiences of these characters.

As the plot unfolds, we learn that Josie and Peter were childhood best friends and the children of mothers who are themselves best friends. In a flashback, the two youngsters show off the house they have built together and declare themselves "married." Josie's mother Alex wistfully watches "Peter curl up on his side, Josie spooned against him, wrapping her arm around his waist" (78). Josie protects frail Peter from bullies, and their loyalty holds through middle school, until Josie's beauty draws her into the orbit of popular kids.

In high school their paths diverge. "What does it feel like? . . . Being at the top?" Peter asks Josie at one point. "Like if you take one wrong step, you're going to fall," she replies (205). Yet despite their different high school positions, both teens display misery. Peter considers killing himself with a gun; Josie ponders taking a cocktail of Ambien and vodka. He despises himself for his lack of social status, whereas she hates her own popularity, perceiving herself as a fraud. Josie verbalizes their cross-identification in the novel's ending, when she tells her mother that "the rest of us are all like Peter. Some of us just do a better job of hiding it" (447).

In *Nineteen Minutes*, then, both the male social outcast and the female queen bee respond to the alienation that they feel with violence. The Columbine narrative has been invoked in many American cultural contexts, sparking conversations about terrorism, bullying, teenaged mental health, violent video games, and more. But as several critics have pointed out, *gender* analysis has been strangely absent in the popular press. "Indeed, whenever there have been school shootings over the past decade there is rarely a discussion of the role of the social construction of masculinity and gun culture in the shooting, and rarely do headlines describe the shooters as 'boys' or 'males,' usually preferring gender-neutral descriptions," comments Douglas Kellner (121). Karla Mantilla also notes the way that boys seem to "lose gender" when they commit violence. "There have been articles in newspapers and discussions on TV earnestly searching for the reasons why *children* kill and wondering what the real cause could be of the increase in such crimes by *children*," she says. "There is very little hope of discovering the answer if we ignore the most salient aspect of these young killers—their gender" ("Child Violence" 5). Michael Kimmel, too, urges us to pay attention to the way gender and race often disappear from analyses of these shootings. "Can you picture the national debate, the headlines, the handwringing," he asks, if rampage shooters "were black girls? The entire focus would be on race, class, and gender. The media would doubtless invent a new term for their behavior, as with wilding two decades ago. We'd hear about the culture of poverty. . . . Someone would likely even blame feminism for causing girls to become violent in a vain imitation of boys" (73).

The cultural erasure of gender in eruptions of school violence is in keeping with the framework of postfeminism. It should be noted, though, that Picoult *does* explore gender's relationship to violence, analyzing how toxic norms of masculinity destroy Peter Houghton's peace. She illustrates how masculinity and femininity can occupy what Carine Mardorossian deems "structural positions rather than biologically derived ones," and how they are driven by positions of domination and submission (*Framing the Rape Victim* 3). Readers see that the slightly built Peter is bullied, even by his own brother, because he expressively cares for his family, friends, and pets. At one point his mother Lacy remarks that she had "always considered herself lucky to have somehow received a child who was not the cookie-cutter American boy, one who was sensitive and emotional and so in tune with what others thought and felt" (197). In the lexicon of high school masculinity, these qualities are deficits, and earn Peter antigay slurs. Two precipitating incidents before the shooting assault Peter's masculinity. His e-mailed love note to Josie is intercepted by another student and broadcast throughout the school as a joke; later, Josie's boyfriend Matt strips him in the cafeteria, publicly exposing his genitals. It is no surprise that Peter's lawyer adapts a former client's defense—battered woman's syndrome—and turns it into *bullied victim*'s syndrome (this is another instance of how Picoult generalizes formerly gendered conditions). To be feminized and to be victimized is apparently one and the same, and this sentiment is echoed in her portrayal of Josie.

The depressed, self-hating teenaged girl is a common archetype in Jodi Picoult's fiction. Prior iterations include *The Tenth Circle*'s Trixie Stone; *Salem Falls*'s (2001) Gillian Duncan, who lies about being sexually assaulted by a teacher to deflect attention from an incestuous father; and *The Pact*'s (1998) Emily Gold, so depressed after an unplanned pregnancy that she shoots herself. Female teens in Picoult's canon also display alarming levels of nihilism and self-directed violence, including cutting and disordered eating. Such figures seem to come straight out of the 1990s "Girl Crisis" narrative, discussed previously in the context of the dead-teen-girl subset of young-adult fiction. Most identified with the work of psychologist Mary Pipher in the book *Reviving Ophelia*, Girl Crisis describes a widespread collapse of confidence in adolescent girls that manifests itself in harmful behaviors.

Josie's story meets the check marks of Girl Crisis. Though she is popular, she is wracked with self-doubt and perceives her social status to be undeserved. "She knew what [boyfriend] Matt saw when he looked at her . . . she just wished she could see it too. The problem was, when Josie looked in the mirror, she noticed what was underneath that raw skin, instead of what had been painted upon it," we learn (8). "If she appeared the same on the outside, it was that much easier to ignore the fact that she didn't really know how she felt on the inside" (17). Hearing the chemistry term *sublimation* makes Josie "afraid she's going to simply vanish"—she thinks of her existence as "a line in the sand" that could be washed away at any point (211).

Like her social doppelgänger Peter, Josie too is bullied. Her older and emotionally manipulative boyfriend Matt coerces Josie into undesired and unprotected sex, and he increasingly controls all aspects of her existence.

Slamming her against a wall after she refuses to leave a party, Matt calls her a slut and a "fucking whore" for talking to another boy, and subsequently threatens to kill himself if she breaks up with him (583). Josie's narrative of violence is not publicly spectacular, as is Peter's. Like most cases of domestic abuse, it unfolds silently as Josie frantically keeps up appearances.

Whereas the typical narrative of Girl Crisis involves despair and, optimally, therapeutic recovery, Josie's story ends in unexpected and suddenly revealed violence. On the stand, Josie testifies that she grabbed one of Peter's guns and shot Matt in the stomach; subsequently, Peter shot him in the head. In the buildup to the murder, Matt's toxic masculine rage assaults both killers: "Josie, for Christ's sake! Are you fucking stupid?" he says, and to Peter, "Shut up, asshole . . . You think she's going to save you?" (440). The identification between the two killers is further emphasized by their childlike conversation—"Don't tell," Peter whispers—and their shared memory of a nursery rhyme.

There are many startling observations about women's violence contained in this scene—for example, what does it mean that Josie needs Peter to help her kill Matt?—but more compelling are the unresolved issues. Since the revelation of Josie's act is saved for the last-minute "twist," there is no space to analyze the gendered conditions that brought her to lash out at Matt. All she will tell her mother is that "I loved Matt. And I hated him" (446). Most troubling is Josie's realization, looking at Peter's murderous rampage, that "she knew exactly what he'd felt as he moved through the school with his backpack and his guns. Every kid in this school played a role: jock, brain, beauty, freak. All Peter had done was what they all secretly dreamed of: be someone, even for just nineteen minutes, who *nobody else was allowed to judge*" (440–41; emphasis added).

What is particularly vexing about the recurring theme of nonjudgment in this novel is that to invoke the word *Columbine* during the past decade-plus has meant to engage in rather judgmental debates about entertainment and youth violence, school bullying, and other flashpoints. But within the frame of Picoult's novel, all attempts at judgment or meaningful distinction between views are collapsed. This lesson is carried out not only through the story of Josie and Peter, but also by Josie's mother, Judge Alex Cormier. Depicted as yet another unfeeling, masculinized lawyer-mother who believed that "everything could be distilled into facts," Alex learns to embrace more traditionally feminine paradigms of listening, nonjudging, and accepting in the wake of the shooting (169). Alex reflects in the novel's conclusion that a job description is not enough to define herself, or anyone. "Nobody ever asked you who you really were, because that changed," she muses. "You might be a judge or a mother or a dreamer. You might be a loner or a visionary or a pessimist. You might be the victim, and you might be the bully. You could be the parent, and also the child. You might wound one day and heal the next" (447).

Picoult here pushes her sentences outward, moving from the omniscient narrator to the second person. The rhythmic repetition of *you* is more than just Alex's free indirect discourse; it is asking, in intimate address to the reader, for sympathy and imaginative exchange. *Nineteen Minutes* itself is a series of sympathetic exchanges. Josie's experience of sexual and domestic violence is like Peter's experience of bullying, which is itself like Columbine, and so on. One effect of these linkages is to raise the visibility of victims like Josie, but another is to flatten its distinctions under a bland assurance that everyone's experiences are similar and equally valid.

Conclusion

In the 2011 novel *Sing You Home*, music therapist Zoe apologizes to her miscarried fetus for "not being able to keep you safe inside me for a few more weeks" (43). Jodi Picoult's world, like those of the other authors working in postfeminist gothic, is one where we are born into risk and pain. Christopher Wilson writes that in contemporary America, it is "always necessary that the pain of the crime victim be opened up, so that it may be appropriated into an ever-vigilant, populist, and sleepless state" (157). Like a literary version of the iconic "security mom," Picoult keeps readers awake at night through her repeated narratives of violated children. She has told Ginia Bellafante that her fascination with this narrative is an attempt to ward off maternal harm. "There is a part of me that believes that if I think about these issues, if I put myself through the emotional wringer, I somehow develop an immunity for my own family. . . . I realize that this kind of thinking is completely ridiculous," she admits ("Jodi Picoult and the Anxious Parent").

Picoult's novels employ hedging strategies that blunt and contain the traumas perpetrated upon her characters. By suffusing traumatic narratives in other stories and other narrators, she often eschews direct confrontations with acts of misogyny. There is no significant discussion, for instance, of what it means for a priest—Father Gwynne—to have raped little Nathaniel in *Perfect Match*. Andrew Hopkins's kidnapping of his daughter Delia is neatly justified in retrospect, and Trixie's experience of rape is sublimated in favor of the spectacular rage and redemption of her father in *The Tenth Circle*. Peter

Houghton's school rampage in *Nineteen Minutes*, which is catalyzed by the persistent homophobia and feminization he endures, is similarly diluted by the narrative's gothic twinning of his character with Josie Cormier. Instead, Picoult maintains faith in the individual's power to overcome horrific traumas and to balance the scales. Her novels conclude happily; in *Perfect Match*, for instance, little Nathaniel tells readers that "I'm going to be okay after all" (352). Individuals do indeed triumph over horrendous circumstances in Picoult's work, but the price to pay for that satisfaction is a willed not-seeing of the larger darkness around them.

Jodi Picoult's digressions represent one response to the ongoing danger of living in a world drenched in sexualized violence. We have seen other lines of flight within the postfeminist gothic. Alice Sebold's *The Lovely Bones* drains outrage over the rape and murder of its main character in narrative arcs as circular as the culs-de-sac that populate Susie Salmon's neighborhood. The young-adult novels following in Susie Salmon's path demonstrate a disturbingly hopeful yearning to remove young heroines from this world and to imagine death as a space of self-re-creation. The exodus of medical examiner Kay Scarpetta to a world of computerized electronics symbolizes another such pathway. Conversely, some postfeminist gothic authors prefer to move headlong toward the threats denied by postfeminism. Sapphire cracks language apart, moving Precious from the barrage of obscenities that define and limit her toward a path where she is written into visibility. Susanna Moore, for her part, gazes at the abyss, repeatedly returning to the unpopular topic of women's physical vulnerability and creating words that whistle like a blade through the air.

Whichever orientation they choose, these gothic novelists are united in troubling the glassy surface of postfeminism. While these literary eruptions might be metaphorical, in recent years the world has also borne witness to the *literal* emergence of female survivors held captive for years. Their memoirs and testimony, coupled with the voices of novelists who reimagined their captive worlds, are joined to provide the final chapter in this story so far.

7

Up from the Basement

Postfeminist Gothic's Captive Imagination

Within the pages of Susanna Moore's novel *In the Cut*, Frannie's student Cornelius asks her why "chicks act the way they do, you know, like captives, 'cause they be scared of male violence?" (32). The theme of captivity resonates throughout the postfeminist gothic. Moore's novel, for instance, details how Frannie's life is circumscribed like that of an inmate in the face of misogynistic threat. Her fears are indeed ultimately realized, and she exits the story as a captive who is bound and tortured to death. Alice Sebold's protagonist Susie Salmon is murdered in a subterranean hole after being kidnapped by her homicidal neighbor. Sapphire's Precious Jones is metaphorically and often literally entombed in her cramped apartment, subject to abuse by both parents. Patricia Cornwell's bloody imagination, meanwhile, frequently conjures up extended captivity scenes, read postmortem by Kay Scarpetta. Within the female gothic more broadly, imprisonment is also an important theme; works as diverse as Ann Radcliffe's *The Romance of the Forest* (1791), Charlotte Perkins Gilman's *The Yellow Wall-paper* (1892), and Daphne du Maurier's *Jamaica Inn* (1936) have all interrogated the captive's fate.

Threats of confinement are frightening for anyone to imagine, but for women, captivity has specifically gendered resonance. Most significantly, untold numbers of enslaved black women, considered chattel, fueled the American slave economy through their reproductive and economic labor. The powerful ideology of domesticity, consigning unknown numbers of women to the boundaries of the home, was often portrayed as a kind of captivity; the portrait of the homemaker as hostage was detailed most famously in Betty Friedan's *The Feminine Mystique* (1963). In the twenty-first century, the threat of *literal* captivity had been viewed as more of a horror trope than a national anxiety until a remarkable cluster of kidnap-recovery cases compelled public attention. In 2002, domestic news media was dominated by the case of Elizabeth Smart, who was taken from bed, forcibly "married" to a religious fundamentalist, and confined for nine months. Abroad, Austria was the site of two notorious cases of long-term domestic imprisonment. In 2006, schoolgirl Natascha Kampusch escaped from eight years in a cellar at the hands of a stranger. Two years later, the world learned of Elisabeth Fritzl, a woman who had endured twenty-four years in a basement as her own father's prisoner. Back on American shores, 2009 saw the discovery of Jaycee Dugard, a former missing child held captive for nearly two decades by a pedophile. In May 2013, in an otherwise unremarkable Cleveland dwelling, three women emerged from a near decade as hostages. Held in close quarters, forcibly restrained, beaten, and repeatedly raped, the survivors, one of whom had borne a daughter to her captor, were instantly splashed across magazines and featured on news programs. Although the Cleveland women are perhaps the most spectacular case in recent history, they are not even the most current; the 2014 return of Abigail Hernandez, aged fourteen when she was abducted for nine months, portends the grim continuation of such crimes. The trauma suffered by these girls and women strains ordinary human belief; rarely has our culture seen such stark examples of human brutality. They serve as powerful reminders that the gothic is not merely dreamscapes and visions. For some women, the nightmare world exists when the dawn breaks, too.[1]

This project concludes by investigating how postfeminist gothic confronts the wounds of female captivity. The accounts of three survivors—Elizabeth Smart, Jaycee Dugard, and Michelle Knight—are explored alongside multiple mass-market novels that have adapted similar premises. Memoir and fiction are blended in this chapter because postfeminist gothic works, while not strictly mimetic, are informed by real-life conditions. Susanna Moore's adaptation of Sylvia Likens's torture in *The Big Girls*, Jodi Picoult's reimagining of Ellie Nesler's vengeance in *Perfect Match*, Sapphire's amalgamation of incest-victim testimonies in *Push*, and Alice Sebold's adaptation of her own rape and beating illustrate how actual events of gendered violence provide context for this particular genre.

Captivity survivors literalize the concept of "women's liberation," demonstrating courage and determination. Having endured the most lurid forms of sexual and physical debasement and returned to tell about it, ex-captives also contribute to the iconography of postfeminist gothic. Many of the heroines studied in this book, including Precious Jones, Frannie, and Susie Salmon, die in their narrative worlds. Others, like Kay Scarpetta and Mamie Clark, live on in a compromised, anaesthetized fog. The circulation of negative affects, we have seen, is a useful way for postfeminist gothic stories to remind audiences of the terror and inequity of violence. Former captives unsettle the glossy postfeminist surface in different ways. Their returns disturb the representational sign of the missing young (white) woman, a figure often abstracted for political ends and compressed into an easy sainthood. As women who have returned from experiences of horror, former captives also alter scripts about whose disappearance matters in America. Ultimately, their works reaffirm what postfeminist gothic *can do*, reifying and analyzing gendered violence against women through the prism of a victim-skeptical, "empowerment"-focused age.

Part of the "writing back" performed by former captives involves disrupting the pervasive *aestheticizing* of captivity found throughout popular culture. In literary genres as diverse as the romance and the thriller, the idea of captivity as either an erotic bonding experience or a form of literal objectification abounds. At the core of these works, which range from innocuous to sadistic, is the claim that captivity tempers a modern life where women have been granted "too much" freedom. The neo-captivity genre, by contrast (I use the descriptor *neo-captivity* to distinguish it from *colonial captivity narrative*, a well-known literary genre), emphatically rejects nostalgia about bondage. Each book straightforwardly documents the painful, ugly ideology at the heart of captivity: the conviction that women and girls are made to be used as sexual and reproductive receptacles. Neo-captivity works provide a powerful critique of patriarchal privilege while also engaging in a project of empathy building that insists on a society more attuned to domestic distress. Calling on imagery of literal and metaphorical trapped spaces like basements and backyards, captivity authors make the unsettling assertion that their individual traumas are merely the tip of a proverbial iceberg. They claim broader community with other victims of gendered violence yet unseen and unheard.

The umbrella of *captivity narrative* under which these stories fall is exceedingly broad. Throughout history and in almost every culture, people have recounted their experiences of being held against their will. The testimonies of African American slaves are part of the legacy of captivity literature, as are the memoirs of British men and women captured by Barbary Coast pirates in the seventeenth century. Pauline Turner Strong points out that many "anonymous Indian captives abducted as tokens of otherness, objects of knowledge, and instruments of conquest" belong in this tradition too, although they are rarely acknowledged (202). In literary history, the term *captivity narrative* is most associated with the genre of white colonial American women's accounts of their trials as political prisoners of Native American tribes. The most famous example belongs to Mary Rowlandson, a Massachusetts settler who was held for eleven weeks during King Philip's War in 1675. Rowlandson recounted her physical trials, which included searing hunger and general ill-treatment, as well as her profound emotional anguish over her young daughter's death. Her narrative, which was prefaced by an anonymous male editor generally credited as Puritan minister Increase Mather, appeared in 1682 and remained in wide circulation for generations. Rowlandson's tale has become, as Gordon Sayre writes, "a model that later texts imitated and the foundation of a myth that transcends literature, reaching deep into Anglo-America's history and psyche" (127).

Blending scripture and personal lamentation, Mary Rowlandson's story is an instructional tale of trials overcome with God's help. Andrea Tinnemeyer reminds us of its religious function; for Puritan audiences, "reading a captivity narrative made the reader a surrogate to the same trials and tribulations and reinforced religious conviction for those among the flock who were straying or backsliding" (xii). Scholars of the genre generally do not think that Rowlandson was sexually abused in captivity; she at one point obliquely alludes to her captors never having "offered me the least abuse of unchastity to me, in word or action" (172).[2] However, the kidnapping of white women like Rowlandson by Native men certainly served as ideological tinder for the fires of nation-burning. Manifest destiny claims, Christopher Castiglia reminds us, have "relied for dramatic tension on the threatened sexualization of white women by men of color who possess uncontrollable, violent, and animalistic lusts" (123). Increase Mather used such agitprop when he shaped Rowlandson's text in order to, in Tiffany Potter's words, "ventriloquize his own political agenda against the Indians and in favor of passive feminine purity" (164).[3]

While acknowledging the very real suffering that Rowlandson underwent, many literary critics have also theorized the captivity narrative as a hybrid space where the captive becomes receptive to new forms of cultural exchange, and perhaps even reassesses her own culture. Potter, for instance, remarks on Rowlandson's keen anthropological gaze, particularly as she documents Native American women. Tara Fitzpatrick contends that Rowlandson comes to a "grudging but undeniable recognition of the suffering she shares with her captors," making her narrative an "intersection in the contest of cultures" (12). Furthermore, Rowlandson's itinerancy (she was not restrained and often wandered from lodging to lodging, bartering with individual tribe members) contrasts with what Christopher Castiglia deems the "subordinating, infantilizing, and immobilizing gender ideologies of white America" to which she and other captives returned (10). Colonial captivity narratives' bracing possibilities of cultural exchange and wilderness adventure, however, are almost entirely absent from the confining, claustrophobic worlds of contemporary neo-captivity.

Political context is another key distinction between colonial captivity narratives like that of Mary Rowlandson and twenty-first-century texts. Many, though certainly not all, colonial captives had some exchange value. Rowlandson, for instance, was a minister's wife of significant status in her New England community; her ransom was assumed. Michelle Burnham writes that "with the eventual exchange of Mary Rowlandson for twenty pounds, her suspended cultural identity and liminal subjectivity appear resolved; she is purchased by her husband and reclaimed by Puritan New England." Burnham acknowledges, of course, that the economic transaction belies "the residual inscription of her body, her text, and her subjectivity by the experience of Indian captivity" (20). Nevertheless, most of those who survived to pen their experiences in colonial America were kidnapped because, as white women, they were strategically and financially useful.

Centuries later, a child named Jaycee Dugard made a similar assumption. In a 2013 television interview with journalist Diane Sawyer, the now-adult Dugard recalls her bewildered eleven-year-old self bargaining with the man who had stunned her with a Taser and snatched her off a local road. She told the man that her mother had money and could pay him. "That's what I [thought]. Kidnap is ransom, right?" Dugard mused to Diane Sawyer. Then her facial expression changed. "No," she said softly. "Not always," ruefully recalling how little that younger self could be prepared for what was ahead. Captives like Jaycee Dugard, Elizabeth Smart, and Michelle Knight were prisoners of a different kind of war. Taken by (mostly) white captors explicitly for sexual slavery and abuse without end, they do not fit neatly into prior established narratives of white female captivity.[4] They do testify to a pervasive, violent sense of entitlement to women's and girls' bodies that might give even the Puritans pause.

Attics and Bell Jars: Where Did Captivity Go?

In the long historical space between Mary Rowlandson's era and the twenty-first century, the theme of women's captivity has circulated through literature in several marked ways. Most notably, slave narratives provided compelling testimony of black men's and women's physical, sexual, and psychological abuse over the course of generations. Most published slave narratives were authored by men, no doubt due in part to social reticence about female authorship and the explosive subject matter of enslaved women's sexual exploitation.[5] In her famous *Incidents in the Life of a Slave Girl* (1861), Harriet Jacobs (writing as Linda Brent) deftly broaches these topics, detailing sexual harassment by her master and explicating how beauty, coveted as the pinnacle of white femininity, only further victimizes the female slave. To evade her master, Jacobs lived in the cramped, suffocating space of her grandmother's attic for seven years, a travail that epitomizes, notes Kari Winter, "the ultimate female Gothic event—one that conjures up women's worst fears of being alive" (103). The slave narrative's powerful literary legacy continues today with an outpouring, first begun in the 1960s, of novels foregrounding female protagonists grappling with slavery's assault on black female bodily autonomy. Such novels, which include Margaret Walker's *Jubilee* (1966), Gayl Jones's *Corregidora* (1975), Octavia Butler's *Kindred* (1979), Sherley Anne Williams's *Dessa Rose* (1986), Toni Morrison's *Beloved* (1987), and J. California Cooper's *Family* (1991), "improvise on and rearrange the complex reaches" of the slave narrative tradition, writes Deborah McDowell (142).

While the slave and neoslave narrative traditions have detailed captivity to provide a richer understanding of American historical conditions, the trope of captivity has also operated in popular genres of the twentieth century, where it has produced affects of pleasure and fear. A prime example of such "cultural junk food" is V. C. Andrews's 1980s Dollanganger series, starting with the book *Flowers in the Attic*, a salacious account of incest between trapped siblings. Within the romance genre, captivity is frequently employed as an erotic metaphor that symbolizes mutual bonds. Kathleen Woodiwiss's landmark 1972 romance *The Flame and the Flower* illustrates this "love's prisoners" dynamic. The novel notoriously begins with the hero Brandon, ostensibly mistaking the heroine Heather for a prostitute, raping and imprisoning her on his sailing ship. Literal captivity soon becomes marital captivity; the pair is forced to wed after the rape results in pregnancy. Brandon's "mastery over her had already begun and she knew that she would never again belong to herself," Heather muses on her wedding day (99). Yet after the pair arrives in colonial America, it is Brandon who is metaphorically "enslaved" to his virtuous wife. Thinking of her, he is "hot and sweating one moment, cold and shaking another," lacking "his cold, logical wit, his easy self-control" (165). The bonds of Heather's captivity are dissolved into mutual submission, which whitewashes the violent past and makes the pair full partners in the new American enterprise.

Captivity remains a booming subgenre of romance, often with racially marked subgenres that scholars have identified as "sand books," "desert fabula," or "sheikh fantasy" (Haddad 44). In such works, white women are kidnapped to unnamed Middle Eastern nations, where they are frequently placed in harems. Racial coding in such novels uses post-9/11 politics to make the "sheikh," rather than the Native American male of the Western captivity tradition, occupy the role of the dangerous other. Emily Haddad describes the heroine's initial rebellion, followed by an "ideological shift" that "dissipates the heroine's feminist dedication to the ideals of personal liberty" in comparison to "the delights of love" (44). Such plots participate in what Diane Negra has termed the broader trope of postfeminist retreatism, in which female protagonists learn to reject their empty professional lives and to instead appreciate domestic delights (*What a Girl Wants?*).

Captivity's place in women's erotic fantasy has been further solidified by the success of the trilogy *Fifty Shades of Grey* (2011). E. L. James's self-published oeuvre chronicles a virginal young woman's literal submission to a wealthy, S&M-obsessed male. The books have incurred the usual vitriolic screeds about women's "trashy" reading taste, but, more interestingly, they have been offered into evidence as examples of women's secret *desires* for domination. Katie Roiphe, for instance, theorizes a causal link between women's increased educational and workplace success and the rise in popularity of mass-market rape and bondage fantasies. She proposes that for some women "the more theatrical fantasies of sexual surrender offer a release, a vacation, an escape from the dreariness and hard work of equality" ("Working Women's Fantasies"). Roiphe's suggestion that women secretly desire romantic subjugation is one more manifestation of a popular cultural belief. It is of course important to acknowledge that the romance genre's portrayal of captivity as pleasurable and educational is rooted in fantasy. Readers of the genre experience sexual exploration without actual danger. Haddad has argued that when political conditions bring realities of captivity home (as they did during the Iraq wars, where several women working abroad were kidnapped), the subgenre "loses its tropic, figurative character" (60). My point is not to politically indict the romance, but rather to suggest that it has shaped our cultural expectations about female captivity.

Romance is not the only genre in love with its captives. The "collection" plot, in which psychotic killers keep women as prized possessions, has become increasingly stock in written thrillers and their filmic counterparts. Some even appear to have influenced true crime: John Fowles's *The Collector* (1963) has been claimed as inspiration by multiple serial killers, and was found on the person of 1980s "beauty queen killer" Christopher Wilder at his apprehension.[6] *The Collector* is a two-person drama set in a claustrophobic cottage basement. Clegg, a timid clerk and butterfly collector made newly wealthy by a lottery win, has drugged and kidnapped Miranda, a vibrant art student he has long coveted. Sonia Saubion writes that "it finally occurs to [Clegg] to make Miranda part of his collection of petrified objects, in the hope that in the long run she will fall in love with him" (99). The language of collection is emphasized throughout Fowles's novel. "Now you've collected me," Miranda reproaches Clegg. "Literally. You've pinned me in this little room and you can come and gloat over me" (42). She later ruminates, "I am one in a row of specimens. It's when I try to flutter out of line that he hates me. I'm meant to be dead, pinned, always the same, always beautiful" (217–18). *The Collector* is a hermetic text, its airlessness mimicking Clegg's aim to enclose Miranda within his world. Katharine Tarbox observes that "the series of nonproductive events in the novel are so many flutterings against the glass of the killing jar" (41). Much of Fowles's plot consists of debates—about art, taste, Jungian archetypes, and language—between the wealthy, bohemian Miranda and the bourgeois Clegg. The material horror of Miranda's confinement is frequently muted: there are only veiled references to her slop bucket, for instance.

In a troubling parallel to the romance/captivity tradition, Clegg does not, as Amit Marcus observes, "deem the other's free will as a necessary precondition for love; rather, he believes that . . . love is the final outcome, the *telos*, of a long and strenuous process of re-education, in which the previously underdeveloped woman matures and realizes that she admires and longs for the man who has made so many efforts for her own good" (84). Indeed, although Miranda never comes to accept her captivity, she problematically admits that "I would not want this [her kidnapping] not to have happened. Because if I escape I shall be a completely different and I think better person. Because if I don't escape, if something dreadful happened, I shall still know that the person I was . . . was not the person I now want to be" (270). Some of Fowles's critics, Marcus notes, similarly suggest that Miranda's captivity has the potential for bildungsroman. Carol Barnum, for instance, writes of Miranda's enclosure as "potentially positive, as womb" and adds that "the metaphor is apt since Miranda will experience rebirth into higher consciousness" (41).

If Fowles's hushed, airless novel reduces captivity narrative to a metaphorical struggle under glass, then James Patterson's *Kiss the Girls* (1995) gorges on a buffet of sexualized violence and unbridled consumption. Patterson, one of America's most prolific and best-selling mass-market fiction writers with over 300 million books in print, pits African American detective Alex Cross against two serial killers self-identified as the "Gentleman Caller" and "Casanova." The duo bond over their imprisonment, rape, and murder of beautiful and professionally accomplished women. *Kiss the Girls* is exploitation fiction through and through. Interchangeable women are shown subject to scenes of intense sadism, including an anal rape by a snake, and the narrative is focalized primarily from the perspective of the psychotic "curators."

"We believe that he might be a *collector*. We think he could be keeping a few of the young women nearby . . . a private harem maybe. His very own harem," a police officer tells Cross of Casanova (68). The kidnapped victims are racially diverse, as if to show a perverse sort of progressiveness, but all are dazzling and extraordinarily high-achieving in their fields.[7] Cross observes that Casanova is "*taking only the heartbreakers . . . the women that everybody wants but nobody ever seems to get*" (93–94). The detective's comment, curiously, reflects the killers' own sense of entitlement toward women. Casanova, for instance, describes a young girl he stalks as "unbearably haughty and *untouchable*," declaring that "tonight he was going to change all that. He was going to take her" (5; emphasis in original). Casanova repeatedly refers to women as "haughty" and "uppity," while his partner, the Gentlemen Caller, selects a random victim in a store because she "had a full and arrogant mouth" and an "aura of self-confidence and competency—which he would absolutely shatter" (228–29).

Casanova and the Gentleman Caller believe they are merely exercising their natural male aggression in order to secure the prizes they are owed. "*Man was born to hunt . . . women*," muses Casanova in the opening pages (23). "*I'm like a killer shark . . . I am a predator without peer, a thinking predator*" (43). All males, he believes, "were all watching, constantly selecting, obsessed with mastering the hunt from puberty to the grave" (45). The killers' shared torturing of women, meanwhile, is described by a detective as "*male bonding as it had never existed*" (385). This particular plotline is retread on iterations of *Criminal Minds* or *CSI* to the point of banality; it has become background noise, another ambient horror in postfeminist popular culture. The collection thriller continues to be consumed by women, in part as the "gaze into the abyss" that Laura Browder has identified as a preventative fear-management strategy (932). Perhaps, like Patricia Cornwell's killer makeover novels, the genre also comments, even if unwittingly, on postfeminist popular culture itself.

Postfeminist sensibility emphasizes the deliberately arranged lifestyle, achievable through the rhetoric of choice. Lifestyle consumerists use the vocabulary of curation to literally sell this idea. One popular site is explained by its founder as "about living a very one-of-a-kind, curated life."[8] Internet flash sales of mass-produced goods are ironically billed as "curated collections."[9] The rise of female-dominated Pinterest, a "social bookmarking site" of "easy curation" in which users create themed galleries about weddings, interior decor, and more, testifies to postfeminist interest in "collecting, sharing, and resharing" (Oler, "Pinned Down"). The curation fad promises that women can selectively order, choose, and arrange broad areas of their lives (certainly a presumption riddled with all kinds of privileges). The sadistic collector trope that runs throughout popular television and mass-market books acts as counternarrative, deeming women-as-objects bereft of any agency. Susan Stewart writes that in order for many collectors to properly assemble the airtight worlds that they control, "it is necessary to obliterate the object's context of origin" (158). Women in collector narratives are indeed extinguished, whether pinned, trapped under glass, or smothered in dirt-filled basements.

What happens, then, when the actual captive speaks? In three memoirs, ex-captives Elizabeth Smart, Jaycee Dugard, and Michelle Knight destroy the notion that captivity is training ground for a fruitful marriage. They do not aestheticize—rather they sharply indict—the violent male sense of entitlement to women's bodies that underpins captivity. Their texts contain individualized political projects that stem from the different circumstances of their cases as well as their varying representations in the media. Elizabeth Smart was a blonde, harp-playing golden child of wealthy Mormon parents, and a symbol of post-9/11 loss. Sharp and unsentimental, Smart's memoir *My Story* demolishes elements of the official narrative surrounding her case. Most strikingly, Smart emphasizes her sexual abuse, returning again and again to the word *rape*. This textual strategy has helped Smart carry her crusade against victim-blaming into the popular sphere, where she has become a strong voice for sexual-assault survivors within a religiously conservative subculture. The second memoirist, Jaycee Dugard, spent nearly two decades as a sexual slave hidden in a backyard compound, eventually bearing two girls fathered by her captor. Dugard's literary style might be termed "maternal"—she reaches out to readers through carefully chosen motifs and metaphors, connecting her painful experience to theirs and arguing for the creation of a more domestically attuned society where there will be no more hidden "backyards." Finally, if Dugard's project is to ask us to interrogate all the hidden places we do not see, then ex-captive Michelle Knight's goal is to challenge Americans' preconceptions about *which victims count.* A runaway fleeing a sexually and physically abusive family, Knight was abducted by a friend's father and held for eleven years. She remained invisible to both the police and her own family, and this anonymity further enraged a captor who fed on public attention. In the interim since her freedom, Knight has made the public *her* family, and she continues to crusade against victim-blaming and victim-ignoring. Elaine Showalter argues that captivity narratives "are the testaments to women's courage, resourcefulness, and strength" ("Dark Places" 35). Smart, Dugard, and Knight offer searing literary testimony that disrupts prevailing captivity tropes and promotes more equitable worlds.

Salt Lake City—Elizabeth Smart

Elizabeth Smart—daughter of an affluent Salt Lake City couple, sister to five picture-perfect blond siblings—was plucked from her bed in the middle of the night on June 5, 2002, by an armed stranger. She vanished, resurfacing nine months later not far from home, in the company of Brian David Mitchell (a man calling himself the prophet Immanuel) and his wife Wanda Barzee. Publicity from sources including *America's Most Wanted* led to citizens' alerts that triggered Smart's rescue by police. Throughout the duration of her kidnapping, she received significant media attention. Elizabeth's telegenic appearance, combined with the storied history of her family, who traced their lineage to Mormon pioneers, contributed to her mass-media appeal. So too did the unease of a post-9/11 America. Shannon Luders-Manuel writes that "just as the world could not tear itself away from the image of the Twin Towers crumbling to the ground in 2001, it could also not tear itself away from the angelic-looking teen who was being deemed 'everyone's daughter' in 2002" (4–5). Smart's media ubiquity and golden-girl image was also noted by media blogger Black Canseco, who invoked her in a 2008 web campaign to highlight missing children of color by reminding the public that they were "just as 'all-american'" as "Elizabeth Smart and all the rest who receive so much focus" (Harding, "We Want Our Kids Back Too").

For nearly a year, Smart was a lost girl, appearing in haunting still footage on the twenty-four-hour cable news cycle. The cultural power of missing and murdered white girls has already been explored in Alice Sebold's *The Lovely Bones*, its young-adult fiction variants, and Jodi Picoult's *Vanishing*

Acts. Rebecca Wanzo comments that the pull exerted by such lost girls is not only cultural, but also *legal*; several pieces of public policy, including Megan's Law (a sex-offender registration statute) and the Amber Alert (an emergency-broadcast system for suspected child abductions), coalesced out of Americans' desires to memorialize the "thwarted future self" of real-life murdered girls and to safeguard "the imagined futures of others" ("Era of Lost [White] Girls" 105). Elizabeth Smart's unlikely return from among the missing on March 12, 2003, wrote a different ending to the lost-girl narrative. News of her freedom from captivity was greeted jubilantly in the public sphere. "The astonishing reappearance of Elizabeth Smart occurred in the jittery days immediately before the invasion of Iraq," writes Jon Krakauer. "Most Americans . . . were desperate for some good news and rejoiced with commensurate intensity when the girl was reunited with her family" (41). A few details became known: during her captivity, Smart had endured starvation, dehydration, and a host of deprivations. Yet because of her youth at the time of her rescue, much explicit detail of her travails remained hidden. "As her parents, we wish to protect our daughter's privacy and will not share the terrifying details of her captivity," begins Ed and Lois Smart's 2003 memoir *Bringing Elizabeth Home* (8).

In the years following Smart's return, public documents about her case emphasized the miraculous nature of her return and placed her in a "fairy princess" narrative of good fortune. Her parents' memoir remained the dominant text defining her abduction. An overtly religious work, *Bringing Elizabeth Home* drew moral lessons from the crisis. The Smarts theorized that "maybe Elizabeth's kidnapping was God's way of showing the world that He can perform miracles. . . . It brought us together as a nation of faithful people from all religions and beliefs. It gave us hope. It made us better people" (204). Other public treatments of Elizabeth Smart focused on her resumption of girlhood. After her rescue, Elizabeth graced the cover of *People* magazine in the tight joint embrace of her parents. The cover story focused on Smart's readjustment to society by way of bubble baths, hot-pink nail polish, and playfully flipped hair (Tresniowski 51). Her wedding in 2012 landed her another *People* magazine cover. "Elizabeth Smart: Happily Ever After!" proclaimed the headline. Amid details of the menu, dress choice, and more, readers learn that Elizabeth "married a prince" and experienced "a love story that has come true" (Free and Dennis 70).

The lost-girl and fairy-princess discourses surrounding Elizabeth Smart were primarily authored by others. In 2013, however, Smart took ownership of her own narrative, smiling directly into the camera on the cover of her memoir *My Story.* Like colonial captivity narratives, the memoir contains regular discussions of religious faith as well as the occasional miracle in the wilderness. Smart writes, for instance, of finding a mysterious glass of water after many days of dehydration in Mitchell's camp. However, her text also hypnotically *foregrounds* her endurance of sexual assaults in order to critique both patriarchal privilege and victim-blaming. Smart's authorial decision to emphasize her corporeal pain and suffering fragments the existing, and often abstract, ways she has been portrayed.

"My life pretty much consisted of three things: getting raped, being forced to drink alcohol, and sitting on a bucket in a clearing in the trees," Smart remarks sardonically of her daily routine in captivity (190). Rape is a near-constant in *My Story*, mentioned on nearly every page. Its textual ubiquity mirrors Smart's own experience of facing sexual assault daily in captivity. Smart recalls being subjected to Mitchell's "incessant talking, sometimes interrupted only long enough that he could rape me before going back to sharing his insights once again" (14). Elsewhere she confides that Mitchell had to abandon a planned campsite construction because he had "too much plundering, raping, and drinking to do" (180). The memoir's use of textual repetition is a constant reminder of Brian David Mitchell's evil; Smart also uses it strategically to speak back against the shaming impact of abstinence-only sexual-education programs on sexual-assault victims.

In the aftermath of her first rape by Mitchell (which occurred on her initial day of captivity), Smart describes her feelings of worthlessness and her anxieties about rejection by her highly devout family. "If they knew what the man had done to me, would they still want me?" she asks. "I felt like I was . . . like not even half, like I was just a portion of a human being. I just felt filthy and disgusting. I felt like, Who would ever want me back? Who would ever want to talk to me? Who would ever be my friend?" (47–48). Deciding that her mother and siblings would definitely continue to love her, she continues, "The more I thought about it, the more I realized that my dad would accept me back as well. I mean, how many times had I crashed one of our snowmobiles into a snowbank? How many other things had I done that he could have gotten mad at me for? But he hadn't" (60–61). Smart's troubling equation between domestic accidents she might have caused or "done" and a forcible rape perpetrated *upon her* by a strange adult illustrates her internalization of shame and self-blame.

Years later, Smart gave a powerful speech at Johns Hopkins University in which she returned to the false correlation between virginity and self-worth. Margaret Talbot writes: "She spoke of a former teacher who had promoted abstinence by saying 'Imagine you're a stick of gum, and when you engage in sex that's like getting chewed. And then if you do that lots of times you're going to become an old piece of gum, and who's going to want you after that?' Smart told the crowd, 'Nobody should ever say that'" (34). It was a resounding remark, and headlines and politicizing followed. Smart pointed out to Talbot that abstinence-based education is but one of many vectors causing sexual-assault survivors pain and shame; the misuse of social media, for instance (Smart cited the 2012 Steubenville case, in which teens broadcast a sexual assault widely over social media) can have dangerous and even fatal consequences. The now-married Smart told Talbot that her goal as a public figure is to make "talking about rape and abuse not such a taboo." She added that "there's a huge difference between rape and sex. Having experienced both, I *know* it's not the same thing" (33).

Smart's text makes the same distinction, showing that her rapes, which Mitchell claimed were maritally sanctioned acts of sexual pleasure, were instead rooted in his need to control and abuse young women. Mitchell first justifies his rape of the child Elizabeth by polygamously "wedding" her in a self-directed ceremony. When she protests against his sexual assaults, he asserts that the marital vows guarantee his possession. "We're man and wife. That's a part of what we do now. It's what we do!" he claims indignantly (74). Later he says again that "we're man and wife. It's an important part of the relationship. If you're sick or something maybe we won't do it, but otherwise, plan on it" (81). Mitchell's vision of marriage is one of literal and sexual captivity for women; he also draws strength from the power imbalance between himself and his "bride." Smart reflects that "my [sexual] rejection didn't bother him. In fact, it seemed to urge him on, being able to dominate me like that. Domination and power. That was always his intent" (75). Indeed, when Mitchell reveals a prophetic vision to take seven more wives, he is very specific about taking ones that are "young and malleable . . . that I can mold into proper servants." "Believe me," he adds, "I have learned that they can't be so old that they will fight me" (147).

Smart repeatedly talks of her captor as a religious hypocrite, a man who "simply used the culture and language of religion to manipulate people in order to get what he wanted" (16). *My Story* points out how Mitchell used religion for self-glorification, all the while indulging in acts ranging from drunkenness to sexual violence. At one point Smart recounts sardonically: "Oh, how we'd pray! Brian David Mitchell had more to say to heaven than any other man in the world. Forty-five minutes was the norm. Kneeling. Eyes closed. Head down. . . . Maybe then he'd rape me. Or maybe he'd wait until the afternoon. Or maybe that night. Or maybe one and then the other" (120).

Smart severs Mitchell from any legitimate connection to her faith, asserting, "He wasn't a prophet. He hadn't received any visions. He hadn't talked to God. All he was was a dirty pedophile who liked living on the streets" (295).

In dismantling Mitchell's self-portrayal as a devout man, Smart changes part of the conversation about her case. The other portion involves a reconsideration of her own presumed meekness. The general public narrative about Smart portrayed her as, in Jon Krakauer's words, "an utterly submissive polygamous concubine" who was "raised to obey figures of Mormon authority unquestioningly . . . [thus] particularly susceptible to the dexterous fundamentalist spin" of Brian David Mitchell (45). News outlets had reported that Smart neglected to capitalize on rescue opportunities when she was in public with Mitchell, denied her identity to police upon rescue, and exhibited great solicitude for her captors. Yet *My Story* assigns Smart particular kinds of agency during her captivity that surprise—and in some ways contradict—official accounts. Smart's memoir reinterprets her "passivity" as a guise of stoic guardedness in the face of Mitchell's repeated threats to kill her family. She recounts thinking to herself, "*Whatever it takes to survive. I will do what he tells me. I will not endanger my family. I will not endanger myself*" (81). *My Story* also depicts acts of psychic resistance, in scenes where Smart and Mitchell gaze upon one another. "He looked at me and held my stare, refusing to look away," Smart writes. "My unspoken words were very clear. '*You tried to kill me. But you didn't. For all your talk of being a mighty prophet, I am stronger than you are. One day, you're going to know that. One day, you're going to see.*' . . . Mitchell was the first one to look away" (248).

Smart's memoir also adjusts the public narrative about her rescue. She asserts that *she* masterminded the group's plan to return to Salt Lake City (where she had a much better chance of being recognized) after their three-month trip to California. In a chapter titled "Manipulating Mitchell," Smart describes faking a revelation about God's desire for them to return home, and stoking Mitchell's ego by asking him, as the divine representative, to query this with God. "After nearly nine months of being enslaved, I had shown that I was more than a bystander in my own life, more than just a puppet in his hands," she rejoices (255). Finally, Smart narrates the story of her resumed identity in a much more dramatic fashion. Upon being asked by the police to write her name, she recalls that "I felt calm. I felt assured. Months of fear and pain seemed to melt before the sun. I felt a sweet assurance. 'I am Elizabeth,' I finally said" (275).

This departure from the prior published accounts (including those of her own parents) shows Smart's desire to resume control of her story. David Sewell suggests that "writing about the captivity experience is, for the author, an attempt to establish once and for all the primacy of the captive's language over the captors,' to reverse the power relationship of the captivity experience" (qtd. in Logan 268). Indeed, Smart begins *My Story* by asserting her right to narrate the kidnapping, arguing that "the keys to the story" are "lying in my hands." "I am the one," she continues, "who lived through nine months of hell. I am the one who was forced to lie beside Mitchell every night. I am the one who had to listen to his stories. . . . I am the one who felt his hot breath on my face. . . . I am the one who saw him play other people like a fiddle. . . . I saw all this, and more. Which is why I know Brian David Mitchell better than any other person in the world" (14–15). Smart's *I,* as textually insistent as her use of the word *rape,* triumphs in one final confrontation with Mitchell—this one years later, inside courtroom walls. Smart describes returning Mitchell's stare. "*No, Brian David Mitchell, I am stronger than you. I'm not afraid of my future. And I'm not afraid of you. Not another second will I give you. I will live and I'll be happy. That is how this story ends*" (295–96).

As Margaret Talbot observes, one of many extraordinary things about Elizabeth Smart is that "she has chosen to remain a public figure and has been unusually successful at doing so on her own terms" (32). Emerging from the media persona of the sheltered, harp-playing daughter, Smart writes her straightforward captivity narrative to expose her captor's misogyny and speak back to victim-shaming culture. Smart has emerged, comments Kristine Haglund, as someone "strong and whole, a modern woman able to address questions of sexuality directly and confidently" (qtd. in Talbot 38).

The basic events of Smart's case have been thematically adapted in novelist Chevy Stevens's neo-captivity work *Still Missing* (2010). Stevens's first-person narrator is Annie O'Sullivan, a former real estate agent abducted at an open house and forced to spend a year atop a mountaintop bunker, held captive by an antigovernment reactionary she calls "The Freak." During this time, Annie gives birth to a daughter, who dies at six weeks of age after the captor refuses her medical aid. Like the real-life Brian David Mitchell, the fictional Freak cleaves to rigidly sexist thinking. He strips Annie of her business suit, telling her, "Don't worry, you never have to go into the office again" (39). She is "cleansed" of her professional identity via his elaborate rituals of bathing, grooming, and dressing her in childlike white dresses with hearts. In between heavy loads of domestic chores, Annie is subjected to violent rape every night until she becomes pregnant as a "real woman" should (69). Like Brian David Mitchell, Annie's captor is aroused by her terror. During a rape, Annie recalls him shouting, "You should be terrified. You should be begging. You should be fighting for your life. *Don't you get it?*" as he pounds her body "with his fists, against my breasts, face, crotch" (53).

"I learned to keep the perfect amount of submissive shame in my expression, forced myself to look down, and curled my shoulders like a beaten dog," Annie narrates (81). Through the figure of Annie, compelled to be literally barefoot and pregnant, Stevens taps into women's fears about the fragility of their economic and social freedoms. As the title suggests, the novel also engages the difficulty of post-captivity trauma, a topic that takes up little space in Smart's memoir. *My Story* eschews talk of formal therapies, instead claiming kinship with Smart's pioneer ancestors. She affirms that "history is replete with stories of human suffering," adding that God "gave us the ability to forgive. To leave our past behind. To look forward instead of back. . . . People have been doing it for generations" (298–99). Stevens's Annie, by contrast, is far from free after she kills "The Freak" and stumbles back to civilization. Unable to readjust to her prior life after having her daily routines (including bathroom breaks) controlled by another, she experiences panic attacks, sleeplessness, crying jags, and other symptoms of posttraumatic stress disorder. "Any little personality quirk I had before has been blown up twenty times and now I'm some weird hybrid of *freakdom*," she tells her doctor, her choice of words alluding to her fear of becoming like her captor (43; emphasis added).

Annie also struggles to place her own stamp of authority on her experiences. In captivity, it was not enough for The Freak to rape and beat her and to cause her daughter's death through medical neglect; he sought to reinterpret her captivity as its own "freedom" from the burdens of modernity. Just like Smart's captor Brian David Mitchell, who lectured her that she was "lucky" because "I brought you out of the ugly world" (Smart 120), The Freak harangues Annie. "You don't think it's possible that people can sometimes come to realize what they thought was a bad event in their life was actually an extremely good event, if they knew the alternative?" he asks (Stevens 23). "Don't you understand what a fantastic gift this is? This is your *redemption*, Annie," he adds (40). Sneering when she counters with her professional success, he contends, "You merely existed. But I'm giving you a second chance" (40). For jailers both fictional and real, captivity corrects a modern world characterized by women's "excessive" liberty. Annie, however, never accepts this line of thinking, and learns gradually to move toward reintegration, largely by mourning her lost daughter.

South Lake Tahoe: Jaycee Dugard

My Story and the fictional *Still Missing* offer glimpses into worlds of male entitlement to women's bodies, whether purportedly justified by religious doctrine or by counterculturalism. Ex-captive Jaycee Dugard's memoir *A Stolen Life* adds another perspective to the genre. Kidnapped at age eleven by pedophile Phillip Garrido with the assistance of his wife Nancy, Dugard endured eighteen years of being raised as both the sexual partner and the daughter of her male captor. Furthermore, she bore and raised two daughters herself, first becoming pregnant at the age of fourteen. Her memoir, then, has the extraordinarily difficult job of excavating severe childhood sexual abuse while sheltering her beloved daughters from the unflinching public eye. Whereas Smart's text is framed around an assertive "I" retaking control of the "America's Daughter" narrative, Dugard's takes an orientation that might be deemed "maternal." She protectively guards her daughters' privacy, and in so doing creates a text of gaps and chronological fissures. Moreover, Dugard takes the *rhetorical* role of mother, crafting empathetic connections between her own singularly horrific experience and readers' own cases of abuse and neglect. *A Stolen Life* ends with a social prescription for community spirit, in the service of making a more compassionate nation attuned to the needs of women and children.

I have mentioned that one project of neo-captivity narratives is to lay bare gruesome details of sexual abuse and assault from the point of view of the dehumanized victim (as opposed to the sadistic "collector" subgenre). This is tough material, and Dugard, like Elizabeth Smart, does not hold back. "What this man had in mind for me was like a foreign language," she recalls. "No amount of preparation could have helped me understand why another human being would do what [Garrido] did to another human being, a little girl, for that matter. I still don't get it" (15). Dugard recounts being raped every day, tied up, and hung from eye hooks in sexual positions, often for hours at a time. She endured Garrido's threats to make her have sex with his dog and his wife. During Garrido's methamphetamine-fueled binges, called "runs," Dugard was ordered to help her captor "fulfill all his fantasies." She remembers: "First he's going to get me dressed the way he wants and then depending on his mood, the rest will consist of me masturbating him, sucking his penis, me in whatever position he desires, and dancing over him while he masturbates" (51). Garrido "has already told me not to cry because it will interfere with his fantasy," she adds solemnly (51).

Dugard connects with her readers *despite* these wrenching scenes because she repeatedly constructs her captivity within a larger spectrum of suffering and, in so doing, creates a more nuanced understanding of victimization. Carine Mardorossian has called for a rethinking of the social construction of the category of *sexual victim*, suggesting we conceive of victims as "people whose vulnerability to others has been abused," as opposed to a class overtaken with a vulnerability virus to which stronger people are immune. If we "came to terms with the fact that we are all, by definition, characterized by vulnerability," Mardorossian continues, "then it becomes more difficult (if not impossible) to hold it against people that they are vulnerable" (*Framing the Rape Victim* 15). Dugard takes up this challenge in a preface that embraces the reader in shared vulnerability. She asserts that she is writing "in the hopes that it will be of help to someone going through, hopefully not similar conditions, but someone facing a difficult situation of their own—whatever that may be" (ix–x). Dugard continues that "it's easy for people to be horrified and shocked when someone is abducted, but what about all the other adults and kids living in sad homes? . . . I know that I am not the only child to be hurt by a crazy adult. I am sure there are still the families that look great on the outside, but if someone were to delve deeper they would discover horrors beyond belief" (x). She constructs a rhetorical parallel between her own backyard—a ramshackle smattering of tents that served as her living space for most of eighteen years—and someone living "in a self-made 'backyard'" that is "tough and scary to venture out" of (x). The preface concludes with Dugard's gesture of solidarity to her readers that they too "can endure tough situations and survive" (x).

Within the narrative of *A Stolen Life*, Dugard works to create bridges between her unspeakable experience and more common forms of suffering. The text repeatedly foregrounds Jaycee Dugard's love of, and identification with, young animals; in so doing, it stresses her childlike earnestness and also her vulnerability to predation. Animals "were a big focus of our lives and they were family," Dugard reminisces, as she thanks, by name, the officer who secured foster homes for her cats after her rescue (165). Vignettes about various cats given to her—usually only temporarily—in captivity recur so frequently throughout the book that the animals' names blur together. Janet Maslin, reviewing the book in the *New York Times*, expresses mild frustration with the "vapid" nature of Dugard's verbal meanderings about "her pets and their sweet personalities" ("Captivity"). Yet these digressions serve a strategic purpose by situating Dugard in moments of accessible space for readers.

Located in the memoir's center is a photocopied reproduction of "Eclipse's Journal," a notebook written by a twelve-year-old Jaycee to her kitten. An all-consuming chronicle of the cat's quotidian behaviors, Eclipse's journal feels startlingly static because there are no outside referents of any sort—friends, activities, or even descriptions of the weather. It is a poignant window into Dugard's isolation. She constantly affirms her love for Eclipse, who is her sole companion: "Eclipse is very special to me because she is always with me for me to talk to, even if she doesn't listen I know she cares," she observes at one point (unpaginated journal). The cat also rescues her from the stretches of intense boredom that accompany her captivity. "Before all I did was sit around and watch T.V. all day, now I watch [Eclipse] all day and play with her, so by the time I go to sleep I'm very tired and I fall right to sleep," Jaycee observes. Yet the kitten, like the vulnerable girl taking care of her, is also disposable in her captor's world. The journal ends with Garrido's abrupt removal of Eclipse, for no reason stated. Pulling us back into the horror of her world, Dugard muses that Eclipse might have met the same fate as her previous cat, who was exiled because "Phillip didn't want cat hair sticking to the Vaseline that he used for masturbating and to lubricate me" (77).

A Stolen Life's animal motif provides a pathway into the darkness of Dugard's torment. Her grim vignettes are not merely about the various acts she was subjected to; they also reveal Phillip Garrido's chilling sense of violent male entitlement. He repeatedly insists that Dugard is performing a societal "service" as the receptacle of his abuse. Initially, she writes that "he explains to me he has a sex problem and that he took me so I could help him with his problem so he wouldn't have to bother anyone else with his problem. He says it consumes his mind and that by me giving him an outlet I am saving others" (53). She later recollects that "he was always saying what a good person he was" but that "society didn't help people like him and that there were a lot of men out there in the world with the same problem as his" (57). When Diane Sawyer asks Dugard if she believed she was protecting other little girls by absorbing Garrido's abuse, she responds, "I think I did. I think at some level I did" (Dugard, interview by Diane Sawyer).[10]

Phillip Garrido manipulated his young victim by exploiting her instincts to protect others. As she grew older, Dugard's sheltering instincts grew to encompass the daughters she bore at ages fourteen and seventeen. Maternal love, and the theme of female generations, suffuses *A Stolen Life*, both in the form of Dugard's longing for her mother, Terry, and in her connection to her daughters. After the birth of her first child, she reminisces that "I rock her for hours and hours and sing 'You Are My Sunshine' just like my mom used to sing to me" (112). In the *20/20* interview, Dugard calls her second daughter "another little piece of my mom to hang onto." While Dugard's parental love is explored at length, the girls themselves, who are identified by the first initial of their names, make only shadowy impressions in the book. The authorial curtain around those who shared her captivity necessarily alters the textual and chronological coherence of *A Stolen Life*. As Ruth Franklin points out, we "get little sense of what, for most outsiders, will be the greatest mystery: How did she manage, assisted only by her captors, to bring up two children who were always kept hidden from the outside world? How did she cope with being solely responsible for them, day in and day out? And how on earth did she explain their situation to them?" ("Jaycee Dugard's Memoir"). Dugard remains unapologetic about protecting her children's names, images, and identifying details fiercely to this day. She has even referred to voracious media interest in her family as a second captivity, writing that "sometimes I feel like I'm still a prisoner. I spent eighteen years hiding and not being seen, and now it almost feels like history is repeating itself" (229–30).

Dugard emphasizes the theme of mother love in her memoir; intriguingly, so too do popular narratives about her rescue from captivity. To recall, for eighteen years Dugard was literally hiding in plain sight, living in a ramshackle assortment of tents in Garrido's backyard. In *A Stolen Life* she muses that it's "funny, how I can look back now, and notice how the 'secret backyard' didn't really look so 'secret.' It wasn't even that well hidden. I was in the middle of a neighborhood. . . . I can't understand why Phillip's parole officers didn't know anything about the property and the size of it. It makes me believe no one cared or was ever really looking for me" (58). Extended interviews with Dugard were secured by *20/20*, which chronicled various failures of law enforcement in her case. Garrido, for instance, received "positive commendations" from parole boards in spite of prior aggravated rapes of young women, and a neighbor's 911 call reporting young girls in Garrido's yard was largely dismissed by authorities. The show also displayed a map charting the movements of the GPS device Garrido was legally bound to wear. The map's data showed unusually concentrated activity in the backyard of the residence. A simple search of the property would have found Dugard.

As *20/20* tells it, it took "two campus cops [to] do what an entire federal bureaucracy had failed to do." When Garrido brought his daughters to the campus of the University of California at Berkeley to spread his religious propaganda, two officials, Ally Jacobs and Lisa Campbell, became concerned by the girls' sallowness and lack of affect. They located Garrido's prior sex-offender convictions and set in motion the chain of events that led to Dugard writing her own name, for the first time in eighteen years, within a police station. In the television special, Officer Jacobs indicates that her actions stemmed from "concern for the girls, from a mother's standpoint. They weren't giving me any kind of sign they were in trouble, but yet I felt that they were." She later reiterates that "I think it comes down to life experience—having that woman's intuition, mother's intuition, work experience, life experience." Finally, Diane Sawyer emphasizes that Dugard was saved by "mother's instinct" and "female intuition." While the television program certainly oversimplifies the politics of Dugard's rescue, its emphasis on using maternal knowledge to recognize, decode, and prevent another's suffering accords with the themes of Dugard's memoir.

A Stolen Life reiterates the theme of maternal care in the conclusion. Dugard discusses her work with the JAYC foundation, which advocates for families rent asunder by trauma, and in particular her desire to shed light on abuses hiding in plain sight within our own communities. She ends by saying: "I'm hoping to rescue many needy families and animals in the years to come. I hope to encourage others to reach out and help other families and animals, too. It's the simple things that count. Just Ask Yourself to Care (JAYC)" (268). Drawing upon maternal authority, Dugard asks us to be in each other's lives and houses, so there will be no more hidden backyards.

Reviewing *A Stolen Life*, Ruth Franklin observes that Dugard "doesn't have the privilege of the novelist's bird's-eye view of her own situation—she is still stuck in the middle of it, trying to make sense of it, as she may well be for the rest of her life" ("Jaycee Dugard's Memoir"). Fiction, however, has more imaginative space to roam. The extraordinary circumstances of Dugard's captive maternity are mirrored in two novels. Emma Donoghue's best-selling novel *Room* (2011) narrates the captivity experience from the perspective of a five-year-old boy born and raised in a small shed. Isla Morley's *Above* (2014) chronicles a life underground as a kidnapped sixteen-year-old gives birth and raises a baby to adolescence within an abandoned missile silo. Both novels explore how captive women negotiate the difficulty of making worlds for well-loved children in the most terrible of circumstances.

"I get on Rocker to take a pin from Kit on Shelf," explains *Room*'s five-year-old Jack in a typical utterance (5). For Jack, life is limited to the contours of the eleven by eleven soundproof shed called Room that he has never left. Objects are capitalized because they are, in his unique life experience, Singular. The circumstances of Jack and Ma's captivity emerge slowly, filtered through a child's perspective. For instance, Ma has created a rigorous schedule of educational and health-related activities for Jack; some of these tasks include daily shouting while standing close to the skylight and a coordination game where they punch random combinations into the keypad by the shed door. Readers (but not Jack) intuit that these are signals for help. So too is Ma's daily Morse code switches of the lamp at nighttime, which Jack only interprets as a stress reliever that "helps her get to sleep again" (27).

The third person in Jack's world is Old Nick, a shadowy figure who "creaks Bed" with Ma until he "makes that gaspy sound" each night as Jack watches from the protective embrace of the wardrobe (37). Like other captors real and fictional, Old Nick, who kidnapped Ma as a college student seven years prior, expects her gratitude for "saving" her from the burdens of modernity. "I don't think you appreciate how good you've got it here," he argues later. "Aboveground, natural light, central air, it's a cut above some places, I can tell you. Fresh fruit, toiletries, what have you, click your fingers and it's there. Plenty girls would thank their lucky stars for a setup like this, safe as houses" (69). Like Jaycee Dugard, Donoghue shows how the presence of a child in captivity gives the captor even more power by creating emotional vulnerability in the mother. Ma, who derides Old Nick in private, becomes instantly subservient whenever she perceives a threat to Jack. When Jack's toy accidentally falls on Old Nick's head, she cries, "I'm sorry, I'm so sorry, I should have put it somewhere it wouldn't fall. I'm really really totally" sorry (48). At another point she distracts him with sex, assuring Old Nick that "I can be quiet. You know how quiet I can be, so long as you leave him alone. It's all I've ever asked" (74).

The pair's escape from Room occurs when Jack executes Ma's heart-stopping plan to feign death, escape from a rolled-up carpet on the back of Old Nick's truck, and run for help. For Jack, the Outside offers new material rewards, but also threatens an end of the protective "cocoon" in which he "has his mother's complete attention all day long" (Franklin, "Jaycee Dugard's Memoir"). For Ma, the challenges of reintegration include figuring out her place in a broken family that resents Jack and negotiating the pitfalls of instant media notoriety. "Do you sometimes wish we didn't escape?" Jack asks Ma toward the end of *Room*, to which she responds, "No, I never wish that" (313). Jack's question is innocent, but the similar one posed by a television interviewer—"Is there a sense in which you miss being behind a locked door?"—seems far more sinister. Ma rejects the idea, by now familiar in women's captivity memoir and fiction, that being "provided for" in captivity is somehow preferable to the uncertain modern world of freedom and choices. "Is she allowed to ask me such stupid questions?" Ma muses aloud (236).

Room's television-interview scene highlights the unsettled iconography of the ex-captive. An unctuous TV presenter expresses her gratitude to Ma for "refusing to be silenced any longer" and telling her story to the world (231). However, throughout the interview, Ma refuses to deliver an easily digestible narrative about heroism or maternity. She tells the hostess that

Jack's birth saved her, but also admits to having had an abortion earlier in life, with no regrets. She parries the interviewer's implication that motherhood without access to education or help was overwhelming, asserting that "I think what babies want is mostly to have their mothers right there" (233). In desperation, the reporter resorts to therapeutic clichés. "Do you realize what a beacon you've become?" she asks Ma. "A beacon of hope." Viewers besieged the show, she continues, "telling us you're an angel, a talisman of goodness" (235). Sounding somewhat like Jaycee Dugard, Ma snaps that "I'm not a saint. I wish people would stop treating us like we're the only ones who ever lived through something terrible. I've been finding stuff on the Internet you wouldn't believe . . . slavery's not a new invention." Refusing to fit into an assumed script of victimization, Ma connects her suffering to other forms of victimization like solitary confinement, abusive orphanages, child labor, and "kids getting raped by Daddy every night" while the interviewer cringes (236). Lost girls who return, like *Room*'s Ma, negotiate a world that struggles to categorize them.

The novel's conclusion literally revisits Room, as Jack and Ma say a final good-bye to the objects that created their world, much as they did each night in captivity. The text and rhythms deliberately play tribute to Margaret Wise Brown's children's classic *Goodnight Moon*. Leonard Marcus writes that Brown's book functions as a "ritual preparation for a journey beyond that world, a leave-taking of the known for the unknown world of darkness and dreams" (187). The moment prepares Jack to move into the real world more fully because it is a recognition of mother love; his old beloved Room, stripped of memory and Ma's sheltering presence, is merely "a crater, a hole where something happened" (321).

The novel *Room* documents the immense wellsprings of maternal love in captivity. So too does Isla Morley's work of fiction, *Above*, which rescripts the events of Jaycee Dugard's story in interesting ways. The novel is told by Blythe, who is kidnapped at sixteen and secreted in an abandoned missile silo by an end-of-days fanatic. In a plot much like other captivity memoirs and novels, Blythe is held prisoner by a man who sexually exploits her while claiming to "protect" her. "We are the Remnant, Blythe," her captor Dobbs intones, claiming the girl for his new Eve. "You and me—we will one day seed the new world" (48). When Blythe angers him by creating a mess in the silo, Dobbs rapes her. In a move reminiscent of Elizabeth Smart's captor Brian David Mitchell, Dobbs "weds" Blythe to self-justify his abuse. He then institutes "Married Time," lecturing her while raping her that "a wife has a duty to her husband" (95). The end product of "Married Time" is Adam, left to Blythe to raise while her captor is gone for long stretches aboveground.

Like other captive children real and fictional, Adam is claimed by his mother as hers alone. "I am going to have a baby, Dobbs," Blythe tells her captor. "And because he had missed it the first go-around, I spelled it out real clear and slow. '*I* am going to have a baby. I. Me.' There was to be no 'we,' I told him" (130). Blythe's solitary claim to the captive child echoes that of *Room*'s Ma, who told the television reporter that "Jack's nobody's son but mine" (234). Jaycee Dugard responded similarly, telling *20/20*'s Diane Sawyer that when she looked at her daughters, "I don't see [Phillip Garrido]. I see my mom. I see me. I don't see him." In *Above*, Morley demonstrates how motherhood necessarily alters the captive woman's worldview. Although Blythe never abandons hope of escape, she realizes that she must create a livable environment for her child. "I have been trying so hard to make it home," she reflects of the silo. "If I can make it home, my son will not grow up a refugee" (135).

The ending third of *Above* morphs into science fiction; the world outside the silo has indeed, during Blythe's years of captivity, been ravaged by postnuclear meltdown. Having finally killed her captor and escaped to the surface with Adam, Blythe now questions herself. "Was he wrong to take me? Was he right to keep us down there?" she asks herself. "Am I not now beholden to him in a way I wasn't before? Will I now never be free of him?" (269). Returning to her family farm, where she learns of the death of her loved ones, Blythe admits that "this is not the world to which I wanted to return" (371). Yet she unabashedly embraces freedom, embracing her new reality and Adam's expanded future.

Neo-captivity narratives involving mothers and children are emotionally difficult texts. Jaycee Dugard's memoir claims her daughters as "the most precious thing in the world" (110). To protect their privacy, she creates spaces of silence in her text, protecting the girls as they encounter the wider world. Neo-captivity novels about motherhood have more textual freedom to examine, as do *Room* and *Above*, daily horrors and daily routines in these unusual circumstances. Both books dismiss the ludicrous idea that captivity is its own simpler form of freedom, much as Dugard's memoir undoes the public assumption that she merely adjusted to oppression over a number of years. While laying bare the harsh misogyny at the root of captivity, all three texts also show how the birth of children brings new emotional ties into the lives of imprisoned mothers.

Cleveland: Michelle Knight

Halfway across the country, four years after Jaycee Dugard left her backyard, another mother in captivity broke down a locked front door. In May 2013 the American public learned of the decade-long imprisonment of three Cleveland-area women. "I've been kidnapped and I've been missing for ten years, and I'm, I'm here, I'm free now," a woman named Amanda Berry told a surprised 911 operator. Neighbors helped Berry smash the door after hearing her screams for help. Inside the squalid house filled with chains and padlocks, police officers encountered two other women. They were Michelle Knight, last seen in 2002, and Gina DeJesus, missing since 2004. All three women had been raped, beaten, and tortured for years. Berry had borne a daughter; Knight had suffered five miscarriages as a result of beatings. The women's captor, former bus driver Ariel Castro, was subsequently charged with over 900 counts of rape and assault.

The "Cleveland kidnapping" case soon riveted the nation. Irin Carmon asserts that the story "fits every societal expectation of what sexual violence looks like: Young girls, abducted off the street, imprisoned by grim-faced perpetrators whose mug shots are straight out of a crime procedural" ("Cleveland Kidnapping"). For others, it was a telling example of societal anomie. "Many neighbors have now reported, in hindsight, screams from Castro's house," writes Debra Houry. "Did any of Mr. Castro's neighbors think it was 'just another' instance of domestic violence and figured it 'wasn't their place' to intervene?" ("Stemming"). Still other critics argued that the actions of neighbor Charles Ramsey—a charismatic African American man whose account of the rescue became extremely popular on social media networks—suggested progress in bystander intervention. Ramsey told the press that he initially believed Berry's cries for help were part of a domestic-violence incident. Amy Davidson notes that "in many times and places, a line like that has been offered as an excuse for walking *away*, not for helping a woman break down your neighbor's door. How many women have died as a result? They didn't yesterday" ("What Charles Ramsey").

Literally bursting into the public consciousness, the three Cleveland women then returned to private life and to physical and emotional healing for the better part of a year. On the symbolic date of her one-year anniversary of freedom (May 6, 2014), Michelle Knight released her memoir, *Finding Me*. Nearly a year later, her cocaptives Amanda Berry and Gina DeJesus brought forth their story entitled *Hope: A Memoir of Survival in Cleveland*. The two works are distinct. Knight's account is a raw first-person account of her ordeal in captivity. *Hope*, which is cowritten with two investigative journalists, alternates the women's voices with narratives of the police and FBI investigations; additionally, it provides insight into Ariel Castro's upbringing and his extensive history of domestic violence. Both narratives are compelling and necessary for a full understanding of the captives' experience; I focus here primarily on Knight's *Finding Me* because of its first-person testimonial structure and its congruency with the social-justice orientation of the Smart and Dugard memoirs.

In the introduction to her memoir, Michelle Knight references both Elizabeth Smart and Jaycee Dugard in a litany of past kidnapping cases. "These kinds of stories are big news," she muses, "but when they fade away, it's easy to forget all the people who are still missing. . . . I want everyone to remember those who are still lost" (ix–x). *Finding Me* is an account of a woman lost, both literally and figuratively. Knight's early years were marked by severe sexual abuse, homelessness, food insecurity, and despair. At one point she lived in a garbage can under a bridge. As a teenager, Knight became pregnant by a sweet-talking boy who already had a girlfriend. "I hoped that at least the baby would love me," she recalls wistfully. "At the time I felt like no one else in the world did" (50). Kidnapped by Castro on her way to a custody meeting about her young son, Knight was plunged into an even deeper nightmare. Like the other captivity memoirs, *Finding Me* is replete with scenes of grim suffering. Initially, Knight spent large chunks of time chained upright to a pole in the basement, her oxygen limited by the metal chain in her mouth and by a motorcycle helmet jammed on her head. Fed scraps fit for a dog, she could not wash her body in any way for over a year, and her skin blackened and mottled from dirt. A few paper napkins were all she had for menstrual care, but, Knight notes, "he never gave me enough, so I had brown blotches of dried blood all over my body." She adds that she "also had so much of his dried semen in my hair that when I touched it, it was hard as a rock" (98). During the frigid Cleveland winters, Castro often left her naked, without blankets or coverings, as he repeatedly raped her. "You're not here to stay warm," he informed a naked and shivering Knight at one point. "You're only here for one thing" (119). At the time of her rescue, it was reported that Knight required reconstructive surgery because of facial beatings; she had also been rendered infertile from sexual abuse, and she weighed only eighty-four pounds.

Knight, unlike Smart and Dugard, endured imprisonment with other strangers. It is clear from both survivor accounts that the Cleveland hostages experienced many interpersonal tensions (some of which continue today) stemming from Castro's emotional manipulation. Castro frequently isolated the women; at times, he appeared to give either Gina DeJesus or Amanda Berry "preferential" treatment.[11] Knight believed herself to be at the bottom of the house of horrors' social hierarchy. "One of the hardest parts about [captivity]," she writes, "was that it seemed to me like [Castro] treated the others better than he did me" (176). She often felt "as if I was the prisoner who got beat down the most. And my perception was that on some days I was the only one he had raped" (177). Though Knight appears infrequently in Berry and DeJesus's book *Hope*, her account of being frequently isolated and subject to severe abuse is supported. DeJesus recalls Castro repeatedly removing Knight from the group to help with what he euphemistically calls "cleaning." "Yeah, right," DeJesus comments sarcastically. "We know what he's really doing with her, and she tells us anyway. So why does he try to hide it?" (126). Berry also hints at Knight's assertive tendency, noting: "Michelle usually stays in her room [during group exercise time] because whenever she's with him they get into a fight. Gina and I have learned it's easier if you don't talk back to him" (229).

Ariel Castro's unfathomable vitriol for Michelle Knight was most sharply revealed in his attitude toward her pregnancy. While he bragged about his daughter with Berry and, incredibly, took the child to church on Sundays, Castro impregnated Knight five times, berated her as "a little slut," and beat her in the stomach each time until she miscarried (*Finding Me* 134). During the fifth ordeal, Knight rescued her fetus from the toilet. Castro screamed that "it's your fault. You aborted my baby. I should go get my gun and blow your head off right now" (211).

Acknowledging that we cannot know what motivated Castro's seemingly boundless rage toward Knight, her status as his "invisible" first victim seems to echo throughout the memoir. Castro's abductions of DeJesus and Berry received widespread publicity on the news; the girls' cases were also featured on the *Oprah Winfrey Show*, the *Montel Williams Show*, and *America's Most Wanted*. The Berry/Serrano and the Ruiz/DeJesus families were also fearless and tireless in the media, holding regular public vigils, contacting reporters and the police regularly, and maintaining an unshakeable faith that their daughters were alive. Eventually, police offered a $25,000 reward for the open cases. Castro thrilled at the media attention surrounding his crimes; he even telephoned Berry's mother to assure her of Amanda's "safety," and he joined search parties for DeJesus.

The captivity of Michelle Knight, by contrast, yielded no similar satisfaction. Deemed a runaway by most people familiar with her case, Knight's information was removed from the National Crime Information Center after only fifteen months. Her disappearance was not connected with those of her fellow captives. In fact, in an odd twist, a *different* third woman (the still-missing Ashley Summers) was sometimes connected to the Berry/DeJesus cases, most prominently on an October 2009 *Oprah Winfrey Show* episode. Similarly, the archived recording of Cleveland police conversing with dispatch before entering Castro's house makes clear the differing levels of public awareness surrounding the cases. The officers are advised that Georgina DeJesus might be in the house as well. After the jubilant "We found them! We found them!" there is an awkward coda as the entering officer reports, in a somewhat confused tone of voice, that there is also "a Michelle Knight in the house . . . I don't know if you want to look that up in the system? Thirty-two years old."

Castro's sadism seemed to be fueled by the lack of public interest in Knight's case. "Nobody is even looking for you. There ain't been any fliers put around the neighborhood, and nothin's been on the news. I can do whatever I want to you. No one gives a crap," Castro tells Knight (95). "Just about every day he reminded me," writes Knight, "that he did not see one single thing on TV or any fliers in the neighborhood about my disappearance. 'You're a nobody,' he always told me" (117). This theme was repeated when Castro's next two victims arrived. "At least someone is looking for [Amanda Berry]. But who's looking for you? Not a soul. That's because you don't mean nothin' to nobody. I can keep you in here forever and nobody will miss you," he jeered (132). After kidnapping DeJesus, Castro told Knight "no one was ever looking for you. That's why I hate you the most" (152).

If Jaycee Dugard's testimony alerts us to *what* we don't see in our own literal and metaphorical "backyards," Knight's story forces us to confront *who* we don't see as missing. Eric Freedman asserts that the archive of fliers and posters highlighting America's missing presents a "crisis of representation as well as a representation of crisis. What I don't see are the statistics on runaways, those missing on a voluntary basis. What I don't see are the statistics on the number of kids abducted by relatives. What I don't see are families in crisis, broken homes" (696). As a former runaway with a troubled family history, Knight was not recognized as a potential crime victim. She is one of many whose stories do not fit the more media-friendly "lost white girl" paradigm. As Rebecca Wanzo has commented, "the loss of some citizens do not become events" ("Era of Lost [White] Girls" 101).

The invisible outcast Knight, however, seems to have practiced the same kind of maternal spirit that permeates the story of Jaycee Dugard. "When you're the oldest one, you have to watch out for the younger ones. That's just what big sisters do," Knight writes of her fellow captives (152). Often physically bound to DeJesus, Knight worried over her and protected her. She recounts how "if the dude started in with [attempts to rape] Gina, I would beg for him to stop. 'Please, take me instead,' I said. 'I'm the one you hate'" (153). Frequently kept apart from Berry, Knight would nonetheless raise the volume of her TV whenever Berry's kidnapping was referenced on the news. "I wanted her to know that people were still looking for her," she recalls (131). She also became an aunt to Berry's daughter.

A mother herself, Knight had already experienced tremendous loss prior to her captivity, when her son was removed from her care. The yearning for her son is palpable in the memoir, and the book's center contains color photographs of poems and pictures she made for him over years in captivity. Yet the story's ending is bittersweet; adopted shortly after Knight's disappearance, Joey has not, as of this time, been reunited with his biological mother. Insightfully connecting her own kidnapping to her son's situation, Knight insists that "I would never rip him out of his world just so he can be in mine" (239). Perhaps because she is estranged from her biological family, Knight has instead made a family of the public. She has emerged as the Cleveland women's visible representative. The only survivor at Castro's sentencing, Knight stared him down and made a long, compelling statement. She was a feisty presence at the demolition of Castro's house, passing out balloons and greeting onlookers. Furthermore, Knight has continued to serve as a public advocate for victimized women. Most recently she took to the airwaves to defend a California woman kidnapped in childhood. The woman, like Jaycee Dugard, had appeared in public with her captor and their child, provoking skepticism from neighbors about the veracity of her story. "Just because you're not chained up and you're not locked in the basement doesn't mean you ain't trapped," Knight told CNN. "I know exactly what it feels like to be trapped in your own mind . . . and told you can't do anything about it, nobody will care about what you say" (Knight, "Stop Doubting").

In the beginning of her memoir, Knight muses that "the man who took away a huge part of my life would have wanted me to stay quiet." But "that's exactly why I shouldn't," she continues. Now "I want to speak up for all those missing women and children who still aren't being heard" (xi). The advocacy of which Knight speaks resurfaces in Carla Norton's 2013 novel *The Edge of Normal* and Chelsea Cain's *One Kick* (2014), which both feature formerly trafficked young women rescuing other children from sex slavery. Injecting an action-adventure sensibility into the neo-captivity fiction subgenre, both novels avow that kidnapped girls can draw strategically on their authoritative knowledge of suffering to help end that of other victims.

A decade after she was rescued from four years of being held hostage as a pedophile's sexual slave, *The Edge of Normal*'s protagonist Reeve LeClaire is surviving but not thriving. She holds a restaurant job, but suffers from severe interpersonal anxiety. Reeve's discussions with her therapist center on her inability to sustain meaningful relationships and her desire to "have a normal life and be a normal adult" (19). Much like *Still Missing*'s Annie, who cracks that there is no support group for "Some Asshole Abducted Me Anonymous, online or off" (15), Reeve is deeply isolated by the singularity of her experience. After being rescued, Reeve recalls feeling like "she'd emerged into a world that felt like an alien planet. No one spoke her language. Not a soul could understand" (36). She connected only with another woman who experienced captivity as a girl. "It sounds corny, but I always think she was like an angel or something," Reeve tells her therapist (37).

The sudden reappearance of a kidnapped girl offers the now-adult Reeve a chance to adopt the role of mentor. She listens as the girl, Tilly, also brought forcibly into the world of adult sexuality, expresses the contradictions of readjusting to freedom after intense trauma. "So here I am, with no TV and no computer and no phone," Tilly complains. "I mean, after spending, like, a year locked up in a dungeon, getting raped and sucking cock, do they really think I can't handle TV?" (103). Reeve's prior captivity experience leads her to correctly intuit Tilly's strange silences; ultimately, she discerns that the girl had a *second* and still at-large captor of whom she remains deeply afraid. Reeve's detective work ultimately leads to her heroic rescue of yet another captive child, Hannah. The locked basement door opens and present meets past, as "a single bulb illuminates a small figure and Reeve gasps, seeing her own ghostly image in the pale girl caught in that dim wash of light" (247).

At the book's conclusion, Reeve, who has primarily pondered the word *intimacy* in terms of sexual connection, reconceives it as an expression of her therapeutic impact. "I actually succeeded in making an intimate connection with another human being . . . who would have guessed that I'd be bonding over scars with another survivor, eh?" she tells her therapist (269). Reeve's therapist encourages her to pursue a trauma-therapy career, arguing that "you already understand more about captivity syndromes than my best graduate students. . . . Do some analysis. Write some papers. Develop your natural insights" (270). Despite the implausibility of several of the action-rescue sequences, at the novel's heart lies the heroine's desire to rebuild her life through attachments to other survivors.

One Kick amplifies the captivity novel's adventure sensibility, but reaches similar conclusions. Heroine Kathleen "Kick" Lannigan was kidnapped as a child into an underground ring of child pornographers. The exploitation films in which she performed, nicknamed "The Beth Movies," remain ubiquitous on the Dark Web. Years removed from her original rescue in a police raid, the now-adult Kick remains isolated. She lives in a state of hyperarousal, spending her free time at target practice or obsessively cuffing and uncuffing her hands. The contents of her purse include "the army fixed-blade survival knife, the recon camo tactical knife, a three-pack of throwing knives, the Leatherman, her lipstick pepper spray, a pouch of throwing stars, the handcuffs, and a pen with a steel tip that could be used as an emergency window breaker" (146). Kick's nervous energy is directed toward mapping other cases of children's disappearances. She constantly downloads Amber Alerts, knowing that, despite the long odds of such actions, she will "drive up and down the interstate until she was exhausted, and stay up half the night refreshing her browser, sorting through every detail, hunting for anything familiar" (24).

When Bishop, a suave, mysterious benefactor with strength, money, and a fleet of helicopters, arrives, Kick is given the opportunity to switch from obsessive self-defense to assertive offense. Bishop values Kick's specialized knowledge and urges her that by "coming with me . . . using your background to see things I can't," the duo can track down two kidnapped children (55). Kick literally and figuratively "taps" her knowledge of dark hideaways, rapping on false walls, closets, and basements to find a sequence of captivity boxes much like the ones she was confined in as a girl. She also draws on her personalized understanding of pedophilia's dynamics when she video-chats an appeal to online predators, flushing out the sadist and facilitating the children's rescue.

The heroines of *One Kick* and *The Edge of Normal* bear some similarities to by-now familiar media tropes of resourceful women, including horror's "final girl," television's ass-kicking action heroine, and the stars of film's rape-revenge genre. Yet they are also distinct in important ways. Unlike most of these figures (and also unlike other captivity novels, which are focused on adult women's sufferings), heroines like Reeve and Kick have survived child rape, prostitution, and pornography, some of the most corrosive topics imaginable to mass-market audiences. Authors Norton and Cain develop literary strategies of displacement that shield the heroines from the psychic burdens of such narration. Norton frequently switches perspective, commenting indirectly on Reeve's own backstory through the narration of the two kidnapped girls, and in particular through the thoughts of their sadistic captor. Cain similarly relies on other characters to sketch elements of Kick's traumatic childhood. Bishop's body, rather than Kick's, absorbs a violent wrist suspension that is earlier discussed as the villain's preferred form of torturing children.

Action-adventure captivity narratives appear more ambivalent about the type and the pleasure of vengeance as well. Both *The Edge of Normal* and *One Kick* are cynical about any kind of happy ending. Each affirms that captivity survivors negotiate what Norton calls "cascading despair" in a society that trumpets but does not embrace them (99). Reeve critiques mainstream media's "perfectly groomed newscasters sitting in well-lit studios" who "pick over the details of her abuse" (33). Norton also indicts armchair social media users who offer "long-winded expositions on post-traumatic shock disorder, plus a few good wishes—posted with lots of exclamation points!!!—that are intended for [Reeve] . . . and every other victim of every other sex crime ever committed" (181). Cain, meanwhile, analyzes the monetization of captivity through the character of Kick's mother, a greedy woman who soaked up media attention after her daughter's reappearance. Despite paying no attention to her daughter's trauma, Cain writes in a grim inside joke that "ever since [Paula Lannigan had] read Elizabeth Smart's book, she acted like she had some psychological insight into Kick's behavior" (125).

For both of these fictional survivors, peace is found not in confrontation with the captor or the violence wreaked upon them, but rather in the opportunity to aid others.[12] In both novels, the men responsible for Reeve's and Kick's kidnappings are jailed. Indeed, Kick's ex-captor remains a compelling source of ambiguity for her because her selective memory often shields herself from his crimes, recalling instead his protective paternalism toward her. Refusing to neatly wrap up the heroine's personal suffering, these action-adventure neo-captivity novels locate the greatest value in reaching out as an avenging angel and sweeping the cobwebs from basements and hidden spaces.

Help Save the Next Girl

"A girl disappeared from Clayton Falls a couple of years before I did, and I used to worry about finding her body in the woods when I was walking [dog] Emma" muses ex-captive Annie in *Still Missing*. "Now I wondered if the world was full of girls like me. Their families had moved on. They weren't front-page news anymore. They were locked up in some cabin or dungeon with their very own freak, still waiting to be rescued" (82). Annie's vision of the world is exceedingly dark. Yet neo-captivity narratives frequently express the unsettling conviction that the world is indeed full of such girls. All three captivity memoirs detail how kidnappers manipulated their victims' fears for other girls. Brian David Mitchell, for instance, later unsuccessfully attempted to kidnap Elizabeth Smart's cousin. Phillip Garrido manipulated Jaycee Dugard by claiming that by serving as his sex slave, she protected other little girls from his attacks. Ariel Castro, as we know, did kidnap multiple women, and the survivor memoir *Hope* goes even further, providing unsettling snapshots about gendered violence in the Cleveland region. In the course of the investigation, the head of a still-unidentified Hispanic girl, originally feared to be Gina DeJesus, is found in a backpack; post-rescue, *another* resident on Castro's street is found to have raped and murdered several young women. The ghosts of future victims also course through *Still Missing* and other neo-captivity novels. *The Edge of Normal*'s Reeve and *One Kick*'s Kathleen literally rescue other young women. *Above*'s Blythe endures her kidnapper's threats to target her sister next, and *Room*'s Ma speculates about young victims in her national television interview.

Neo-captivity's recurring refrain of a "next girl" to save returns us to the crux of postfeminist gothic. Narrating accounts of being trapped, beaten, raped, and sometimes impregnated, neo-captivity survivors testify to the starkest realities of violence against women. They frame their experiences within a larger context of other forms of victimization and abuse and encourage us to create an American society more attuned to problems of sexual and physical violence hidden behind closed doors. Like other postfeminist gothic texts, they also provide us with tools to critically dissect postfeminist culture.

Yvonne Tasker and Diane Negra remind us that feminist inquiry is needed more than ever "at a time when women face significant challenges to their economic well-being, hard-won reproductive rights, and even authority to speak, while popular culture blithely assumes that gender equality is a given" (12). In a victim-denying and victim-blaming age, postfeminist gothic's abject protagonists—socially invisible, physically broken, or deceased—demand our attention. These texts maintain a pessimistic bent, as seen when Susanna Moore's Mamie despairs of sexual violence's inevitability ("vagina as fate"), or when Cornwell's Kay Scarpetta retreats into a numbing, computerized wall of words. Empowerment-oriented postfeminist popular culture tries to turn these stories "right side up," as we have seen in the colonization of Sebold's *The Lovely Bones* by young-adult fiction for its own ends. The texts themselves often express these tensions on their pages; Jodi Picoult, for instance, tempers stories of gendered violence through her literary practice of open-ended indeterminacy. Postfeminist gothic novels, though, all resist readings as progress-oriented bildungsromans or as empowerment narratives. Sapphire abruptly kills off her beloved heroine, and Alice Sebold's protagonist Helen experiences psychosis, foreclosing—as do most of the other novels—the traditional happy ending. Neo-captivity memoirs and novels certainly express joy and relief about restoration, but they also present ongoing scenes of trauma and unnerving fears for the "next girl."

To end as we began, let us return to Morgan Harrington, the college student from Virginia who left a rock concert and never came back. Morgan's mother, Gil Harrington, invoked Alice Sebold's postfeminist gothic novel *The Lovely Bones* in her press comments about her own daughter's "lovely bones." In the novel, Sebold's narrator Susie reinterprets her physical body as a site of skeletal "connections—sometimes tenuous, sometimes made at great cost, but often magnificent—that happened after I was gone" (320). The Harringtons have taken that concept to heart, creating the Help Save the Next Girl foundation to "spread safety information and prevent future crimes against young women." The national nonprofit publicizes missing-person cases, works directly with affected families, and provides safety training for women. In a tone similar to that of Jaycee Dugard's memoir, the mission statement claims that "as a community we must know our neighbors, be responsible for one another, and cherish precious family."

The phantom of the "next girl" recently became manifest in a new and tragic twist in Morgan's story. Five years later, another young college student in Charlottesville was assaulted, murdered, and left in a rural area. Police subsequently announced a significant forensic link between the cases of Hannah Graham and Morgan Harrington, and arrested a suspect. While the legal case involving Morgan's murder achieved resolution, the family's ongoing story of loss and grief, articulated with such grace and power by her parents over the years, continues unabated. Gil Harrington conveyed her relief at an arrest, but noted that it didn't "change a lot for us, in some ways." She continued: "Our bedroom is still empty upstairs. We're still not going to have the grandchildren, the wedding, those things" (Ford, "Family of Morgan Harrington"). In becoming her daughter's storyteller, and in her willingness to publicly share grief's wild, jagged power, Gil Harrington refuses tidy models of closure. For her family, she has said, "resistance rather than surrender was the right response" (Adams, "Resistance"). Postfeminist gothic work offers literary resistance, asking us to acknowledge an ongoing story of loss and violence that has enveloped Morgan Harrington and so many others. In a sun-dappled world, women writers challenge us to acknowledge the presence of breathtaking darkness, and far too many bones.

Notes

Chapter 1. Terror and Brightness

1. Use of the term *postfeminist* is also increasingly frequent in work that defines itself as feminist. "Are girls going wild in this postfeminist era?" ask Meda Chesney-Lind and Katherine Irwin in *Beyond Bad Girls*, a study of feminist criminology that takes on the "mean girl" narrative of the 1990s popular press (183). In "Pleasures and Problems of the 'Angry Girl,'" Kim Roberts begins her exploration of the limits of the phrase *Girl Power* by asserting that "today's postfeminism looks quite different from the feminism of the 1970s and 1980s" (220). I draw attention to this phenomenon in order to show the general agreement among feminist scholars that the set of cultural conditions shaping millennial young women and men are quite different than those of twenty or thirty years ago.

2. See also Pearce, "Beyond Redemption?," on feminist reading for agency and postfeminism, and Maher, "Post-Feminist Mystique," and Modleski, *Feminism without Women,* on the overuse of empowerment tropes.

3. The phrase *strong woman* has separate resonance in the African American tradition, where it is linked to an ethos of the "superwoman" or "STRONGBLACK-WOMAN" who is forced to bear multiple personal and professional roles without complaint. See, for instance, Morgan, *Biology of Horror*; Parks, *Fierce Angels*; and Michele Wallace, *Black Macho*. I am speaking here of a more vague and open phrase of substitution, where the speaker swaps the word *feminist* for something that appears less political.

4. On the development of female gothic criticism, see DeLamotte, *Perils of the Night*; Doody, "Deserts, Ruins and Troubled Waters"; Ellis, *Contested Castle*; Fleenor, "Introduction"; Showalter, "Dark Places" and *Sister's Choice*; Smith and Wallace, "Female Gothic: Then and Now"; Diana Wallace, *Female Gothic Histories*; and Winter, *Subjects of Slavery*.

5. See also Pain, "Space, Sexual Violence and Social Control"; Stanko, "Women, Crime, and Fear"; and Valentine, "Geography of Women's Fear."

6. See also Meyers's *Femicidal Fears* (2001) for discussion of others writing the female gothic experience during the 1960s to 1980s, including Beryl Bainbridge, Angela Carter, Diane Johnson, Edna O'Brien, and Muriel Spark.

7. See Oates's short stories "Where Are You Going, Where Have You Been?" (1970),"The Girl" (1974), and "Faithless" (1997), along with the novels *Black Water* (1992), *Foxfire: Confessions of a Girl Gang* (1993), *Zombie* (1995), *We Were the Mulvaneys* (1996), *Rape: A Love Story* (2003), *Missing Mom* (2005), *My Sister, My Love* (2008), and *Little Bird of Heaven* (2009).

8. See Neuman, "'Just a Backlash,'" for a sustained discussion of feminist waves in the novel.

9. See, for example, Gillis, Howie, and Munsford, *Third Wave Feminism*; Negra, "Quality Postfeminism?"; Projansky, *Watching Rape*; and Tasker and Negra, "Introduction."

10. See Gamble, "Postfeminism," for a discussion of British reporter Justine Picardie's attempt to test young women's identification with a postfeminist label.

11. See Greene, *Changing the Story*, for a discussion of Nancy Cott's discovery of a 1919 journal's use of "post-feminism" as a humanist term.

12. Third wave subjects affirm a relationship to feminism. For theoretical texts and anthologies of the period, see Baumgardner and Richards, *Manifesta*; Dicker and Piepmeier, "Introduction"; Findlen, *Listen Up*; Gillis, Howie, and Munford, *Third Wave Feminism*; Hernández and Rehman, *Colonize This!*; Heywood and Drake, *Third Wave Agenda*; and Walker, *To Be Real*.

13. On therapeutic rhetorics and gender, see also Cloud, *Control and Consolation*; Ouellette, "Take Responsibility"; Rapping, *Culture of Recovery*; Sandell, "Adjusting to Oppression"; and Travis, *Language of the Heart*.

14. See in particular the work of Frost, "Theorizing the Young Women"; Gill, "Postfeminist Media Culture"; Negra, *What a Girl Wants?*; McRobbie, *Aftermath of Feminism*; and Tasker and Negra, "Introduction."

15. On postfeminism and recession-era austerity, see Nathanson, "Dressed for Economic Distress," and Thoma, "What Julia Knew."

16. See also Warren Farrell, *Myth of Male Power*; Sommers, *War against Boys*; Parker, *Save the Males*; and Venker, "War on Men." See also Leonard, "Escaping the Recession," for a helpful compilation of many such titles.

17. See also the critiques of Caryl Rivers and Rosalind Barnett in *New Soft War on Women*.

18. See particularly the work of Banet-Weiser, "What's Your Flava?"; Patricia Hill Collins, *On Intellectual Activism*; Elam, *Souls of Mixed Folk*; McGary, *Post-Racial Ideal*; Senna, "Mulatto Millennium"; Sexton, *Amalgamation Schemes*; and Rainier Spencer, *Reproducing Race*.

19. See also Butler, "For White Girls Only?," on postfeminism's strategic inclusions of women of color.

20. See also Hirshman, "Homeward Bound," and Whelehan, *Overloaded.*

21. See also Crowley, *Feminism's New Age.*

22. See Cole, *Cult of True Victimhood,* on the broader historical context of Reagan-era antivictimization rhetoric.

23. See Cole, *Cult of True Victimhood,* and Mardorossian, "Toward a New Feminist Theory of Rape," on the historical rise of a broad range of antivictimist discourses in the 1990s.

24. See Meyers, *Femicidal Fears,* for an author-by-author discussion; also see DeMott, *Killer Woman Blues*; Kinahan, "Women Who Run from the Wolves"; Pollitt, "Not Just Bad Sex"; Sorisio, "Tale of Two Feminisms"; and Stringer, "Rethinking the Critique of Victim Feminism."

25. See Joseph, "Tyra Banks Is Fat," for an analysis of how Banks uses this sort of rhetorical shrug.

26. See the Twitter hashtag #SurvivorPrivilege; see also Dusenberry, "#SurvivorPrivilege Shows George Will"; Rosenberg, "George Will's Distasteful Conclusions"; and Solnit, "Cassandra among the Creeps."

27. See Weisman, "Measure to Protect Women," and Louise Erdrich's novel *The Round House* (2013).

28. See Whittier, *Politics of Child Sexual Abuse,* on the professionalization of many former grassroots feminist groups, and Wright and Hearn, "Neutralizing Gendered Violence," on "human rights" language displacing feminist language.

29. See also Boren, "Hope Solo and the Domestic Violence Case"; Echo Chambers, "Hope Solo"; Hess, "No, Women's Soccer"; and Macur, "In Hope Solo Case," on gender-symmetry arguments in the sports world.

30. Consequently, I have chosen to focus my analysis on texts, rather than the film versions that have followed from several of the novels studied here. One exception is Peter Jackson's version of *The Lovely Bones* (2009), since that film's strange repurposing as a Christmas offering for teenaged girls furthers my argument that postfeminist popular culture seeks to lighten up traumatic issues.

31. See in particular Rosenfelt, "Feminism, 'Postfeminism,' and Contemporary Women's Fiction," and Greene, *Changing the Story*; on the rape novel of the second wave era, see Field, "Writing the Victim." See also Leonard, "I Really Must Be an Emma Bovary," for a different view of feminist fiction's historical congruencies.

32. See also Meyers's *Femicidal Fears* on Joyce Carol Oates and contemporaries discussing sexual violence. See also Rubenstein, "Bodily Harm," on Margaret Atwood; Melley, "Stalked by Love," on Diane Johnson; and the uses of paranoia to reveal misogyny.

33. See Whelehan's discussion in *The Feminist Bestseller* of the bonkbuster, and Hogland's depiction in *Feminism and Its Fictions* of the "shopping and fucking novel." See also Langer, "Whatever Happened to Feminist Fiction?," on 1980s modalities of women's literature.

34. See Mazza's introduction to Mazza, DeShell, and Sheffield, *Chick-Lit,* in which she writes that their anthology of women's writing was the first to use the term.

35. See also Harzewski, *Chick Lit and Postfeminism,* and Benstock, "Afterword: The New Woman's Fiction," on chick lit's literary ancestors.

Chapter 2. Uneasy Lie the Bones

1. See also Bliss, "Share Moments," who contends that snapshots of Susie work as "substitutes for her missing body" (862).
2. See also Bliss, "Share Moments," on photographs and disruption in *The Lovely Bones*.
3. See also Beirne, *Lesbians in Television*; Hamer and Budge, "Introduction"; and McKenna, "Queer Insistence," on the circulation of lesbian chic in postfeminist discourses.
4. See Walters, "From Here to Queer."
5. See also Tallent, "Trouble with Postmortality."
6. Wave issues are widely discussed within contemporary feminist theory; see Baumgardner and Richards, *Manifesta*; Dicker and Piepmeier, "Introduction"; Findlen, *Listen Up*; Gillis, Howie, and Munford, *Third Wave Feminism*; Astrid Henry, *Not My Mother's Sister*; Hernández and Rehman, *Colonize This!*; Heywood and Drake, *Third Wave Agenda*; Looser and Kaplan, *Generations*; Maglin and Perry, *"Bad Girls"/"Good Girls"*; Reger, *Different Wavelengths*; Deborah Siegel, *Sisterhood Interrupted*; and Walker, *To Be Real*.
7. See also Belkin, "Opt-Out Revolution"; Faludi, *Backlash*; and Hirshman, "Homeward Bound."
8. In Forman's novel, protagonist Mia eventually wakes up from her coma. I include it here because for the majority of the novel she is perceived by others as dead or on the boundary of death.
9. See Baumgardner and Richards's feminist critique of Girl Crisis, *Manifesta,* and Sommers's conservative critique of Girl Crisis, *War against Boys*.

Chapter 3. A Woman Might as Well Be Brave

1. Moore has also written two historical novels, *One Last Look* (2003) and *The Life of Objects* (2012), which are not covered in this chapter because of their thematic difference.
2. As told by Moore to interviewer Joyce Wadler (Moore, "At Home with Susanna").
3. See Early and Kennedy, *Athena's Daughters*; Heinecken, *Warrior Women of Television*; Inness, *Tough Girls* and *Action Chicks*; and Mainon and Ursini, *Modern Amazons*.
4. The scene is also discussed in Montemurro, "Charlotte Chooses Her Choice," and in Hirshman, "Homeward Bound."
5. See Michele Wallace, *Black Macho*; see also Harris-Perry, *Sister Citizen*; hooks, "Dig Deep"; Morgan, *Biology of Horror*; and Parks, *Fierce Angels*.
6. See also Clare Chambers, *Sex, Culture, and Justice,* on the limits of liberal theory and choice feminism; Ferguson, "Choice Feminism," on dissent; and Negra, *What a Girl Wants?,* on implicit conservativism behind many home/career "choice" narratives.

7. A list of important primary documents central to the Barnard conference and its aftermath is contained in Basiliere, "Political Is Personal."

8. The film, directed by Jane Campion, was neither a critical nor commercial success. Moore wrote the first draft of the screenplay, which ends with Rodriguez's death and Frannie's reunion with Malloy. Moore told interviewer Robert Birnbaum that Frannie "should have died," while also acknowledging that such a dark film would most likely not have been financially backed (Moore, "Birnbaum v. Susanna Moore").

9. See Moore, "Birnbaum v. Susanna Moore," where Moore says to Birnbaum, "It's a cop phrase. The original phrase would have been 'in the cunt.'"

10. For "vengeful equity," see Bloom and Chesney-Lind, "Women in Prison." For more on "equality with a vengeance," see Chesney-Lind and Pollock, "Women's Prisons." Similar topics are also taken up by Dragiewicz in *Equality with a Vengeance* and Alexander in "Crushing Equality."

11. See also the novels *Let's Go Play at the Adams'* (1975), *By Sanction of the Victim* (1976), and *The Girl Next Door* (1989). See also the films *The Girl Next Door* and *An American Crime,* both released in 2007.

Chapter 4. Break Through to Me

1. On the gothic's use of racialized others, see also Anolik, "Introduction: The Dark Unknown"; Arata, *Fictions of Loss*; Bergland, "Diseased States"; Burley, "Death of Zofloya"; Edwards, *Gothic Passages*; Halberstam, *Skin Shows*; and Malchow, *Gothic Images*.

2. See also Bodziock, "Cage of Obscene Birds" and "Richard Wright and Afro-American Gothic," and Goddu, "To Thrill the Land."

3. Mane's text is focused on anthologies and other texts authored by women who claim a third wave feminist identity. Nevertheless, I would argue that the strategies she describes with regard to whiteness apply to postfeminist culture as well.

4. See also Ibrahim, "Toward Black and Multiracial 'Kinship,'" and Joseph, *Transcending Blackness*. For the figure in literature, see Chen, "Postmodern Hybridity." For the figure in television, see McConnell, "Dark Angel."

5. See in particular the work of Young, "Black 'Like Me.'"

6. See also Harris-Perry, *Sister Citizen*; Jordan-Zachery, *Black Women, Cultural Images*; Patricia Bell Scott, "Debunking Sapphire"; Springer, "Divas"; and Zook, "Manifesto of Sorts."

7. See also Pough, *Check It While I Wreck It.*

8. Alice Walker and Maya Angelou are most famous for their writings. Both have produced works overtly influenced by spiritualism: Walker has written a pamphlet called *Sent by Earth: A Message from the Grandmother Spirit after the Bombing of the World Trade Center and Pentagon* (2001), and Angelou created a "Life Mosaic" collection of greeting cards for Hallmark.

9. See Whittier, *Politics of Child Sexual Abuse,* on the de-emphasis of a feminist perspective in incest-survivor support work.

10. In response to criticism, the line is written differently in different editions of this text. The 1994 third edition directly addresses public debate in a section titled "Honoring the Truth: A Response to the Backlash." The line in question there reads, "If you genuinely think you were abused and your life shows the symptoms, there's a strong likelihood that you were" (26).

11. See also Doane and Hodges, *Telling Incest,* on Roiphe's view of African American women's incest narrative.

12. McLennan, *Nature's Ban,* contains a thorough literary history.

13. Everett's frame novel *We's Lives in Da Ghetto* contains character names like "Clareece" and references to children with "Down Sinder," further suggesting connections to Sapphire's work.

14. See Higginbotham, *Righteous Discontent,* on the development of the politics of respectability.

15. See also Michlin for thorough discussion of the relationship between educational labor, the push metaphor, and self-rebirth.

16. See also Cooper, "'Maybe I'll Be a Poet, Rapper.'" Additionally, see Michlin's extended discussion of the literary relationship between Walker's and Sapphire's text. Sapphire has openly admitted her literary debt to Alice Walker, saying in an interview with Mark Marvel, "I wanted to let this whole new generation who's gonna read *Push* know that it was born out of *The Color Purple* . . . and the other books I mention. I don't think I could have written *Push* if Alice Walker had not written *The Color Purple*, or if Toni Morrison had not written *The Bluest Eye*. They kicked open the door" (Sapphire, "Sapphire's Big Push" 29). "Where my color purple?" Precious asks herself at one point (86).

17. See also Cooper, "'Maybe I'll Be a Poet, Rapper,'" on hip-hop literary aesthetics at work in *Push.*

18. Maternal offenders remain rare in literature; see Mardorossian, *Framing the Rape Victim,* on maternal sexual assault in recent fiction.

19. See also Dalsgard, "Disrupting the Black Feminist Consensus?"

20. See Kellogg, "Review: 'The Kid,'" who places *The Kid* amid Flannery O'Connor and William Faulkner in the Southern gothic tradition.

21. I focus here on the negative discourse surrounding the black rear end because of the particular way that Precious Jones is demonized as "waste" in Sapphire's text. However, scholars have also explicated it as a site of resistance and affirmation. See Collins, *Black Sexual Politics*; Hobson, "Nicki Minaj"; Miller-Young, *Taste for Brown Sugar*; Nash, *Black Body in Ecstasy*; and Parasecoli, "Bootylicious."

Chapter 5. Waking the Dead

1. See also Cargill and Kaufman's comprehensive bibliography of feminist detective fiction. In the wake of Scarpetta's success, female medical examiners have become lucrative literary heroines. Kathy Reichs's Bones series (1997–) features a petite, blonde, and blue-eyed fifty-something forensic anthropologist working

both in North Carolina and Canada. Successfully reinterpreted on television, *Bones* (2005–) has a breezier style. Former physician Tess Gerritsen's Rizzoli and Isles series (2001–) pairs a working-class detective with an elegant medical examiner similar to Scarpetta. It has been eponymously and successfully adapted to television (2010–).

2. The television shows *Bones* and *Rizzoli and Isles* rescript the medical professionals as younger women in their thirties. Actress Angelina Jolie has long been attached to play Scarpetta in a film adaptation of Cornwell's work, but this project is still in progress as of this writing.

3. For some foundational third wave–era print texts, see Brumberg, *Body Project*; Amy Erdman Farrell, *Fat Shame*; Gimlin, *Body Work*; Heywood, *Dedication to Hunger*; Hobson, *Venus in the Dark*; Peiss, *Hope in a Jar*; Price and Shildrick, *Feminist Theory and the Body*; Becky Thompson, *Hunger So Wide and So Deep*; Thomson, *Extraordinary Bodies*; Wallace-Sanders, *Skin Deep, Spirit Strong*; Weitz and Kwan, *Politics of Women's Bodies*; and Wolf, *Beauty Myth*. See also the websites Jezebel, Crunk Feminist Collective, and Everyday Feminism.

4. While the makeover narrative addresses all women, it takes a white and middle-class subject as normative. See McRobbie, *Aftermath of Feminism*; see also Ringrose and Walkerdine, "Regulating the Abject," on the denigration of lower-class subjects by makeover "experts"; and also Weber and Tice, "Are You Finally Comfortable in Your Own Skin?," on white normativity within the genre. I focus here on the normative white middle-class narrative because it is the experience of the particular victims in Cornwell's literary universe.

5. Cornwell has accused painter Walter Sickert (1860–1942) of being Jack the Ripper. See also her *Portrait of a Killer: Jack the Ripper—Case Closed* (2002). She allegedly spent millions of dollars purchasing dozens of Sickert paintings and hiring forensic experts to examine them.

6. Cornwell's universe does contain a few female villains, although they are rarely involved in sexual murder. Of women who are sexually sadistic, one is in thrall to serial murderer Temple Gault, and the other is delusional and identifies as an angel. The vast majority of predators in Cornwell's fiction are white males.

7. See also Cargill, "Chief Medical Examiner Kay Scarpetta." In Cornwell's universe, the single childless young woman is overwhelmingly the victim.

8. See also Gay, "Great 2014 Celebrity Nude Photos Leak," on Internet body policing.

9. See also Mantilla, "Gendertrolling," and Buni and Chemaly, "Unsafety Net," on quantifying misogyny online.

Chapter 6. Hedging Her Bets

1. Twitter, @jodipicoult, 16 August 2010, 5:26 a.m.

2. On priv-lit and Gilbert in particular, see Ruth Williams, "*Eat, Pray, Love*: Producing the Female Neoliberal Spiritual Subject," as well as Sanders and Barnes-Brown, "Eat, Pray, Spend."

3. See Duncan, "Black Women and Motherhood," for a persuasive reading of how science fiction diversifies the representation of black female subjectivity.

4. For the history of the term *soccer mom*, see MacFarquhar's article "What's a Soccer Mom Anyway?"

5. See Morin and Balz, "'Security Mom' Bloc Proves Hard to Find," on the hype surrounding the security-mom label.

6. For more on kidnapped children in recent female-oriented fiction, see Lee Martin, *The Bright Forever* (2005), Heather Gudenkauf, *The Weight of Silence* (2008), Jennifer McMahon, *Island of Lost Girls* (2008), and Cara Hoffman, *So Much Pretty* (2011).

7. See Cuklanz, *Rape on Prime Time*, on 1970s and 1980s procedurals. This figure seems most strikingly represented today by Detective Elliot Stabler of *Law and Order: Special Victims Unit* (1999–), who for twelve seasons physically assaulted and openly fantasized about killing sexual predators.

8. See Lewin, "Are These Parties for Real?," for a historical analysis of the controversy and relationship to moral panic.

9. See Mardorossian, *Framing the Rape Victim*, for a helpful summation of politicians' comments about rape during the 2012 election cycle.

Chapter 7. Up from the Basement

1. Victims of kidnappings have certainly not always been female. Public narratives about rescued young men abducted by nonfamily members and subjected to ordeals of sexual and physical abuse include the stories of Paul Martin Andrews, kidnapped and rescued in 1973; Steven Stayner, held from 1972 to 1980; and Shawn Hornbeck, missing between 2002 and 2007. I have focused on female kidnap victims here because of the book's overall thematic concerns, the congruency of rhetoric about misogyny across the female survivor memoirs, and the relative paucity of information about male survivor experiences. It is my hope that more will be written about male victims.

2. See also Namias, *White Captives*, and Faery, *Cartographies of Desire*, for fuller explanations of captives' status, adoption, and incest taboos in colonial America.

3. See also Hoeveler, "Female Captivity Narrative," on sixteenth- and seventeenth-century British nation-building and the racial dynamics of white women's captivity in harems.

4. Luders-Manuel, in "Captive America," argues that the unkempt image of Brian David Mitchell was compared in the press to Osama bin Laden and "used as a way to foster increased American patriotism against any who would attempt to hinder the freedom of its countrymen" in the post-9/11 era (10).

5. See the work of Hartman, *Scenes of Subjection*, and Abdur-Rahman, "This Horrible Exhibition," on depictions of sexual terror in slave narratives.

6. Serial killers Leonard Lake and Charles Ng, as well as Robert Berdella, have also professed to find the novel inspirational, as many true-crime documents attest.

7. The underground chambers where the women are tortured were formerly used as places of sanctuary by the Underground Railroad. Patterson draws a parallel between the captive women and slaves; Alex Cross thinks of "the extraordinary kidnapping and subjugation of more than four million Africans who were originally brought to America. They had been *abducted*. Against their will" (207; emphasis in original).

8. See Niven, "What's Next for Blake?"

9. See also arts blogger Caltabiano's "Curated: The New Buzzword" for a critique of the word.

10. Ariel Castro, the captor of three Cleveland women, utilized similar rhetoric. In *Hope*, Amanda Berry recounts begging to die after a particularly brutal rape. Castro then shouts, "I don't want to kill you! This is just about my sexual problem!" (42). Gina DeJesus similarly recalls Castro externalizing his abuse onto his penis "Charlie." "He blames Charlie. He's always saying, 'What Charlie wants, Charlie gets,'" DeJesus recalls (122).

11. There is no "worst" captivity in Cleveland; all captives faced horrible, unique trials. See Berry and DeJesus, *Hope*, for a fuller account of the particular ordeals of Amanda Berry and Gina DeJesus. Berry, for instance, was terrifyingly dependent on Castro for her daughter's material needs and safety. DeJesus, younger than the other two captives, faced a barrage of insults daily about her intelligence and learning ability.

12. See also Read, *New Avengers*, on rape revenge.

Works Cited

Aapola, Sinikka, Marnina Gonick, and Anita Harris. *Young Femininity: Girlhood, Power and Social Change*. Basingstoke, UK: Palgrave Macmillan, 2005. Print.

Abdur-Rahman, Aliyyah I. "This Horrible Exhibition: Sexuality in Slave Narratives." *The Oxford Handbook of the African-American Slave Narrative.* Ed. John Ernest. Oxford: Oxford University Press, 2014. 235–47. Print.

Adams, Duncan. "'Resistance Rather Than Surrender' Was Right Path for Family of Morgan Harrington." *Roanoke Times,* 10 October 2014. Web. 24 November 2015. http://www.roanoke.com/news/crime/resistance-rather-than-surrender-was-right-path-for-family-of/article_86e9e9da-4d9f-54ff-9f2c-e8ffa88c9712.html.

Ahmed, Sara. "Creating Disturbance: Feminism, Happiness and Affective Differences." *Working with Affect in Feminist Readings: Disturbing Differences.* Eds. Marianne Liljeström and Susanna Paasonen. London: Routledge, 2010. 31–44. Print.

Alcoff, Linda Martín. "Dear Congressman Akin." *Feminist Wire,* 21 August 2012. Web. 24 November 2015. http://thefeministwire.com/2012/08/dear-congressman-akin/.

———. "Rethinking Rape and Resistance." Twenty-First Annual Women and Society Conference. Marist College, Poughkeepsie, NY. 19 October 2012. Keynote address.

Alexander, Christopher M. "Crushing Equality: Gender Equal Sentencing in America." *American University Journal of Gender, Social Policy and the Law* 6.1 (1997): 199–229. Print.

Allen, Mary. *The Necessary Blankness: Women in Major American Fiction of the Sixties*. Urbana: University of Illinois Press, 1976. Print.

Annesley, James. *Blank Fictions: Consumerism, Culture and the Contemporary American Novel*. London: St. Martin's Press, 1998. Print.

Anolik, Ruth Bienstock. "Introduction: The Dark Unknown." *The Gothic Other: Racial and Social Construction in the Literary Imagination.* Eds. Ruth Bienstock Anolik and Douglas L. Howard. Jefferson, NC: McFarland, 2004. 1–16. Print.

Arata, Stephen. *Fictions of Loss in the Victorian Fin-de-Siècle*. Cambridge: Cambridge University Press, 1996. Print.

Armitt, Lucie. "Dark Departures: Contemporary Women's Writing after the Gothic." *Postfeminist Gothic: Critical Interventions in Contemporary Culture*. Eds. Benjamin A. Brabon and Stéphanie Genz. Basingstoke, UK: Palgrave Macmillan, 2007. 16–29. Print.

Atwood, Margaret. *Bodily Harm*. Toronto: McClelland and Stewart, 1981. Print.

———. *The Handmaid's Tale*. 1985. New York: Fawcett Crest, 1986. Print.

———. *Lady Oracle*. 1976. New York: Anchor Books, 1998. Print.

Banet-Weiser, Sarah. "What's Your Flava? Race and Postfeminism in Media Culture." *Interrogating Postfeminism*. Eds. Yvonne Tasker and Diane Negra. Durham, NC: Duke University Press, 2007. 201–26. Print.

Barrera, Magdalena. "Hottentot 2000: Jennifer Lopez and Her Butt." *Sexualities in History: A Reader*. Eds. Kim M. Phillips and Barry Reay. New York: Routledge, 2001. 407–17. Print.

Barnum, Carol M. *The Fiction of John Fowles: A Myth for Our Time*. Greenwood, FL: Penkeville, 1988. Print.

Basiliere, Jenna. "Political Is Personal: Scholarly Manifestations of the Feminist Sex Wars." *Politics and Performativity* 22.1 (2008–9): n.p. Web. 24 November 2015. http://hdl.handle.net/2027/spo.ark5583.0022.101.

Bass, Ellen, and Laura Davis. *The Courage to Heal*. New York: Harper and Row, 1988. Print.

Baumgardner, Jennifer, and Amy Richards. *Manifesta: Young Women, Feminism, and the Future*. 2000. New York: Farrar, Straus and Giroux, 2010. Print.

Bean, Kellie. *Post-Backlash Feminism: Women and the Media since Reagan-Bush*. Jefferson, NC: McFarland, 2007. Print.

Becker, Susanne. *Gothic Forms of Feminine Fictions*. Manchester, UK: Manchester University Press, 1999. Print.

Beirne, Rebecca. *Lesbians in Television and Text after the Millennium*. Basingstoke, UK: Palgrave Macmillan, 2008. Print.

Belkin, Lisa. "The Opt-Out Revolution." *New York Times Magazine*, 26 October 2003. Web. 24 November 2015. http://www.nytimes.com/2003/10/26/magazine/26WOMEN.html.

Bellafante, Ginia. "Jodi Picoult and the Anxious Parent." *New York Times*, 17 June 2009. Web. 24 November 2015. http://www.nytimes.com/2009/06/21/magazine/21picoult-t.html.

Benstock, Shari. "Afterword: The New Woman's Fiction." *Chick Lit: The New Woman's Fiction*. Eds. Suzanne Ferriss and Mallory Young, New York: Routledge, 2006. 253–56. Print.

Bergland, Renée L. "Diseased States, Public Minds: Native American Ghosts in Early National Literature." *The Gothic Other: Racial and Social Construction in the Literary Imagination*. Eds. Ruth Bienstock Anolik and Douglas L. Howard. Jefferson, NC: McFarland, 2004. 90–103. Print.

Berlant, Lauren. *The Female Complaint: The Unfinished Business of Sentimentality in American Culture.* Durham, NC: Duke University Press, 2008. Print.

———. *The Queen of America Goes to Washington City: Essays on Sex and Citizenship.* Durham, NC: Duke University Press, 1997. Print.

Berry, Amanda, and Gina DeJesus, with Mary Jordan and Kevin Sullivan. *Hope: A Memoir of Survival in Cleveland.* New York: Viking, 2015. Print.

Bliss, Ann V. "Share Moments, Share Life: The Domestic Photograph as a Symbol of Disruption and Trauma in *The Lovely Bones*." *Women's Studies* 37.7 (2008): 861–84. Print.

Bloom, Barbara, and Meda Chesney-Lind. "Women in Prison: Vengeful Equity." *It's a Crime: Women and Criminal Justice*, 4th ed. Ed. Roslyn Muraskin. New York: Prentice Hall, 2007. 542–63. Print.

Bloom, Harold. "Introduction." *Margaret Atwood.* 3rd ed. Ed. Harold Bloom. New York: Infobase, 2009. 1–2. Print.

Blum, Virginia L. *Flesh Wounds: The Culture of Cosmetic Surgery.* Berkeley: University of California Press, 2003. Print.

Bodziock, Joseph. "The Cage of Obscene Birds: The Myth of the Southern Garden in Frederick Douglass's *My Bondage and My Freedom*." *The Gothic Other: Racial and Social Construction in the Literary Imagination.* Eds. Ruth Bienstock Anolik and Douglas L. Howard. Jefferson, NC: McFarland, 2004. 251–63. Print.

———. "Richard Wright and Afro-American Gothic." *Richard Wright: Myths and Realities.* Ed. C. James Trotman. New York: Garland, 1988. 27–42. Print.

Bolotin, Susan. "Voices from the Post-Feminist Generation." *New York Times Magazine,* 17 October 1982, 28–31. Print.

Bordo, Susan. *Unbearable Weight: Feminism, Western Culture, and the Body.* Berkeley: University of California Press, 1993. Print.

Boren, Cindy. "Hope Solo and the Domestic Violence Case No One Is Talking About." *Washington Post,* 19 September 2014. Web. 24 November 2015. http://www.washingtonpost.com/blogs/early-lead/wp/2014/09/19/hope-solo-and-the-domestic-violence-case-no-one-is-talking-about/.

Botting, Fred. "Flight of the Heroine." *Postfeminist Gothic: Critical Interventions in Contemporary Culture.* Eds. Benjamin A. Brabon and Stéphanie Genz. Basingstoke, UK: Palgrave Macmillan, 2007. 170–85. Print.

Box Office Mojo. "The Lovely Bones." IMDb, n.d. Web. 24 November 2015. http://www.boxofficemojo.com/movies/?id=lovelybones.htm.

Brabon, Benjamin A., and Stéphanie Genz. "Introduction: Postfeminist Gothic." *Gothic Studies* 9.2 (2007): 1–6. Print.

———. "Introduction: Postfeminist Gothic." *Postfeminist Gothic: Critical Interventions in Contemporary Culture.* Eds. Benjamin A. Brabon and Stéphanie Genz. Basingstoke, UK: Palgrave Macmillan, 2007. 1–15. Print.

Braithwaite, Ann. "Politics of/and Backlash." *Journal of International Women's Studies* 5.5 (June 2004): 18–33. Print.

Bray, Abigail. "Governing the Gaze: Child Sexual Abuse Moral Panics and the Post-Feminist Blindspot." *Feminist Media Studies* 9.2 (2009): 173–91. Print.

———. *Misogyny Re-Loaded*. Victoria, Australia: Spinifex Press, 2014. Print.

Broeske, Pat H. "A Midwest Nightmare, Too Depraved to Ignore." *New York Times*, 14 January 2007. Web. 24 November 2015. http://www.nytimes.com/2007/01/14/movies/14broes.html?pagewanted=all&_r=0.

Bronfen, Elisabeth. *Over Her Dead Body: Death, Femininity and the Aesthetic*. New York: Routledge, 1992. Print.

Brooks, Ann. *Postfeminisms: Feminism, Cultural Theory, and Cultural Forms*. London: Routledge, 1997. Print.

Browder, Laura. "Dystopian Romance: True Crime and the Female Reader." *Journal of Popular Culture* 39.6 (2006): 928–53. Print.

Brown, DeNeen. "Book Review: 'The Kid,' by Sapphire." *Washington Post*, 15 July 2011. Web. 24 November 2015. http://www.washingtonpost.com/entertainment/books/book-review-the-kid-by-sapphire/2011/06/27/gIQAHVM3GI_story.html.

Brown, Ivana. "Ambivalence of the Motherhood Experience." *Twenty-First-Century Motherhood: Experience, Identity, Policy, Agency*. Ed. Andrea O'Reilly. New York: Columbia University Press, 2010. 121–39. Print.

Brown, Wendy. *States of Injury: Power and Freedom in Late Modernity*. Princeton, NJ: Princeton University Press, 1995. Print.

Brownley, Martine Watson. *Deferrals of Domain: Contemporary Women Novelists and the State*. New York: St. Martin's Press, 2000. Print.

Brumberg, Joan Jacobs. *The Body Project: An Intimate History of American Girls*. New York: Vintage, 1998. Print.

Buni, Catherine, and Soraya Chemaly. "The Unsafety Net: How Social Media Turned Against Women." *Atlantic*, 9 October 2014. Web. 24 November 2015. http://www.theatlantic.com/technology/archive/2014/10/the-unsafety-net-how-social-media-turned-against-women/381261/.

Burley, Stephanie. "The Death of Zofloya; or, The Moor as Epistemological Limit." *The Gothic Other: Racial and Social Construction in the Literary Imagination*. Eds. Ruth Bienstock Anolik and Douglas L. Howard. Jefferson, NC: McFarland, 2004. 197–211. Print.

Burnham, Michelle. *Captivity and Sentiment: Cultural Exchange in American Literature, 1682–1861*. Hanover, NH: University Press of New England, 1997. Print.

Butler, Jess. "For White Girls Only? Postfeminism and the Politics of Inclusion." *Feminist Formations* 25.1 (2013): 35–58. Print.

Butler, Pamela, and Jigna Desai. "Manolos, Marriage, and Mantras: Chick-Lit Criticism and Transnational Feminism." *Meridians: feminism, race, transnationalism* 8.2 (2008): 1–31. Print.

Cain, Chelsea. *One Kick*. New York: Simon and Schuster, 2014. Print.

Callus, Ivan. "(Auto)Thanatography or (Auto)Thanatology? Mark C. Taylor, Simon Critchley and the Writing of the Dead." *Modern Language Studies* 41.4 (2005): 427–38. Print.

Caltabiano, Andrea. "Curated: The New Buzzword." *Calta Creative*. 6 May 2014. Web. 24 November 2015. http://www.caltacreative.com/blog/2014/5/6/curated-the-new-buzzword.

Cameron, Deborah. "That's Entertainment? Jack the Ripper and the Selling of Sexual Violence." *Femicide: The Politics of Woman Killing*. Eds. Jill Radford and Diana E. H. Russell. New York: Twayne, 1992. 184–88. Print.

Caputi, Jane. *The Age of Sex Crime*. Bowling Green, OH: Bowling Green University Popular Press, 1987. Print.

Cargill, Ann Sanders. "Chief Medical Examiner Kay Scarpetta." *Clues* 22.2 (2001): 35–48. Print.

Cargill, Ann Sanders, and Natalie Hevener Kaufman. "Feminism and Formula Fiction: The Ends." *Clues* 19.1 (1998): 61–77. Print.

Carmon, Irin. "The Cleveland Kidnapping Could Have Been Stopped." *Salon*, 9 May 2013. Web. 24 November 2015. http://www.salon.com/2013/05/09/the_cleveland_kidnapping_could_have_been_stopped/.

———. "*The Lovely Bones* Wins by Targeting Twihards." *Jezebel*, 19 January 2010. Web. 24 November 2015. http://jezebel.com/5452008/the-lovely-bones-wins-by-targeting-twihards.

Cassidy, Marsha F. "The Cinderella Makeover: *Glamour Girl*, Television Misery Shows, and 1950s Femininity." *The Great American Makeover: Television, History, Nation*. Ed. Dana Heller. Basingstoke, UK: Palgrave Macmillan, 2006. 125–40. Print.

Castiglia, Christopher. *Bound and Determined: Captivity, Culture-Crossing, and White Womanhood from Mary Rowlandson to Patty Hearst*. Chicago: University of Chicago Press, 1996. Print.

Chambers, Clare. *Sex, Culture, and Justice: The Limits of Choice*. University Park: Pennsylvania State University Press, 2008. Print.

Chambers, Echo. "Hope Solo: Does Domestic Abuse Have a Double Standard?" *BBC News Online*, 25 September 2014. Web. 24 November 2015. http://www.bbc.com/news/blogs-echochambers-29352322.

Champagne, Rosaria. *The Politics of Survivorship: Incest, Women's Literature, and Feminist Theory*. New York: New York University Press, 1996. Print.

Chen, Fu-Jen. "Postmodern Hybridity and Performing Identity in Gish Jen and Rebecca Walker." *Critique* 50.4 (2009): 377–96. Print.

Chesney-Lind, Meda, and Katherine Irwin. *Beyond Bad Girls: Gender, Violence and Hype*. New York: Routledge, 2008. Print.

Chesney-Lind, Meda, and Joycelyn M. Pollock. "Women's Prisons: Equality with a Vengeance." *Women, Law, and Social Control*. Eds. Alida V. Merlo and Joycelyn M. Pollock. Boston: Allyn and Bacon, 1995. 155–75. Print.

Clark-Flory, Tracy. "The 'Gray Rape' Myth." *Salon*, 1 March 2008. Web. 24 November 2015. http://www.salon.com/2008/03/01/ctv_flory_grayrape/.

Cloud, Dana L. *Control and Consolation in American Culture and Politics*. Thousand Oaks, CA: Sage, 1998. Print.

Coady, Roxane J., and Joy Johannessen, eds. *The Book That Changed My Life: 71 Remarkable Writers Celebrate the Books That Matter Most to Them*. New York: Gotham Books, 2006. Print.

Coates, Ta-Nehisi. "No, Hope Solo Is Not 'Like' Ray Rice." *Atlantic*, 23 September 2014. Web. 24 November 2015. http://www.theatlantic.com/entertainment/archive/2014/09/no-hope-solo-is-not-like-ray-rice/380626/.

Cobb, Shelley. "Adaptable Bridget: Generic Intertextuality and Postfeminism in *Bridget Jones's Diary*." *Authorship in Film Adaptation*. Ed. Jack Boozer. Austin: University of Texas Press, 2008. 281–304. Print.

———. "Mother of the Year: Kathy Hilton, Lynne Spears, Dina Lohan and Bad Celebrity Motherhood." *Genders* 48 (2008): n.p. Web. 15 August 2014. https://web.archive.org/web/20140719003857/http://www.genders.org/recent.html

Cole, Alyson. *The Cult of True Victimhood: From the War on Welfare to the War on Terror*. Stanford, CA: Stanford University Press, 2007. Print.

Collins, Gerard. "Contagion and Technology in Patricia Cornwell's Scarpetta Novels." *The Devil Himself: Villainy in Detective Fiction and Film*. Eds. Stacy Gillis and Philippa Gates. Westport, CT: Greenwood Press, 2002. 160–69. Print.

Collins, Jim. *Bring On the Books for Everybody: How Literary Culture Became Popular Culture*. Durham, NC: Duke University Press, 2010. Print.

Collins, Patricia Hill. *Black Sexual Politics: African Americans, Gender, and the New Racism*. New York: Routledge, 2005. Print.

———. *On Intellectual Activism*. Philadelphia: Temple University Press, 2012. Print.

Connelly, Sherryl. "Women on the Inside." *New York Daily News*, 29 April 2007. Final ed. 15. Print.

Cooper, Brittney. "Feminism's Ugly Internal Clash: Why Its Future Is Not up to White Women." *Salon*, 24 September 2014. Web. 24 November 2015. http://www.salon.com/2014/09/24/feminisms_ugly_internal_clash_why_its_future_is_not_up_to_white_women/.

———. "'Maybe I'll Be a Poet, Rapper': Hip-Hop Feminism and Literary Aesthetics in *Push*." *African American Review* 46.1 (2013): 55–69. Print.

Cornwell, Patricia. *All That Remains*. New York: Pocket Star, 1992. Print.

———. *Black Notice*. New York: G. P. Putnam's Sons, 1999. Print.

———. *Blow Fly*. New York: G. P. Putnam's Sons, 2003. Print.

———. *The Body Farm*. New York: Charles Scribner's Sons, 1994. Print.

———. *Body of Evidence*. New York: Pocket Books, 1991. Print.

———. *Book of the Dead*. 2008. New York: G. P. Putnam's Sons, 2007. Print.

———. *Cause of Death*. New York: Berkley Books, 1996. Print.

———. *Cruel and Unusual*. New York: Charles Scribner's Sons, 1993. Print.

———. *From Potter's Field*. New York: Scribner, 1995. Print.

———. "I Created a Monster: Interview with Patricia Cornwell." Interview by James Kidd. *Observer* (UK), 7 December 2008. Web. 24 November 2015. http://www.guardian.co.uk/books/2008/dec/07/patricia-cornwell-interview.

———. "Killer Queen: Patricia Cornwell Interview." Interview by Nigel Farndale. *Telegraph* (UK), 16 November 2009. Web. 15 August 2014. http://www.telegraph.co.uk/culture/books/6560751/Killer-Queen-Patricia-Cornwell-Interview.html.

———. *The Last Precinct*. New York: G. P. Putnam's Sons, 2000. Print.

———. "Patricia Cornwell's Extraordinary Life." Interview by Janice Turner. *Times Online* (UK), 19 April 2008. Web. 15 August 2014. http://entertainment.timesonline.co.uk/tol/arts_and_entertainment/books/article3743717.ece.

———. *Point of Origin*. New York: G. P. Putnam's Sons, 1998. Print.

———. *Port Mortuary*. New York: G. P. Putnam's Sons, 2010. Print.

———. *Portrait of a Killer: Jack the Ripper—Case Closed*. New York: Berkley Books, 2002. Print.

———. *Postmortem*. New York: Pocket Books, 1990. Print.

———. *Predator*. New York: G. P. Putnam's Sons, 2005. Print.

———. *Scarpetta*. New York: G. P. Putnam's Sons, 2008. Print.

———. *The Scarpetta Factor*. New York: Berkley, 2009. Print.

———. *Trace*. New York: G. P. Putnam's Sons, 2004. Print.

———. *Unnatural Exposure*. New York: G. P. Putnam's Sons, 1997. Print.

Covino, Deborah Caslav. *Amending the Abject Body: Aesthetic Makeovers in Medicine and Culture*. Albany: State University of New York Press, 2004. Print.

"Crime in the United States." Federal Bureau of Investigation 2009 Report. *Table 37. Current Year over Previous Year Arrest Trends by Sex*. Web. 24 November 2015. http://www2.fbi.gov/ucr/cius2009/data/table_37.html.

Crowley, Karlyn. *Feminism's New Age: Gender, Appropriation, and the Afterlife of Essentialism*. Albany: State University of New York Press, 2011. Print.

Cuklanz, Lisa M. *Rape on Prime Time: Television, Masculinity, and Sexual Violence*. Philadelphia: University of Pennsylvania Press, 2000. Print.

Cvetkovich, Ann. *Depression: A Public Feeling*. Durham, NC: Duke University Press, 2012. Print.

Dalsgard, Katrine. "Disrupting the Black Feminist Consensus? The Position of Sapphire's *Push* in the African American Women's Tradition." *After Consensus: Critical Challenge and Social Change in America*. Eds. Hans Lofgren and Alan Shima. Gothenburg, Sweden: Acta Universitatis Gothoburgensis, 1998. 171–87. Print.

Daly, Brenda. "Seeds of Shame or Seeds of Change? When Daughters Give Birth to Their Father's Children." *This Giving Birth*. Eds. Julie Tharp and Susan MacCallum-Whitcomb. Bowling Green, OH: Bowling Green University Press, 2000. 103–23. Print.

Davidson, Amy. "Michelle Knight, Missing." *New Yorker*, 9 May 2013. Web. 24 November 2015. http://www.newyorker.com/news/amy-davidson/michelle-knight-missing.

———. "What Charles Ramsey and Amanda Berry Knew." *New Yorker,* 7 May 2013. Web. 24 November 2015. http://www.newyorker.com/news/amy-davidson/what-charles-ramsey-and-amanda-berry-knew.

Davis, Kathy. *Dubious Equalities and Embodied Differences: Cultural Studies on Cosmetic Surgery.* Lanham, MD: Rowman and Littlefield, 2003. Print.

Dean, Jonathan. *Rethinking Contemporary Feminist Politics.* Basingstoke, UK: Palgrave Macmillan, 2010. Print.

Dean, Jodi. "Coming Out as an Alien: Feminists, UFOs, and the Oprah Effect." *"Bad Girls"/"Good Girls": Women, Sex, and Power in the Nineties.* Eds. Nan Bauer Maglin and Donna Perry. New Brunswick, NJ: Rutgers University Press, 1996. 90–105. Print.

DeLamotte, Eugenia. *Perils of the Night: A Feminist Study of Nineteenth-Century Gothic.* New York: Oxford University Press, 1990. Print.

———. "White Terror, Black Dreams: Gothic Constructions of Race in the Nineteenth Century." *The Gothic Other: Racial and Social Construction in the Literary Imagination.* Eds. Ruth Bienstock Anolik and Douglas L. Howard. Jefferson, NC: McFarland, 2004. 17–31. Print.

DeMott, Benjamin. *Killer Woman Blues.* Boston: Houghton Mifflin, 2000. Print.

Denfeld, Rene. *The New Victorians: A Young Woman's Challenge to the Old Feminist Order.* New York: Warner Books, 1995. Print.

D'Erasmo, Stacey. "Jailhouse Flock." *New York Times,* 13 May 2007. Web. 24 November 2015. http://www.nytimes.com/2007/05/13/books/review/DErasmo.html?ref=susanna_moore.

DeVolder, Beth. "Overcoming the Overcoming Story: A Case of 'Compulsory Heroism.'" *Feminist Media Studies* 13.4 (2013): 746–54. Print.

Dicker, Rory, and Alison Piepmeier, "Introduction." *Catching a Wave: Reclaiming Feminism for the 21st Century.* Eds. Rory Dicker and Alison Piepmeier. Boston: Northeastern University Press, 2003. 3–28. Print.

Dilworth, Sharon. "There's Nothing Lovely about Novelist's Latest." *Pittsburgh Post-Gazette,* 21 October 2007. Web. 24 November 2015. http://www.post-gazette.com/ae/book-reviews/2007/10/21/The-Almost-Moon-by-Alice-Sebold/stories/200710210240.

Dirda, Michael. "The Wand of the Enchanter." *New York Review of Books,* 20 December 2007. Web. 24 November 2015. http://www.nybooks.com/articles/archives/2007/dec/20/the-wand-of-the-enchanter/.

Doane, Janice, and Devon Hodges. *Telling Incest: Narratives of Dangerous Remembering from Stein to Sapphire.* Ann Arbor: University of Michigan Press, 2001. Print.

Donaldson, Elizabeth. "Handing Back Shame: Incest and Sexual Confession in Sapphire's *Push.*" *Transgression and Taboo: Critical Essays.* Eds. Vartan P. Messier and Nandita Batra. Mayaguez, PR: College English Association Caribbean Chapter Publications, 2005. 51–60. Print.

Donoghue, Emma. *Room*. New York: Little, Brown, 2010. Print.

Doody, Margaret Anne. "Deserts, Ruins and Troubled Waters: Female Dreams in Fiction and the Development of the Gothic Novel." *Genre* 10.4 (1977): 529–72. Rpt. in *The Eighteenth-Century English Novel*. Ed. Harold Bloom. New York: Chelsea House, 2004. 71–111. Print.

Douglas, Susan. *The Rise of Enlightened Sexism: The Seductive Message That Feminism's Work Is Done*. New York: Times Books, 2010. Print.

Douglas, Susan J., and Meredith W. Michaels. *The Mommy Myth: The Idealization of Motherhood and How It Has Undermined All Women*. New York: Free Press, 2004. Print.

Dragiewicz, Molly. *Equality with a Vengeance: Men's Rights Groups, Battered Women, and Antifeminist Backlash*. Boston: Northeastern University Press, 2011. Print.

Dugard, Jaycee. Interview by Diane Sawyer. *20/20*. ABC. 10 July 2011. Television.

———. *A Stolen Life: A Memoir*. New York: Simon and Schuster, 2011. Print.

Duncan, Carol B. "Black Women and Motherhood in Contemporary Cinematic Science Fiction." *Journal of the Association for Research on Mothering* 5.1 (2003): 45–52. Print.

Dusenberry, Maya. "#SurvivorPrivilege Shows George Will Just How Fun It Is to Be a Rape Survivor." *Feministing*, 9 June 2014. Web. 24 November 2015. http://feministing.com/2014/06/09/survivorprivilege-shows-george-will-the-many-perks-of-being-a-rape-survivor/.

Early, Frances, and Kathleen Kennedy, eds. *Athena's Daughters: Television's New Warrior Women*. Syracuse, NY: Syracuse University Press, 2003. Print.

Ebert, Roger. "The Lovely Bones." *RogerEbert.com*, 13 January 2010. Web. 24 November 2015. http://www.rogerebert.com/reviews/the-lovely-bones-2010.

Edwards, Justin D. *Gothic Passages: Racial Ambiguity and the American Gothic*. Iowa City: University of Iowa Press, 2003. Print.

Ehrenreich, Barbara. *Bright-Sided: How Positive Thinking Is Undermining America*. New York: Picador, 2010. Print.

Elam, Michele. *The Souls of Mixed Folk: Race, Politics, and Aesthetics in the New Millennium*. Stanford, CA: Stanford University Press, 2011. Print.

Ellis, Kate. *The Contested Castle: Gothic Novels and the Subversion of Ideology*. Urbana: University of Illinois Press, 1989. Print.

Erdrich, Louise. *The Round House*. New York: Harper, 2013. Print.

Eugenides, Jeffrey. "I Don't Know Why Jodi Picoult Is Belly-Aching." Interview with David Daley. *Salon*, 26 September 2012. Web. 24 November 2015. http://www.salon.com/2012/09/26/jeffrey_eugenides_i_dont_know_why_jodi_picoult_is_belly_aching/.

Evans, Danielle. "In Sapphire's New Novel, Life without Precious." *New York Times*, 29 July 2011. Web. 24 November 2015. http://www.nytimes.com/2011/07/31/books/review/the-kid-by-sapphire-book-review.html.

Evans, Sara M. "Feminism in the 1980s: Surviving the Backlash." *Living in the Eighties*. Eds. Gil Troy and Vincent J. Cannato. Oxford: Oxford University Press, 2009. 85–97. Print.

Everett, Percival. "Colour Bind." Interview by Sean O'Hagan. *Observer* (UK), 15 March 2003. Web. 24 November 2015. http://www.guardian.co.uk/books/2003/mar/16/fiction.features.

———. *Erasure*. Minneapolis: Graywolf Press, 2001. Print.

Faery, Rebecca Blevins. *Cartographies of Desire: Captivity, Race, and Sex in the Shaping of an American Nation*. Norman: University of Oklahoma Press, 1999. Print.

Fairclough, Kirsty. "Fame Is a Losing Game: Celebrity Gossip Blogging, Bitch Culture and Postfeminism." *Genders* 48 (2008): n.p. Web. 15 August 2014. https://web.archive.org/web/20140719003857/http://www.genders.org/recent.html

Faludi, Susan. *Backlash: The Undeclared War against American Women*. New York: Anchor Books, 1991. Print.

Farrell, Amy Erdman. *Fat Shame: Stigma and the Fat Body in American Culture*. New York: New York University Press, 2011. Print.

Farrell, Warren. *The Myth of Male Power*. Sydney: Finch, 1993. Print.

Fellela, Toni. "Bombs Cost More Than Welfare: Rethinking 'Responsibility' in Sapphire's *PUSH*." *Sapphire's Literary Breakthrough: Erotic Literacies, Feminist Pedagogies, Environmental Justice Perspectives*. Eds. Elizabeth McNeil, Neal A. Lester, DoVeanna S. Fulton, and Lynette D. Myles. Basingstoke, UK: Palgrave Macmillan, 2012. 29–46. Print.

Felski, Rita. "Redescriptions of Female Maoschism." *Minnesota Review* 63/64 (2005): 127–41. Print.

Ferguson, Michaele L. "Choice Feminism and the Fear of Politics." *Perspectives on Politics* 8.1 (2010): 247–53. Print.

Field, Robin. "Writing the Victim: Rescripting Rape in Contemporary American Fiction since 1970." PhD diss., University of Virginia, 2006. Print.

Findlen, Barbara, ed. *Listen Up: Voices from the Next Feminist Generation*. Emeryville, CA: Seal Press, 1995. Print.

Fineman, Martha L. "The Politics of Custody and Gender: Child Advocacy and the Transformation of Custody Decision Making in the USA." *Child Custody and the Politics of Gender*. Eds. Carol Smart and Selma Sevenhuijsen. London: Routledge, 1989. 27–50. Print.

Fitzpatrick, Tara. "The Figure of Captivity: The Cultural Work of the Puritan Captivity Narrative." *American Literary History* 3.1 (1991): 1–26. Print.

Fleenor, Juliann. "Introduction." *The Female Gothic*. Ed. Juliann Fleenor. Montreal: Eden Press, 1983. 3–30. Print.

Ford, Dana. "The Family of Morgan Harrington—A 'True Original'—Searches for Answers." CNN. 1 October 2014. Web. 24 November 2015. http://www.cnn.com/2014/09/29/us/morgan-harrington-virginia-tech/index.html?iref=allsearch.

Ford, Susan Allen. "Tracing the Other in Patricia D. Cornwell: Costs and Accommodations." *Clues* 20.2 (1999): 27–34. Print.

Forman, Gayle. *If I Stay*. New York: Speak/Penguin Group, 2009. Print.
Fowles, John. *The Collector*. 1963. New York: Little, Brown, 1997. Print.
Fraiman, Susan. *Unbecoming Women: British Women Writers and the Novel of Development*. New York: Columbia University Press, 1993. Print.
Frank, Russell. "The Making and Unmaking of a Folk Hero: The Ellie Nesler Story." *Western Folklore* 59.3–4 (2000): 197–214. Print.
Franklin, Ruth. "Jaycee Dugard's Memoir, an Acclaimed Novel, and the Art of Writing about Captivity." *New Republic*, 27 July 2011. Web. 24 November 2015. http://www.newrepublic.com/article/the-read/92702/jaycee-dugard-stolen-life-emma-donoghue-room.
Free, Cathy, and Alicia Dennis. "Elizabeth Smart: Happily Ever After!" *People*, 5 March 2012, 65–70. Print.
Freedman, Eric. "'Have You Seen This Child?': From Milk Carton to *Mise-en-Abime*." *Hop on Pop: The Politics and Pleasures of Popular Culture*. Eds. Henry Jenkins, Tara McPherson, and Jane Shattuc. Durham, NC: Duke University Press, 2002. 689–99. Print.
Freeman, Meghan A. "Disarticulated Figures: Language and Sexual Violence in Contemporary Crime Fiction." *Rape in Stieg Larsson's Millennium Trilogy and Beyond*. Eds. Berit Astrom, Katarina Gregersdotter, and Tanya Horeck. Basingstoke, UK: Palgrave Macmillan, 2012. 117–35. Print.
Fritz, Ben, and Claudia Eller. "Paramount Nixes Plan to Expand 'The Lovely Bones' for Christmas." *Los Angeles Times*, 23 December 2009. Web. 24 November 2015. http://latimesblogs.latimes.com/entertainmentnewsbuzz/2009/12/paramount-nixes-plan-to-expand-the-lovely-bones-for-christmas.html.
Frost, Liz. "Theorizing the Young Women in the Body." *Body and Society* 11.1 (2005): 63–85. Print.
Fudge, Rachel. "The Buffy Effect." *Bitch* 10 (1999): 18–20. Print.
Galioto, Erica D. "'Shame, thas a shame': The Anti-Sentiment of Sapphire's *Push* and *The Kid*." *The Sentimental Mode: Essays in Literature, Film and Television*. Eds. Jennifer A. Williamson, Jennifer Larson, and Ashley Reed. Jefferson, NC: McFarland, 2014. 134–50. Print.
Gamble, Sarah. "Postfeminism." *The Routledge Critical Dictionary of Feminism and Postfeminism*. Ed. Sarah Gamble. New York: Routledge, 2000. 43–54. Print.
Gay, Roxane. "The Great 2014 Celebrity Nude Photos Leak Is Only the Beginning." *Guardian*, 30 September 2014. Web. 24 November 2015. http://www.theguardian.com/commentisfree/2014/sep/01/celebrity-naked-photo-leak-2014-nude-women.
Genz, Stéphanie. *Postfemininities in Popular Culture*. Basingstoke, UK: Palgrave Macmillan, 2009. Print.
Gerhard, Jane. "*Sex and the City*: Carrie Bradshaw's Queer Postfeminism." *Feminist Media Studies* 5.1 (2005): 37–49. Print.
Gerritsen, Tess. *The Mephisto Club*. New York: Ballantine, 2007. Print.
———. *The Sinner*. New York: Ballantine, 2003. Print.
———. *Vanish*. New York: Ballantine, 2006. Print.

Gilbert, Sandra, and Susan Gubar. *The Madwoman in the Attic: The Woman Writer and the Nineteenth-Century Literary Imagination.* Hartford, CT: Yale University Press, 1979. Print.

Gill, Rosalind. "Postfeminist Media Culture: Elements of a Sensibility." *European Journal of Cultural Studies* 10.2 (2007): 147–66. Print.

Gill, Rosalind, and Christina Scharrf. "Introduction." *New Femininities: Postfeminism, Neoliberalism and Subjectivity.* Ed. Rosalind Gill and Christina Scharrf. Basingstoke, UK: Palgrave Macmillan, 2011. 1–20. Print.

Gillis, Stacy. "The (Post)Feminist Politics of Cyberpunk." *Gothic Studies* 9.2 (2007): 7–19. Print.

Gillis, Stacy, Gillian Howie, and Rebecca Munford, eds. *Third Wave Feminism: A Critical Exploration.* Basingstoke, UK: Palgrave Macmillan, 1997. Print.

Gimlin, Debra L. *Body Work: Beauty and Self-Image in American Culture.* Berkeley: University of California Press, 2002. Print.

Goddu, Teresa A. *Gothic America: Narrative, History, and Nation.* New York: Columbia University Press, 1997. Print.

———. "To Thrill the Land with Horror: Antislavery Discourse and the Gothic Imagination." *Gothic Topographies: Language, Nation Building and "Race."* Eds. P. M. Mehtonen and Matti Savolainen. Surrey, UK: Ashgate, 2013. 73–86. Print.

Gordon, Avery. *Ghostly Matters: Haunting and the Sociological Imagination.* Minneapolis: University of Minnesota Press, 1997. Print.

Gordon, Michael. "Sexual Slang and Gender." *Women and Language* 16.2 (Fall 1993): 16–26. Print.

Greene, Gayle. *Changing the Story: Feminist Fiction and the Tradition.* Bloomington: Indiana University Press, 1991. Print.

Gregoriou, Christiana. *Deviance in Contemporary Crime Fiction.* Basingstoke, UK: Palgrave Macmillan, 2007. Print.

Grossman, Lev. "Fall Arts Preview: *The Almost Moon.*" *Time,* 24 August 2 2007. Web. 24 November 2015. http://www.time.com/time/specials/2007/article/0,28804,1655968_1655989_1656008,00.html.

Grosz, Elizabeth. *Volatile Bodies: Toward a Corporeal Feminism.* Bloomington: Indiana University Press, 1994. Print.

Haaken, Janice. "Heretical Texts: *The Courage to Heal* and the Survivor Movement." *New Versions of Victims: Feminists Struggle with the Concept.* Ed. Sharon Lamb. New York: New York University Press, 1999. 13–41. Print.

Haddad, Emily A. "Bound to Love: Captivity in Harlequin Sheikh Novels." *Empowerment versus Oppression: Twenty-First Century Views of Popular Romance Novels.* Ed. Sally Goade. Newcastle, UK: Cambridge Scholars, 2007. 42–64. Print.

Halberstam, Judith. "Neo-Splatter: *Bride of Chucky* and the Horror of Heteronormativity." *Postfeminist Gothic: Critical Interventions in Contemporary Culture.* Eds. Benjamin A. Brabon and Stéphanie Genz. Basingstoke, UK: Palgrave Macmillan, 2007. 30–42. Print.

———. *The Queer Art of Failure*. Durham, NC: Duke University Press, 2011. Print.

———. *Skin Shows: Gothic Horror and the Technology of Monsters*. Durham, NC: Duke University Press, 1995. Print.

Hamer, Diane, and Belinda Budge. "Introduction." *The Good, the Bad, and the Gorgeous: Popular Culture's Romance with Lesbianism*. Eds. Diane Hamer and Belinda Budge. London: Pandora, 1994. 1–14. Print.

Hansen, Elaine Tuttle. "Fiction and (Post)Feminism in Atwood's 'Bodily Harm.'" *Novel: A Forum on Fiction* 19.1 (1985): 5–21. Print.

Harding, Kate. "We Want Our Kids Back Too." *Salon*, 15 August 2008. Web. 24 November 2015. http://www.salon.com/2008/08/15/missing_children_of_color/.

Harkins, Gillian. *Everybody's Family Romance: Reading Incest in Neoliberal America*. Minneapolis: University of Minnesota Press, 2009. Print.

Harris, Lynn. "Is Female-on-Male Violence on the Rise?" *Salon*, 23 November 2010. Web. 24 November 2015. http://www.salon.com/2010/11/24/women_more_violent/.

Harris-Perry, Melissa V. *Sister Citizen: Shame, Stereotypes, and Black Women in America*. New Haven, CT: Yale University Press, 2011. Print.

Hartman, Saidiya. *Scenes of Subjection: Slavery, Terror, and Self-Making in Nineteenth-Century America*. New York: Oxford University Press, 1997. Print.

Harzewski, Stephanie. *Chick Lit and Postfeminism*. Charlottesville: University of Virginia Press, 2011. Print.

Haskell, Molly. "NYPD Blue." *New York Times Book Review*, 12 November 1995, 9. Print.

Head, Beth. "A Normal Pathology? Patricia Cornwell's Third-Person Novels." *The Millennial Detective: Essays on Trends in Crime Fiction, Film and Television*. Ed. Malcah Effron. Jefferson, NC: McFarland, 2011. 36–49. Print.

Heiland, Donna. *Gothic and Gender: An Introduction*. Malden, MA: Blackwell, 2004. Print.

Heinecken, Dawn. *The Warrior Women of Television*. New York: Peter Lang, 2003. Print.

Heinze, Ruediger. "Violations of Mimetic Epistemology in First-Person Narrative Fiction." *Narrative* 16.3 (October 2008): 279–97. Print.

Hemmings, Clare. *Why Stories Matter: The Political Grammar of Feminist Theory*. Durham, NC: Duke University Press, 2011. Print.

Henry, Astrid. *Not My Mother's Sister: Generational Conflict and Third Wave Feminism*. Bloomington: Indiana University Press, 2004. Print.

Henry, Claire. "*The Girl with the Dragon Tattoo*: Rape, Revenge, and Victimhood in Cinematic Translation." *Rape in Stieg Larsson's Millennium Trilogy and Beyond*. Eds. Berit Åström, Katarina Gregersdotter, and Tanya Horeck. Basingstoke, UK: Palgrave Macmillan, 2012. 175–92. Print.

Hernández, Daisy, and Bushra Rehman, eds. *Colonize This! Young Women of Color on Today's Feminism*. Emeryville, CA: Seal Press, 2002. Print.

Hess, Amanda. "No, Women's Soccer Does Not Have a Domestic Violence Problem." *Slate*, 22 September 2014. Web. 24 November 2015. http://www.slate.com/articles/

double_x/doublex/2014/09/hope_solo_domestic_violence_it_is_very_very_stupid_to_compare_the_soccer.html.

Hewitt, Nancy, ed. *No Permanent Waves: Recasting Histories of U.S. Feminism*. Rutgers, NJ: Rutgers University Press, 2010. Print.

Heyes, Cressida J. "Cosmetic Surgery and the Televisual Makeover: A Foucauldian Feminist Reading." *Feminist Media Studies* 7.1 (2007): 17–32. Print.

Heywood, Leslie. *Dedication to Hunger: The Anorexic Aesthetic in Modern Culture*. Berkeley: University of California Press, 1996. Print.

Heywood, Leslie, and Jennifer Drake, eds. *Third Wave Agenda: Being Feminist, Doing Feminism*. Minneapolis: University of Minnesota Press, 1997. Print.

Higginbotham, Evelyn. *Righteous Discontent: The Women's Movement in the Black Baptist Church, 1880–1920*. Cambridge, MA: Harvard University Press, 1993. Print.

Highberg, Nels P. "The (Missing) Faces of African American Girls with AIDS." *Feminist Formations* 22.1 (2010): 1–20. Print.

Hillsburg, Heather. "Compassionate Readership: Anger and Suffering in Sapphire's *Push*." *Canadian Review of American Studies* 44.1 (2014): 122–47. Print.

Hirsch, Marianne. "Spiritual *Bildung*: The Beautiful Soul as Paradigm." *The Voyage In: Fictions of Female Development*. Eds. Elizabeth Abel, Marianne Hirsch, and Elizabeth Langland. Hanover, NH: University Press of New England, 1983. 23–48. Print.

Hirshman, Linda. "Homeward Bound." *American Prospect*, 21 November 2005. Web. 24 November 2015. http://prospect.org/article/homeward-bound-0.

Hobson, Janell. "Nicki Minaj: A Brown Sugar Sphinx Riddle." *Ms. Magazine Blog*, 30 July 2014. Web. 24 November 2015. http://msmagazine.com/blog/2014/07/30/nicki-minaj-a-brown-sugar-sphinx-riddle/.

———. *Venus in the Dark: Blackness and Beauty in Popular Culture*. New York: Routledge, 2005. Print.

Hodgkins, John. "A Dark-Adapting Eye: Susanna Moore, Jane Campion, and the Fractured World of Postmodern Noir." *College Literature* 39.4 (2012): 46–68. Print.

Hoeveler, Diane Long. "The Female Captivity Narrative: Blood, Water, and Orientalism." *Interrogating Orientalism*. Eds. Diane Long Hoeveler and Jeffrey Cass. Columbus: Ohio State University Press, 2006. 46–71. Print.

———. *Gothic Feminism: The Professionalization of Gender from Charlotte Smith to the Brontës*. University Park: Pennsylvania State University Press, 1998. Print.

———. "The Postfeminist Filmic Female Gothic Detective: Reading the Bodily Text in *Candyman*." *Postfeminist Gothic: Critical Interventions in Contemporary Culture*. Eds. Benjamin A. Brabon and Stéphanie Genz. Basingstoke, UK: Palgrave Macmillan, 2007. 99–113. Print.

Hogland, Lisa Maria. *Feminism and Its Fictions: The Consciousness-Raising Novel and the Women's Liberation Movement*. Philadelphia: University of Pennsylvania Press, 1998. Print.

Hollows, Joanne, and Rachel Moseley, eds. *Feminism in Popular Culture*. Oxford: Berg, 2006. Print.

hooks, bell. "Dig Deep: Beyond Lean In." *Feminist Wire,* 28 October 2013. Web. 24 November 2015. http://thefeministwire.com/2013/10/17973/.

———. "Dissident Heat: *Fire with Fire.*" *"Bad Girls"/"Good Girls": Women, Sex, and Power in the Nineties.* Eds. Nan Bauer Maglin and Donna Perry. New Brunswick, NJ: Rutgers University Press, 1996. 57–64. Print.

Hopkins, Susan. *Girl Heroes: The New Force in Popular Culture.* Annandale, Australia: Pluto Press, 2002. Print.

Horeck, Tanya. "Lost Girls: The Fiction of Joyce Carol Oates." *Contemporary Women's Writing* 4.1 (2010): 24–39. Print.

Houry, Debra. "Stemming the Domestic Abuse Epidemic." *Atlantic,* 31 July 2013. Web. 24 November 2015. http://www.theatlantic.com/health/archive/2013/07/stemming-the-domestic-abuse-epidemic/278166/.

"How Far Would You Go to Protect Your Child?" *Oprah.* Harpo. 18 October 2010. Web. 24 November 2015. http://www.oprah.com/oprahshow/How-Far-Would-You-Go-to-Protect-Your-Child_1/3#ixzz2MDzj2wZi.

Humble, Nicola. *The Feminine Middlebrow Novel, 1920s to 1950s: Class, Domesticity, and Bohemianism.* Oxford: Oxford University Press, 2001. Print.

Hurley, Dorothy L., and E. Anthony Hurley. *Constructing Incest Stories: Black Women's Voices in Fact and Fiction.* Trenton, NJ: Africa World Press, 2009. Print.

Hyman, Eric. "The Nonliteral, Non-Gluteal, Semi-Referential, Off-Standard, Synecdochic, Supermetonymic, Paradoxical, Existential, Ever-Lovin' Ass." *Journal of Popular Culture* 26.3 (1992): 203–10. Print.

Ibrahim, Habiba. "Toward Black and Multiracial 'Kinship' after 1997, or How a Race Man Became 'Cablinasian.'" *Black Scholar* 39.3–4 (2009): 23–31. Print.

Inness, Sherrie A, ed. *Action Chicks: New Images of Tough Women in Popular Culture.* Basingstoke, UK: Palgrave McMillan, 2004. Print.

———. *Tough Girls: Women Warriors and Wonder Women in Popular Culture.* Philadelphia: University of Pennsylvania Press, 1999. Print.

Jackson, Peter. "Peter Jackson: 'Lovely Bones' Was Lovely to Make." Interview with Scott Bowles. *USA Today,* 19 April 2009. Web. 24 November 2015. http://www.usatoday.com/life/movies/news/2009-04-19-bones-jackson_N.htm.

Jenkins, Candice M. *Private Lives, Proper Relations: Regulating Black Intimacy.* Minneapolis: University of Minnesota Press, 2007. Print.

Jenks, Chris. *Childhood.* 2nd ed. London: Routledge, 2005. Print.

Jordan, Tina. "Book Review: *The Kid.*" *Entertainment Weekly,* 27 July 2011. Web. 24 November 2015. http://www.ew.com/article/2011/07/27/kid-review-sapphire.

Jordan-Zachery, Julia S. *Black Women, Cultural Images, and Social Policy.* New York: Routledge, 2009. Print.

Joseph, Ralina L. *Transcending Blackness: From the New Millennium Mulatta to the Exceptional Multiracial.* Durham, NC: Duke University Press, 2013. Print.

———. "Tyra Banks Is Fat: Reading (Post-)Racism and (Post-)Feminism in the New Millennium." *Critical Studies in Media Communication* 26.3 (2009): 237–54. Print.

Kakutani, Michiko. "He's a Vessel Overflowing with Rage (And He's the Orphan Son of Precious)." *New York Times,* 4 July 2011. Web. 24 November 2015. http://www.nytimes.com/2011/07/05/books/the-kid-by-sapphire-review.html.

———. "Instability Passes from Mother to Daughter with Sudden, Deadly Consequences." *New York Times,* 9 October 2007. Web. 24 November 2015. http://www.nytimes.com/2007/10/09/books/09kaku.html?n=Top/Reference/Times%20Topics/People/K/Kakutani,%20Michiko.

———. "She Has an Ear for Slang and an Eye for Trouble." *New York Times,* 31 October 1995. Web. 24 November 2015. http://www.nytimes.com/1995/10/31/books/books-of-the-times-she-has-an-ear-for-slang-and-an-eye-for-trouble.html?ref=susannamoore.

Kane, Thomas H. "The Deaths of the Authors: Literary Celebrity and Automortography in Acker, Barthelme, Bukowski, and Carver's Last Acts." *Lit: Literature Interpretation Theory* 15 (2004): 409–43. Print.

Kavka, Misha. "Feminism, Ethics, and History, or What Is the 'Post' in Postfeminism?" *Tulsa Studies in Women's Literature* 21.1 (2002): 29–44. Print.

Kellner, Douglas. *Guys and Guns Amok: Domestic Terrorism and School Shootings from the Oklahoma City Bombing to the Virginia Tech Massacre.* New York: Paradigm, 2008. Print.

Kellogg, Carolyn. "Review: 'The Kid' by Sapphire." *Los Angeles Times,* 3 July 2011. Web. 24 November 2015. http://articles.latimes.com/2011/jul/03/entertainment/la-ca-sapphire-20110703.

Kenny, Lorraine. *Daughters of Suburbia: Growing Up White, Middle Class, and Female.* New Brunswick, NJ: Rutgers University Press, 2000. Print.

Kimmel, Michael. *Angry White Men: American Masculinity at the End of an Era.* New York: Nation Books, 2013. Print.

Kinahan, Anne-Marie. "Women Who Run from the Wolves: Feminist Critique as Post-Feminism." *Canadian Review of American Studies* 31 (2001): 31–46. Print.

"Kirkus Review: *The Kid.*" *Kirkus Reviews,* 20 May 2011. Web. 24 November 2015. http://www.kirkusreviews.com/book-reviews/fiction/sapphire/kid/#review.

Klein, Kathleen Gregory. "*Habeas Corpus*: Feminism and Detective Fiction." *Feminism in Women's Detective Fiction.* Ed. Glenwood Irons. Toronto: University of Toronto Press, 1995. 171–90. Print.

Knight, Michelle. "Stop Doubting California Woman on Kidnapping, Michelle Knight Says." Interview by Kate Bolduan. *New Day.* CNN. 23 May 2014. Television. 24 November 2015. http://www.cnn.com/2014/05/23/us/california-kidnap-victim-found-knight/.

Knight, Michelle, with Michelle Burford. *Finding Me: A Decade of Darkness, a Life Reclaimed—A Memoir of the Cleveland Kidnappings.* New York: Weinstein Books, 2014. Print.

Kornfield, Sarah. "The E-man-ci-pation of Jeannie: Feminist Doppelgangers on U.S. Television." *Communication, Culture and Critique* 5.3 (2012): 445–62. Print.

Kowalewski, Michael. *Deadly Musings: Violence and Verbal Form in American Fiction.* Princeton, NJ: Princeton University Press, 1993. Print.

Krakauer, Jon. *Under the Banner of Heaven: A Story of Violent Faith.* New York: Doubleday, 2003. Print.

Kristjansson, Margitte. "Fashion's 'Forgotten Woman': How Fat Bodies Queer Fashion and Consumption." *Queering Fat Embodiment.* Eds. Cat Pausé, Jackie Wykes, and Samantha Murray. Farnham, UK: Ashgate, 2014. 131–46. Print.

LaBrie, Sarah. "Sapphire's *The Kid: Push* Author Discusses Sex, Violence and Child Abuse in Her New Novel about Precious' Son." *L.A. Weekly,* 11 July 2011. Web. 24 November 2015. http://blogs.laweekly.com/arts/2011/07/sapphire_the_kid.php.

Lamb, Sharon. "Constructing the Victim." *New Versions of Victims: Feminists Struggle with the Concept.* Ed. Sharon Lamb. New York: NYU Press, 1999. 108–38. Print.

Lane, Harriet. "Tough on Crime." *Observer,* 19 October 2003. Web. 24 November 2015. http://www.guardian.co.uk/books/2003/oct/19/crime.patriciacornwell/print.

Langer, Elinor. "Whatever Happened to Feminist Fiction?" *New York Times,* 4 March 1984, BR1, 34–35. Print.

Larsson, Stieg. *The Girl with the Dragon Tattoo.* Trans. Reg Keeland. New York: Knopf, 2008. Print.

Lauret, Maria. *Liberating Literature: Feminist Fiction in America.* London: Routledge, 1994. Print.

Leonard, Suzanne. "Escaping the Recession? The New Vitality of the Woman Worker." *Gendering the Recession: Media and Culture in an Age of Austerity.* Eds. Diane Negra and Yvonne Tasker. Durham, NC: Duke University Press, 2014. 31–58. Print.

———. "I Really Must Be an Emma Bovary: Female Literacy and Adultery in Feminist Fiction." *Genders* 51 (2010): n.p. Web. 21 February 2014. https://web.archive.org/web/20140719003857/http://www.genders.org/recent.html

Lewin, Tamar. "Are These Parties for Real?" *New York Times,* 30 June 2005. Web. 24 November 2015. http://www.nytimes.com/2005/06/30/fashion/thursdaystyles/30rainbow.html?pagewanted=all&_r=0.

Liddell, Janice Lee. "Agents of Pain and Redemption in Sapphire's *Push.*" *Arms Akimbo: Africana Women in Contemporary Literature.* Gainesville: University of Florida Press, 1999. 135–46. Print.

Lidoff, Joan. "Domestic Gothic: The Imagery of Anger, Christina Stead's *The Man Who Loved Children.*" *The Female Gothic.* Ed. Juliann Fleenor. Montreal: Eden Press, 1983. 109–22. Print.

Lloyd, Rachel. *Girls Like Us: Fighting for a World Where Girls Are Not for Sale, an Activist Finds Her Calling and Heals Herself.* New York: HarperCollins, 2011. Print.

Logan, Lisa. "Mary Rowlandson's Captivity and the 'Place' of the Woman Subject." *Early American Literature* 28.3 (1993): 255–77. Print.

Looser, Devoney, and Ann E. Kaplan. *Generations: Academic Feminists in Dialogue.* Minneapolis: University of Minnesota Press, 1997. Print.

Lucas, Rose. "Anxiety and Its Antidotes: Patricia Cornwell and the Forensic Body." *Lit: Literature Interpretation Theory* 15.2 (2004): 207–22. Print.

Luders-Manuel, Shannon. "Captive America: Smart, Rowlandson and the Colonial Sentiment." *AmeriQuests* 7.1 (2010): 1–12. Print.

Luscombe, Belinda. "Ayelet Waldman: Bad Mother." *Time,* 8 May 2009. Web. 24 November 2015. http://www.time.com/time/arts/article/0,8599,1896848,00.html.

MacFarquhar, Neil. "What's a Soccer Mom Anyway?" *New York Times,* 20 October 1996. Web. 24 November 2015. http://www.nytimes.com/1996/10/20/weekinreview/what-s-a-soccer-mom-anyway.html.

Macur, Juliet. "In Hope Solo Case, Soccer Turns a Blind Eye toward Domestic Violence." *New York Times,* 19 September 2014. Web. 24 November 2015. http://www.nytimes.com/2014/09/20/sports/soccer/in-hope-solo-case-us-soccer-doesnt-get-it-right-either.html?_r=1?.

Maglin, Nan Bauer, and Donna Perry, eds. *"Bad Girls"/"Good Girls": Women, Sex, and Power in the Nineties.* New Brunswick, NJ: Rutgers University Press, 1996. Print.

Maher, Jennifer. "The Post-Feminist Mystique." *College Literature* 35.3 (Summer 2007): 193–202. Print.

Mainon, Dominique, and James Ursini. *The Modern Amazons: Warrior Women On-Screen.* Pompton Plains, NJ: Limelight Editions, 2006. Print.

Malchow, H. L. *Gothic Images of Race in Nineteenth-Century Britain.* Stanford, CA: Stanford University Press, 1996. Print.

Mane, Rebecca L. Clark. "Transmuting Grammars of Whiteness in Third-Wave Feminism: Interrogating Postrace Histories, Postmodern Abstraction, and the Proliferation of Difference in Third-Wave Texts." *Signs* 38.1 (2012): 71–98. Print.

Mantilla, Karla. "Child Violence: It's a Male Thing." *Off Our Backs* 28.5 (1998): 5. Print.

———. "Gendertrolling: Misogyny Adapts to New Media." *Feminist Studies* 39.2 (2013): 563–70. Print.

Marcus, Amit. "Narrative Ethics and Incommensurable Discourses: Lyotard's *The Differend* and Fowles' *The Collector.*" *Mosaic: A Journal for the Interdisciplinary Study of Literature* 41.4 (2008): 77–94. Print.

Marcus, Leonard. *Margaret Wise Brown: Awakened by the Moon.* Boston: Beacon Press, 1992. Print.

Mardorossian, Carine M. *Framing the Rape Victim: Gender and Agency Reconsidered.* New Brunswick, NJ: Rutgers University Press, 2014. Print.

———. "Toward a New Feminist Theory of Rape." *Signs* 27.3 (2002): 743–75. Print.

Marshall, Christine, and Kiran Pienaar, "'You Are Not Alone': The Discursive Construction of the 'Suffering Victim' Identity on *The Oprah Winfrey Show.*" *Southern African Linguistics and Applied Language Studies* 26.4 (2008): 525–46. Print.

Martin, Bradford. *The Other Eighties: A Secret History of America in the Age of Reagan.* New York: Hill and Wang, 2011. Print.

Maslin, Janet. "After the Shooting Is Over." *New York Times,* 16 March 2007. Web. 24 November 2015. http://www.nytimes.com/2007/03/16/books/16book.html?_r=0.

———. "A Captivity No Novelist Could Invent." *New York Times,* 17 July 2011. Web. 24 November 2015. http://www.nytimes.com/2011/07/18/books/jaycee-dugards-stolen-life-18-years-of-abuse-review.html?_r=0.

Massé, Michelle. "Gothic Repetition: Husbands, Horrors, and Things That Go Bump in the Night." *Signs* 15.4 (1990): 679–709. Print.

———. *In the Name of Love: Women, Masochism, and the Gothic.* Ithaca, NY: Cornell University Press, 1992. Print.

Mazza, Cris, Jeffrey DeShell, and Elizabeth Sheffield, eds. *Chick-Lit: Postfeminist Fiction.* Normal, IL: Fiction Collective 2, 1995. Print.

McAfee, Noelle. *Julia Kristeva.* New York: Routledge, 2004. Print.

McCarthy, Anna. *Ambient Television: Visual Culture and Public Space.* Durham, NC: Duke University Press, 2001. Print.

McCarthy, Todd. "Review: 'The Lovely Bones.'" *Variety,* 24 November 2009. Web. 24 November 2015. http://variety.com/2009/film/reviews/the-lovely-bones-2-1200477283/.

McClintock, Pamela. "'Lovely Bones' Does About-Face." *Variety,* 18 January 2010. Web. 24 November 2015. http://www.variety.com/article/VR1118013956?refCatId=13.

McConnell, Kathleen. "Dark Angel: A Recombinant Pygmalion for the Twenty-First Century." *Gothic Studies* 4.2 (2002): 178–90. Print.

McDonough, Katie. "The Domestic Violence Gender Trap: Hope Solo, Ray Rice and the Tired Myopia of 'Women Do It Too.'" *Salon,* 25 September 2014. Web. 24 November 2015. http://www.salon.com/2014/09/25/the_domestic_violence_gender_trap_hope_solo_ray_rice_and_the_tired_myopia_of_women_do_it_too/.

McDowell, Deborah. *The Changing Same: Black Women's Literature, Criticism, and Theory.* Bloomington: Indiana University Press, 1995. Print.

McGary, Howard, Jr. *The Post-Racial Ideal (Aquinas Lecture).* Milwaukee: Marquette University Press, 2012. Print.

McKenna, Susan E. "The Queer Insistence of *Ally McBeal*: Lesbian Chic, Postfeminism, and Lesbian Reception." *Communication Review* 5 (2002): 285–314. Print.

McLennen, Karen Jacobsen. *Nature's Ban: Women's Incest Literature.* Boston: Northeastern University Press, 1996. Print.

McRobbie, Angela. *The Aftermath of Feminism: Gender, Culture, and Social Change.* Los Angeles: Sage, 2009. Print.

McWilliams, Ellen. *Margaret Atwood and the Female Bildungsroman.* Surrey, UK: Ashgate, 2009. Print.

Melley, Timothy. "Stalked by Love: Female Paranoia and the Stalker Novel." *Differences: A Journal of Feminist Cultural Studies* 8.2 (1996): 68–100. Print.

Mendelsohn, Daniel. "Novel of the Year." *New York Review of Books,* 16 January 2003. Web. 24 November 2015. http://www.nybooks.com/articles/archives/2003/jan/16/novel-of-the-year/.

Merrick, Elizabeth. "Why Chick Lit Matters." *This Is Not Chick Lit: Original Stories by America's Best Women Writers.* Ed. Elizabeth Merrick. New York: Random House, 2006. vii–xi. Print.

Messent, Peter. "Authority, Social Anxiety and the Body in Crime Fiction: Patricia Cornwell's *Unnatural Exposure*." *The Art of Detective Fiction*. Eds. Warren Chernaik, Martin Swales, and Robert Vilain. New York: St. Martin's, 2000. 124–37. Print.

Messud, Claire. "Nightmare on Mean Street." *Guardian* (UK), 20 April 1996, sec. Features, 30. Print.

Meyers, Helene. *Femicidal Fears: Narratives of the Female Gothic Experience*. Albany: State University of New York Press, 2001. Print.

Michlin, Monica. "Narrative as Empowerment: *Push* and the *Signifying* on Prior African-American Novels on Incest." *Études Anglaises* 59.2 (2006): 170–85. Print.

Miller-Young, Mireille. *A Taste for Brown Sugar: Black Women in Pornography*. Durham, NC: Duke University Press, 2014. Print.

Millett, Kate. *The Basement: Meditations on a Human Sacrifice*. New York: Simon and Schuster, 1979. Print.

Mizejewski, Linda. "Illusive Evidence: Patricia Cornwell and the Body Double." *South Central Review* 18.3–4 (2001): 6–20. Print.

Modleski, Tania. *Feminism without Women: Culture and Criticism in a 'Postfeminist' Age*. New York: Routledge, 1991. Print.

Moers, Ellen. *Literary Women: The Great Writers*. New York: Doubleday, 1976. Print.

Montemurro, Beth. "Charlotte Chooses Her Choice: Liberal Feminism on *Sex and the City*." *Scholar and Feminist Online* 3.1 (2004): n.p. Web. 24 November 2015. http://sfonline.barnard.edu/hbo/montemurro_01.htm.

Moore, Susanna. "At Home with Susanna Moore: Dark Work in a Sunny Spot." Interview by Joyce Wadler. *New York Times*, 21 June 2007. Web. 24 November 2015. http://www.nytimes.com/2007/06/21/garden/21moore.html?scp=2&sq=Susanna+Moore&st=nyt.

———. *The Big Girls*. New York: Vintage, 2008. Print.

———. "Birnbaum v. Susanna Moore." Interview by Robert Birnbaum. *Morning News*, 25 September 2007. Web. 24 November 2015. http://www.themorningnews.org/archives/birnbaum_v/susanna_moore.php.

———. "Dead End with a Life of Its Own: Interview: Susanna Moore." Interview by Christine Cremen. *Spectrum* (Australia), 22 November 2003, late ed., 15. Print.

———. *I Myself Have Seen It: The Myth of Hawaii*. Washington, DC: National Geographic Society, 2003. Print.

———. *In the Cut*. New York: Plume, 1995. Print.

———. "A Kind of Craziness: Susanna Moore on Women, Writing, Sex and Feminism." Interview by Maya Linden. *Writers in Conversation* 1.1 (2014): 1–5. Print.

———. *Light Years: A Girlhood in Hawaii*. New York: Grove, 2007. Print.

———. *My Old Sweetheart*. 1982. New York: Vintage, 1997. Print.

———. *Sleeping Beauties*. 1993. New York: Vintage, 2003. Print.

———. *The Whiteness of Bones*. 1989. New York: Vintage, 2003. Print.

———. "Write the Good Fight." Interview by Kate Kellaway. *Observer* (UK), 14 December 2003. Web. 24 November 2015. http://www.guardian.co.uk/books/2003/dec/14/fiction.features2.

Moran, Ginger. "Mother Gaze: Gil Harrington and Her Lovely Daughter Morgan." GingerMoran.com, 19 February 2012. Web. 24 November 2015. http://gingermoran.com/2015/12/mother-gaze-gil-harrington-and-her-lovely-daughter-morgan/.

Morgan, Jack. *The Biology of Horror: Gothic Literature and Film.* Carbondale: Southern Illinois University Press, 2002. Print.

Morin, Richard, and Dan Balz. "'Security Mom' Bloc Proves Hard to Find: The Phenomenon May Be a Myth." *Washington Post,* 1 October 2004. Web. 24 November 2015. http://www.washingtonpost.com/wp-dyn/articles/A63197-2004Sep30.html.

Morley, Isla. *Above.* New York: Gallery Books, 2014. Print.

Morris, Susana M. *Close Kin and Distant Relatives: The Paradox of Respectability in Black Women's Literature.* Charlottesville: University of Virginia Press, 2014. Print.

Morrison, Toni. *Beloved.* New York: Alfred A. Knopf, 1987. Print.

———. *The Bluest Eye.* 1970. New York: Plume, 1994. Print.

———. *A Mercy.* New York: Knopf, 2008. Print.

———. *Sula.* New York: Knopf, 1973. Print.

Mundy, Liza. *The Richer Sex: How the New Majority of Female Breadwinners Is Transforming Our Culture.* New York: Simon and Schuster, 2012. Print.

Munt, Sally. *Murder by the Book? Feminism and the Crime Novel.* London: Routledge, 1994. Print.

Murley, Jean. *The Rise of True Crime: 20th-Century Murder and American Popular Culture.* Westport, CT: Praeger, 2008. Print.

Murphy, Caryn. "Getting Even: Feminist Agency and Postfeminist Containment in Girl Power Narratives." *MP: An Online Feminist Journal* 3.2 (2010): 98–132. Print.

Namias, June. *White Captives: Gender and Ethnicity on the American Frontier.* Chapel Hill: University of North Carolina Press, 1993.

Nash, Jennifer Christine. *The Black Body in Ecstasy: Reading Race, Reading Pornography.* Durham, NC: Duke University Press, 2014. Print.

Nathanson, Elizabeth. "Dressed for Economic Distress: Blogging and the 'New' Pleasures of Fashion." *Gendering the Recession: Media and Culture in an Age of Austerity.* Eds. Diane Negra and Yvonne Tasker. Durham, NC: Duke University Press, 2014. 136–60. Print.

Naugler, Diane. "Credentials: Breast Slang and the Discourse of Femininity." *Atlantis* 34.1 (2009): 100–110. Print.

Negra, Diane. "Quality Postfeminism? Sex and the Single Girl on HBO." *Genders* 39 (2004): n.p. Web. 15 August 2014. https://web.archive.org/web/20140719003857/http://www.genders.org/recent.html

———. *What a Girl Wants? Fantasizing the Reclamation of Self in Postfeminism.* New York: Routledge, 2008. Print.

Neuman, Shirley. "'Just a Backlash': Margaret Atwood, Feminism, and *The Handmaid's Tale.*" *University of Toronto Quarterly* 75.3 (2006): 857–68. Print.

Newman, Melanie. "Feminist or Misogynist?" Review of *The Girl with the Dragon Tattoo,* by Stieg Larsson. *The F Word,* 2 September 2009. Web. 24 November 2015. http://www.thefword.org.uk/reviews/2009/09/larrson_review.

Niven, Lisa. "What's Next for Blake?" *Vogue*, 25 September 2013. Web. 24 November 2015. http://www.vogue.co.uk/news/2013/09/25/blake-lively-new-business-and-marriage-since-gossip-girl.

Norman, Brian. *Dead Women Talking: Figures of Injustice in American Literature*. Baltimore: Johns Hopkins University Press, 2013. Print.

Norton, Carla. *The Edge of Normal*. New York: Minotaur, 2013. Print.

Nunn, Heather, and Anita Biressi. "*Silent Witness*: Detection, Femininity, and the Post-Mortem Body." *Feminist Media Studies* 3.2 (2003): 193–206. Print.

Nussbaum, Emily. "Trauma Queen: The Pulp Appeal of 'Law and Order: SVU.'" *New Yorker*, 10 June 2013. Web. 24 November 2015. http://www.newyorker.com/magazine/2013/06/10/trauma-queen.

Oates, Joyce Carol. *Black Water*. 1992. New York: Plume Books, 1993. Print.

———. *Rape: A Love Story*. New York: Carroll and Graf, 2003. Print.

———. *We Were the Mulvaneys*. New York: Penguin, 1996. Print.

Ofshe, Richard, and Ethan Watters. *Therapy's Delusions: The Myth of the Unconscious and the Exploitation of Today's Walking Worried*. New York: Scribner, 1999. Print.

Oler, Tammy. "Pinned Down." *Bitch* 56 (2012): n.p. Web. 24 November 2015. http://bitchmagazine.org/article/pinned-down.

Oliver, Lauren. *Before I Fall*. New York: Harper, 2010. Print.

Orwell, George. "Bookshop Memories." *The Collected Essays, Journalism and Letters of George Orwell*. Eds. Sonia Orwell and Ian Angus. Vol 1. New York: Harcourt Brace and World, 1968. 242–46. Print.

Ouellette, Laurie. "Take Responsibility for Yourself: *Judge Judy* and the Neoliberal Citizen." *Reality TV: Remaking Television Culture*. Eds. Susan Murray and Laurie Ouellette. New York: New York University Press, 2004. 231–50. Print.

Paglia, Camille. *Sex, Art, and American Culture: Essays*. New York: Vintage, 1992. Print.

Pain, Rachel. "Space, Sexual Violence and Social Control: Integrating Geographical and Feminist Analyses of Women's Fear of Crime." *Progress in Human Geography* 15.4 (1991): 415–31. Print.

Parasecoli, Fabio. "Bootylicious: Food and the Female Body in Contemporary Black Pop Culture." *Women's Studies Quarterly* 35.1–2 (2007): 110–25. Print.

Parker, Kathleen. *Save the Males: Why Men Matter, Why Women Should Care*. New York: Random House, 2008. Print.

Parks, Sheri. *Fierce Angels: The Strong Black Woman in American Life and Culture*. New York: One World, 2010. Print.

Pastor, Jennifer, Jennifer McCormick, and Michelle Fine. "Makin' Homes: An Urban Girl Thing." *Urban Girls Revisited: Building Strengths*. Eds. Bonnie J. Ross Leadbeater and Niobe Way. New York: New York University Press, 2007. 75–96. Print.

Patterson, James. *Kiss the Girls*. New York: Warner Books, 1995. Print.

Payant, Katherine B. *Becoming and Bonding: Contemporary Feminism and Popular Fiction by American Women Writers*. Westport, CT: Greenwood Press, 1993. Print.

Pearce, Lynne. "Beyond Redemption? Mobilizing Affect in Feminist Reading." *Working with Affect in Feminist Readings: Disturbing Differences*. Eds. Marianne Liljestrom and Susanna Paasonen. London: Routledge, 2010. 151–64. Print.

Peiss, Kathy. *Hope in a Jar: The Making of America's Beauty Culture*. Philadelphia: University of Pennsylvania Press, 2011. Print.

Pelaud, Isabelle Thuy. *This Is All I Choose to Tell: History and Hybridity in Vietnamese American Literature*. Philadelphia: Temple University Press, 2011. Print.

Perry, Ruth. "Incest as the Meaning of the Gothic Novel." *Eighteenth Century* 30.3 (1998): 261–78. Print.

Peterson, Latoya. "Of Push, Precious, Percival, and 'My Pafology.'" *Racialicious*, 10 November 2009. Web. 24 November 2015. http://www.racialicious.com/2009/11/10/of-push-precious-percival-and-my-pafology/.

Picoult, Jodi. "Jodi Picoult." Interview with Bob Abernethy and Bob Faw. *Religion and Ethics Newsweekly*, 24 April 2009. Web. 24 November 2015. http://www.pbs.org/wnet/religionandethics/episodes/april-24-2009/jodi-picoult/2753/.

———. *Nineteen Minutes*. New York: Washington Square Press, 2007. Print.

———. *Perfect Match*. New York: Atria, 2002. Print.

———. *Sing You Home*. New York: Washington Square Press, 2011. Print.

———. "Sisterhood's Keeper." Interview with Andrew Goldman. *New York Times Magazine*, 10 February 2013, MM12. Print.

———. *The Tenth Circle*. New York: Washington Square Press, 2006. Print.

———. *Vanishing Acts*. New York: Atria, 2005. Print.

Pipher, Mary. *Reviving Ophelia: Saving the Selves of Adolescent Girls*. New York: Ballantine, 1994. Print.

Pollitt, Katha. "Not Just Bad Sex." *New Yorker*, 4 October 1993. Rpt. in *Reasonable Creatures: Essays on Women and Feminism*. By Katha Pollitt. New York: Knopf, 1994. 157–68. Print.

Potter, Tiffany. "Writing Indigenous Femininity: Mary Rowlandson's Narrative of Captivity." *Eighteenth-Century Studies* 36.2 (2003): 153–67. Print.

Pough, Gwendolyn. *Check It While I Wreck It: Black Womanhood, Hip-Hop Culture, and the Public Sphere*. Boston: Northeastern University Press, 2004. Print.

Press, Joy. "Susanna Moore's 'In the Cut': Not for the Faint of Heart." *Baltimore Sun*, 3 December 1995. Web. 24 November 2015. http://articles.baltimoresun.com/1995-12-03/news/1995337120_1_susanna-moore-frannie-Malloy.

Price, Janet, and Margrit Shildrick, eds. *Feminist Theory and the Body: A Reader*. London: Routledge, 1998. Print.

Probyn, Elspeth. "New Traditionalism and Post-Feminism: TV Does the Home." *Screen* 31.2 (1990): 147–59. Print.

Projansky, Sarah. *Watching Rape: Film and Television in Postfeminist Culture*. New York: New York University Press, 2001. Print.

Quindlen, Anna. "Playing God on No Sleep." *Newsweek*, 1 July 2001, 62. Print.

Rapping, Elayne. *The Culture of Recovery: Making Sense of the Self-Help Movement in Women's Lives.* Boston: Beacon Books, 1996. Print.

Read, Jacinda. *The New Avengers: Feminism, Femininity and the Rape-Revenge Cycle.* New York: St. Martin's, 2000. Print.

Reger, Jo. *Different Wavelengths: Studies of the Contemporary Women's Movement.* London: Routledge, 2005. Print.

Reichs, Kathy. *Cross Bones.* New York: Pocket Star, 2005. Print.

Ringrose, Jessica, and Valerie Walkerdine. "Regulating the Abject: The TV Make-Over as Site of Neo-Liberal Reinvention towards Bourgeois Femininity." *Feminist Media Studies* 8.3 (2008): 227–46. Print.

Rivers, Caryl, and Rosalind C. Barnett. *The New Soft War on Women: How the Myth of Female Ascendance Is Hurting Women, Men—and Our Economy.* New York: Tarcher, 2013. Print.

Roberts, Kimberley. *Girls in Black and White: The Iconography of Teenage Girls.* PhD diss., University of Virginia, 2002. Ann Arbor: UMI, 2002. Print.

———. "Pleasures and Problems of the 'Angry Girl.'" *Sugar and Spice and Everything Nice: Cinemas of Girlhood.* Eds. Frances Gateward and Murray Pomeroy. Detroit: Wayne State University, 2002. 217–34. Print.

Robinson, Bobbie. "Playing Like the Boys: Patricia Cornwell Writes Men." *Journal of Popular Culture* 39.1 (2006): 95–108. Print.

Rodgers, Peter. "In the Cut" (review). *Richmond Times* (UK), n.d. Web. 15 August 2014. http://www.richmondreview.co.uk/books/inthecut.html.

Rodino-Colocino, Michelle. "Man Up, Woman Down: Mama Grizzlies and Anti-Feminist Feminism during the Year of the (Conservative) Woman and Beyond." *Women and Language* 35.1 (2012): 79–95. Print.

Rodino, Michelle. "War Mothering." *Feminist Media Studies* 5.3 (2005): 380–85. Print.

Roiphe, Katie. "Making the Incest Scene." *Harpers* 291 (1995): 68–71. Print.

———. *The Morning After: Sex, Fear, and Feminism.* Boston: Little, Brown, 1993. Print.

———. "Working Women's Fantasies." *Newsweek,* 16 April 2012. Web. 24 November 2015. http://www.newsweek.com/working-womens-fantasies-63915.

Rose, Tricia. "Race, Class, and the Pleasure/Danger Dialectic: Rewriting Black Female Teenage Sexuality in the Popular Imagination." *Black Renaissance* 1.3 (1998): 171–90. Print.

Rosenberg, Alyssa. "George Will's Distasteful Conclusions about Sexual Assault." *Washington Post,* 10 June 2014. Web. 24 November 2015. http://www.washingtonpost.com/news/act-four/wp/2014/06/10/george-wills-distasteful-conclusions-about-sexual-assault/.

Rosenfelt, Deborah Silverton. "Feminism, 'Postfeminism,' and Contemporary Women's Fiction." *Tradition and the Talents of Women.* Ed. Florence Howe. Urbana: University of Illinois Press, 1991. 268–91. Print.

Rosin, Hanna. *The End of Men: And the Rise of Women.* New York: Riverhead, 2012. Print.

Roskowski, Susan. "The Novel of Awakening." *The Voyage In: Fictions of Female Development*. Eds. Elizabeth Abel, Marianne Hirsch, and Elizabeth Langland. Hanover, NH: University Press of New England, 1983. 49 68. Print.

Rothenberg, Jess. *The Catastrophic History of You and Me*. New York: Dial Books, 2012. Print.

Rottenberg, Catherine. "Happiness and the Liberal Imagination: How Superwoman Became Balanced." *Feminist Studies* 40.1 (2014): 144–68. Print.

Rountree, Wendy A. "Overcoming Violence: Blues Expression in Sapphire's *Push*." *Atenea* 24.1 (2004): 133–43. Print.

Rowlandson, Mary. "The Sovereignty and Goodness of God." 1682. *Olaudah Equiano, Mary Rowlandson, and Others: American Captivity Narratives*. Ed. Gordon M. Sayre. Boston: Houghton Mifflin, 2000. 137–76. Print.

Rubenstein, Roberta. "Bodily Harm: Paranoid Vision in Contemporary Fiction by Women." *Lit: Literature Interpretation Theory* 1.1–2 (1989): 137–49. Print.

Ruddick, Sara. "Preservative Love and Military Destruction." *Mothering: Essays in Feminist Theory*. Ed. Joyce Trebilcot. Totowa, NJ: Rowman and Littlefield, 1983. 231–62. Print.

Russ, Joanna. "Somebody's Trying to Kill Me and I Think It's My Husband: The Modern Gothic." *The Female Gothic*. Ed. Juliann Fleenor. Montreal: Eden Press, 1983. 123–37. Print.

Russell, Alec. "Mortgage Moms May Hold Key to a Democrat Win." *Telegraph* (UK), 6 September 2006. Web. 24 November 2015. http://www.telegraph.co.uk/news/1528202/Mortgage-Moms-may-hold-key-to-a-Democrat-win.html.

Sacco, Lynn. *Unspeakable: Father-Daughter Incest in American History*. Baltimore: Johns Hopkins University Press, 2009. Print.

Safire, William. "Soccer Moms." *New York Times*, 27 October 1996. Web. 24 November 2015. http://www.nytimes.com/1996/10/27/magazine/soccer-moms.html.

Sales, Leila. "The Problem with Dead Narrators: 'The Catastrophic History of You and Me.'" *Daily Beast*, 26 April 2012. Web. 24 November 2015. http://www.thedailybeast.com/articles/2012/04/26/the-problem-with-dead-narrators-the-catastrophic-history-of-you-and-me.html.

Sandberg, Sheryl, with Nell Scovall. *Lean In: Women, Work, and the Will to Lead*. New York: Alfred A. Knopf, 2013. Print.

Sandell, Jillian. "Adjusting to Oppression: The Rise of Therapeutic Feminism in the United States." *"Bad Girls"/"Good Girls": Women, Sex, and Power in the Nineties*. Eds. Nan Bauer Maglin and Donna Perry. New Brunswick, NJ: Rutgers University Press, 1996. 21–35. Print.

Sapphire. "Artist with a Mission: A Conversation with Sapphire." Interview by Owen Keehnen. *Queer Cultural Center*, n.d. Web. 24 November 2015. http://www.queerculturalcenter.org/Pages/Keehnen/Sapphire.html.

———. *The Kid*. New York: Penguin, 2011. Print.

———. *Push*. New York: Vintage, 1996. Print.

———. "Sapphire Releases Graphic Sequel to 'Push.'" Interview with *National Public Radio*, 6 July 2011. Web. 24 November 2015. http://www.npr.org/2011/07/06/137646847/sapphire-releases-graphic-sequel-to-push.

———. "Sapphire's Big Push." Interview by Mark Marvel. *Interview* 26.6 (1996): 28–30. Print.

———. "Sapphire's Story: How 'Push' Became 'Precious.'" Interview with *National Public Radio*, 6 November 2009. Web. 24 November 2015. http://www.npr.org/templates/story/story.php?storyId=120176695.

Sanders, Joshunda, and Diana Barnes-Brown. "Eat, Pray, Spend: Priv-Lit and the New, Enlightened American Dream." *Bitch* 47 (2010): n.p. Web. 24 November 2015. http://bitchmagazine.org/article/eat-pray-spend.

Saubion, Sonia. "From Logorrhea to Silence in John Fowles's *The Collector*." *Voice and Silence in the Contemporary Novel in English*. Ed. Vanessa Guignery. Newcastle, UK: Cambridge Scholars, 2009. 99–111. Print.

Sayre, Gordon M. "The Foundational Narrative of Mary Rowlandson." *Olaudah Equiano, Mary Rowlandson, and Others: American Captivity Narratives*. Ed. Gordon M. Sayre. Boston: Houghton Mifflin, 2000. 127–31. Print.

Schreiber, Evelyn Jaffe. *Race, Trauma, and Home in the Novels of Toni Morrison*. Baton Rouge: Louisiana State University Press, 2010. Print.

Schwartz, Jennifer. "A 'New' Female Offender or Increasing Social Control of Women's Behavior? Cross-National Evidence." *Feminist Studies* 39.3 (2013): 790–821. Print.

Scott, A. O. "Gazing Down, from a Suburb of Heaven, at an Earthly Purgatory." *New York Times*, 10 December 2009. Web. 24 November 2015. http://www.nytimes.com/2009/12/11/movies/11lovelybones.html.

Scott, Patricia Bell. "Debunking Sapphire: Toward a Non-Racist and Non-Sexist Social Science." *All the Men Are Black, All the Women Are White, but Some of Us Are Brave*. Eds. Gloria T. Hull, Patricia Bell Scott, and Barbara Smith. New York: Feminist Press, 1982. 85–92. Print.

Sebold, Alice. "Above and Beyond." Interview by Katharine Viner. *Guardian* (UK), 24 August 2002. Web. 24 November 2015. http://www.theguardian.com/books/2002/aug/24/fiction.features.

———. *The Almost Moon*. New York: Little, Brown, 2007. Print.

———. *The Lovely Bones*. New York: Back Bay Books/Little, Brown, 2002. Print.

———. *Lucky*. 1999. New York: Back Bay Books/Little, Brown, 2002. Print.

———. "A Summer Must-Read with Eerie Echoes." Interview by Cathy Horyn. *New York Times*, 2 September 2002. Web. 24 November 2015. http://query.nytimes.com/gst/fullpage.html?res=9906E4DC123FF932A3575AC0A9649C8B63&scp=1&sq=Cathy+Horyn+Sebold&st=nyt.

Senna, Danzy. "The Mulatto Millennium." *Half and Half: Writers on Growing Up Biracial and Bicultural*. Ed. Claudine Chiawei O'Hearn. New York: Pantheon Books, 1998. 12–27. Print.

Sexton, Jared. *Amalgamation Schemes: Antiblackness and the Critique of Multiculturalism*. Minneapolis: University of Minnesota Press, 2008.

Shelton, Jen. *Joyce and the Narrative Structure of Incest*. Gainesville: University Press of Florida, 2006. Print.

Shockley, Evie. "Buried Alive: Gothic Homelessness, Black Women's Sexuality and (Living) Death in Ann Petry's 'The Street.'" *African-American Review* 40.3 (2006): 439–60. Print.

Showalter, Elaine. "Dark Places." *New York Times Book Review*, 9 June 2013, sec. BR, 35. Print.

———. *Sister's Choice: Traditions and Change in American Women's Writing*. Oxford: Oxford University Press, 1991. Print.

Siegel, Deborah. *Sisterhood Interrupted: From Radical Women to Grrls Gone Wild*. Basingstoke, UK: Palgrave Macmillan, 2007. Print.

Siegel, Lee. "Mom's in the Freezer." *New York Times*, 21 October 2007. Web. 24 November 2015. http://www.nytimes.com/2007/10/21/books/review/Siegel-t.html?_r=1&.

———. "Thank You for Sharing." *New Republic*, 5 June 2006. Web. 24 November 2015. http://www.newrepublic.com/article/books-and-arts/thank-you-sharing#.

Silverman, Stephen. "Morgan Harrington's Parents Grateful for Closure." *People*, 29 January 2010. Web. 24 November 2015. http://www.people.com/people/article/0,20340261,00.html.

Skinner, David. "Andrea Yates: Not a Women's Issue." *Weekly Standard*, 14 March 2002. Web. 24 November 2015. http://www.weeklystandard.com/Content/Public/Articles/000/000/001/010agmve.asp.

Slaughter, Anne-Marie. "Why Women Still Can't Have It All." *Atlantic Monthly*, July/August 2012.Web. 24 November 2015. http://www.theatlantic.com/magazine/archive/2012/07/why-women-still-cant-have-it-all/309020/.

Smart, Carol. "Power and the Politics of Child Custody." *Child Custody and the Politics of Gender*. Ed. Carol Smart and Selma Sevenhuijsen. London: Routledge, 1989. 1–26. Print.

Smart, Ed, and Lois Smart, with Laura Morton. *Bringing Elizabeth Home*. New York: Doubleday, 2003. Print.

Smart, Elizabeth, with Chris Stewart. *My Story*. New York: St. Martin's Press, 2013. Print.

Smigiel, Frank. "The Queen Is Dead: Style, *Salomé*, and the Death of the Woman." *Staging the Rage: The Web of Misogyny in Modern Drama*. Eds. Katherine H. Burkman and Judith Roof. Cranbury, NJ: Associated University Press, 1998. 248–66. Print.

Smith, Andrew, and Diana Wallace. "The Female Gothic: Then and Now." *Gothic Studies* 6.1 (2004): 1–7. Print.

Solinger, Rickie. *Beggars and Choosers: How the Politics of Choice Shapes Adoption, Abortion, and Welfare in the United States*. New York: Hill and Wang, 2001. Print.

Solnit, Rebecca. "Cassandra among the Creeps." *Harper's* 329 (2014): 4–10. Print.

———. "The Longest War." *TomDispatch*, 24 January 2013. Web. 24 November 2015. http://www.tomdispatch.com/post/175641/.

Sommers, Christina Hoff. *The War against Boys: How Misguided Policies Are Harming Our Young Men*. 2000. New York: Simon and Schuster, 2013. Print.

———. *Who Stole Feminism? How Women Have Betrayed Women.* New York: Simon and Schuster, 1994. Print.

Sorisio, Carolyn. "A Tale of Two Feminisms: Power and Victimization in Contemporary Feminist Debate." *Third Wave Agenda: Being Feminist, Doing Feminism.* Eds. Leslie Heywood and Jennifer Drake. Minneapolis: University of Minnesota Press, 1997. 134–54. Print.

Spencer, Hawes. "Black Ribbon: Harrington's Parents Express Emotions." *Hook,* Better Publications, 27 January 2010. Web. 24 November 2015. http://www.readthehook.com/68925/black-ribbon-harringtons-parents-express-emotions.

Spencer, Rainier. *Reproducing Race: The Paradox of Generation Mix.* Boulder, CO: Lynne Rienner, 2011. Print.

Spillers, Hortense. "Mama's Baby, Papa's, Too." *Trans-Scripts* 1 (2011): n.p. Web. 24 November 2015. http://sites.uci.edu/transscripts/files/2014/10/2011_01_02.pdf.

Springer, Kimberly. "Divas, Evil Black Bitches, and Bitter Black Women: African American Women in Postfeminist and Post-Civil-Rights Popular Culture." *Interrogating Postfeminism: Gender and the Politics of Popular Culture.* Eds. Yvonne Tasker and Diane Negra. Durham, NC: Duke University Press, 2007. 249–77. Print.

———. "Waiting to Set It Off: African American Women and the Sapphire Fixation." *Reel Knockouts: Violent Women in the Movies.* Eds. Martha McCaughey and Neal King. Austin: University of Texas Press, 2001. 172–99. Print.

Stallings, L. H. "Sapphire's *PUSH* for Erotic Literacy and Black Girl Sexual Agency." *Sapphire's Literary Breakthrough: Erotic Literacies, Feminist Pedagogies, Environmental Justice Perspectives.* Eds. Elizabeth McNeil, Neal A. Lester, DoVeanna S. Fulton, and Lynette D. Myles. Basingstoke, UK: Palgrave Macmillan, 2012. 113–39. Print.

Stanford, Ann Folwell. *Bodies in a Broken World: Women Novelists of Color and the Politics of Medicine.* Chapel Hill: University of North Carolina Press, 2003. Print.

Stanko, Elizabeth A. "Women, Crime, and Fear." *Annals of the American Academy of Political and Social Science* 539 (1995): 46–58. Print.

Stein, Karen F. "A Left-Handed Story: The Blind Assassin." *Margaret Atwood's Textual Assassinations: Recent Poetry and Fiction.* Ed. Sharon Rose Wilson. Columbus: Ohio State University Press, 2003. 135–53. Print.

———. "Monsters and Madwomen: Changing Female Gothic." *The Female Gothic.* Ed. Juliann Fleenor. Montreal: Eden Press, 1983. 123–37. Print.

Stepp, Laura Sessions. "A New Kind of Date Rape." *Cosmopolitan,* 11 September 2007. Web. 24 November 2015. http://www.cosmopolitan.com/sex-love/advice/a1912/new-kind-of-date-rape/.

Stevens, Chevy. *Still Missing.* New York: St. Martin's Griffin, 2010. Print.

Stewart, Susan. *On Longing: Narratives of the Miniature, the Gigantic, the Souvenir, the Collection.* 1984. Durham, NC: Duke University Press, 1993. Print.

Steyn, Mark. "Moms Defend a Baby-Killer." *Spectator,* 30 June 2001, 18–19. Print.

Strengell, Heidi. "'My knife is so nice and sharp I want to get to work right away if I get a chance': Identification between Author and Serial Killer in Patricia Cornwell's Kay Scarpetta Series." *Studies in Popular Culture* 27.1 (2004): 73–90. Print.

Stringer, Rebecca. "Rethinking the Critique of Victim Feminism." *Victim No More: Women's Resistance to Law, Culture and Power.* Eds. Ellen Faulkner and Gayle MacDonald. Halifax, NB: Fernwood, 2009. 20–27. Print.

Strong, Pauline Turner. *Captive Selves, Captivating Others: The Politics and Poetics of Colonial American Captivity Narratives.* Boulder, CO: Westview Press, 1999. Print.

Summers-Bremner, Eluned. "Post-Traumatic Woundings: Sexual Anxiety in Patricia Cornwell's Fiction." *New Formations: A Journal of Culture/Theory/Politics* 43 (2001): 130–47. Print.

Sweeney, Kathleen. *Maiden USA: Girl Icons Come of Age.* New York: Peter Lang, 2008. Print.

Talbot, Margaret. "Gone Girl." *New Yorker,* 21 October 2013, 32–38. Print.

Tallent, Elizabeth. "The Trouble with Postmortality." *Threepenny Review* (Spring 2005): n.p. Web. 24 November 2015. http://www.threepennyreview.com/samples/tallent_sp05.html.

Tarbox, Katharine. *The Art of John Fowles.* Athens: University of Georgia Press, 1989. Print.

Tasker, Yvonne, and Diane Negra. "Introduction." *Interrogating Postfeminism: Gender and the Politics of Popular Culture.* Eds. Yvonne Tasker and Diane Negra. Durham, NC: Duke University Press, 2007. 1–26. Print.

Thoma, Pamela. "Buying Up Baby: Modern Feminine Subjectivity, Assertions of 'Choice,' and the Repudiation of Reproductive Justice in Postfeminist Unwanted Pregnancy Films." *Feminist Media Studies* 9.4 (2009): 409–22. Print.

———. "What Julia Knew: Domestic Labor in the Recession-Era Chick Flick." *Gendering the Recession: Media and Culture in an Age of Austerity.* Eds. Diane Negra and Yvonne Tasker. Durham, NC: Duke University Press, 2014. 107–35. Print.

Thompson, Becky. *A Hunger So Wide and So Deep: A Multiracial View of Women's Eating Problems.* Minneapolis: University of Minnesota Press, 1996. Print.

Thompson, Mary. "Third Wave Feminism and the Politics of Motherhood." *Genders* 43 (2006): n.p. Web. 15 August 2014. https://web.archive.org/web/20140719003857/http://www.genders.org/recent.html

Thomson, Rosemarie Garland. *Extraordinary Bodies: Figuring Physical Disability in American Literature and Culture.* New York: Columbia University Press, 1996. Print.

Thornham, Sue. "Starting to Feel Like a Chick: Revisioning Romance in *In the Cut.*" *Feminist Media Studies* 7.1 (2007): 33–46. Print.

Thornton, Carolyn I., and James H. Carter. "Treatment Considerations with Black Incestuous Families." *Journal of the National Medical Association* 78.1 (1986): 49–53. Print.

Timmermans, Stefan. *Postmortem: How Medical Examiners Explain Suspicious Deaths.* Chicago: University of Chicago Press, 2006. Print.

Tinnemeyer, Andrea. *Identity Politics of the Captivity Narrative after 1848.* Lincoln: University of Nebraska Press, 2006. Print.

Tolan, Fiona. "Sucking the Blood out of Second Wave Feminism: Postfeminist Vampirism in Margaret Atwood's *The Robber Bride.*" *Gothic Studies* 9.2 (2007): 45–57. Print.

Tompkins, Jane. *Sensational Designs: The Cultural Work of American Fiction 1790–1860*. New York: Oxford University Press, 1985. Print.

Travis, Trysh. *The Language of the Heart: A Cultural History of the Recovery Movement from Alcoholics Anonymous to Oprah Winfrey*. Chapel Hill: University of North Carolina Press, 2009. Print.

Treichler, Paula, and Catherine Warren. "Maybe Next Year: Feminist Silence and the AIDS Epidemic." *The Visible Woman: Imaging Technologies, Gender, and Science*. Eds. Paula A. Treichler, Lisa Cartwright, and Constance Penley. New York: New York University Press, 1998. 83–129. Print.

Tresniowski, Alex. "The Miracle Girl." *People*, 31 March 2003, 44–51. Print.

Tyler, Anne. "The Growing Up of Lily Shields." *New York Times*, 17 October 1982, sec. 7, 14. Print.

Valenti, Jessica. "Ending Rape Illiteracy." *Nation*, 23 October 2012. Web. 24 November 2015. http://www.thenation.com/blog/170767/ending-rape-illiteracy.

Valentine, Gill. "The Geography of Women's Fear." *Area* 21.4 (1989): 385–90. Print.

Van Wormer, Katherine. "Anti-Feminist Backlash and Violence against Women Worldwide." *Social Work and Society* 6.2 (2008): n.p. Web. 24 November 2015. http://www.socwork.net/sws/article/view/64/366.

Van Wormer, Katherine Stuart, and Clemens Bartollas. *Women and the Criminal Justice System*. 3rd ed. Boston: Prentice Hall, 2011. Print.

Venker, Suzanne. "The War on Men." FoxNews, 24 November 2012. Web. 24 November 2015. http://www.foxnews.com/opinion/2012/11/24/war-on-men/.

Villalobos, Ana. "Mothering in Fear: How Living in an Insecure-Feeling World Affects Parenting." *Twenty-First-Century Motherhood: Experience, Identity, Policy, Agency*. Ed. Andrea O'Reilly. New York: Columbia University Press, 2010. 57–71. Print.

Vint, Sherryl. "The New Backlash: Popular Culture's 'Marriage' with Feminism, or Love Is All You Need." *Journal of Popular Film and Television* 34.4 (2007): 160–68. Print.

Von Czarnowsky, Laura-Marie. "The Postmortal Rape Survivor and the Paradox of Female Agency across Different Media: Alice Sebold's Novel 'The Lovely Bones' and Its 2009 Film Adaptation." *Gender Forum* 41 (2013): n.p. Web. 24 November 2015. http://www.genderforum.org/issues/gender-and-force-in-the-media/the-postmortal-rape-survivor-and-the-paradox-of-female-agency-across-different-media-alice-sebolds-novel-the-lovely-bones-and-its-2009-film-adaptation/.

Walker, Rebecca, ed. *To Be Real: Telling the Truth and Changing the Face of Feminism*. New York: Anchor, 1995. Print.

Walkowitz, Judith R. "Jack the Ripper and the Myth of Male Violence." *Feminist Studies* 8.3 (1982): 542–74. Print.

Wallace, Diana. *Female Gothic Histories: Gender, History and the Gothic*. Cardiff, UK: University of Wales Press, 2013. Print.

Wallace, Michele. *Black Macho and the Myth of the Superwoman*. 2nd ed. London: Verso, 1991. Print.

Wallace-Sanders, Kimberly. *Skin Deep, Spirit Strong: The Black Female Body in American Culture*. Ann Arbor: University of Michigan Press, 2002. Print.

Walters, Suzanna Danuta. "From Here to Queer: Radical Feminism, Postmodernism, and the Lesbian Menace (Or, Why Can't a Woman Be More Like a Fag?)." *Signs* 21.4 (1996): 830–69. Print.

Wanzo, Rebecca. "The Era of Lost (White) Girls: On Body and Event." *Differences: A Journal of Feminist Cultural Studies* 19.2 (2008): 99–126. Print.

———. *The Suffering Will Not Be Televised: African American Women and Sentimental Political Storytelling*. Albany: State University of New York Press, 2009. Print.

Warkentin, Elyssa. "Jack the Ripper Strikes Again: The 'Ipswich Ripper' and the 'Vice Girls' He Killed." *Feminist Media Studies* 10.1 (2010): 35–49. Print.

Warner, Judith. *Perfect Madness: Motherhood in the Age of Anxiety*. New York: Riverhead, 2005. Print.

Warner, Lionel. "Rising Paranoia: Child-Theft in Three 1980s Novels." *Uses of English* 52.1 (2000): 49–55. Print.

Wearing, Sadie. "Subjects of Rejuvenation: Aging in Postfeminist Culture." *Interrogating Postfeminism: Gender and the Politics of Popular Culture*. Eds. Yvonne Tasker and Diane Negra. Durham, NC: Duke University Press, 2007. 277–310. Print.

Webb, Jen. "Who Is Kevin, and Why Do We Need to Talk about Him? Lionel Shriver, *Kevin*, and the Problem of Representation." *Australian Literary Studies* 24. 3–4 (2009): 133–43. Print.

Weber, Brenda R., and Karen W. Tice. "Are You Finally Comfortable in Your Own Skin? The Raced and Classed Imperatives for Somatic/Spiritual Salvation in *The Swan*." *Genders* 49 (2009). n.p. Web. 15 August 2014. https://web.archive.org/web/20140719003857/http://www.genders.org/recent.html

Weese, Katherine. *Feminist Narrative and the Supernatural*. Jefferson, NC: McFarland, 2008. Print.

Weisman, Jonathan. "Measure to Protect Women Stuck on Tribal Land Issue." *New York Times*, 10 February 2013. Web. 24 November 2015. http://www.nytimes.com/2013/02/11/us/politics/violence-against-women-act-held-up-by-tribal-land-issue.html.

Weitz, Rose, and Samantha Kwan, eds. *The Politics of Women's Bodies: Sexuality, Appearance, and Behavior*. 1998. Oxford: Oxford University Press, 2013. Print.

Wester, Maisha L. *African American Gothic: Screams from Shadowed Places*. Basingstoke, UK: Palgrave Macmillan, 2012. Print.

Whelehan, Imelda. *The Feminist Bestseller: From "Sex and the Single Girl" to "Sex and the City."* Basingstoke, UK: Palgrave Macmillan, 2005. Print.

———. *Overloaded: Popular Culture and the Future of Feminism*. London: Women's Press, 2000. Print.

Whittier, Nancy. *The Politics of Child Sexual Abuse: Emotion, Social Movements, and the State*. Oxford: Oxford University Press, 2009. Print.

Will, George. "Colleges Become the Victims of Progressivism." *Washington Post*, 6 June 2014. Web. 24 November 2015. http://www.washingtonpost.com/opinions/george-will-college-become-the-victims-of-progressivism/2014/06/06/e90e73b4-eb50-11e3-9f5c-9075d5508f0a_story.html.

Williams, Anne. *Art of Darkness: A Poetics of Gothic*. Chicago: University of Chicago Press, 1995. Print.

Williams, Linda Meyer. "Race and Rape: The Black Woman as Legitimate Victim." *National Institutes of Mental Health* report. Rockville, MD: DHHS, 1986. Print.

Williams, Mary Elizabeth. "Why Etan Patz Still Haunts Us." *Salon*, 25 May 2012. Web. 24 November 2015. http://www.salon.com/2012/05/25/why_etan_patz_still_haunts_us/.

Williams, Ruth. "*Eat, Pray, Love*: Producing the Female Neoliberal Spiritual Subject." *Journal of Popular Culture* 47.3 (2014): 613–33. Print.

Wilson, Christopher P. *Learning to Live with Crime: American Crime Narrative in the Neoconservative Turn*. Columbus: Ohio State University Press, 2010. Print.

Wilson, Melba. *Crossing the Boundary: Black Women Survive Incest*. Seattle: Seal Press, 1993. Print.

Winch, Alison. *Girlfriends and Postfeminist Sisterhood*. Basingstoke, UK: Palgrave Macmillan, 2013. Print.

Winter, Kari J. *Subjects of Slavery, Agents of Change: Women and Power in Gothic Novels and Slave Narratives, 1790–1865*. Athens: University of Georgia Press, 1992. Print.

Witt, Doris. *Black Hunger: Food and the Politics of U.S. Identity*. New York: Oxford University Press, 1999. Print.

Wolcott, James. "Hear Me Purr." *New Yorker* 72.12 (1996): 54–59. Print.

Wolf, Naomi. *The Beauty Myth: How Images of Beauty Are Used against Women*. New York: Vintage, 1992. Print.

———. *Fire with Fire: The New Female Power and How It Will Change the 21st Century*. New York: Random House, 1993. Print.

Wolitzer, Meg. "The Second Shelf: On the Rules of Literary Fiction for Men and Women." *New York Times*, 30 March 2012. 24 November 2015. http://www.nytimes.com/2012/04/01/books/review/on-the-rules-of-literary-fiction-for-men-and-women.html?pagewanted=all&_r=0.

Woodiwiss, Kathleen. *The Flame and the Flower*. 1972. New York: Avon, 2007. Print.

Wright, Carole, and Jeff Hearn. "Neutralizing Gendered Violence: Subsuming Men's Violence against Women into Gender-Neutral Language." *Framing Sexual and Domestic Violence through Language*. Ed. Renate Klein. Basingstoke, UK: Palgrave Macmillan, 2013. 21–40. Print.

Wright, Richard. "How 'Bigger' Was Born." 1940. Web. 24 November 2015. http://xroads.virginia.edu/~ma01/white/anthology/bigger.html.

Young, Hershini Bhana. "Black 'Like Me': (Mis)Recognition, the Racial Gothic, and the Post-1967 Mixed-Race Movement in Danzy Senna's 'Symptomatic.'" *African American Review* 42.2 (2008): 287–305. Print.

Zacharek, Stephanie. "'The Lovely Bones': Be Very Afraid." *Salon,* 10 December 2009. Web. 24 November 2015. 2014. http://www.salon.com/2009/12/11/the_lovely_bones/.

Zaslow, Emilie. *Feminism, Inc.: Coming of Age in Girl Power Media Culture.* Basingstoke, UK: Palgrave Macmillan, 2009. Print.

Zevin, Gabrielle. *Elsewhere.* New York: Farrar, Straus and Giroux, 2005. Print.

Zook, Kristal Brent. "A Manifesto of Sorts for a Black Feminist Movement." *New York Times Magazine,* 12 November 1995, 86–89. Print.

Index

SARAH E. WHITNEY is a lecturer in English and women's studies at Penn State Behrend.

The University of Illinois Press
is a founding member of the
Association of American University Presses.

University of Illinois Press
1325 South Oak Street
Champaign, IL 61820-6903
www.press.uillinois.edu